THE PSALMS

THE PSALMS

Songs of Faith and Praise

THE REVISED GRAIL PSALTER
WITH COMMENTARY AND PRAYERS

Gregory J. Polan, OSB

Paulist Press
Mahwah, NJ / New York

Cover design by Brother Michael Marcotte, OSB
Cover art by Rev. Eugene Plaisted, OSC and kind permission of the Chapter of Ripon Cathedral. Used with permission.

Book design by Lynn Else

Library of Congress Cataloging-in-Publication Data

Bible. Psalms. English. Revised Grail Psalms. 2014
    The psalms songs of faith and praise : the Revised Grail Psalter with commentary and prayers / Abbot Gregory J. Polan, OSB.
        pages cm
    Includes bibliographical references.
    ISBN 978-0-8091-4882-0 (alk. paper)
    1. Psalters. 2. Bible. Psalms—Devotional literature. 3. Catholic Church—Liturgy. I. Polan, Gregory J., 1950– II. Title.
    BX2033.A4C66 2014
    223`.2077—dc23

                                                            2014006482

ISBN 978-0-8091-4882-0 (paperback)

Published by Paulist Press
997 Macarthur Boulevard
Mahwah, New Jersey 07430

www.paulistpress.com

Printed and bound in the
United States of America

To the Benedictine Monks of Conception Abbey,
my brothers with whom I have learned
to love the psalms,
and
In memory of the Reverend Lawrence E. Boadt, CSP,
biblical scholar, past president of Paulist Press,
and dear friend,
who invited me to write this book.

CONTENTS

ACKNOWLEDGMENTS

This book is dedicated both to my confreres, the Benedictine Monks of Conception Abbey, and to the memory of Rev. Lawrence Boadt, CSP, who first invited me to write this book. My confreres in monastic life have fostered in me a love of the Scriptures, and especially of the Psalms, for which I am most grateful. Father Larry Boadt, an eminent biblical scholar and a dear friend, encouraged me to share with others my love of the psalms, which has made them for me such a rich avenue to prayer. And I sincerely thank my secretary, Brother Jude Person, OSB, whose careful editing of these texts has enhanced them both in style and in clarity of expression, making them more inviting and accessible to the reader. His skill with words has been applied with care, dedication, and patience, for which I am most grateful. Finally, I offer a word of appreciation to my confrere, Father Hugh Tasch, OSB, who carefully proofread this manuscript and asked some poignant questions; his own love of the Psalms has been an incentive to read this text with interest and attention to detail, for which I am most grateful.

INTRODUCTION

When *The Grail Psalms* appeared in the early 1960s, their value to the Church's prayer and spiritual life was quickly recognized. A special edition was prepared in 1968 by Deus Books in association with Paulist Press: *The Psalms: A New Translation—Singing Version* included introductions by Rev. Joseph Gelineau, SJ, and Dom A. Gregory Murray, OSB. Gelineau provided background information on this new translation: originating in France, the translation had been specifically proposed and developed so that the psalms could be chanted in a manner closely approximating the original Hebrew rhythmic patterns. Murray provided some basic instruction regarding the application of Gelineau's chant tones to the new English translation. A further special feature of this edition was the inclusion of brief introductions to each individual psalm, contributed by British biblical scholars Rev. Alexander Jones and Rev. Leonard Johnston. These were intended to help readers recognize key motifs distinguishing each of these ancient prayers. For many Roman Catholics, this edition provided the opportunity for their first serious reflection on the Book of Psalms—for centuries a familiar and integral part of the Church's liturgy, but up to this time encountered primarily in Latin, which few could readily understand. Short, insightful introductions to a fresh new translation opened to the reader the profound meanings available in these important biblical and liturgical texts.

With the promulgation in 2001 of *Liturgiam Authenticam* (an instruction from the Congregation for Divine Worship and the Discipline of the Sacraments [CDWDS] for the translation of liturgical texts), it became apparent that an updated revision of *The 1963 Grail Psalms* would be necessary. At the request of the United States Conference of Catholic Bishops, *The Revised Grail Psalms* was prepared by the monks of Conception Abbey, and in 2010 the CDWDS issued a *recognitio* for the revision's use in the liturgy. As abbot and spiritual father of the monks of Conception, I was closely involved with the production of *The Revised Grail Psalms*. While the process of revision was under way, Rev. Lawrence Boadt, CSP, then president of Paulist Press, as well as a long-time friend and professional colleague, approached me to ask if I would consider writing an introduction to each of the psalms similar to those provided in the Deus/Paulist edition of 1968, for a special edition of *The Revised Grail Psalms*. Such an edition, he felt, would provide a new generation with a spiritual *entrée* to these ancient Hebrew prayers that had become pillars of the Church's liturgy. This edition of *The Revised Grail Psalms* originated from that conversation.

What is significant about this revision of the *1963 Grail Psalms*? The translation bears the distinction of being a "liturgical psalter." It differs in some points from many recent translations of the Bible. It takes the Hebrew text of the psalms as its base for translation, but because it is specifically intended for liturgical use, other cultural and historical factors have a bearing on particular formulations. For example, when in the third century BC the Hebrew Bible was translated into Greek (the Septuagint or LXX), the dominant Hellenistic culture of the Mediterranean world at the time, with its particular philosophical and anthropological outlook, had a significant bearing on how that text was formed in both vocabulary and intellectual concepts. Every translation is also in some sense an interpretation. In the Christian era, when St. Jerome was commissioned to prepare a Latin translation of the Scriptures (the Vulgate), both the original Hebrew and the Greek Septuagint were consulted in his "interpretation." The Vulgate's version of the Psalter then had its own significant influence on how the texts of the psalms were incorporated into various ancient missals, and finally in the Roman Missal that became the Western Church's standard. As the Missal was developed and refined, specific psalm texts came to be directly associated with specific theological themes and concepts, and with specific liturgical celebrations, both in seasonal contexts (Advent/Christmas, Lent/Easter) and for special feasts and solemnities of the liturgical year. For that reason, certain key words have been translated in a specific way so that these traditional associations are not lost, and the Latin tradition remains in concord with the Hebrew and Greek versions of the psalms, as well as with the Scriptures as a whole.

The introductions to each of the psalms in this edition have been written for anyone who might wish to cultivate a deeper spiritual understanding of this "prayer-book of the Bible." No advanced technical knowledge of exegesis or historical-critical method is necessary. Although these introductions do impart information culled from biblical scholarship, they seek to express those ideas in a language geared both to intellectual understanding and spiritual appreciation. The psalms are *poetry*—the ancient compositions of the Jewish people, adopted by the Christian Church in its earliest years and revered through all ages since. Of all the texts of the Old Testament, the Book of Psalms is the one most frequently quoted in the New Testament. The psalms appear on the lips of Jesus himself, becoming expressions of his own prayer to God, manifesting his own human experiences and articulating his own insights into his life and mission. These introductions seek to explain the biblical background for understanding individual psalms with attention to imagery, rhetorical style, and distinctive vocabulary; furthermore, each psalm is linked to the message of the New Testament, keeping alive in the mind of the reader how relevant these ancient prayers are to our Christian faith.

An additional feature of this edition is a psalm-prayer following each of the psalms. These prayers are intended to bring the readers full circle in their experience by reiterating some of the themes and images of the particular psalm in a way that brings them into his or her current spiritual practice. It is helpful to know that from the time of the early Church, psalm-prayers have been a part of the Liturgy of the Hours or Divine Office, the Church's official daily prayer. The Liturgy of the Hours consecrates the various parts of a day—Morning, Noon, Evening, and Night—with the recitation of psalms and canticles in communion with the whole Church. The psalms have always been understood as a springboard for personal prayer; the images, themes, and motifs of the psalms draw the one who prays them into a reflective response to God. As God has spoken to the person in his or her recitation of a psalm, so the psalm-prayer is the individual's response to God's word, a reply from a heart illuminated by the word. The *General Instruction* of the renewed Liturgy of the Hours speaks of the importance of the "sacred silence" associated with such prayer: "The purpose of this silence is to allow the voice of the Holy Spirit to be heard more fully in our hearts, and to unite our personal prayer more closely with the word of God and the public voice of the Church" (*General Instruction on the Liturgy of the Hours*; Section XII, "The Sacred Silence"). The psalm-prayers presented here are examples for the reader's use; the hope is that by praying the psalms again and again, those praying will gradually be moved into spontaneous responses arising from their own hearts with ever-greater facility.

This edition also provides for each psalm a title, a name by which it might come to be known and remembered. Again, the hope is that each person who recites and prays these psalms will eventually create a distinctive and personal title for each of these texts from the prayer-book of the Bible, reflecting his or her own appropriation of the ancient song-prayer. By that means, each psalm may take on a unique character for each person who reads and reflects on it, a special meaning, a distinctive link to one's own spiritual life. Some of the titles given here are drawn from the text of the psalm itself; others come from personal reflection on its images and language, thoughts and recollections mustered from life experiences. No one should hesitate to be creative in giving a psalm a "title" distinctively one's own; such a practice has the potential to draw the one who prays into the rich world of meaning that the Psalms have borne for both church and synagogue for thousands of years. Make each psalm special to you, yourself.

READING THE BOOK OF PSALMS

The Hebrew name for the Book of Psalms is *Sepher Tehillim*, which literally means "A Book of Praises." For those who have read or prayed all 150 psalms, this may seem an odd or even inaccurate designation; after all, there are more Laments in the Psalter than any other type of psalm. Can a prayer of lament be at the same time an offering of praise? A theological understanding of the Psalter helps us appreciate the rich Hebrew tradition behind the title "A Book of Praises." For the mind of the ancient Hebrews, any words addressed to God, even in lamentation—cries from the heart arising from pain or discouragement, anger, or dismay—all of them constitute praise. Why? Because these words come from one who looks to God as the source of all blessing, the foundation of all hope. So often, the sufferings and hardships of life are beyond our power to understand or resolve. When we turn to our Creator in time of need, we do so acknowledging that God alone can transform a situation that is impossible for us to alter or amend. For the Hebrew mind, turning to God becomes in itself an act of praise, an affirmation of our faith and confidence that God will hear us and act on our behalf, taking us out of our helpless situation and moving us in a new direction. When we ask someone to do something for us that we cannot do for ourselves, we honor that person by our request; the request for something significant offers implicit praise for their magnanimity. So whether we raise a hymn or a lament, whether we praise the wonders of creation or deplore a life-threatening situation, such prayers offer praise to God as the source of all blessing.

We have referred to the Psalter as "the prayer-book of the Bible." These ancient prayers reflect every situation imaginable in human life—situations we find recounted both in the prose narratives and in the poetry of the Bible. The psalms, then, are the prayer-responses to those situations. They are the songs of both the nation and the individual; after conflicts with foreign foes or personal adversaries, they give voice to gratitude both collective and personal—for return to the land once lost, for restoration of peace once shattered. Certain psalms bring together the wisdom of the elders regarding how life may be lived in such a way as to bring blessings, cautioning us against dangers besetting that path. Some psalms give us words acclaiming the wonders of creation, its inexplicable rhythm of seasons that may bring either benefit or calamity. Others draw us into the drama of human experience—from deception and betrayal in potentially fatal circumstances, to joys eliciting profound gratitude and unbounded praise. One way in which we can begin to appreciate the countless variety of the Psalter is by noting carefully how the psalms are integrated into the Mass. Each First Reading at the Eucharist is followed by a Responsorial Psalm, which voices a prayer responding to what God has said to us through the words of Scripture. Each time we listen to the cantor sing or the lector read the text of the Responsorial Psalm, each time we sing or recite the refrain, we are drawn together into the prayer of God's people, expressing the faith that comprehends everything from anger and dismay to joy and thanksgiving before God—the faith that unites us in time and space through countless generations.

We learn from the psalms the language of prayer that has characterized both synagogue and church for centuries. Sometimes we may be surprised or even shocked at the imagery employed, so different from the way we tend to portray our own experience in today's world. But by studying the context and meaning of those images and metaphors, we can come to see how even these images of violence and hostility, suffering and sadness, can speak to us as poetry imbued with the beauty of faith and hope. For example, when the Psalmist says that God is aware of our wanderings and collects "our tears in a flask" (Ps 56:9), we are touched by this Hebraic image of tenderness; yes, God knows our every footstep; each tear of sadness and disappointment is collected and retained by the One who cares so deeply for us. Or again in this same psalm, we truly appreciate the words of the Psalmist that speak of walking "in the presence of God," and enjoying "the light of the living" (v. 14): when we experience a reprieve after great challenges, it is then that light breaks through the dark clouds, and God's presence is revealed to us. Such images speak to our own journey through life, in times that threaten, challenge, and exhilarate us.

A further element of Hebrew poetry that may be unfamiliar or surprising is its characteristic rhetorical style, so different from what we know and use today. Although English has an astoundingly rich and expressive vocabulary, scholars note that biblical Hebrew comprises only about five thousand words. Also, the ancient Hebrews did not have access to the vast number of texts we have at our disposal today. This makes a difference in the way a biblical text is rendered: in those days, people remembered key ideas through the *repetition* of specific words. Such words in the texts of a psalm bring focus to important themes and motifs. By means of such repetition, the Psalmist impressed upon those who used the texts exactly what they should remember about it. Also, the texts of the Bible were composed and brought together in a primarily oral culture; written texts were rare or largely nonexistent during this early period. What was conveyed in a dynamic and repetitive form was more readily retained in the minds and hearts of the hearers. Repetition focuses thought and gives continuity to the progression of a passage. Often a psalm is composed so as to begin and end with the same word or phrase; such inclusion signals a key idea in the mind of the Psalmist. Sometimes the Psalmist will repeat a term by means of a pun, a play on words that draws attention to and develops an idea. Repetition resides in the "genetic pool" of biblical literature; examples of these are noted in many of the introductions to individual psalms.

THE FORMATION OF THE BOOK OF PSALMS

The Book of Psalms is divided into five smaller sections or books within the *Sepher Tehillim* or "Book of Praises." As the *Torah* (what we call the Pentateuch) is divided into five books, so this pattern is reproduced in the Book of Psalms. The word *torah* means "instruction," so the Pentateuch is a book of instruction on the life and experience of the people in their encounter with God; we can consider the fivefold division of the Psalter a corresponding "instruction in prayer." The five books are distinguished thus:

Book One: Psalms 1–41
Book Two: Psalms 41–72
Book Three: Psalms 73–89
Book Four: Psalms 90–106
Book Five: Psalms 107–50

Each of the five books concludes with a characteristic *doxology*—an expression of praise and blessing to God. Some have suggested that the last few psalms of the Psalter (Pss 148–50) serve as a grand doxology to the whole Book of Psalms.

In the nineteenth and twentieth centuries, biblical scholars offered a method of reading the psalms in terms of what they designated the "literary forms" of the Psalter. The function of this might be understood by way of analogy. In our own day and age, a particular form for writing business letters is widely observed; it includes the date, the recipient's name and address, a salutation and greeting, followed by the body of the letter, and concluding with closing remarks and the name and signature of the sender. An internal memo will have a different, yet equally recognizable, form. In the ancient world of the Bible, many texts, both narrative and poetic, were composed according to particular literary forms. These literary forms might be classified according to a pattern of elements or topics within the text, to thematic material, or both. The following list presents the most common literary forms of the Psalter and designates some of the psalms included in the respective categories.

The Hymn of Praise. These psalms follow a simple pattern of (a) an initial invitation to praise God, followed by (b) an extended list of reasons for this acclaim, and concludes with (c) a final call to give praise, often echoing the opening words or phrases of the psalm. The Hymns of the Psalter include Psalms 8, 33, 66, 100, 104, and 150.

The Individual Lament. These comprise the most numerous of the Psalter's literary forms. They speak of human trials and sufferings of the Psalmist's experience, calling out to God for the help that the Lord alone can give. The form includes the following elements: (a) a direct address to God, calling on the name of the Lord; (b) an account of the troubles facing the individual who calls; (c) the request for divine assistance, knowing that human assistance cannot be sufficient; this is often followed by (d) an expression of trust in God's help and intervention; many times, the conclusion voices (e) an expression of praise for what God has done in the past, and will, the Psalmist hopes, do now. Noteworthy here is the progression from complaint and distress to expressions of faith and confidence in God's action. Some of the more recognizable Individual Laments are Psalms 3, 7, 17, 22, 31, 51, 54, 55, 69, 88, and 130.

The Communal Lament. Obvious similarities exist between the Individual and Communal Laments. The distinguishing characteristic of this literary form arises in the context of the community's historical experience of exile: siege by foreign enemies, invasion, destruction of land and holy places, and a critical loss of hope. The Communal Laments include Psalms 44, 74 and 79 (recounting the destruction of the temple), 77, and 80.

The Thanksgiving Song. Scholars align this literary form to the concluding element of the Lament: an expression of gratitude for the action of God's saving hand, bringing the Psalmist out of a situation of distress. The form comprises the following elements: (a) a word of gratitude to God; (b) an account of the state of affairs from which the Psalmist has been delivered; (c) an acknowledgment of the divine intervention that has brought blessing for the Psalmist; and (d) a call for others to join in the acclamations of the Psalmist's deliverance. The Thanksgiving Songs of the Psalter include Psalms 30, 57, 92, 116, and 138.

Psalms of Confidence. In contrast to the preceding forms, the Psalms of Confidence are recognized by the vocabulary and imagery included in the text. These psalms have a special spiritual significance as expressions of faith in God's goodness and action in human lives: they may be bold or gentle, forceful or sedate. The Psalms of Confidence include Psalms 4, 16, 23, 62, and 91.

Royal or Messianic Psalms. The content of these psalms focuses on the life of the anointed one, the king, with prayers for his well-being, protection, and victory in battle, and may refer to royal ceremonies (coronation, military spectacles or parades, a wedding, royal adjudication, etc.). Those falling into this category include Psalms 2, 19, 20, 72, 89, 110, and 132.

Songs of Zion/Enthronement Psalms. Like the Royal Psalms, these are grouped by reference to their content. They proclaim the reign of God as sovereign Lord of creation, and Jerusalem as the dwelling place of God on earth, the chosen city of divine rest. These texts tell of God's universal rule over the created world and all that dwells in it. Psalms 29, 46, 47, 93, 95—99 are designated Songs of Zion or Enthronement Psalms.

Historical Psalms. Several psalms tell the story of Israel in the language of poetry, highlighting God's saving action and expressing regret at Israel's failure to respond faithfully to the offer of God's love. These include Psalms 78, 105—7, 135, and 136.

Wisdom Psalms. The whole Bible, including the Psalter, is replete with proverbial sayings. Several psalms offer the pithy maxims of instruction and behavior perhaps most characteristic of the Books of Proverbs and Sirach. These succinct, sober expressions bear a wealth of spiritual wisdom for living life well and profitably in accord with God's law and the divine will. Such messages are apparent in Psalms 19, 25, 34, 37, 111, 112, and 119 (the longest psalm of the Psalter).

This catalog of literary forms is not meant to be exhaustive. It is rather a brief consideration of the various classifications of psalms that have been identified in the field of form criticism. The Annotated Bibliography offers suggestions for further reading for those who might benefit from deeper investigation of this analytical approach to the texts of the psalms.

FOR THE BEGINNER

Some people are uneasy with reading and praying the psalms. They may make observations such as, "The ancient imagery is difficult for me to understand....The violent language at certain points makes me uncomfortable....We don't talk in that kind of language today....These prayers don't speak to my personal experience as a person of faith....I don't seem to find much about Christ's new commandment of love in these ancient prayers....Isn't the faith of the Psalmist very different from my own experience of faith?...I find too much subversive language in the Psalms." This book seeks to address each of these questions and concerns in an effort to help everyone appreciate the rich tradition of faith we can discover in the Psalms. It is not without good reason that the Church has revered these prayers from her earliest days and continues to use them in her liturgy even to the present day.

Each introduction to the individual psalms seeks to address briefly those elements of the text that may be unfamiliar to the reader. Matters of language, imagery, literary style, historical context, and Christian application are also dealt with in these passages. For those who wish to become more familiar with the Book of Psalms as a whole, I include here a list of thematic topics that might be helpful for using the psalms to find words for our own situations and needs for prayer. No single psalm is likely to say everything you need to say in any given moment, but certain lines in the Psalter will prove, once we encounter them, so appropriate to so many familiar circumstances that they will remain in our hearts forever. Our faith affirms that the psalms, with all of Scripture, are truly inspired, and thus possess the unique character of God's very word: they are the means by which God speaks directly to us as beloved children.

1. A Morning Prayer: Psalms 3, 5, 63, 143
2. An Evening Prayer: Psalms 130, 141
3. A Night Prayer: Psalms 4, 91, 134
4. Praise of God: Psalms 8, 66, 104, 135—36, 145, 148, 150
5. Thanksgiving to God: Psalms 30, 34, 92, 111, 116, 118, 138
6. Prayer for Upright Living: Psalms 1, 15, 24, 37, 112
7. Prayer for Forgiveness: Psalms 32, 51, 80, 86
8. Longing for Union with God: Psalms 12, 27, 42, 63, 139
9. The Vanity of Human Life: Psalms 39, 49, 73, 90
10. Laments to Life's Struggles: Psalms 22, 25, 31, 40, 90
11. Confidence in God: Psalms 4, 16, 23, 25, 46, 131, 139
12. Hymns about the Messiah: Psalms 2, 23, 45, 89, 110, 132
13. Prayer in Old Age: Psalms 71, 90, 139
14. Historical Psalms: Psalms 78, 105, 106, 135, 136
15. Prayer in Times of Danger: Psalms 7, 28, 35, 38, 54, 56, 140

When we use the Psalms daily as a source of inspiration and prayer, we are using the very prayers that Jesus learned as a child, and which so influenced his own relationship with the One whom he addressed as *Abba*. For some, the imagery and language may be challenging initially. But poetic language is evocative: it moves us to reflect on the profound meanings that these images and metaphors have borne through time and now place before us. That experience has the power to bring forth in us that "prayer of the heart" that is most deeply satisfying and enriching. May this be so for you.

Book One
of the
Psalter

℘salm 1

THE TWO WAYS

Psalm 1 is both prayer and instruction. As it opens the Book of Psalms, Psalm 1 tells us in a nutshell what is to follow: a collection of prayers that show us a way of living in accord with God's justice and righteousness. The image of a flourishing and fruitful tree underscores the blessings that come to a life fully rooted in the ways of God. St. Augustine tells us that the Just One spoken of in this psalm is Jesus Christ, who models for us the way of righteous living. St. Jerome tells us that this very same tree should be every man and woman washed in the waters of baptism and called to be like Jesus Christ. We cannot fail to note the description of the wicked given in Psalm 1: they are like discarded chaff carried away by the wind; they perish in the end from lack of rootedness in the word of God. The Acts of the Apostles speaks of Christian life as "the way," the path for living out the gospel (cf. Acts 9:2; 18:25–26; 19:9, 23; 22:4; 24:14, 22; Ps 1:6). Each day the Christian renews the promises made at baptism by following the way; Psalm 1 sets out the markers of this daily path. St. Paul expands the theme: "As God's chosen ones, holy and beloved, clothe yourselves with compassion, kindness, humility, meekness, and patience. Bear with one another and, if anyone has a complaint against another, forgive each other; just as the Lord has forgiven you, so you also must forgive. Above all, clothe yourselves with love, which binds everything together in perfect harmony" (Col 3:12–14).

PSALM 1

1 Bléssed indéed is the mán
who fóllows not the cóunsel of the wícked,
nor stánds in the páth with sínners,
nor abídes in the cómpany of scórners,
2 but whose delíght is the láw of the LÓRD,
and who pónders his láw day and níght.

3 Hé is like a trée that is plánted
besíde the flówing wáters,
that yíelds its frúit in due séason,

and whose léaves shall néver fáde;
and áll that he dóes shall prósper.

4 Not só are the wícked, not só!
For théy, like wínnowed cháff,
shall be dríven awáy by the wínd.

5 When the wícked are júdged they shall not ríse,
nor shall sínners in the cóuncil of the júst;
6 for the LORD knóws the wáy of the júst,
but the wáy of the wícked will pérish.

PRAYER

Just and righteous God, enliven your word within us that it may be our constant source of strength, our vision for living, and our hope for peace. Make us a people founded on your word, so that we may become living words in the likeness of our Lord, Jesus Christ, who lives and reigns forever and ever. Amen.

Psalm 2

GOD'S ANOINTED ONE

As people who embrace both the Old and New Testaments, Christians read Psalm 2 on two levels: in its historical setting, as speaking of David and his descendants, and also as fulfilled in the person of Jesus Christ, Son of David, Son of God, the Messiah. Historically, this psalm was a prayer for the protection of the Davidic king in the face of pressures from foreign rulers. The psalm presents these rulers with a warning: as the wicked will perish (Ps 1:6), so will those who try to thwart God's anointed one (Ps 2:12). The psalm affirms the election of the Davidic line as God's chosen ones, who are to rule the people of God. The authors of the New Testament saw in this psalm a prophecy announcing the coming of Jesus as God's Anointed One. The Epistle to the Hebrews, drawing from Old Testament texts to demonstrate the divinity of Jesus, quotes Psalm 2:7: "To which of the angels did God ever say, 'You are my Son; today I have begotten you'?" (Heb 1:5). Psalms 1 and 2 are understood to function in tandem: note that Psalm 1 begins with "blessed," and Psalm 2 closes with "blessed." " "Lord, look at the threats, and grant to your servants to speak your word with all boldness, while you stretch out your hand to heal, and signs and wonders are performed through the name of your holy servant, Jesus" (Acts 4:29–30).

PSALM 2

¹ Whý do the nátions conspíre,
and the péoples plót in váin?
² They aríse, the kíngs of the éarth;
princes plót against the LÓRD and his Anóinted.
³ "Let us búrst asúnder their fétters.
Let ús cast óff their cháins."

⁴ He who síts in the héavens láughs;
the LÓRD derídes and mócks them.
⁵ Thén he will spéak in his ánger,
his ráge will stríke them with térror.
⁶ "It is Í who have appóinted my kíng
on Síon, my hóly móuntain."

⁷ I will annóunce the decrée of the LÓRD:
The LORD sáid to me, "Yóu are my Són.
It is Í who have begótten you this dáy.

⁸ Ásk of mé and I will gíve you
the nátions as yóur inhéritance,
and the énds of the éarth as your posséssion.
⁹ With a ród of íron you will rúle them;
like a pótter's jár you will shátter them."

¹⁰ So nów, O kíngs, understánd;
take wárning, rúlers of the éarth.
¹¹ Sérve the LÓRD with féar;
exult with trémbling, páy him your hómage,
¹² lest he be ángry and you pérish on the wáy,
for súddenly his ánger will bláze.
Blessed are áll who trúst in Gód!

PRAYER

Jesus Christ, Son of David, Son of God, Holy and Anointed One, we acknowledge your lordship over all creation and all peoples who place their trust in you. As you served your Father through the fulfillment of his will and brought to fulfillment the paschal mystery, so enable us to follow you faithfully. With you, may we one day come to glory in the kingdom where you live and reign, forever and ever. Amen.

Psalm 3

I WILL NOT FEAR

For centuries, this psalm has been prayed each day by monks and nuns who rise in the dark of night to celebrate the Office of Vigils. The words of verse 6, "I lie down, I sleep, and I wake," make it a perfect psalm to begin each new day in God's grace. In reading this psalm, one is struck by the many indications that the Psalmist sees himself as being surrounded by foes who rise up to harm him. And yet interspersed among his expressions of fear are expressions of trust in God: "You, LORD, are a shield about me" (v. 4); "he answers me" (v. 5); "the LORD upholds me" (v. 6); "Salvation belongs to the LORD" (v. 9). This kind of confidence in God's ever-present care and protection is embodied in the most frequent injunction of Jesus in the New Testament, "Do not fear." We all face difficult situations that weave their way in and out of our lives, some more challenging and some less. But regardless of their magnitude, persevering prayer offered in trust and confidence enables us to live the gospel's teaching with fidelity. We can imagine an echo of this psalm in Jesus' own mind after his death and resurrection: "I lie down, I sleep and I wake, for the LORD upholds me" (v. 6).

PSALM 3

¹ *A Psalm of David as he is fleeing from his son Absalom.*

² How mány are my fóes, O LÓRD!
How mány are rísing up agáinst me!
³ How mány are sáying abóut me,
"There is no hélp for hím in Gód."
⁴ But yóu, LORD, are a shíeld abóut me,
my glóry, who líft up my héad.

⁵ I crý alóud to the LÓRD.
From his hóly móuntain he ánswers me.
⁶ I lie dówn, I sléep and I wáke,
for the LÓRD uphólds me.
⁷ I will not féar even thóusands of péople
who are ránged on every síde agáinst me.

Aríse, LORD; sáve me, my Gód,
⁸ you who stríke all my fóes on the chéek,
you who bréak the téeth of the wícked!
⁹ Salvátion belóngs to the LÓRD;
may your bléssing bé on your péople!

PRAYER

Lord of our salvation, you guard and protect us on our journey through life. In the face of life's challenges, our temptations to sin, and our personal fears, show us the way to peace through an ever greater trust in your faithful mercy and your gracious care. We pray through Christ our Lord. Amen.

𝒫salm 4

DWELL IN SAFETY

As the previous psalm is appropriate for the early morning, Psalm 4 is suitable for prayer at night. The Church has long used this psalm at Compline, or Night Prayer, the last office of prayer for the day. Those who pray it close the day with an expression of reliance on divine providence. Though we find in Psalm 4 some elements of a Lament, the striking language of this psalm can be characterized as voicing assurance, trust, and confidence in God's providential care. The Psalmist affirms the conviction that if we offer a just sacrifice and trust in the Lord, he will provide for our needs. We hear this psalm echoed in Jesus' own words at the Sermon on the Mount, reminding his followers that just as God cares for the small creatures of the world, so his care for us is even more assured. "Look at the birds of the air; they neither sow nor reap nor gather into barns, and yet your heavenly Father feeds them. Are you not of more value than they?" (Matt 6:26). We can assert with the Psalmist that we have much cause for hope.

PSALM 4

¹ *For the Choirmaster. With stringed instruments.*
A Psalm of David.

² I cálled, the Gód of jústice gave me ánswer;
from ánguish you reléased me, have mércy and héar me!
³ Children of mán, how lóng will my glóry be dishónored,
will you lóve what is fútile and séek what is fálse?
⁴ Knów that the LÓRD works wónders for his fáithful one;
the LÓRD will héar me whenéver I cáll him.

⁵ Tremble, do not sín: pónder on your béd and be stíll.
⁶ Óffer right sácrifice, and trúst in the LÓRD.
⁷ "What can bríng us háppiness?" mány sáy.
Lift up the líght of your fáce on ús, O LÓRD.

⁸ You have pút into my héart a gréater jóy
than abúndance of gráin and new wíne can províde.
⁹ In péace I will lie dówn and fall asléep,
for yóu alone, O LÓRD, make me dwéll in sáfety.

PRAYER

Lord Jesus, foreseen by the Psalmist as the Faithful One of God, teach us the way of genuine trust according to your new law of love. As we grow in the ways of hope and confidence, may your love grow ever stronger in us so that we, too, may pray with confidence, "You, alone, O Lord, make us dwell in peace and security." In your holy name, we pray. Amen.

$Psalm\ 5$

LEAD ME, LORD

As previous examples have illustrated, we find among the earliest psalms several compositions intended for use at specific times of day. Psalm 5 is a morning psalm (cf. v. 4), distinguished by two themes: first, the importance of the temple for the Psalmist's religious life; and second, the contrast between God and the wicked. Devotion to God's house, the temple, where the Psalmist experiences the divine presence, is affirmed (vv. 4c, 8). In verses 12–13, the verbs *shelter* and *surround* indicate that there is a place in God's house for the just. The Scriptures elsewhere affirm that in biblical times, those who were oppressed could find refuge in the temple precincts (cf. Exod 21:13; 1 Kgs 1:50; 2:28). The Psalmist seeks this protective union with God and enters the divine presence to renew inner strength and peace. While God is described in terms of merciful love and justice, bestowing gladness and joy, the wicked are portrayed as deceitful, flattering liars, rebellious and bloodthirsty. St. Paul reports that, for the sake of the gospel, he endured lies, mistreatment, and imprisonment, all the while seeking to draw closer to Christ by following God's will for him. He implores the Galatians, "Have I now become your enemy by telling you the truth?...My little children, for whom I am again in the pain of giving birth, until Christ is formed in you" (Gal 4:16, 19).

PSALM 5

¹ *For the Choirmaster. With flutes. A Psalm of David.*

² To my wórds give éar, O LÓRD;
give héed to my síghs.
³ Atténd to the sóund of my crý,
my Kíng and my Gód.

⁴ To yóu do I práy, O LÓRD.
In the mórning you héar my vóice;
in the mórning I pléad and watch befóre you.

⁵ You are no Gód who delíghts in évil;
no sínner is your guést.
⁶ The bóastful shall not stánd their gróund
befóre your éyes.
⁷ Áll who do évil you despíse;
all who líe you destróy.
The decéitful and thóse who shed blóod,
the Lórd detésts.

⁸ Yet through the gréatness of your mérciful lóve,
I énter your hóuse.
I bow dówn before your hóly témple,
in áwe of yóu.

⁹ Léad me, Lórd, in your jústice,
becáuse of my fóes;
make stráight your wáy befóre me.

¹⁰ No trúth can be fóund in their móuths,
their héart is all málice,
their thróat a wide-ópen gráve;
with their tóngue they flátter.

¹¹ Declára them guílty, O Gód.
Let them fáil in their desígns.
Drive them óut for their mány transgréssions,
for against yóu have they rebélled.

¹² All who take réfuge in yóu shall be glád,
and ever crý out their jóy.
You shélter them; in yóu they rejóice,
those who lóve your náme.
¹³ It is yóu who bless the júst one, O Lórd,
you surróund him with your fávor like a shíeld.

PRAYER

O just God, who never delight in evil, show us the way to live in truth, mercy, and peace. In our encounters with those who act contrary to your word, strengthen us to do only what is just, to rejoice in our calling to be your servants, and to find peace in following your will. We ask this through Christ our Lord. Amen.

Psalm 6

EXHAUSTED WITH GROANING

Psalm 6 is the first of what are known as the Church's Seven Penitential Psalms (6, 32, 38, 51, 102, 130, and 143). These psalms lament a painful situation that has befallen them, while also feeling the absence of God's presence and assistance. In biblical times, the number seven was a symbol of perfection and completion. In this prayer, the Psalmist calls out the divine name "Lord" (YHWH) seven times. The Psalmist is at the end of his rope; life's trials have left him exhausted, shaken, and in tears. In the midst of this difficult situation, he appeals to God to reassert the covenant love (Hebrew, *hesed*) that marks God's relationship with those who seek to follow in the way of the Lord. "Save me in your merciful love" (v. 5b) is the Psalmist's cry. We sometimes find it difficult to pray such a psalm when our own lives are not so severely desperate and anguished. Yet we know that in our world, these words are painfully true for some of our fellow members of the Body of Christ; their lives are troubled daily by oppressive political regimes, threats of war, and ongoing acts of violence. We can pray psalms such as these in the names of our brothers and sisters who face such threats and whose lives are vulnerable and in danger through no fault of their own. St. Paul encouraged his young disciple, Timothy, along these same lines: "Fight the good fight of faith; take hold of the eternal life, to which you were called and for which you made the good confession in the presence of many witnesses" (1 Tim 6:12). Each of us can also pray this psalm with meaning when we encounter times of sickness, interior sadness, and rejection by others. With the Psalmist we can say, "Have mercy...save me...turn to me...deliver me."

PSALM 6

¹ *For the Choirmaster. With stringed instruments, upon the Eighth Chord. A Psalm of David.*

² O Lórd, do not rebúke me in your ánger;
repróve me nót in your ráge.

³ Have mércy on me, LÓRD, for I lánguish.
Lord, héal me; my bónes are sháking,
⁴ and my sóul is gréatly sháken.

But yóu, O LÓRD, how lóng?
⁵ Retúrn, LORD, réscue my sóul.
Sáve me in your mérciful lóve.
⁶ For in déath there is nó remémbrance of yóu;
from the gráve, whó can gíve you práise?

⁷ Í am exháusted with my gróaning;
every níght I drench my béd with téars,
I bedéw my cóuch with wéeping.
⁸ My éyes waste awáy with gríef;
I have grown óld surróunded by áll my fóes.

⁹ Léave me, áll who do évil,
for the LORD héeds the sóund of my wéeping.
¹⁰ The LÓRD has héard my pléa;
the LÓRD will recéive my práyer.
¹¹ All my fóes will be shámed and greatly sháken,
súddenly pút to sháme.

PRAYER

Almighty and eternal God, who strengthen us in time of trial, be with all who suffer in witness to the gospel. Keep us strong in proclaiming the message of hope that your merciful love will conquer the power of hatred and pride, and free all people to live in accord with your word of life. We ask this through Christ our Lord. Amen.

ℙsalm 7

A PLEA FOR JUSTICE

When an accusation is made against us, and we have to admit it is true, it stings. But when a false accusation is leveled at us, we feel pain both in wondering where the falsehood came from and how the situation can be corrected. Here the Psalmist calls out to God in a state of confusion and helplessness. But the person of faith can turn to our all-knowing God with firm trust that a reversal of this injustice will come about. Our God is righteous, and tests mind and heart to ensure that justice will prevail in the end (v. 10). Though we know of no one named Cush in the biblical narratives of David, as indicated in the superscription of this psalm, David knew his innocence before Saul. When jealousy and revenge overtook Saul's heart against David, he suffered the cause of an innocent yet besieged servant. Hearing the Psalmist's plea of innocence also recalls one of the unsung heroes of the Bible beset by this very situation, the prophet Jeremiah. As a faithful prophet, he announced God's word to the people of Jerusalem, but they responded with mockery and derision; even worse, his words were willfully misconstrued as a subversive plot against the leaders of Jerusalem (see Jer 18:18–23). These painful circumstances will be familiar, too, to any Christian recalling the trial of Jesus before the Sanhedrin. Yet Jesus was a model of righteousness, trusting that the Just Judge would set him free. "Then the high priest said to him, 'I order you to tell us under oath before the living God whether you are the Messiah, the Son of God.' Jesus said to him in reply, 'You have said so. But I tell you: From now on you will see "the Son of Man seated at the right hand of the Power" and "coming on the clouds of heaven"'" (Matt 26:63–64).

PSALM 7

¹ *A Lament of David that he chanted to the Lord on account of Cush, the Benjaminite.*

² O LORD, my Gód, I take réfuge in yóu.
Save and réscue me from áll my pursúers,
³ lest they téar me apárt like a líon,
and drag me óff with nó one to réscue me.

⁴ If I have dóne this, O LÓRD, my Gód,
⁵ if I have páid back évil for góod,
I who sáved my unjúst oppréssor:
⁶ then let my fóe pursúe my soul and séize me;
let him trámple my lífe to the gróund,
and láy my hónor in the dúst.

⁷ O LÓRD, rise úp in your ánger;
be exálted against the fúry of my fóes.
Awáke, my Gód, to enáct
the jústice you órdered.

8 Let the cómpany of péoples gather róund you,
as you táke your seat abóve them on hígh.

9 The LÓRD is júdge of the péoples.
Give júdgment for mé, O LÓRD,
for I am júst and blámeless of héart.

10 Put an énd to the évil of the wícked!
Make the just man stand fírm;
It is yóu who test mínd and héart,
O Gód of jústice!

11 Gód is a shíeld befóre me,
who sáves the úpright of héart.
12 God is a júdge, just and pówerful and pátient,
not éxercising ánger every dáy.

13 Against sómeone who does nót repént,
Gód will shárpen his swórd;
he bénds his bów and makes réady.
14 For such a óne he prepáres deadly wéapons;
he bárbs his árrows with fíre.

15 Here is óne who concéives iníquity;
pregnant with málice, he gives bírth to líes.
16 He digs a pít and bóres it déep;
and in the tráp he has máde he fálls.
17 His málice recóils on his héad;
on his own skúll his víolence fálls.

18 I thánk the LÓRD for his jústice,
singing to the náme of the LÓRD, the Most Hígh.

PRAYER

*O just and upright God, who know the twisting paths of the human
heart, help us to judge all things rightly. When faced with fearful circumstances, enable us to place our confidence in your mercy and truth,
and to find our only source of hope in you, who live and reign, forever
and ever. Amen.*

Psalm 8

THE MAJESTIC NAME

This psalm begins and concludes with a refrain exalting the divine name of YHWH (indicated in this translation as LORD). This is the name that God revealed to Moses (Exod 3:13–15), and by which the people of Israel were to know, pray to, and acclaim their God. In the Bible, one's name is an encapsulation of one's destiny, mission, and calling. The majestic name of the Lord, transcendent in its meaning, reveals the greatness, righteousness, and power belonging alone to the God of Israel. In his famous christological hymn, St. Paul propounds the significance of the name of God's Son: "At the name of Jesus every knee should bend, in heaven and on earth and under the earth, and every tongue should confess that Jesus Christ is Lord, to the glory of God the Father" (Phil 2:10–11). Psalm 8 is cited in the Epistle to the Hebrews to explain the manner in which God has subjected everything to the resurrected Christ, who "for a little while was made lower than the angels, is now crowned with glory and honor" (Heb 2:9; Ps 8:6). Psalm 8 appears frequently in the liturgies of both Christmas and Easter. The New Testament authors read this psalm as a prophecy of the mystery of Christ to come in the fullness of time. At Christmas, we celebrate the One who shared fully in our humanity, who, while yet still God, was made lower than the angels (see vv. 5–6). At Easter, we celebrate the manner in which Jesus was crowned with glory and honor, and given power over the works of God's hands (vv. 6–7), all things being put under Christ's feet (see also 1 Cor 15:27; Eph 1:22). From beginning to end, this psalm praises God for the wonders of creation, and for the new creation accomplished in Jesus Christ. We also find here the great dignity that is found in each human person in God's creation of man and woman as the summit of the whole creative plan. Knowing the dignity and nobility of the human person enables each of us to believe we have a role to play in the unfolding plan of God's continuing creative redemption.

PSALM 8

[1] *For the Choirmaster. Upon the* gittith.
A Psalm of David.

² O Lᴏ́ʀᴅ, our Lórd, how majéstic
is your náme through áll the éarth!

Your májesty is sét above the héavens.
³ From the móuths of chíldren and of bábés
you fáshioned praise to fóil your énemy,
to sílence the fóe and the rébel.

⁴ When I see the héavens, the wórk of your fíngers,
the móon and the stárs which you arránged,
⁵ what is mán that you should kéep him in mínd,
the son of mán that you cáre for hím?

⁶ Yet you have máde him little lówer than the ángels;
with glóry and hónor you crówned him,
⁷ gave him pówer over the wórks of your hánds:
you put áll things únder his féet,

⁸ Áll of them, shéep and óxen,
yes, éven the cáttle of the fíelds,
⁹ birds of the áir, and físh of the séa
that máke their wáy through the wáters.

¹⁰ O Lᴏ́ʀᴅ, our Lórd, how majéstic
is your náme through áll the éarth!

PRAYER

*To your name, almighty and eternal God, whose glory fills the world,
we lift up joyous and thankful praise. In fashioning us as the summit
of creation, you formed us to be your image on earth. Strengthen us in
our witness to the gospel of Jesus Christ, that we may become your new
creation, giving glory to you in all that we say and do. This we ask
through Christ our Lord. Amen.*

Psalm 9

GOD, THE STRONGHOLD FOR THE POOR AND OPPRESSED

The Psalmist affirms that the God of Israel is the God of the poor and oppressed. We find in this psalm the tender and loving language proper to those who acknowledge their need for God's care. "Those who know your name will trust you; you will not forsake those who seek you, O LORD...he has not forgotten the cry of the poor" (vv. 11, 13). The psalm opens with words of thanksgiving, words that rise from a heart filled with gratitude for the universal justice of God, who never forsakes those who seek divine protection but brings judgment on those who have laid snares for others. As the psalm tells us, "[God] will judge the world with justice; he will govern the peoples with equity" (v. 9). In this psalm, we hear an echo of Luke's beatitudes: "And raising his eyes toward his disciples [Jesus] said: "Blessed are you who are poor, for yours is the kingdom of God. Blessed are you who are hungry now, for you will be filled. Blessed are you who weep now, for you will laugh" (Luke 6:20–21). Jesus is truly God's ambassador of divine justice.

PSALM 9

¹ *For the Choirmaster. In the manner of a Chant* Mut Labben. *A Psalm of David.*

² I will práise you, LÓRD, with all my héart;
all your wónders Í will conféss.
³ I will rejóice in yóu and be glád,
and sing psálms to your náme, O Most Hígh.

⁴ Sée how my énemies turn báck,
how they stúmble and pérish befóre you.
⁵ You uphéld the jústice of my cáuse;
you sat enthróned, an úpright júdge.

⁶ You have rebúked the nátions, destróyed the wícked;
you have wíped out their náme foréver and éver.

⁷ The fóe is destróyed, etérnally rúined.
You upróoted their cíties; their mémory has pérished.

⁸ But the Lᴏʀᴅ sits enthróned foréver;
he has sét up his thróne for júdgment.
⁹ He will júdge the wórld with jústice;
he will góvern the péoples with équity.

¹⁰ For the oppréssed, the Lᴏʀᴅ will be a strónghold,
a strónghold in tímes of distréss.
¹¹ Those who knów your náme will trúst you;
you will not forsáke those who séek you, O Lᴏʀᴅ.

¹² Sing psálms to the Lᴏʀᴅ who dwells in Síon.
Téll his mighty wórks among the péoples,
¹³ for the Avénger of Blóod has remémbered them,
has not forgótten the crý of the póor.

¹⁴ Have mércy on mé, O Lᴏʀᴅ;
sée how I súffer from my fóes,
you who ráise me from the gátes of déath,
¹⁵ that Í may recóunt all your práise
at the gátes of dáughter Síon,
and rejóice in yóur salvátion.

¹⁶ The nátions have fállen in the pít which they máde;
their féet have been cáught in the snáre they láid.
¹⁷ The Lᴏʀᴅ has revéaled himself; hé has given júdgment.
The wícked are snáred by the wórk of their hánds.

¹⁸ Let the wícked go dówn to the gráve,
all the nátions forgétful of Gód:
¹⁹ for the néedy shall not álways be forgótten,
nor the hópes of the póor ever pérish.

²⁰ Arise, O Lᴏʀᴅ, let human stréngth not prevávil!
Let the nátions be júdged befóre you.
²¹ Stríke them with térror, O Lᴏʀᴅ;
let the nátions knów they are but mén.

PRAYER

*O just and merciful God, who govern the world with equity and love,
show us the path to justice in our daily lives. May we mirror the goodness of Jesus in all we say and do, and one day come to know the peace*

that you have promised to those who seek you above all things. We ask this through Christ our Lord. Amen.

Psalm 10

THE SCHEMING OF THE WICKED

In their earliest form, Psalms 9 and 10 may well have been a single psalm. As an alphabetic psalm that begins each new verse with a succeeding letter of the Hebrew alphabet, we can see how Psalm 10 completes what is begun in Psalm 9. We also see the same motifs in both: concern for the poor and needy in contrast to anger at the evil plots of the wicked. In the Septuagint, the earliest translation of the Hebrew Scriptures into Greek, Psalms 9 and 10 are one psalm; St. Jerome followed this tradition in his translation of the Vulgate. In noting the differences between Psalms 9 and 10, we see that Psalm 10 focuses more attention on the plotting and scheming of the wicked, doing so in vivid and descriptive language: they wait in ambush to prey upon the innocent (v. 8); they lurk in hiding like a lion, ready to seize victims and drag them away (v. 9); and in their hearts, they have forgotten God and abandoned his way of justice (v. 11). St. Paul bemoans a situation in which his own converts have been thus preyed upon, drawn by others to a way of life that differs from what Paul taught them: "You foolish Galatians! Who has bewitched you? It was before your eyes that Jesus Christ was publicly exhibited as crucified!" (Gal 3:1). This psalm prays for the Lord to act quickly to right what is wrong, and to defend those in need.

PSALM 10 *(9:22–39)*

¹ O LÓRD, whý; do you stánd afar óff,
and híde yoursélf in tímes of distréss?
² The póor are devóured by the príde of the wícked;
they are cáught in the schémes that óthers have máde.

3 For the wícked bóasts of his sóul's desíres;
the cóvetous blasphémes and spúrns the LÓRD.
4 The wicked sáys in his pride, "Gód will not púnish.
There ís no Gód." Súch are his thóughts.

5 His páth is éver untróubled;
your júdgments are on hígh, far remóved.
All thóse who oppóse him, he derídes.
6 In his héart he thinks, "Néver shall I fálter;
néver shall misfórtune be my lót."

7 His móuth is full of cúrsing, guíle, oppréssion;
únder his tóngue are decéit and évil.
8 He síts in ámbush in the víllages;
in hidden pláces, he múrders the ínnocent.

The éyes of the wícked keep wátch for the hélpless.
9 He lúrks in híding like a líon in his láir;
he lúrks in híding to séize the póor;
he séizes the póor one and drágs him awáy.

10 He cróuches, prepáring to spríng,
and the hélpless fall préy to his stréngth.
11 He sáys in his héart, "God forgéts,
he hides his fáce, néver will he sée."

12 Arise, O LÓRD; lift up your hánd, O Gód!
Do nót forgét the póor!
13 Whý; should the wícked spurn Gód,
saying in his héart, "You will not cáll to accóunt"?

14 But you have séen the tróuble and sórrow.
You nóte it; you táke it in your hánds.
The hélpless one relíes on yóu,
for yóu are the hélper of the órphan.

15 Break the árm of the wícked and the sínner!
Pursue their wíckedness till nóthing remáins!
16 The LORD is kíng foréver and éver.
The nátions shall pérish from his lánd.

17 O LÓRD, you have héard the desíre of the póor.
You stréngthen their héarts; you túrn your éar
18 to gíve right júdgment for the órphan and oppréssed,
so that nó one on éarth may strike térror agáin.

Judge of all, Defender of the poor, hear our earnest prayer, O God. Come to the aid of those who stand ever in need of your saving help. You, who are ever merciful, help the widow and the orphan to find justice in their time of need, and come to the aid of all who call out to you in faith, through Christ who is Lord, forever and ever. Amen.

Psalm 11

THE JUST LORD LOVES JUST DEEDS

Moments of crisis sometimes seem to shake the very order of the world in which we live. Foundations of political power and moral rectitude are called into question when justice and uprightness are ignored. This psalm seems to address that situation. And when such a situation arises, when "might makes right" and we know it is wrong, we too ask, "What can the just do?" It is true, we often feel individually that the powers of the world are beyond our sway, but what we can do is "to do justice, and to love kindness, and to walk humbly with your God" (Mic 6:8b). We must trust that, in the end, the justice of God will prevail. The images appearing in verses 5–7 of this psalm tell us that God's judgment will indeed come to all, and those who have done evil will be forced to drink from the cup of divine wrath, an image that appears elsewhere in the Scriptures, promising death to the wicked (cf. Ps 75:9; Ezek 23:32). We detect in this psalm foreshadowings of the judgment to be given by Jesus at the end of time, as presented in the Gospel according to Mark: "In those days, after that suffering, the sun will be darkened, and the moon will not give its light, and the stars will be falling from heaven, and the powers in the heavens will be shaken. Then they will see 'the Son of Man coming in clouds' with great power and glory. Then he will send out the angels, and gather his elect from the four winds, from the ends of the earth to the ends of heaven" (13:24–27). On that day the upright shall surely behold the face of God, as the concluding verse of this psalm asserts.

PSALM 11 *(10)*

¹ *For the Choirmaster. Of David.*

In the LÓRD I have táken réfuge.
Hów can you sáy to my sóul,
"Flý like a bírd to the móuntain!

² "Look, the wícked are bénding their bów!
They are fíxing their árrow on the stríng,
to shoot the úpright of héart in the dárk.
³ Foundátions ónce destróyed,
whát can the júst man dó?"

⁴ The LÓRD is in his hóly témple;
the thróne of the LÓRD is in héaven.
His éyes behóld the wórld;
his gáze probes the chíldren of mén.

⁵ The LORD inspécts the júst and the wícked;
the lóver of víolence he hátes.
⁶ He sends fíre and brímstone on the wícked,
a scorching wínd to fíll their cúp.
⁷ For the LORD is júst and lóves deeds of jústice;
the úpright shall behóld his fáce.

PRAYER

Almighty and eternal God, just Judge of the world, hear the prayer of your people who seek to establish your justice in our day. Drive out the forces of evil, soften the hearts of the arrogant, and bring to our world that peace promised by your risen Christ, who lives with you and the Holy Spirit, world without end. Amen.

Psalm 12

WORDS BOTH CUNNING AND TRUSTWORTHY

The words of the Psalmist anticipate the teaching of the Letter of James, which includes a forceful lesson on the power of the tongue both for evil and for good. "So also the tongue is a small member, yet it boasts of great exploits. How great a forest is set ablaze by a small fire! And the tongue is a fire. The tongue is placed among our members as a world of iniquity; it stains the whole body, sets on fire the cycle of nature, and is itself set on fire by hell" (3:5b–6). Here the Psalmist draws a sharp contrast between the words of evildoers and the words of God. "Cunning lips" and "boastful hearts" are contrasted with the character of the words of the Lord: "without alloy," like "silver from the furnace, seven times refined" (v. 7). The number seven is employed frequently in the Bible as an image of perfection, completeness, and wholeness. Two lessons may be learned here. First, wicked and cunning speech leads to a divided heart, which is far from the ways of God, and those who possess a wicked and arrogant tongue destroy themselves in the end; it is they who will vanish from among the children of Adam (v. 2). Second, the pure and untaintable word of God brings salvation. At the center of this psalm is a brief but life-giving oracle of the Lord: "For the poor and oppressed, I will arise, and I will grant them salvation" (v. 6). This is the psalm's message of great hope: God's saving hand will lift up those oppressed by the vicious tongues of the unscrupulous. This is God's word of promise, and it will surely come to pass.

PSALM 12 (11)

¹ *For the Choirmaster. Upon the Eighth Chord.*
A Psalm of David.

² Save me, O LÓRD, for the hóly ones áre no móre;
the fáithful have vánished from the sóns of mén.
³ They bábble vánities, óne to anóther,
with cúnning líps, with divíded héart.

⁴ May the LÓRD destróy all cúnning líps,
the tóngue that útters bóastful wórds,
⁵ thóse who sáy, "We preváil with our tóngue;
our líps are our ówn, whó is our máster?"

⁶ "For the póor who are oppréssed and the néedy who gróan,
nów will Í aríse," says the LÓRD;
"I will gránt them the salvátion for whích they lóng."
⁷ The wórds of the LÓRD are wórds without álloy,
sílver from the fúrnace, séven times refíned.

⁸ It is yóu, O LÓRD, who will kéep us sáfe,
and protéct us foréver from thís generátion.
⁹ The wícked prówl on évery síde,
while báseness is exálted by the sóns of mén.

PRAYER

Lord, Jesus Christ, living and eternal Word of God, show us the way to truth and mercy, kindness and compassion in the words we speak. May we imitate you in speaking words of life that we may serve as instruments in the building up of your kingdom, where you live and reign, forever and ever. Amen.

Psalm 13

HOW LONG, O LORD?

One means of getting a quick understanding of the message of a psalm is to read the opening and the closing verses. Are they similar, or do they contrast? In Psalm 13 we see a striking difference. The Psalmist opens his prayer with expressions of dejection, frustration, and near despair. Four times the question is posed, "How long, O LORD?" This rhetorical repetition emphasizes the force and urgency of the message. In sum, the Psalmist feels forgotten by God: separated from God's presence (v. 2a: "How long will you hide your face?"), alienated in personal anguish (v. 3a–b: "sorrow in my heart"; "grief in my soul"), and crushed by enemies

(v. 3c). It is an expression of utter misery and distress. What becomes the Psalmist's doorway to hope? It is trust in God's merciful love. "Merciful love" is the English rendering of the Hebrew word *hesed*, expressing the idea of God's covenant love marked by fidelity, steadfastness, loyalty, and devotion. When we have known the persevering love and kindness of someone in our own experience, it becomes a lifeline for us, a focus for ongoing hope even in the face of difficult or threatening times. St. Paul speaks of God's faithfulness in the same way in accounts of the challenges he faced. "[I have been] on frequent journeys, in danger from rivers, danger from bandits, danger from my own people, danger from Gentiles, danger in the city, danger in the wilderness, danger at sea, danger from false brothers and sisters; in toil and hardship, through many a sleepless night, hungry and thirsty, often without food, cold and naked (2 Cor 11:26–27). The miracle attending this trust in God is the unexpected bounty that comes to us in the midst of this confidence. This is the source of our blessing, and it gives us the reason for offering to God a sacrifice of praise in response.

PSALM 13 *(12)*

¹ *For the Choirmaster. A Psalm of David.*

² How lóng, O Lórd? Will you forgét me foréver?
How lóng will you híde your fáce from mé?
³ How lóng must I bear gríef in my sóul,
have sórrow in my héart all day lóng?
How lóng shall my énemy prevául over mé?

⁴ Lóok, ánswer me, Lórd my Gód!
Give líght to my éyes lest I fáll asleep in déath;
⁵ lest my énemy sáy, "Í have overcóme him";
lest my fóes rejóice when they sée me fáll.

⁶ As for mé, I trúst in your mérciful lóve.
Let my héart rejóice in yóur salvátion.
⁷ I will síng to the Lórd who has been bóuntiful with mé.
I will sing psálms to the náme of the Lórd Most Hígh.

PRAYER

Lord God of our salvation, we look to you in our every need. Strengthen us always to trust in your bountiful mercy and compassion, that we may experience the power of your saving grace and acclaim your faithful love. We ask this through Christ our Lord. Amen.

$\mathcal{P}$salm 14

ARE THERE ANY
WHO SEEK GOD?

Sometimes the text of a particular psalm, whole or in part, appears elsewhere in the Psalter. Such is the case with Psalm 14. The only major difference between Psalm 14 and Psalm 53 is that the latter consistently uses "God" to refer to the Almighty, while Psalm 14 uses both "God" and "Lord." This very distinction embodies an element of Hebraic literary style that bears a subtle but important message—one that might easily be missed in translation. The Psalmist begins by quoting the fool who says, "There is no God." In what then follows, we note that the names "God" or "Lord" appear seven times, the number seven being that frequent indication of fullness, perfection, or completion in the Hebraic imagination of the Psalter. Thus the Psalmist subtly contradicts the fool in the very structure of this prayer, asserting that the God of Israel lives, acts, and saves all who find their refuge in him. Every age seems to grapple with the ultimate question of God's existence, action, and presence in the world. The Psalmist here calls the one who denies the existence of God a "fool." St. Paul addresses this same question in the opening of his First Letter to the Corinthians, distinguishing "worldly wisdom" (which he calls "folly") from the wisdom of God that leads to eternal life. "God's foolishness is wiser than human wisdom, and God's weakness is stronger than human strength" (1 Cor 1:25). According to this psalm, those who seek God are among the wise (v. 2b). Though it is a lifelong search, it is the promise of our salvation.

PSALM 14 *(13)*

¹ *For the Choirmaster. A Psalm of David.*

The fóol has sáid in his héart,
"There ís no Gód."
Their déeds are corrúpt, depráved;
no one dóes any góod.

² From héaven the LÓRD looks dówn
on the húman ráce,
to sée if ány are wíse,
if ány seek Gód.

³ Áll have góne astráy,
depráved, every óne;
there is nó one who dóes any góod;
nó, not even óne.

⁴ Do nóne of the évil-doers únderstánd?
They eat úp my péople as if éating bréad;
they néver call óut to the LÓRD.

⁵ Thére they shall trémble with féar,
for God is wíth the generátion of the júst.
⁶ You may móck the pláns of one that is póor,
but his réfuge is the LÓRD.

⁷ O that Ísrael's salvátion might cóme from Síon.
When the LÓRD delívers his péople from bóndage,
then Jácob will be glád and Ísrael rejóice.

PRAYER

God of wisdom and truth, hidden in the beauty of creation yet active in the lives of your people, enable us to perceive clearly your presence in our lives and in our world. Manifest to us the wonders of your faithful love, that we may praise and thank you for the blessings you bring to our lives each day. We ask this through Christ our Lord. Amen.

Psalm 15

THE WAYS OF JUSTICE

Imagine the scene the Psalmist paints here. Gathered before the temple, a crowd addresses the Lord through the voice of the priest who stands before them, posing an urgent question: "Lord, who may abide in your tent, and dwell on your holy mountain?" The people formulate the question as a matter of their relationship to God, yet each reply has to do with how the people are to relate to one another: love of neighbor, the second great commandment. The psalm reminds us that communion with God takes for granted that we treat our neighbor as we would wish to be treated ourselves. How perfectly Jesus embodies this attitude. Consider the manner in which he dealt with those who came to him in need. "As he went ashore, he saw a great crowd; and he had compassion for them, because they were like sheep without a shepherd; and he began to teach them many things" (Mark 6:34). When we undertake the acts of kindness, mercy, and justice of which this psalm speaks, we act as instruments of God's goodness, offering to others the love that is ours as God's gift: the Spirit dwelling in us (Rom 5:5).

PSALM 15 (14)

¹ *A Psalm of David.*

Lord, whó may abíde in your tént,
and dwéll on your hóly móuntain?
² Whoéver wálks without fáult;
who dóes what is júst,
and spéaks the trúth from his héart.

³ Whoéver does not slánder with his tóngue;
who dóes no wróng to a néighbor,
who cásts no slúr on a fríend,
⁴ who lóoks with scórn on the wícked,
but hónors those who féar the Lórd.

Who keeps an óath, whatéver the cóst,
⁵ who lénds no móney at ínterest,
and accépts no bríbes against the ínnocent.
Such a óne shall néver be sháken.

PRAYER

Ever-faithful God, who have shown us the depth of your love by sending your Son as our model and example, strengthen us to follow your Christ as disciples. May it be our joy to speak as he spoke, to act as he acted, and to love as he loved. In his holy name, we pray. Amen.

Psalm 16

LORD, YOU ARE
MY PORTION AND MY CUP

This psalm affirms a deep and steady trust in God, both in and out of season. The Psalmist is troubled by those who engage in the worship and reverence of idols; he will have no part in their sacrifices, nor even in the mention of their names. For the Psalmist, the one true God is the only source of happiness, security, and counsel. In every age, men and women are tempted to create idols of whatever suggests power to them: money, possessions, prestige, success, control. This psalm places before us the inner happiness that comes with putting our trust in God and holding God's word as our hope. The writers of the New Testament saw the resurrection foreshadowed in the closing words of this psalm (vv. 9–11): St. Peter quotes them in his speech on Pentecost, asserting that they attest the promise of the resurrection: "But God raised [Christ] up, having freed him from death, because it was impossible for him to be held in its power. For David says concerning him,…'You will not abandon my soul to Hades, or let your Holy One experience corruption. You have made known to me the ways of life; you will make me full of gladness with your presence'" (Acts 2:24–25a, 27–28). St. Paul also cites this psalm in his speech at the synagogue in Antioch, explaining to the Jews that the mystery of the resurrection, hidden in their sacred texts, is now being fulfilled in Christ: "[David] has also said in another psalm, 'You will not let your Holy One experience corruption'" (Acts 13:35). This psalm also appears in the liturgy of the Holy Saturday Vigil as a response to the second reading (Gen 22:1–18 or 22:1–2, 9a, 10–13, 15–18), expressing trust that the resurrection is the future glory for all who place their trust in God's unfolding plan of salvation for each of us.

PSALM 16 *(15)*

¹ *A* Miktam. *Of David.*

Presérve me, O Gód, for in yóu I take réfuge.
² I sáy to the LÓRD, "Yóu are my Lórd.
My háppiness líes in yóu alóne."

³ As for the hóly ones who dwéll in the lánd,
they are nóble, and in thém is all my delíght.
⁴ Those who chóose other góds incréase their sórrows.
I will nót take párt in their ófferings of blóod.
Nór will I táke their námes upon my líps.

⁵ O LORD, it is yóu who are my pórtion and cúp;
yóu yoursélf who secúre my lót.
⁶ Pléasant pláces are márked out for mé:
a pleasing héritage indéed is míne!

⁷ I will bléss the LORD who gíves me cóunsel,
who éven at níght dirécts my héart.
⁸ I kéep the LORD befóre me álways;
with hím at my ríght hand, I shall nót be móved.

⁹ And so, my héart rejóices, my sóul is glád;
éven my flésh shall rést in hópe.
¹⁰ For yóu will not abándon my sóul to héll,
nor lét your hóly one sée corrúption.

¹¹ You will shów me the páth of lífe,
the fúllness of jóy in your présence,
at your ríght hand, blíss foréver.

PRAYER

Lord God, my portion and my cup, in you alone lies the fullness of happiness and peace. May my trust in your merciful love grow ever stronger in witnessing the power of your grace at work in the lives of all who call themselves your servants. May our great hope be the future glory you hold out to all who, with fidelity and perseverance, follow your Son Jesus, in whose holy name we pray. Amen.

Psalm 17

SEARCH MY HEART, TEST ME BY FIRE

Here the Psalmist suffers under false accusations that will bring him before a tribunal of human judges. In the watches of the night (v. 3), before he is to face his detractors, the Psalmist appeals to God for a just hearing of his case. Most important, the Psalmist presents his case directly to God, the true Judge, who will deliver him and show him righteous mercy. Who of us has not at one time or another been willfully misunderstood, maliciously misquoted, or harshly misjudged? This psalm calls us to a persevering faith in God as the single most important Judge in our life. The situation recalls one of the most sorely abused and maltreated heroes of the Bible, the prophet Jeremiah. Among Jeremiah's lasting legacies are those passages collectively known as "The Confessions of Jeremiah," those great prayers of lament in which he pours out his heart, allowing all who read them to witness the struggle between his pain and his faith, his affliction and his trust, his failures and his hopes (cf. Jer 11:18; 12:6; 15:10–21; 17:14–18; 18:18–23; 20:7–18). It is also worth noting that this psalm, like Psalm 16 immediately preceding, ends on a prayer that the Psalmist will come, in the end, before God's face, to share in an experience of the divine presence. Let others pursue worldly wealth in the present moment, but for the Psalmist, what lies ahead is what counts—a vision founded on a resolute trust in God.

PSALM 17 *(16)*

¹ *A Prayer of David.*

O Lᴏʀᴅ, hear a cáuse that is júst,
pay héed to my crý.
Túrn your éar to my práyer:
no decéit is on my líps.
² From yóu may my jústice come fórth.
Your eyes discérn what is úpright.

³ Search my héart and vísit me by níght.
Test me by fíre, and you will fínd no wrong in mé.

⁴ My móuth does not transgréss as others dó;
on accóunt of the wórds of your líps,
I closely wátched the páths of the víolent.

⁵ I képt my steps fírmly in your páths.
My féet have néver fáltered.

⁶ To you I cáll; for you will súrely héed me, O Gód.
Túrn your éar to me; héar my wórds.
⁷ Displáy your mérciful lóve.
By your right hánd you delíver from their fóes
those who pút their trúst in yóu.

⁸ Guárd me as the ápple of your éye.
Híde me in the shádow of your wíngs
⁹ from the víolent attáck of the wícked.

My foes encírcle me with déadly intént.
¹⁰ Their hearts tight shút, their móuths speak próudly.
¹¹ They advánce agáinst me, and nów they surróund me.
Their eyes wátch to stríke me to the gróund.
¹² They are like a líon réady to cláw,
like some young líon cróuched in híding.

¹³ Arise, O LORD, confrónt them, stríke them dówn!
Let your swórd delíver my sóul from the wícked!
¹⁴ Let your hánd, O LORD, delíver me from thóse
whose pórtion in this présent lífe is fléeting.

May you gíve them their fíll of your tréasures;
may their óffspring rejóice in plénty,
and léave their wéalth to their chíldren.
¹⁵ As for mé, in jústice I shall behóld your fáce;
when I awáke I shall be fílled with the vísion of your présence.

PRAYER

*You guard us, O Lord, as the apple of your eye, displaying for us a
mercy beyond our comprehension. Grant me patience when I am misunderstood; grant me peace when I am falsely accused, that in renew-
ing my trust in your providential ways, I may proclaim you as the God
of justice and truth, who live and reign, forever and ever. Amen.*

Psalm 18

O LORD, MY ROCK, MY FORTRESS, MY SAVIOR

The beginning (vv. 2–4) and the end (vv. 47–51) of this psalm echo one another in expressions of praise, gratitude, and thanksgiving to God, the refuge and strength of the Psalmist. The repeated use of the possessive pronoun *my* conveys the close personal nature of the Psalmist's relationship with God: it appears eight times in verse 3 alone: "my rock, my fortress, my savior, my God, my rock, my shield, my saving strength, my stronghold." Every passage of this psalm announces and celebrates the "living God," who is bound intimately to David and his family line, as well as to the entire people of the covenant. The superscript (v. 1) indicates that this psalm is linked to the divine assistance that enabled David, God's anointed, to be victorious over the forces of evil, citing in particular his escape from Saul. Rarely should such superscriptions be read as instances of reliable historical data; rather they suggest an appropriate tone for reading the psalm. Such a psalm could well have been used at some national celebration recalling God's deliverance of Israel. One is encouraged to form the impression that God has coordinated all the cosmic forces to work in concert for the welfare and success of David. Language on a mythic scale is abundant here: God is described as bending back the heavens to come down from the celestial throne to participate in this conquest, soaring on the wings of the wind (vv. 10–11). Among the ancients, the dark and deep waters were symbolic of any life-threatening dangers; here the Psalmist describes God's personal intervention (vv. 16–18) to allay such threats. The second half of the psalm employs language that, even today, can symbolize God's power over the dangers that menace us. We can identify with images like: "It is you who give light to my lamp; the LORD my God lightens my darkness. With you I can break through a barrier. With my God I can scale a wall" (vv. 29–30). All these terms express confidence in God's care, guidance, and protection in the midst of life's challenges. The rich and varied poetic imagery of this psalm invites us to reflect on God's presence amid both the blessings and the challenges of life.

PSALM 18 *(17)*

¹ *For the Choirmaster. Of David, the servant of the Lord, who spoke the words of this canticle to the Lord when he had been freed from the power of all his enemies and from the hand of Saul.* ² *He said:*

I lóve you, LÓRD, my stréngth;
³ O LORD, my róck, my fórtress, my sávior;
my Gód, my róck where I take réfuge;
my shíeld, my saving stréngth, my strónghold.
⁴ I cry óut, "Práised be the LÓRD!"
and sée, I am sáved from my fóes.

⁵ The wáves of déath rose abóut me;
the tórrents of destrúction assáiled me;
⁶ the snáres of the gráve surróunded me;
the tráps of déath confrónted me.

⁷ In my ánguish I cálled to the LÓRD;
I críed to my Gód for hélp.
From his témple he héard my vóice;
my crý to him réached his éars.

⁸ The éarth then réeled and rócked;
the móuntains were sháken to their báse;
they quáked at his térrible ánger.

⁹ Smóke came fórth from his nóstrils,
and scórching fíre from his móuth;
from hím were kíndled live cóals.

¹⁰ He bént the héavens and came dówn,
a black clóud was únder his féet.
¹¹ On a chérub, he róde and he fléw;
he sóared on the wíngs of the wínd.

¹² He máde the dárkness his cóvering,
the dark wáters of the clóuds, his tént.
¹³ A bríghtness shóne out befóre him,
with háilstones and fláshes of fíre.

¹⁴ The LÓRD then thúndered in the héavens;
the Most Hígh let his vóice be héard,
with háil and cóals of fíre.

¹⁵ He shot his árrows, scáttered the fóe,
flashed his líghtnings, and pút them to flíght.

¹⁶ The béd of the ócean was revéaled;
the foundátions of the wórld were laid báre
at yóur rebúke, O LORD,
at the blást of the bréath of your nóstrils.

¹⁷ From on hígh he reached dówn and séized me;
he drew me fórth from the míghty wáters.
¹⁸ He sáved me from my pówerful fóe,
from my énemies, whose stréngth I could not mátch.

¹⁹ They assáiled me in the dáy of my misfórtune,
but the LORD was my stróng suppórt.
²⁰ He brought me óut to a pláce of fréedom;
he sáved me becáuse he lóved me.

²¹ The LORD rewárded me becáuse I was júst,
repáid me, for my hánds were cléan,
²² for I have képt the wáys of the LORD,
and have not fállen awáy from my Gód.

²³ For his júdgments are áll befóre me:
his commánds I have not cást asíde.
²⁴ Í have been blámeless befóre him;
I have képt mysélf from guílt.
²⁵ The LORD repáid me becáuse I was júst,
and my hánds were cléan in his éyes.

²⁶ With the fáithful you shów yourself fáithful;
with the blámeless you shów yourself blámeless.
²⁷ With the sincére you shów yourself sincére,
but the cúnning you outdó in shréwdness;
²⁸ for you sáve a lówly péople,
but bring lów the éyes that are próud.

²⁹ It is yóu who give líght to my lámp;
the LORD my God líghtens my dárkness.
³⁰ With yóu I can bréak through a bárrier,
with my Gód I can scále a wáll.

³¹ As for Gód, his wáy is blámeless;
the wórd of the LORD is púre.

Hé indéed is the shíeld
of áll who trúst in hím.

³² For whó is Gód but the LORD?
Whó is a róck but our Gód?
³³ It is Gód who gírds me with stréngth,
and kéeps my páth free of bláme.

³⁴ My féet he makes swíft as the déer's;
he has máde me stand fírm on the héights.
³⁵ He has tráined my hánds for báttle,
and my árms to bénd the bronze bów.

³⁶ You gáve me your sáving shíeld;
with your right hánd, you gáve me suppórt;
you bent dówn to máke me gréat.
³⁷ You léngthened my stéps benéath me;
and my féet have néver slípped.

³⁸ I pursúed and overtóok my fóes,
néver turning báck till they were sláin.
³⁹ I strúck them so they cóuld not ríse;
they féll benéath my féet.

⁴⁰ You gírded me with stréngth for báttle;
you made my énemies fáll benéath me.
⁴¹ You máde my fóes take flíght;
those who háted mé I destróyed.

⁴² They cried óut, but there was nó one to sáve them,
cried to the LORD, but he díd not ánswer.
⁴³ I crúshed them fine as dúst before the wínd,
trod them dówn like dírt in the stréets.

⁴⁴ From the féuds of the péople you delívered me,
and pút me at the héad of the nátions.
Péople unknówn to me sérved me;
⁴⁵ when they héard of mé, they obéyed me.

Foreign nátions cáme to me crínging;
⁴⁶ foreign nátions fáded awáy.
Trémbling, they came fórth from their stróngholds.

⁴⁷ The LORD líves, and blést be my Róck!
May the Gód of my salvátion be exálted,

⁴⁸ the Gód who gíves me redréss
and subdúes the péoples únder me.

⁴⁹ You sáved me from my fúrious fóes;
you sét me abóve my assáilants;
you sáved me from the víolent mán.

⁵⁰ So I will práise you, LÓRD, among the nátions;
to your náme will I síng a psálm.

⁵¹ The LORD gíves great víctories to his kíng,
and shows mérciful lóve for his anóinted,
for Dávid and his séed foréver.

PRAYER

Almighty and eternal God, our refuge and our strength, make us aware of the ways in which you touch our lives so as to assure us of your saving presence among us. May our response to you always be filled with gratitude and praise for the wonders of your power by which you demonstrate your gracious mercy and compassion toward all your creatures. To you be all praise and glory, now and forever. Amen.

Psalm 19

A TALE OF TWO REVELATIONS

A quick glance at this psalm makes it evident that two different psalms have been joined together (vv. 2–7 and vv. 8–15). Though the two parts differ in poetic style and in the images employed, both treat the same subject: the form under which God's revelation is manifested to the human imagination. In verses 2–7, God's revelation is perceived through the wonders of creation, in particular through the sun and the cycle of the day; in verses 8–15, it is made known through the Law of Moses, the divine word. The heavens, the firmament, the passage from day to night all reveal who God is: the Creator of all the world, the Master of the universe, a God of wonder and majesty. The Psalmist tells us that though none of these elements of creation speaks a word, their being and place in the universe tell us a great deal about the one who created them. Beyond this, we also recognize in the marvelous gift of the Law a form of God's revelation. The Law is humanity's response to God's invitation to relationship in the covenant, and in the Law itself we perceive much about the Lawgiver. God's Law is described in such superlative terms that anyone would want to be the beneficiary of its blessings: it is perfect, steadfast, righteous, clear, pure, true, more precious than quantities of gold, and sweeter than honey. The Law, when observed faithfully, teaches us the path we must follow to obtain life's reward. Both images of revelation portrayed here: the sun and the Law—promise life; the sun warms the earth to bring forth life in all its forms, and the Law illuminates our way to blessings gained from the covenant. Last, it is most enriching to consider the Church's christological application of this psalm. During the season of Christmas, our reading of this psalm foretells the mystery of the incarnation: it is the sun/Son who comes forth from the heavens like a bridegroom, or like a champion running his course. Likewise, the Law of the elder covenant becomes the living Word in Jesus Christ, who has fulfilled the Law by bringing it to life in both his teaching and his deeds. In the Sermon on the Mount, Jesus himself says, "Do not think that I have come to abolish the law or the prophets; I have come not to abolish but to fulfill" (Matt 5:17). He satisfies the greatest of the commandments in his love of God (fulfilling God's will) and neighbor (healings, loving acts of kindness).

PSALM 19 *(18)*

¹ *For the Choirmaster. A Psalm of David.*

² The héavens decláre the glóry of Gód,
and the firmament procláims the wórk of his hánds.
³ Dáy unto dáy convéys the méssage,
and níght unto níght impárts the knówledge.

⁴ No spéech, no wórd, whose vóice goes unhéeded;
⁵ their sóund goes fórth through áll the éarth,
their méssage to the útmost bóunds of the wórld.

⁶ Thére he has pláced a tént for the sún;
it comes fórth like a brídegroom cóming from his tént,
rejóices like a chámpion to rún his cóurse.

7 At one énd of the héavens is the rísing of the sún;
to its fúrthest énd it rúns its cóurse.
There is nóthing concéaled from its búrning héat.

* * *

8 The láw of the LÓRD is pérfect;
it revíves the sóul.
The decrées of the LÓRD are stéadfast;
they give wísdom to the símple.

9 The précepts of the LÓRD are ríght;
they gládden the héart.
The commánd of the LÓRD is cléar;
it gives líght to the éyes.

10 The féar of the LÓRD is púre,
abíding foréver.
The júdgments of the LÓRD are trúe;
they are, áll of them, júst.

11 They are móre to be desíred than góld,
than quántities of góld.
And swéeter are théy than hóney,
than honey flówing from the cómb.

12 So in thém your sérvant finds instrúction;
great rewárd is in their kéeping.
13 But whó can detéct their own érrors?
From hídden faults acquít me.

14 From presúmption restráin your sérvant;
máy it not rúle me.
Thén shall Í be blámeless,
cléan from grave sín.

15 May the spóken wórds of my móuth,
the thóughts of my héart,
win fávor in your síght, O LÓRD,
my róck and my redéemer!

PRAYER

*O Christ, Word of the eternal God, who came among us to share fully
in our humanity, help us to know and put into practice your new law*

of love, that we may always be ambassadors of your goodness and mercy. You live and reign, forever and ever. Amen.

Psalm 20

PRAYER BEFORE THE BATTLE

A common theme connects Psalms 20 and 21: the first offers a prayer before battle and the second a prayer after victory has been won. Psalm 20 presents a fervent plea for God to answer their request: three times, at the beginning, middle, and end of the psalm, the verb *answer* is employed to underscore the urgency of the appeal: "May the LORD answer you" (v. 2), "[The LORD] answers from his holy heaven" (v. 7b), and, "O LORD, give answer on the day we call" (v. 10). We perceive a growing intensity in this reiteration, beginning with an initial statement of hope, moving then to an assertion of fact, and finally a direct appeal to the Divine Name. Each time the Psalmist links this "answer" to the name of God (represented as "LORD" in verses 2, 6, and 8). Reference in the Bible to the name of God implies appeal to God's very nature and identity; such references presuppose that God's name possesses the power, force, and vitality to accomplish whatever is being asked. We also see here that the name of God may be employed to manifest praise and thanksgiving for what God has done for those in need. Human powers and resources, particularly military ones, pale here by comparison to divine strength. The enemy places their trust in the power of horses and chariots, but the faithful rely on the name of the Lord alone. In the Letter to the Ephesians, St. Paul also employs military terminology when speaking of the opposition we encounter in our earthly pilgrimage to the heavenly kingdom. "Our struggle is not against enemies of blood and flesh, but against the rulers, against the authorities, against the cosmic powers of this present darkness, against the spiritual forces of evil in the heavenly places. Therefore take up the whole armor of God, so that you may be able to withstand on that evil day, and having done everything, to stand firm" (Eph 6:12–13). The forces of evil that we must face each and every day remind us that war can be closer to us than we may think—

an interior war by which we seek to take hold of the grace given us in Christ. Psalm 20 is a reminder that life is sometimes a battle.

PSALM 20 *(19)*

¹ *For the Choirmaster. A Psalm of David.*

² May the LORD ánswer you in tíme of tríal;
may the náme of Jacob's Gód protéct you.
³ May he sénd you hélp from the hóly place,
and gíve you suppórt from Síon.

⁴ May he remémber áll your ófferings,
and recéive your sácrifice with fávor.
⁵ May he gíve you your héart's desíre,
and fulfíll every óne of your pláns.

⁶ May we ríng out our jóy at your víctory,
and raise bánners in the náme of our Gód.
May the LÓRD grant áll your práyers.

⁷ Now I knów the LORD sáves his anóinted,
and ánswers from his hóly héaven
with the míghty víctory of his hánd.

⁸ Sóme put their trúst in cháriots or hórses,
but wé in the náme of the LÓRD, our Gód.
⁹ Théy will cóllapse and fáll,
but wé shall rise úp and hold fírm.
¹⁰ Grant salvátion to the kíng, O LÓRD,
give ánswer on the dáy we cáll.

PRAYER

Provident and ever-faithful God, strengthen our trust in your guidance, help, and support in the struggles of life. May our heart's desire be to fulfill your holy plan for our life as you lead us in the ways of peace and faith. We ask this through Christ our Lord. Amen.

Psalm 21

REJOICING IN GOD'S VICTORY

Psalm 21 blends thankful praise for God's victory on the king's behalf with an affirmation of the king's unfailing trust in God's saving action. To these are added vivid expressions of the terrible destruction that is to fall upon the king's foes (vv. 9–13). The psalm opens and closes with references to God's strength, in which the king rejoices and upon which he depends for deliverance in time of trouble. In the ancient pagan civilizations of biblical times, kings were held to possess in themselves some portion of the divinity of their gods. This was not so in Israel, as Psalm 21 clearly shows. Though the king enjoys many blessings, they all arise directly from his relationship with the one God of Israel, the LORD (YHWH). As God's chosen one, the king enjoys divine favor, but he does not share in God's divinity. Rather, as this psalm indicates, the king's successes and victories come from God, the source of all blessing. Verse 8 expresses succinctly that all the good that comes to the king arises from God's mercy—in Hebrew, *hesed*, that term used to denote particularly God's faithful love and steadfast mercy (cf. Ps 13). St. Paul expresses the same understanding of his own experience as the undeserving recipient of God's goodness and blessing. "We have this treasure in clay jars, so that it may be made clear that this extraordinary power belongs to God and does not come from us" (2 Cor 4:7). St. Paul's great achievement is not to be credited to his own abilities, but rather the grace of God at work in him. In the end, we must recognize that everything we have is the gift of God—unmerited, yes, but gratefully accepted.

PSALM 21 *(20)*

¹ *For the Choirmaster. A Psalm of David.*

² In your stréngth, O LÓRD, the kíng rejóices;
how gréatly your salvátion mákes him glád!
³ You have gránted hím his héart's desíre;
you have nót withhéld the práyer of his líps.

⁴ You cáme to méet him with bléssings of prospérity;
you have sét on his héad a crówn of pure góld.
⁵ He ásked you for lífe and thís you have gíven:
dáys that will lást from áge to áge.

⁶ By your sáving help gréat is his glóry;
you have bestówed upon him májesty and spléndor;
⁷ you have gránted him bléssings foréver,
made him rejóice with the jóy of your présence.

⁸ The kíng has pláced his trúst in the Lᴏʀᴅ.
Through the mércy of the Móst High, hé is unsháken.

⁹ Your hánd will find óut all your fóes,
your right hánd will find óut those that háte you.
¹⁰ You will búrn them like a blázing fúrnace
on the dáy when yóu appéar,
and the Lᴏʀᴅ will consúme them in his ánger:
fíre will swállow them úp.

¹¹ You will wípe out their descéndants from the éarth,
and their óffspring from the húman ráce.
¹² Thóugh they planned évil agáinst you,
though they plótted, they shall nót preváil.

¹³ For yóu will fórce them to retréat;
at thém you will áim with your bów.
¹⁴ O Lᴏʀᴅ, aríse in your stréngth;
we shall síng and práise your pówer.

PRAYER

Almighty God, Source of blessing and every good gift, may we never cease to acknowledge the good things with which you have favored us. Just as you never cease to bestow on us your gracious care, so continue to expand the vision of our faith, that we may see ever more clearly your hand at work in our lives. To you be all praise and honor, glory and thanksgiving, now and forever. Amen.

Psalm 22

FROM DEATH TO LIFE

With this psalm, the reader moves with the Psalmist from the deepest distress to the heights of praise. The Psalmist employs a variety of images to evoke the manifold perils of his situation: scorned by everyone (v. 7), surrounded by bulls (v. 13), menaced by a roaring lion (v. 14), laid in the dust of death (v. 16), beset by a band of wicked (v. 17), wasted to skin and bones (v. 18), endangered by the sword (v. 21). These images underscore in forceful language how life-threatening his circumstances are. And in the midst of this dreadful situation the Psalmist twice repeats the plea, "Stay not far from me" (vv. 12, 20), expressing a devastated sense of God's remoteness and inaccessibility in the midst of this unbearable anguish. This alarm at God's absence is rendered more acute by the repeated entreaty "my God" (vv. 2, 3, 11), implying that the relationship, once close and intimate, now seems altered and distant. The opening line of this psalm is poignantly repeated by Jesus in St. Matthew's account of the passion as he hangs up on the cross: "My God, my God, why have you forsaken me?" (Ps 22:2/Matt 27:46). In addition to this memorable usage, several other verses of the psalm appear elsewhere in the passion narrative: Ps 22:8/Matt 27:39; Ps 22:9/Matt 27:43; Ps 22:19/Matt 27:35). The Psalmist's description of his condition emphasizes the sense of being on the margin of life: a worm and not even human (v. 7), like water poured out upon the ground (v. 15), his heart like melted wax (v. 15), his throat parched (v. 16), his hands and feet mutilated (v. 17), and nakedness before his enemies (v. 19). And then, when this situation is at its lowest ebb, something changes, suddenly and drastically. As we move into the final section of the psalm (vv. 23–43), the very one who cried in despair at the psalm's outset now raises exalted praise to God who has lifted him from his isolation and placed him in the midst of the assembly (vv. 23, 26). His new situation bespeaks a significant precept of biblical anthropology: to be without a place in the community is to be a nonperson; to be restored to the community is to be restored to personhood. The Psalmist has been reunited with the community that gives him both identity and security; his restoration is accomplished by God alone. The Psalmist now proclaims a vision not only of the descendants of Jacob, but of all nations, coming before God in worship, even those who have died and gone down into the dust (v. 30). This psalm is suited to bear a significant role in today's world scene: it can articulate the cry of many people whose pain is so great that they are unable to find words to express it. Psalm 22 gives meaning to suffering along with the promise of great hope that in God's good time a reversal of human misfortune can and will be wrought, as we live out the great paschal mystery in our own lives.

PSALM 22 *(21)*

¹ *For the Choirmaster. In the manner of "The Doe at Daybreak."*
A Psalm of David.

² My God, my Gód, whý have you forsáken me?
Why are you fár from sáving mé,
so fár from my wórds of ánguish?
³ O my Gód, I call by dáy and you dó not ánswer;
I cáll by níght and I fínd no repriéve.

⁴ Yet yóu, O Gód, are hóly,
enthróned on the práises of Ísrael.
⁵ In you our fórebears pút their trúst;
they trústed and you sét them frée.
⁶ When they críed to yóu, they escáped;
in you they trústed and were nót put to sháme.

⁷ But Í am a wórm and no mán,
scorned by éveryone, despísed by the péople.
⁸ Áll who sée me deríde me;
they curl their líps, they tóss their héads:
⁹ "He trústed in the LÓRD, let him sáve him;
let him reléase him, for in hím he delíghts."

¹⁰ Yes, it was yóu who tóok me from the wómb,
entrústed me to my móther's bréast.
¹¹ To yóu I was commítted from bírth;
from my móther's womb, yóu have been my Gód.
¹² Stáy not fár from mé;
trouble is néar, and there is nó one to hélp.

¹³ Mány búlls have surróunded me,
fierce bulls of Báshan close me ín.
¹⁴ Agáinst me they ópen wide their móuths,
like a líon, rénding and róaring.

¹⁵ Like wáter Í am poured óut,
disjóinted are áll my bónes.
My héart has becóme like wáx,
it is mélted withín my bréast.

¹⁶ Párched as burnt cláy is my thróat,
my tóngue cléaves to my jáws.
You láy me in the dúst of déath.
¹⁷ For dógs have surróunded mé;
a bánd of the wícked beséts me.
They tear hóles in my hánds and my féet;

¹⁸ I can cóunt every óne of my bónes.
They stáre at mé and glóat.
¹⁹ They divíde my clóthing amóng them,
théy cast lóts for my róbe.

²⁰ But you, O LÓRD, do not stáy afar óff;
my stréngth, make háste to hélp me!
²¹ Réscue my sóul from the swórd,
my lífe from the gríp of the dóg.
²² Save my lífe from the jáws of the líon,
my poor sóul from the hórns of wild búlls.

²³ I will téll of your náme to my kín,
and práise you in the mídst of the assémbly;
²⁴ "Yóu who fear the LÓRD, give him práise;
all descéndants of Jácob, give him glóry;
revére him, all you descéndants of Ísrael.

²⁵ For hé has néver despísed
nor scórned the póverty of the póor.
From hím he has not hídden his fáce,
but he héard him whenéver he críed."

²⁶ Yóu are my práise in the gréat assémbly.
My vóws I will páy before thóse who féar him.
²⁷ The póor shall éat and shall háve their fíll.
They shall práise the LÓRD, thóse who séek him.
May their héarts live ón foréver and éver!

²⁸ All the éarth shall remémber and retúrn to the LÓRD,
all fámilies of the nátions wórship befóre him,
²⁹ for the kíngdom is the LÓRD's, he is rúler of the nátions.

³⁰ They shall wórship him, áll the míghty of the éarth;
befóre him shall bów all who go dówn to the dúst.

³¹ And my sóul shall líve for him, my óffspring sérve him.
They shall téll of the LÓRD to generátions yet to cóme,
³² decláre his saving jústice to péoples yet unbórn:
"Thése are the thíngs the LÓRD has dóne."

PRAYER

O God, who never despise the poverty of the poor, look with compassion on all those whose suffering may move them to doubt your presence in their lives. Enthroned on the praises of your people, hear the pleas of all who call out to you in faith; heed their prayer, and renew them with your loving hand and outstretched arm. Through Christ our Lord. Amen.

Psalm 23

THE SHEPHERD AND THE HOST

Psalm 23, like Psalm 4, is classified as a Psalm of Confidence. Throughout the psalm, the words and images evoke security, trust, and blessing that come from God, the model of the Good Shepherd. Though some today may be critical of the "shepherd" image as passé, or belonging to a distant culture and time, we dare not neglect or abandon this rich theological motif, recurring so frequently in both the Old and New Testaments. An understanding of the roles and responsibilities of the shepherd in the biblical imagination opens up ideas and concepts rich in potential for spiritual reflection. Among Ancient Near Eastern cultures, the shepherd image was applied to both gods and kings. Notions of protection, guidance, and watchful care of a flock were eminently applicable to any significant position of authority or leadership to ensure that the needs of those entrusted to his guardianship will be provided for. One way of approaching Psalm 23 is to compare it with what precedes it in Psalm 22. Both psalms speak of the bonds that relate God and the Psalmist; expressions like "my God" and "my shepherd" embody this relationship clearly. In Psalm 22, the anguished sense of God's absence that opens the psalm is only later relieved with a conclusion of ebullient praise. But from the beginning to the end of Psalm 23, the Psalmist speaks confidently of God's intimacy with and care for him; when traversing the potentially threatening "valley of the shadow of death," the Psalmist's assertion that "you are with me" conveys a confidence and closeness that characterizes this trustful relationship. In verses 5–6, the imagery changes, and the Lord is portrayed as bearing the traits of a typical Middle Eastern host, significant in a culture that sets great value on extending familial warmth and welcome to others. Images of preparing a meal, anointing the head with oil, and providing an overflowing cup all bespeak Semitic hospitality and graciousness. The early Christian Church found rich symbolism in this psalm, using its imagery as catechesis on the sacraments of initiation: the waters tell of baptism, the anointing of confirmation, and meal of Eucharist. And the closing line has long been the source of hope for many when used as a prayer on the occasion of the death of a loved one. The New Testament authors saw in this psalm a fundamental image of Jesus Christ himself, who is the good shepherd of the Church, never leaving his flock untended (Matt 9:35–38/Mark 6:34–44; Luke 15:4–7; John 10:1–42; Heb 13:20–21; 1 Pet 2:24–25; 5:1–4). For all of this and more, Psalm 23 continues to speak vitally to people of faith.

PSALM 23 *(22)*

[1] *A Psalm of David.*

The LÓRD is my shépherd;
there is nóthing I shall wánt.
[2] Frésh and gréen are the pástures
where he gíves me repóse.
Near réstful wáters he léads me;
[3] he revíves my sóul.

He guídes me alóng the right páth,
for the sáke of his náme.
[4] Though I should wálk in the válley of the shádow of déath,
no évil would I féar, for you are wíth me.
Your cróok and your stáff will give me cómfort.

[5] You have prepáred a táble befóre me
in the síght of my fóes.

My héad you have anóinted with óil;
my cúp is overflówing.

6 Surely góodness and mércy shall fóllow me
all the dáys of my lífe.
In the LÓRD's own hóuse shall I dwéll
for léngth of days unénding.

PRAYER

Lord Jesus, you are my shepherd. You lead with graciousness and fidelity, and you tend to the needs of your whole flock with loving care and devotion. May your goodness inspire your flock to follow you in bestowing on others the same devotion and loving care. To you be our constant thanksgiving and praise, forever and ever. Amen.

Psalm 24

PRAYER FOR THE CLEAN OF HANDS AND PURE OF HEART

Psalm 24 appears to have been associated with a ritual of entry into the temple, and thus compares with Psalm 15. Two sets of inquiries beginning with the interrogative pronoun *who* mark this psalm: Who shall climb the mountain of the LORD? Who shall stand in his holy place? (v. 3); Who is this king of glory? (vv. 8, 10). This psalm can be divided into three sections. The first acclaims the God of Israel as the God of creation, who has set the world upon its base and possesses all that is in it (vv. 1–2). The second section poses a rhetorical inquiry regarding who may appropriately enter the holy place, and responds with an enumeration of the ethical and righteous deeds that distinguish those who truly seek God (vv. 3–6). The third section poses a further question that evokes in response an acclamation that the God of Jacob named in the previous section (v. 6) is the King of Glory (vv. 7–10). Though the people of ancient Israel did have a monarchical period in their history, the prophets and the liturgy (see Pss 95—99) constantly reminded them that

God was their only true King. This closing section of the psalm presents a ritual expressing the people's enthusiastic praise for the One who bestows life, blessing, and prosperity on them. The references to "the clean of hands and pure of heart" link this psalm to the Beatitudes enumerated by Christ in the Sermon on the Mount (Matt 5:3–10), where Jesus reveals to his disciples and the people the new law of love, a law present but hidden in the words of the Old Testament. The list of requirements for entry into God's holy place in the middle section of the psalm concludes by noting that those who follow these precepts are the ones who "seek the face of the God of Jacob" (v. 6b). "To seek the face of God" is to cultivate the desire to abide in the divine presence, to live out the unfolding plan of God in one's own life, and to experience the blessing that comes in being righteous before the Righteous One.

PSALM 24 (23)

¹ *A Psalm of David.*

The LÓRD's is the éarth and its fúllness,
the wórld, and thóse who dwéll in it.
² It is hé who sét it on the séas;
on the rívers he máde it firm.

³ Who shall clímb the móuntain of the LÓRD?
Who shall stánd in his hóly pláce?
⁴ The clean of hánds and púre of héart,
whose sóul is not sét on vain thíngs,
who has not swórn decéitful wórds.

⁵ Bléssings from the LÓRD shall he recéive,
and right rewárd from the Gód who sáves him.
⁶ Súch are the péople who séek him,
who seek the fáce of the Gód of Jácob.

* * *

⁷ O gátes, lift hígh your héads;
grow hígher, áncient dóors.
Let him énter, the kíng of glóry!

⁸ Whó is this kíng of glóry?
The LÓRD, the míghty, the váliant;
the LÓRD, the váliant in wár.

⁹ O gátes, lift hígh your héads;
grow hígher, áncient dóors.
Let him énter, the kíng of glóry!

¹⁰ Whó is this kíng of glóry?
Hé, the Lórd of hósts,
hé is the kíng of glóry.

PRAYER

O Master of the universe, who have brought all things into being and made us in your own image, grant that our desire to be clean of hands and pure of heart bear fruit in the actions of our lives, that by such deeds we may offer you constant praise, through Christ our Lord. Amen.

Psalm 25

I LIFT UP MY SOUL

Psalm 25 belongs to a special category of psalms known as "acrostics." In an acrostic, each new line (or verse or set of verses) begins with a consecutive letter of the Hebrew alphabet. This Hebrew rhetorical device was meant to express the notion of fullness or completeness; the use of every letter of the alphabet suggests symbolically the idea of breadth, comprehensiveness, and abundance. Often a complex interplay of ideas or motifs could be expressed in an acrostic psalm. Acrostic psalms are associated with the Wisdom tradition: like proverbs, they often present seemingly unconnected teachings on widely varied matters pertaining to proper conduct and faithful living. One further element frequently found in the Wisdom literature appears here in verse 14, which alludes to "the Lord's secret." A lifelong pursuit of wisdom is the secret that opens the way to abundant blessings; "the ways of wisdom are pleasant ways" (Prov 3:17). The Psalmist begins here with an expression of complete confidence in God: "To you, O Lord, I lift up my soul" (v. 1). The "soul" (Hebrew, *nefesh*) was conceived as the life force in a person, from which life and vitality flowed. "Lifting up the soul" places before God all that gives a person life, all that animates one's existence, all that fosters one's own vitality. The Psalmist asks for guidance and instruction, so as to know the ways of God. For the Hebrew mind, "to know" is to experience something or someone first hand, such that the impact of the encounter leaves a lasting impression, a profound knowledge. The Psalmist then moves on to express how God's goodness has been made known: through compassion, merciful love (*hesed*), faithfulness, and uprightness (vv. 7–10). From here to the end of the psalm, a variety of requests are made of God, all of which demonstrate the Psalmist's intimacy with God. What a beautiful model of open and reflective prayer we find in Psalm 25, arising from the heart of one whose purpose is to abide always in the presence of the God of goodness and truth.

PSALM 25 *(24)*

¹ *Of David.*

To you, O LÓRD, I líft up my sóul.
² In yóu, O my Gód, I have trústed;
let me nót be pút to sháme;
let not my énemies exúlt over mé.
³ Let none who hópe in yóu be put to sháme;
but shámed are those who wántonly break fáith.

⁴ O LÓRD, make me knów your wáys.
Téach me your páths.
⁵ Guíde me in your trúth, and téach me;
for yóu are the Gód of my salvátion.
I have hóped in yóu all day lóng.

⁶ Remémber your compássion, O LÓRD,
and your mérciful lóve,
for théy are from of óld.

⁷ Do not remémber the síns of my yóuth,
nor mý transgréssions.
In your mérciful lóve remémber me,
becáuse of your góodness, O LÓRD.

⁸ Góod and úpright is the LÓRD;
he shóws the wáy to sínners.
⁹ He guídes the húmble in right júdgment;
to the húmble he téaches his wáy.

¹⁰ All the LORD's páths are mércy and fáithfulness,
for those who kéep his cóvenant and commánds.
¹¹ O LÓRD, for the sáke of your náme,
forgíve my guílt, for it is gréat.

¹² Who is thís that féars the LÓRD?
He will shów him the páth to chóose.
¹³ His sóul shall líve in háppiness,
and his descéndants shall posséss the lánd.
¹⁴ The LORD's sécret is for thóse who féar him;
to thém he revéals his cóvenant.

¹⁵ My éyes are álways on the LÓRD,
for he réscues my féet from the snáre.
¹⁶ Turn to mé and have mércy on mé,
for Í am alóne and póor.

¹⁷ Relíeve the ánguish of my héart,
and sét me frée from my distréss.
¹⁸ Sée my lówliness and súffering,
and táke away áll my síns.

¹⁹ Sée how mány are my fóes:
with a víolent hátred they háte me.
²⁰ Presérve my lífe and réscue me.
Let me nót be pút to sháme,
for in yóu I trúst.

²¹ May intégrity and vírtue protéct me,
for I have hóped in yóu, O LÓRD.
²² Redéem Ísrael, O Gód,
from áll its distréss.

PRAYER

Lord God, good and upright, merciful and just, we turn to you in our every need, for you have shown yourself daily to be our source of salvation. As it is your joy to guide us in your truth, so lead us in the path of justice and mercy, so that our hearts may be set on the pilgrimage that leads to you, who live and reign forever. Amen.

Psalm 26

WALKING IN INTEGRITY

In both the opening and the closing sections of Psalm 26, the Psalmist asserts, "I have walked in my integrity." Much like the proverbs characteristic of the Wisdom literature, the Psalmist uses the metaphor of "walking" to speak of progress through life; specifically, he indicates here the manner in which a person should live when striving to uphold and embody God's precepts. In the Hebrew mind, "to walk" is to act, to establish purpose and direction in one's life. Psalm 26 is the declaration of a person who claims to walk in the ways of integrity, uprightness, and righteousness in life. The Psalmist intersperses his assertions of righteous living with passages in which he turns to God, asking that God vindicate and confirm the righteousness of his deeds: "Give judgment for me, examine me, test my mind and my heart" (vv. 1–2). These phrases and images echo Psalm 1, which describes the blessings that attend one who renounces association with the wicked; the Psalmist asserts here that he has done just that, avoiding the company of liars, hypocrites, evildoers, and the bloodthirsty. This manner of living fits a person to take part in the liturgy of the temple, where one may wash one's hands in innocence (v. 6) and lift up a song of praise for God's wondrous deeds. When speaking of the temple "where [God's] glory abides" (v. 8), the Psalmist provides a point for further reflection. In the Hebrew imagination, the meaning of "glory" (*kabod*) is multivalent; it includes the notion of something weighty, heavy, or significant. Here it refers to the immense significance of God's presence; to be in the divine presence is a weighty matter indeed for a person of faith. The very act of coming before the Lord demands an attitude and posture that emerges naturally from having lived according to God's precepts. Being part of the sacred assembly is of great importance for the Psalmist; it is there God is blest by the community of faith for the divine goodness and loving mercy (*hesed*) bestowed on his people. This psalm encourages us to examine our own lives, to assess our actions, to conform to God's way, and to join in blessing the God of our salvation.

PSALM 26 (25)

 Of David.

Give júdgment for mé, O LÓRD,
for Í have wálked in my intégrity.
I have trústed in the Lórd; I have not wávered.

² Exámine me, LÓRD, and trý me.
O tést my héart and my mínd.
³ Your mércy is befóre my éyes,
and I wálk accórding to your trúth.

⁴ I néver take my séat with líars,
and with hýpocrites I sháll not gó.
⁵ I háte the évil-doer's cómpany;
I will not táke my séat with the wícked.

⁶ I wásh my hánds in ínnocence
and táke my pláce around your áltar,
⁷ sínging a sóng of thanksgíving,
recóunting áll your wónders.
⁸ O LÓRD, I love the hóuse where you dwéll,
the pláce where your glóry abídes.

⁹ Do not swéep away my sóul with sínners,
nor my lífe with thóse who shed blóod,
¹⁰ in whose hánds are évil plóts,
whose right hánds are filled with a bríbe.

¹¹ As for mé, I have wálked in my intégrity.
Redéem me and have mércy on mé.
¹² My fóot stands on lével gróund:
I will bléss the LÓRD in the assémbly.

PRAYER

O God whose glory fills both your temple and your whole creation, test our minds and our hearts; guide us in the ways of integrity, that our thoughts, words, and deeds may reflect our deep desire for your presence, and so build up your kingdom among us, through Christ our Lord. Amen.

Psalm 27

YOUR FACE, O LORD, I SEEK

Psalms 26 and 27 are linked by references to the temple (Pss 26:6, 8; 27:4–5) and the songs of grateful praise lifted up there (Pss 26:7, 12; 27:6). While Psalm 26 asserts a readiness to come before God in the temple, Psalm 27 articulates both the need for God's assistance in the face of enemy threats (vv. 2, 6, 12) and the tender longing for a greater sense of closeness to God (vv. 4–6). In verses 8–9, the word *face* appears three times, emphasizing the desire to "seek [God's] face"—that is, be in God's presence. The Hebrew expression translated as "heart" carries something beyond our contemporary concept of the seat of the emotions. Biblically, the "heart" brings together that which comprises for us today both mind and heart: the human will. Thus it expresses the deep desire to be with God: to take part with the community of worshipers at the temple; to pray, reflect, and share in the divine presence. An interesting word appears in verse 4c, "to inquire" (in Hebrew, *darash*), sometimes translated "to seek." But appearances in other contexts in the Old Testament suggest that this word also bears the specific meaning of going to the temple to make an inquiry of God, to seek divine counsel, to find the mind of God (see also Isa 58:2; 65:10). In more familiar language, we may speak of knowing God's will and striving to follow it. At the outset of this psalm, the frequent use of the possessive pronoun *my* with reference to the speaker's relationship to God (my light, my salvation, stronghold of my life) highlights the intimacy of the connection. This usage recurs as the psalm draws to a close: "O God my savior" (v. 9). The level of familiarity with God mounts progressively with the many terms suggestive of the Psalmist's trust: Whom should I fear or dread (v. 1); my heart would not fear, even then would I trust (v. 3); he keeps me safe, he hides me (v. 5); though father or mother forsake me, the LORD will receive me (v. 10); I believe I shall see the LORD's goodness (v. 13). St. Paul speaks similarly of his own intimacy with Christ and his trust in the unfolding plan of God when he writes to the Philippians: "For to me, living is Christ and dying is gain. If I am to live in the flesh, that means fruitful labor for me; and I do not know which I prefer" (1:21–22). Let us all take inspiration from such fervent desire for God and the divine will.

PSALM 27 *(26)*

¹ *Of David.*

The LORD is my líght and my salvátion;
whóm shall I féar?
The LORD is the strónghold of my lífe;
whóm should I dréad?

² When thóse who do évil draw néar
to devóur my flésh,
it is théy, my énemies and fóes,
who stúmble and fáll.

³ Though an ármy encámp agáinst me,
my héart would not féar.
Though wár break óut agáinst me,
even thén would I trúst.

⁴ There is óne thing I ásk of the LORD,
only thís do I séek:
to líve in the hóuse of the LORD
all the dáys of my lífe,
to gáze on the béauty of the LORD,
to inquíre at his témple.

⁵ For thére he keeps me sáfe in his shélter
in the dáy of évil.
He hídes me under cóver of his tént;
he sets me hígh upon a róck.

⁶ And nów my héad shall be ráised
above my fóes who surróund me,
and I shall óffer withín his tént
a sácrifice of jóy.
I will síng and make músic for the LORD.

⁷ O LORD, hear my vóice when I cáll;
have mércy and ánswer me.
⁸ Of yóu my héart has spóken,
"Séek his fáce."

It is your fáce, O LORD, that I séek;
⁹ hide not your fáce from mé.
Dismíss not your sérvant in ánger;
yóu have been my hélp.

Dó not abándon or forsáke me,
O Gód, my Sávior!
¹⁰ Though fáther and móther forsáke me,
the LORD will recéive me.

¹¹ Instrúct me, LORD, in your wáy;
on an éven path léad me
becáuse of my énemies.
¹² Do not léave me to the wíll of my fóes,
for false wítnesses rise úp agáinst me,
and they bréathe out víolence.

¹³ I belíeve I shall sée the LORD's góodness
in the lánd of the líving.
¹⁴ Wáit for the LORD; be stróng;
be stouthéarted, and wáit for the LORD!

PRAYER

O God, our light and our salvation, inspire us to seek the mercy you promise to all who trust in you. Grant us perseverance in times of struggle, so that we may come to know the sweetness of your blessings in the land of the living. We ask this in the name of Christ, who is Lord, forever and ever. Amen.

Psalm 28

WHEN GOD IS SILENT

The psalm opens with a passionate plea to the Lord, "Be not deaf to me," specifying the dire consequence that must come to pass "if you are silent to me." The Psalmist's language presents a desperate situation requiring

God's immediate help and guidance. A gesture of the "lifting up of hands" toward God's holy place marks verse 2. To raise and hold the hands upright is a familiar gesture of prayer; it was a frequent element of the temple liturgy, and is something we continue to see enacted today by the presider in Christian and Jewish liturgies. The Psalmist appears to be the object of someone's malicious comments, which stir up his anguish and fear. In verses 3–5, we encounter harsh words of imprecation from the Psalmist, a fairly common element in parts of the Psalter. Twice in verse 4 the phrase "repay them" is invoked against these enemies: first for the inherent malice of their deeds, and then to accord with the harm these deeds have done to others. One often finds this kind of retributive curse in the psalms; the words ask that the harm intended by the wicked for others be let to fall back upon themselves. It is noteworthy that in English editions of the Liturgy of the Hours, these extreme expressions of violence and hatred are excised from the text of the psalms; this is true of verses 3–5 in Psalm 28. The tone changes abruptly with verse 6, when the Psalmist turns to an acclamation of praise for God, blessing the Lord for having heard the plea. God's silence is ended, and the Psalmist breaks forth into laudatory thanksgiving. Twice God is referred to as a source of "strength" (vv. 7, 8). The psalm concludes with a fourfold petition to save, bless, shepherd, and carry the people. Such prayers of pleading typically begin with a drastic situation and conclude with words of gratitude for what God has done, followed by a petition for God to continue with the saving help he has bestowed. The reference in verse 8 to "your anointed" is an example of the frequent intercessions for the king, God's lieutenant on earth, which are scattered throughout much of the Psalter. When God seems silent in the face of our pleadings, we can follow the examples of both the Psalmist and Jesus, who reminds us, "I say to you, Ask, and it will be given you; search, and you will find; knock, and the door will be opened for you" (Luke 11:9).

PSALM 28 (27)

[1] *Of David.*

To yóu, O LÓRD, I cáll;
my róck, be not déaf to mé.
I shall go dówn to thóse in the pít,
if yóu are sílent to mé.

[2] Héar the vóice of my pléading
as I cáll to you for hélp,
as I ráise my hánds
toward your hóly pláce.

³ Do not drág me awáy with the wícked,
with thóse who do évil,
who speak wórds of péace to their néighbors,
but with málice in their héarts.

⁴ Repáy them accórding to their déeds,
accórding to the évil of their áctions.
Accórding to their hándiwork, repáy them;
retúrn to thém their desérts.

⁵ For they ignóre the déeds of the LÓRD
and the wórk of his hánds.
May he rúin them and néver rebuíld them.

⁶ Blést be the LÓRD, for he has héard
the sóund of my appéal.

⁷ The LÓRD is my stréngth and my shíeld;
in hím my heart trústs.
I was hélped; my héart rejóices,
and I práise him with my sóng.

⁸ The LÓRD is the stréngth of his péople,
a saving réfuge for hís anóinted.
⁹ Save your péople and bléss your héritage.
Shépherd them and cárry them foréver.

PRAYER

Lord God, our saving refuge, be not silent before our pleading; hear and answer us in our time of need. Stir up our trust in you, for you are the strength of your people. Save us, bless us, shepherd us, and carry us along the way of life's pilgrimage to your heavenly kingdom, where you live and reign, forever and ever. Amen.

Psalm 29

THE VOICE OF THE LORD

Previous psalms have described the glory of God in the temple; Psalm 29 tells of God's glory in the phenomenon of nature. The rhetorical style of Psalm 29 reveals much about its message. Seven times "the voice of the LORD" is invoked; the number seven being the symbol of perfection and completion in biblical terms (cf. Pss 6, 12, 14). Thus, "the voice of the LORD" becomes a point of emphasis in this hymn. "YHWH," the divine name revealed to Moses (represented in English as LORD), is repeated eighteen times, underscoring the preeminence of the God of Israel among the assembly of heavenly powers (v. 1), the majestic name presiding over the entire cosmos. Similarly, the four repetitions of "glory" work in concert with other expressions of splendor and strength that run through this psalm. While other psalms call the people of Israel to lift up praise and glory to God, this psalm calls upon the heavenly powers, the assembly of angelic messengers and holy beings, to give God the honor and exaltation due to the One who choreographs in beauty and wonder the very motions of the universe. The concluding verse makes a prayer for strength and peace to be conferred upon God's people. "Peace" refers in its biblical usage to well-being on every level—body, mind, spirit. To the biblical mind the blessing of peace was considered the perfection of life, God's greatest blessing. This psalm appears in the Church's liturgy at the feast of the Baptism of the Lord. The majestic imagery of this psalm is well suited to the significance of that New Testament event, including as it does the voice of the Lord, the waters, and divine glory. "When Jesus had been baptized, just as he came up from the water, suddenly the heavens were opened to him and he saw the Spirit of God descending like a dove and alighting on him. And a voice from heaven said, 'This is my Son, the Beloved, with whom I am well pleased'" (Matt 3:16–17; see also Mark 1:9–11; Luke 3:21–22; John 1:29–34). Thus the God of glory is the One who holds sway over and calms the storms within the human heart, the God of glory to whom we cry, "Bring us your peace."

PSALM 29 (28)

¹ *A Psalm of David.*

Ascríbe to the LORD, you héavenly pówers,
Ascríbe to the LORD glóry and stréngth.
² Ascríbe to the LORD the glóry of his náme;
bow dówn before the LORD, majéstic in hóliness.

³ The vóice of the LORD upon the wáters,
the Gód of glóry thúnders;
the LORD on the imménsity of wáters;
⁴ the vóice of the LORD full of pówer;
the vóice of the LORD full of spléndor.

⁵ The vóice of the LORD shatters cédars,
the LORD shátters the cédars of Lébanon;
⁶ he makes Lébanon léap like a cálf,
and Sírion like a yóung wild óx.

⁷ The vóice of the LORD flashes flámes of fíre.
⁸ The vóice of the LORD shakes the wílderness,
the LORD shákes the wílderness of Kádesh;
⁹ the vóice of the LORD rends the óak tree
and stríps the fórest báre.
In his témple they áll cry, "Glóry!"

¹⁰ The LORD sat enthróned above the flóod;
the LORD sits as kíng foréver.
¹¹ The LORD will give stréngth to his péople,
the LORD will bless his péople with péace.

PRAYER

*Creator and Lord of the universe, whose Word bears through all time
and space a message of faithful love and unending compassion, be close
to us. Bring an end to the violence that holds sway our world, and calm
the storms that beset the human heart, that we may be a people of that
peace whose source is your own heart. To you be glory and praise, now
and forever. Amen.*

Psalm 30

THE DAWN BRINGS JOY

Psalm 30 is a reflection rich in contrasts. In the opening verse, the Psalmist has prayed that the LORD will not allow his enemies to rejoice over him (v. 2b); he concludes having been moved from mourning to dancing, now girded by the Lord with joy (v. 12). In verses 3–4, the Psalmist's being lifted up and restored to life are in striking contrast to the depth of the grave and the pit. In verse 6, God's anger, of a mere moment's duration, is opposed to the divine favor that lasts a lifetime; similarly do the tears of the nighttime differ from the joy that comes with dawn. In verses 7–8, we see the divergence between the assurance of good fortune and the confusion brought about by God's absence. In verse 12, mourning is changed into dancing, and garments of sackcloth removed as one is enveloped in joy. The mounting effect of these rhetorical oppositions increases our sense of the importance of God in the life of the Psalmist; the One called "LORD my God" at both the beginning and end (vv. 3, 13) is fully cognizant of the pain and struggle faced by those he has created. These contrasts further illustrate the movement of the paschal mystery in the lives of God's people. The transformation from sickness to health, from sadness to joy, from confusion to certainty, from fear to trust, from imminent death to new life all encompass experiences of paschal grace at work in human lives. Yet the psalm's images do not ignore that human tendency to overconfidence about the paths we choose for ourselves. "I will never be shaken" (v. 7b) bespeaks the pride that goes before a fall; and when the Psalmist asks God, "Can dust give you praise?" (v. 10b), he means, "Who will offer you praise if you let me die?" The straightforward humanity expressed in such words makes this psalm appropriate for anyone's prayer. The Church's liturgy interprets the opening line of the psalm, "You have raised me up," as a christological anticipation of the resurrection, giving it a place at the Easter Vigil as a response to the fourth reading (Isa 54:5–14).

PSALM 30 (29)

1 *A Psalm. A Canticle for the Dedication of the Temple. Of David.*

2 I will extól you, LORD, for you have ráised me úp,
and have nót let my énemies rejóice over mé.

3 O LORD my Gód, I críed to you for hélp,
and yóu have héaled me.
4 O LORD, you have lífted up my sóul from the gráve,
restóred me to lífe from those who sínk into the pít.

5 Sing psálms to the LORD, you fáithful ones;
give thánks to his hóly náme.
6 His ánger lasts a móment; his fávor all through lífe.
At níght come téars, but dáwn brings jóy.

7 I sáid to mysélf in my good fórtune:
"Í shall néver be sháken."
8 O LORD, your fávor had sét me like a móuntain
strónghold.
Then you híd your fáce, and I was pút to confúsion.

9 To yóu, O LORD, I críed,
to my Gód I appéaled for mércy:
10 "What prófit is my lífeblood, my góing to the gráve?
Can dúst give you thánks, or procláim your
fáithfulness?"

11 Hear, O LORD, and have mércy on mé;
bé my hélper, O LORD.
12 You have chánged my móurning into dáncing,
removed my sáckcloth and gírded me with jóy.
13 So my sóul sings psálms to you, and wíll not be sílent.
O LORD my Gód, I will thánk you foréver.

PRAYER

Christ Jesus, Lord of life, by your cross and resurrection you have set us free from the silent darkness of sin and death. By our dying to self may we participate in your paschal mystery, and so in beholding your redemptive grace at work in us, sing endless psalms of praise to you who live and reign with the Father and the Holy Spirit, one God, forever and ever. Amen.

Psalm 31

YOU ARE MY GOD

Psalm 31 is to be remembered as the source of the words (v. 6) that Jesus recited on the cross in the Passion Narrative of St. Luke: "Then Jesus, crying with a loud voice, said, 'Father, into your hands I commend my spirit.' Having said this, he breathed his last" (Luke 23:46). We may note that Jesus alters the text slightly by inserting "Father" in place of the psalm's "LORD" in referring to God. Even in the midst of agony, Jesus calls out in trust to the One he has come to know as Abba. In Hebrew poetry, particular words and phrases may be positioned to indicate key motifs. At the very center of Psalm 31, we encounter the expression, "You are my God" (v. 15). Amid trials and tribulations, fears and anxieties, poor health and inner turmoil, the Psalmist acclaims God as the source of all hope, trust, and confidence. It is a powerful acclamation of faith arising from the firm conviction that whatever our circumstances, wherever we are, we are not alone; the God who created and fashioned us stands with us. At the same time, the Lord of the covenant calls for a response in fidelity to the fidelity God has shown to us. We are reminded in verse 7 that God "detests" all who have turned away to worship "false gods." We know how easy it is today to turn any number of things into such "empty idols": wealth, success, promotion, personal possessions, fashions, accomplishments. When we do this, we have failed to recognize that all we have is given us by God, and we are never more than the stewards of these divine blessings. And should not this very realization enliven an ever-deepening trust in us, affirming our belief that God's greatest gifts to us are mercy, faithfulness, persevering love, and divine guidance? Psalm 31 provides us with words of grateful praise to God for the countless times we have been touched by his saving and redeeming love. In the moment of his greatest suffering, Jesus took the words of this psalm and made them his own. That should be evidence enough of the profound truth available to us in this psalm's assertion of trust in the hour of deepest need.

PSALM 31 *(30)*

¹ *For the Choirmaster. A Psalm of David.*

² In yóu, O LÓRD, I take réfuge.
Let me néver be pút to sháme.
In your jústice, sét me frée;
³ incline your éar to me, and spéedily réscue me.

Be a róck of réfuge for mé,
a míghty strónghold to sáve me.
⁴ For yóu are my róck, my strónghold!
Lead me, guíde me, for the sáke of your náme.

⁵ Reléase me from the snáre they have hídden,
for yóu indéed are my réfuge.
⁶ Into your hánds I comménd my spírit.
You will redéem me, O LÓRD, O faithful Gód.

⁷ You detést those who sérve empty ídols.
As for mé, I trúst in the LÓRD.

⁸ Let me be glád and rejóice in your mércy,
for yóu who have séen my afflíction
and taken héed of my sóul's distréss,
⁹ have not léft me in the hánds of the énemy,
but sét my féet at lárge.

¹⁰ Have mércy on mé, O LÓRD,
for Í am in distréss.
My éyes are wásted with gríef,
my sóul and my bódy.

¹¹ For my lífe is spént with sórrow,
and my yéars with síghs.
Afflíction has bróken down my stréngth,
and my bónes waste awáy.

¹² Becáuse of áll my fóes
I have becóme a repróach,
an óbject of scórn to my néighbors
and of féar to my fríends.

Thóse who sée me in the stréet
flée from mé.

¹³ I am forgótten, like sómeone déad,
and have becóme like a bróken véssel.

¹⁴ I have héard the slánder of the crówd;
térror all aróund me,
as they plót togéther agáinst me,
as they plán to take my lífe.

¹⁵ But as for mé, I trúst in you, O LORD;
I say, "Yóu are my Gód.
¹⁶ My lót is in your hánds, delíver me
from the hánds of my énemies
and thóse who pursúe me.

¹⁷ Let your fáce shíne on your sérvant.
Sáve me in your mérciful lóve.
¹⁸ Let me nót be put to sháme, O LORD,
for I cáll on yóu;
Lét the wícked be shámed!
Let them be sílenced in the gráve!

¹⁹ Let lýing líps be stílled,
that speak háughtily agáinst the júst man
with príde and contémpt."

²⁰ How gréat is the góodness, LORD,
that you kéep for thóse who féar you,
that you shów to thóse who trúst you
in the síght of the chíldren of mén.

²¹ You híde them in the shélter of your présence,
secúre from human schéming;
you kéep them sáfe within your tént
from dispúting tóngues.

²² Blést be the LORD for he has wóndrously shówn me
his mérciful lóve in a fórtified cíty!

²³ "I am fár remóved from your síght,"
I sáid in my alárm.
Yet you héard the vóice of my pléa
when I críed to you for hélp.

²⁴ Lóve the LORD, all you his sáints.
The LORD guards the fáithful.

But the LORD will repáy to the fúll
the one who ácts with príde.
²⁵ Be stróng, let your héart take cóurage,
all who hópe in the LORD.

PRAYER

O God of peace and justice, who by your bountiful kindness make plain
to us the ways of righteousness, inspire us to imitate your generosity,
so that we might serve as ambassadors of your mercy to all we meet,
through Christ our Lord. Amen.

Psalm 32
THE BLESSING OF FORGIVENESS

Sin has a powerful, even deadening effect in our lives. We do wrong, and
something deep within us wells up in self-knowledge—"I am guilty"—but
our habit is to repress or deny such self-knowledge. Our conscience serves
as an inner guide for distinguishing what is righteous and good from what
is unrighteous and evil, but all too often we ignore its promptings. Psalm
32 gives us insight into the human struggle with sin and the need for forgiveness. We sense the inner conflict that the Psalmist felt: "I kept it
secret and my frame was wasted....My strength was dried up" (vv. 3.4).
Though we think of sin as something we do, its effects may become a burden that itself draws life out of us. The wrong we have done infects us in
mind, spirit, and soul; we know too well its power to bring us down in
sadness and discouragement. Prideful silence in the face of our sinfulness
saps us of the spiritual energy that enables us to do good, to hope, to love.
The Psalmist's acknowledgment of sin brings him to the point of new
inner freedom and blessing (v. 5). His words make clear that the inner
turmoil of self-doubt and fear loses its power over us when we honestly
admit that we have indeed sinned and stand in need of forgiveness (v. 6).
To come before God in honesty and truth with an admission of guilt and
a desire to "begin again" is a profound experience of who God is for us.

The Psalmist affirms with newfound conviction and spiritual freedom: "You are a hiding place for me; you keep me safe from distress; you surround me with cries of deliverance" (v. 7). His words of newly found forgiveness speak of the tremendous gift that God offers to those who seek reconciliation with him. St. Paul insists that such a gift is to be shared with others: "In Christ God was reconciling the world to himself, not counting their trespasses against them, and entrusting the message of reconciliation to us. So we are ambassadors for Christ, since God is making his appeal through us; we entreat you on behalf of Christ, be reconciled to God" (2 Cor 5:19–20). What we have found in God's forgiveness makes us ambassadors of God's reconciliation to others. How well the closing lines of Psalm 32 express the joy of being forgiven, and the blessing of being ourselves a source of forgiveness to others: "Rejoice in the LORD; exult, you just! Ring out your joy, all you upright of heart!" (v. 11).

PSALM 32 (31)

¹ *Of David. A* Maskil.

Blessed is hé whose transgréssion is forgíven,
whose sín is remítted.
² Blessed the mán to whom the LÓRD imputes no guílt,
in whose spírit is no guíle.

³ I kept it sécret and my fráme was wásted.
I gróaned all day lóng,
⁴ For your hánd, by dáy and by níght,
lay héavy upón me.
Indéed, my stréngth was dried úp
as by the súmmer's héat.

⁵ To yóu I have acknówledged my sín;
my guílt I did not híde.
I sáid, "I will conféss my transgréssion to the LÓRD."
And yóu have forgíven the guílt of my sín.

⁶ So let each fáithful one práy to yóu
in the tíme of néed.
The flóods of wáter may reach hígh,
but such a óne they shall not réach.

⁷ Yóu are a híding place for mé;
you kéep me sáfe from distréss;
you surróund me with críes of delíverance.

⁸ Í will instrúct you and téach you
the wáy you should gó;
I will fíx my éyes upón you.

⁹ Be not like hórse and múle, unintélligent,
needing brídle and bít,
or élse they will nót appróach you.

¹⁰ Mány sórrows has the wícked,
but lóving mércy surróunds
óne who trústs in the LÓRD.

¹¹ Rejóice in the LÓRD; exult, you júst!
Ring out your jóy, all you úpright of héart!

PRAYER

O God of holiness, whose reign is marked by faithfulness and mercy, and welcomes back with unmerited forgiveness even those who sin against your goodness: Continue to instruct us in the way of forgiveness and reconciliation, so that we may be your ambassadors to others, bringing to them the peace that comes from knowing your forgiveness. We ask this through Christ our Lord. Amen.

Psalm 33

THE HEART OF GOD
FROM AGE TO AGE

The concluding imperative of Psalm 32, "Ring out your joy," is repeated at the opening of Psalm 33, directing us to lift up a new song of praise and thanks for wonders of God's blessings. Psalm 33 is a Hymn: it tells of God's wondrous deeds as experienced by the Psalmist on a deeply personal level. Psalm 33 is unique in speaking of the heart of God (v. 11), an image found nowhere else in the Psalter. In the Hebrew imagination, the heart is understood not merely as the seat of emotions, but is also conceived as the bodily location of the mind, will, and rational faculty. This psalm expresses the belief that God has a divine plan for the world, a design that has been in place forever and continues to unfold in our own day and age. Coupled with references to the divine plan are assertions of God's merciful love (Hebrew *hesed*; vv. 5, 18, 22) that fills the earth; thus God's plan for the world, and his people in it, is loving mercy and faithfulness in a covenant of mutual trust and expectation. God shapes the human heart (v. 15), keeping watch over us with love and concern. God's watchfulness continues to manifest the majesty and power that created the world by a single word (v. 9; cf. Gen 1) and continues to sustain it. While God's glorious majesty and power are clearly manifest in the greatness of creation, the Psalmist takes care to remind us that God holds a genuine and intimate concern for each of us (vv. 14–15). This understanding of God is the heart of Jesus' own ministry and revelation: in Christ himself we can know that our God intimately loves and cares for each of us. "Come to me, all you that are weary and are carrying heavy burdens, and I will give you rest. Take my yoke upon you, and learn from me; for I am gentle and humble in heart, and you will find rest for your souls" (Matt 11:28–29). "When [Jesus] saw the crowds, he had compassion for them, because they were harassed and helpless, like sheep without a shepherd" (Matt 9:36). Jesus reveals to us the sensitive and all-knowing Abba who cares for all our needs, who listens to our prayers, and who continues to teach us through the Spirit that dwells within us.

PSALM 33 *(32)*

¹ Ring out your jóy to the LÓRD, O you júst;
for práise is fítting for the úpright.
² Give thánks to the LÓRD upon the hárp;
with a tén-stringed lúte sing him sóngs.
³ O síng him a sóng that is néw;
play skíllfully, with shóuts of jóy.

⁴ For the wórd of the LÓRD is fáithful,
and áll his wórks to be trústed.
⁵ The LÓRD loves jústice and ríght,
and his mérciful lóve fills the éarth.

⁶ By the wórd of the LÓRD the héavens were máde,
by the bréath of his móuth all their hóst.
⁷ As in a flásk, he collécts the wáves of the ócean;
he stóres up the dépths of the séa.

⁸ Let áll the earth féar the LÓRD,
all who líve in the wórld revére him.
⁹ He spóke, and it cáme to bé.
He commánded; it stóod in pláce.

¹⁰ The LORD frústrates the desígns of the nátions;
he deféats the pláns of the péoples.
¹¹ The desígns of the LÓRD stand foréver,
the pláns of his héart from age to áge.

¹² Blessed the nátion whose Gód is the LÓRD,
the péople he has chósen as his héritage.
¹³ From the héavens the Lórd looks fórth;
he sées all the chíldren of mén.

¹⁴ From the pláce where he dwélls he gázes
on áll the dwéllers on the éarth,
¹⁵ he who shápes the héarts of them áll,
and consíders áll their déeds.

¹⁶ A kíng is not sáved by his great ármy,
nor a wárrior presérved by his great stréngth.
¹⁷ A vain hópe for sáfety is the hórse;
despite its pówer it cánnot sáve.

¹⁸ Yes, the LORD's éyes are on thóse who féar him,
who hópe in his mérciful lóve,
¹⁹ to réscue their sóuls from déath,
to kéep them alíve in fámine.

²⁰ Our sóul is wáiting for the LÓRD.
Hé is our hélp and our shíeld.
²¹ In hím do our héarts find jóy.
We trúst in his hóly náme.
²² May your mérciful lóve be upón us,
as we hópe in yóu, O LÓRD.

PRAYER

O God, Creator and Savior, source of hope and trust, we offer our praise and thanksgiving for your goodness to us. As you create and sustain each of us in your loving care, so help us to recognize your loving presence, that our trust and gratitude for your blessings may increase each day, through Christ our Lord. Amen.

Psalm 34

SEEK AFTER PEACE

Like Psalm 25, Psalm 34 is an acrostic: each verse begins with a consecutive letter of the Hebrew alphabet. This literary device suggests that the psalm is to be associated with the Wisdom tradition of the later Old Testament period. Like other biblical texts of the Wisdom tradition, Wisdom Psalms express frequent pithy mandates and instructions for advancing in wisdom and living life well. The Wisdom tradition held that all creation, made and shaped by God, was imbued with a message for those who sought it with diligence, a message teaching us the very wisdom that sustains the harmony of the world in all its constitutive parts. The title we provide for this introduction, taken from the psalm itself, expresses the heart of the Wisdom tradition: Seek after peace (v. 15). Directives and instructions in the Wisdom style run through this psalm from beginning to end: Glorify the LORD (v. 4), Look toward him (v. 6), Taste and see (v. 9), Fear the LORD (v. 10), Come children and hear me (v. 12), Guard your tongue from evil (v. 14), Turn aside from evil and do good, Seek after peace and pursue it (v. 15). In addition to these teachings, there are numerous other proverbial sayings for living in accord with God's law. All this is Wisdom. Jesus himself employs such expressions in a moment of prayer: "At that time Jesus said, 'I thank you, Father, Lord of heaven and earth, because you have hidden these things from the wise and the intelligent and have revealed them to infants; yes, Father, for such was your gracious will'" (Matt 11:25–26). All too often, the wisdom that God's word teaches is utterly simple, direct, and clear; it is our challenge to follow it in faith and confidence, so as to obtain the blessings it promises. Psalm 34 was important to the early Church. It appears frequently in the liturgy, especially as an antiphon for communion: Taste and see that the Lord is good. The Gospel of John finds in verse 21 of this psalm a prophecy fulfilled at the crucifixion of Jesus: "These things occurred so that the scripture might be fulfilled, 'None of his bones shall be broken'" (John 19:36). Psalm 34 is a rich source for reflection and prayer in the Wisdom tradition.

PSALM 34 (33)

¹ *Of David, when he feigned madness before Abimelech, so that he drove him out, and he went away.*

² I will bléss the Lórd at all tímes,
práise of him is álways in my móuth.
³ In the Lórd my sóul shall make its bóast;
the húmble shall héar and be glád.

⁴ Glórify the Lórd with mé;
togéther let us práise his náme.
⁵ I sóught the Lórd, and he ánswered me;
from all my térrors he sét me frée.

⁶ Lóok towards hím and be rádiant;
let your fáces nót be abáshed.
⁷ This lówly one cálled; the Lord héard,
and réscued him from áll his distréss.

⁸ The ángel of the Lórd is encámped
around thóse who féar him, to réscue them.
⁹ Taste and sée that the Lórd is góod.
Blessed the mán who seeks réfuge in hím.

¹⁰ Féar the Lórd, you his hóly ones.
They lack nóthing, thóse who féar him.
¹¹ The rích suffer wánt and go húngry,
but thóse who seek the Lórd lack no bléssing.

¹² Cóme, chíldren, and héar me,
that I may téach you the féar of the Lórd.
¹³ Who ís it that desíres lífe
and lóngs to see prósperous dáys?

¹⁴ Guárd your tóngue from évil,
and your líps from spéaking decéit.
¹⁵ Turn asíde from évil and do góod.
Séek after péace, and pursúe it.

¹⁶ The Lórd turns his éyes to the júst,
and his éars are ópen to their crý.
¹⁷ The Lórd turns his fáce against the wícked
to destróy their remémbrance from the éarth.

¹⁸ When the júst cry óut, the LORD héars,
and réscues them in áll their distréss.
¹⁹ The LORD is clóse to the bróken-héarted;
those whose spírit is crúshed he will sáve.

²⁰ Mány are the tríals of the júst man,
but from them áll the LÓRD will réscue him.
²¹ He will keep guárd over áll his bónes;
not óne of his bónes shall be bróken.

²² Évil brings déath to the wícked;
those who háte the júst are dóomed.
²³ The LORD ránsoms the sóuls of his sérvants.
All who trúst in him shall nót be condémned.

PRAYER

We glorify you, O God of heavenly wisdom, for the life-giving ways in which you guard us from evil and deceit. Grant each day that we may taste and see your goodness, confident that those who seek you lack no blessing. Renew our trust in your guiding hand as you teach us the ways of righteousness. In all we do, may we seek after peace, and so come to the joy of your kingdom, where you live and reign, forever and ever. Amen.

Psalm 35

SAY TO MY SOUL, "I AM YOUR SALVATION"

Though this psalm is classified as a Lament, arising from a situation of distress, it is nonetheless filled with expressions of hope that God will indeed come and fight the battles faced by the speaker. In the Hebrew poetry of the Bible, the sacred authors are adept at puns, plays on words that repeat in close proximity words formed from a single Hebrew root. Such repetitions function to reinforce the expression—and the petition that employs it—in the memory of the one to whom it is addressed; in this case, the Psalmist wants God to hear and remember his pleas. In the opening line, "Contend, O Lord, with my contenders; fight those who fight me," the Psalmist repeats forms of the words translated here as "contend" and "fight." Playing with the notion that relief will come to him only if God "contends with [his] contenders, and fights those who fight [him]," the Psalmist ironically suggests the coming surprise for those who, in fighting him, are actually fighting the Lord (vv. 4, 5–6, 8). The psalm expresses genuine fear that the speaker's life is threatened (v. 4) and that only God can intervene and make the difference that will turn the situation around. Even amid all the imagery of fear and danger the Psalmist makes three assertions of sincere trust and confidence that the almighty and powerful God will intervene and bring about a reversal of this situation (vv. 9–10, 18, 27–28). These are profound affirmations of faith that God stands with the Psalmist, knows the trials that are before him, and will carry him through these difficult times. We read in Psalm 35 that "Lying witnesses arise, asking me questions I cannot understand. They repay me evil for good; my soul is forlorn" (vv. 11–12). The words turn our thoughts to the passion narratives of the Gospels, where Jesus is brought before his accusers who try to trap him by his answers. For Jesus, this was the moment of ultimate truth with regard to his person, his teaching, and his lived example. We read in St. Luke's account: "They said, 'If you are the Messiah, tell us.' He replied, 'If I tell you, you will not believe; and if I question you, you will not answer. But from now on the Son of Man will be seated at the right hand of the power of God.' All of them asked, 'Are you, then, the Son of God?' He said to them, 'You say that I am.' Then they said, 'What further testimony do we need? We have heard it ourselves from his own lips!'" (22:67–71). Christ's confidence in God is not misplaced; for us too, the Lord will be our refuge and strength in moments when we feel fearful and utterly alone. The example of the Psalmist, an example made perfect in Jesus, entreats us to place all our confidence in the God who saves us.

PSALM 35 (34)

¹ *Of David.*

Conténd, O Lórd, with my conténders;
fíght those who fight me.
² Táke up your búckler and shíeld;
aríse in my defénse.

³ Táke up the jávelin and the spéar
against thóse who pursúe me.
Say to my sóul, "Í am your salvátion."

⁴ Let thóse who séek my lífe
be shámed and disgráced.
Let thóse who plan évil agáinst me
be róuted in confúsion.

⁵ Let them bé like cháff before the wínd;
let the LORD's ángel trip them úp.
⁶ Let their páth be slíppery and dárk;
let the LORD's ángel pursúe them.

⁷ Unprovóked, they have hídden a nét for me;
they have dúg a pit for mé.
⁸ Let rúin fáll upón them,
and táke them by surpríse.
Let them be cáught in the nét they have hídden;
let them fáll in their own pít.

⁹ Then my sóul shall rejóice in the LORD,
and exúlt in his salvátion.
¹⁰ Áll my bónes will sáy,
"LORD, whó is like yóu
who réscue the wéak from the stróng
and the póor from the oppréssor?"

¹¹ Lýing wítnesses aríse,
asking me quéstions I cánnot understánd.
¹² They repáy me évil for góod;
my sóul is forlórn.

¹³ When they were síck I dréssed in sáckcloth,
afflícted my sóul with fásting,
and with práyer ever anéw in my héart,
¹⁴ as for a bróther, a fríend.
I wént as though móurning a móther,
bowed dówn with gríef.

¹⁵ Now that I stúmble, they gládly gáther;
they gáther, and móck me.
Í mysélf do not knów them,
yet strangers téar at me céaselessly.
¹⁶ They provóke me with móckery on móckery,
and gnásh their teeth at mé.

¹⁷ O LORD, how lóng will you look ón?
Réscue my lífe from their rávages,

my sóul from these líons.
¹⁸ Then I will thánk you in the gréat assémbly;
amid the míghty thróng I will práise you.

¹⁹ Do not lét my lýing fóes
rejóice over mé.
Do not lét those who háte me without cáuse
wink éyes at each óther.

²⁰ They spéak no péace to the quíet ones
who líve in the lánd.
Rather, they máke decéitful plóts,
²¹ and, with móuths wide ópen,
they útter their crý agáinst me:
"Yes, yes! Our éyes have séen it!"

²² O LÓRD, you have séen; do not be sílent;
Lórd, do not stánd afar óff!
²³ Awáke! And stír to my defénse,
to my cáuse, O my Gód and my Lórd!

²⁴ Víndicate me, LÓRD, my Gód,
in accórd with your jústice;
and lét them not rejóice over mé.

²⁵ Dó not let them thínk in their héarts,
"Yés, we have wón."
Dó not lét them sáy,
"Wé have destróyed him!"

²⁶ Let them be shámed and bróught to disgráce
who rejóice at my misfórtune.
Let them be cóvered with sháme and confúsion
who ráise themselves agáinst me.

²⁷ Lét them exúlt and be glád
who delíght in my delíverance.
Lét them sáy without énd,
"Gréat is the LÓRD who delíghts
in the péace of his sérvant."

²⁸ Then my tóngue shall spéak of your jústice,
and all day lóng of your práise.

Almighty and all-loving God, we acknowledge ourselves your servants, always in need of your protection. Guide us amid the dangers of this life; help us keep our eyes fixed on Jesus, the pioneer of our faith, that in all our struggles his courage may be our only strength and source of hope. We ask this through the same Christ our Lord. Amen.

Psalm 36

IN YOU, O GOD, IS THE FOUNTAIN OF LIFE

Psalm 36 speaks of depths—the depths of sin in the human heart, and the depths of God's mercy that reaches from the heavens to the "great deep" of the ocean. The Psalmist opens with haunting words about the overwhelming power that words may exert in our lives. Words that flatter may be discovered to have arisen from evil intentions (v. 3). The Letter of James speaks of the tongue as the instrument of such destructive words: "How great a forest is set ablaze by a small fire! And the tongue is a fire. The tongue is placed among our members as a world of iniquity; it stains the whole body, sets on fire the cycle of nature, and is itself set on fire by hell....No one can tame the tongue—a restless evil, full of deadly poison. With it we bless the Lord and Father, and with it we curse those who are made in the likeness of God. From the same mouth come blessing and cursing. My brothers and sisters, this ought not to be so" (Jas 3:5b–10). The Psalmist asserts the direct connection between what comes forth from the tongue and what follows in our deeds: the one who "plots iniquity" is the very one who "sets his foot" on the way of wickedness, accepting all that leads to evil (v. 5). In other words, what comes out of the mouth comes forth from the heart; and what comes from the heart is borne out in our deeds. In contrast to this pattern of evil is the loving mercy of God that spans the cosmos from top to bottom. The use of two images here to describe divine justice, the lofty mountain and the great depth of the sea, is a poetic device called a *merism*: it brings together two opposed extremes to express the idea of fullness, completeness, the abundant extent of the matter thus described. In other words, the scope of divine justice for all God's people and creatures is from the heights to the depths (v. 7). Reflection on this imagery opens a way into the mystery of God's limitless love and care. We live in a world touched both by God's goodness and by the power of evil. Daily we face decisions that can preserve our lives in the benevolence of God's providence or imprison us under the tyranny of evil; it remains our choice which path we will follow.

PSALM 36 (35)

¹ *For the Choirmaster. Of David, the servant of the Lord.*

² Transgréssion spéaks to the sínner
in the dépths of his héart.
There ís no féar of Gód
befóre his éyes.

³ In his own éyes, he flátters himsélf,
not to sée and detést his own guílt.
⁴ The wórds of his móuth are míschief and decéit.
He has céased to be prúdent and do góod.

⁵ In béd he plóts iníquity.
He sets his fóot on évery wicked wáy;
no évil does hé rejéct.

⁶ Your mércy, LORD, réaches to héaven,
your trúth to the clóuds.
⁷ Your jústice is líke God's móuntains;
like the great déep, your jústice.
Both man and béast you sáve, O LÓRD.

⁸ How précious is your mércy, O Gód!
The chíldren of mén seek shélter
in the shádow óf your wíngs.

⁹ They féast on the ríches of your hóuse;
you give them drínk from the stréam of your delíght.
¹⁰ For with yóu is the fóuntain of lífe,
and ín your líght we see líght.

¹¹ Maintain your mércy for thóse who knów you,
your saving jústice to úpright héarts.
¹² Let the fóot of the próud not tréad on me
nor the hánd of the wícked drive me óut.

¹³ Thére have the évildoers fállen;
flung dówn, unáble to ríse!

PRAYER

Just and merciful God, whose faithful love reaches to the heavens, whose truth touches the clouds, sustain in your righteousness all who know you and call upon your name. Let the power of sin not hold sway in our lives, but rather let your loving kindness show us the way to life and light in that kingdom where you live, forever and ever. Amen.

Psalm 37

THE HUMBLE SHALL POSSESS THE LAND

The acrostic formats of Psalms 25 and 34 are preparation for this extended acrostic psalm. In the previous acrostics, each verse began with a consecutive letter of the Hebrew alphabet; in Psalm 37, each pair of verses begins with the Hebrew letter following the initial letter of the previous pair. Like its predecessors in the Psalter, this acrostic psalm evinces the Wisdom tradition's mandates, instructions, and rules for good living. A distinctive feature of Psalm 37 is its emphasis on the "land" as God's gift to the chosen people. The directive of verse 3 ("trust in the LORD and do good") promises in consequence a secure life in the land that God has given. Likewise, verse 9 promises that those who hope in the LORD will have the land as an inheritance. And again, in verse 11, those who are humble are told that they will own the land and dwell there in peace. All of the assertions about possession of the land in this psalm follow a long-standing tradition in the Scriptures. In Genesis 12, God calls Abram to leave his own land to go to a land that was to be shown him. Moses is chosen to lead the Hebrew slaves out of Egypt and back to the land God had given their ancestors. And after the people had again lost the land to Babylonian conquerors, the words of Ezekiel, prophet of the Exile, offer yet another invitation to return to the land God had given their ancestors, where they would again receive the land's many blessings (Ezek 36:22–

30). During the Roman occupation against the chosen people's hold on the land, Jesus reveals a new insight regarding the matter: "Blessed are the meek, for they shall possess the land" (Matt 5:5; author's translation). Christ's beatitudes give new meaning to possession of the land: he envisions it as the place where those who follow the new law of love can live in peace, hope, and security. Psalm 37 is a mixed bag of sayings and teachings in which one finds the "rules of the road" for arriving at God's kingdom, worthy of much reflection and prayer.

PSALM 37 *(36)*

¹ *Of David.*

Do not frét becáuse of the wícked;
do not énvy thóse who do évil,
² for they wíther quíckly like gráss
and fáde like the gréen of the fíelds.

³ Trúst in the Lórd and do góod;
then you will dwéll in the lánd and safely pásture.
⁴ Fínd your delíght in the Lᴏʀᴅ,
who gránts your héart's desíre.

⁵ Commít your wáy to the Lᴏʀᴅ;
trúst in him, and hé will áct,
⁶ and make your úprightness shíne like the líght,
the jústice of your cáuse like the nóon-day sún.

⁷ Be stíll before the Lᴏʀᴅ and wait in pátience;
do not frét at the óne who próspers,
the óne who makes évil plóts.

⁸ Calm your ánger and forgét your ráge;
do not frét, it ónly leads to évil.
⁹ For thóse who do évil shall pérish.
But thóse who hópe in the Lᴏʀᴅ,
théy shall inhérit the lánd.

¹⁰ A little longer—and the wícked one is góne.
Lóok at his pláce: he is not thére.
¹¹ But the húmble shall ówn the lánd
and delíght in fúllness of péace.

¹² The wícked one plóts against the júst man
and gnáshes his téeth agáinst him;

¹³ but the LORD láughs at the wícked,
for he sées that his dáy is at hánd.

¹⁴ The wícked draw the swórd, bend their bóws,
to sláughter the póor and néedy,
to sláy those whose wáys are úpright.
¹⁵ Their swórd shall píerce their own héarts,
and their bóws shall be bróken to píeces.

¹⁶ Better the féw posséssions of the júst,
than the abúndant wéalth of the wícked;
¹⁷ for the árms of the wícked shall be bróken,
and the LORD will suppórt the júst.

¹⁸ The LORD takes nóte of the dáys of the blámeless;
their héritage will lást foréver.
¹⁹ They shall nót be put to sháme in evil dáys;
in time of fámine they shall háve their fill.

²⁰ But áll the wícked shall pérish;
the énemies of the LORD shall be consúmed.
Théy are like the béauty of the méadows;
they shall vánish, they shall vánish like smóke.

²¹ The wicked bórrows and does nót repáy,
but the úpright is génerous and gíves.
²² Those blessed by hím shall inhérit the lánd,
but those cúrsed by hím shall be cut óff.

²³ By the LORD are the stéps made fírm
of óne in whos páth He delíghts.
²⁴ Though he stúmble he shall néver fáll,
for the LORD will hóld him by the hánd.

²⁵ I was yóung and nów I am óld,
but I have néver seen the júst man forsáken
nor his chíldren bégging for bréad.
²⁶ All the dáy he is génerous and lénds,
and his chíldren becóme a bléssing.

²⁷ Then túrn away from évil and do góod,
and yóu may abíde foréver;
²⁸ for indéed, the LORD loves jústice,
and will néver forsáke his fáithful.

The unjúst shall be wíped out foréver,
and the descéndants of the wícked destróyed.
29 The júst shall inhérit the lánd;
thére they shall abíde foréver.

30 The móuth of the júst man utters wísdom,
and his tóngue tells fórth what is júst.
31 The láw of his Gód is in his héart;
his stéps shall be sáved from stúmbling.

32 The wícked keeps wátch for the júst,
and séeks an occásion to destróy him.
33 The LÓRD will not léave him in his pówer,
nor lét him be condémned when he is júdged.

34 Then wáit for the LÓRD, keep to his wáy.
He will exált you to inhérit the lánd,
and you will sée the wícked destróyed.

35 I have séen the wícked one triúmphant,
tówering like a cédar of Lébanon.
36 I pássed by agáin; he was góne.
I séarched; he was nówhere to be fóund.

37 Mark the blámeless, obsérve the úpright;
for the péaceful man a fúture lies in stóre,
38 but sínners shall áll be destróyed.
No fúture lies in stóre for the wícked.

39 But from the LÓRD comes the salvátion of the júst,
their strónghold in tíme of distréss.
40 The LORD hélps them and réscues thém,
réscues and sáves them from the wícked:
becáuse they take réfuge in hím.

PRAYER

*O God, Master of the universe, who created the earth and all it holds,
bestow your blessings upon the people you have made your own. As
you once called a people from slavery to freedom, so form by the waters
of baptism a new people summoned from darkness to light. Grant us
the wisdom to use well this earth and its blessings, so that we may walk
uprightly toward the land of promise, where you live and reign forever.
Amen.*

Psalm 38

ALL MY LONGING
LIES BEFORE YOU

The psalms incorporate many keen insights into the experience of profound human suffering. The Hebrew poets gave voice to the pain of alien-
ation, insult, betrayal, loss of friendship, physical illness, and oppressive
fear. We hope, of course, that we may be spared such burdensome trials;
but when they do come, the psalms provide the comfort of knowing that
others have encountered just such sorrows and lived through them, and
in the end could thank God for the divine protection that sustained them
during their trials, the guidance that led through them, and the wisdom
that came from having endured them. Psalm 38 expresses a remarkable
intimacy with God, a closeness rich in consolation. When the Psalmist
says, "O Lord, all my longing lies before you; my groans are not hidden
from you (v. 10), the words are addressed to the Creator of the universe,
at once both transcendently almighty and utterly near to one who calls out
in faith and trust. The Psalmist brings before God candid expressions of a
sense of personal guilt (v. 5), anguish of heart (v. 9), loss of strength (v.
11), fear of those who plot against him (v. 13), and an acknowledgment of
sin (v. 19). The Psalmist gives us an example of how to come before God
in utter trust and confidence, in confident belief that what we say before
the Lord is heard and understood, and will receive a response—sometimes
mysterious, sometimes not clearly foreseen, but always manifesting God's
unchanging love. Thus Jesus encourages us in the Sermon on the Mount:
"Ask, and it will be given you; search, and you will find; knock, and the
door will be opened for you. For everyone who asks receives, and everyone
who searches finds, and for everyone who knocks, the door will be opened"
(Matt 7:7–8). The sense of these verbs in the original Greek suggests a
more complete rendering might be: "Keep on asking, don't stop searching,
and never cease knocking." Christ encourages us to pray without ceasing,
fully engaging our heart, mind, soul, and will. The final line of the psalm
addresses God as "my Lord and my salvation." Ours is a God who saves
time and time again; in the spirit of this assurance we can pray with con
fidence and trust.

PSALM 38 (37)

¹ *A Psalm of David. For a Memorial.*

² O LÓRD, do not rebúke me in your ánger;
repróve me nót in your ráge.
³ For your árrows have sunk déep in mé;
your hánd has come dówn upón me.

⁴ Thére is no sóundness in my flésh
becáuse of your ánger:
thére is no héalth in my límbs
becáuse of my sín.

⁵ My guílt towers hígher than my héad;
it is a wéight too héavy to béar.
⁶ My wóunds are fóul and féstering,
the resúlt of mý own fólly.
⁷ I am bówed and bróught to my knées.
I go móurning áll the day lóng.

⁸ All my fráme is búrning with féver;
thére is no sóundness in my flésh.
⁹ I am spént and útterly crúshed,
I cry alóud in ánguish of héart.

¹⁰ O LÓRD, all my lónging lies befóre you;
my gróans are not hídden from yóu.
¹¹ My heart thróbs, my stréngth is spént;
the very líght has góne from my éyes.

¹² Friends and compánions stand alóof from my páin;
those clósest to me stánd afar óff.
¹³ Those who plót against my lífe lay snáres;
those who séek my rúin speak of hárm,
planning tréachery áll the day lóng.

¹⁴ But Í, like someone déaf, do not héar;
ke someone múte, I do not ópen my móuth.
am like óne who hears nóthing,
hose móuth is nó defénse.

in yóu, O LÓRD, I hópe;
ι, LORD my Gód, who will ánswer.

¹⁷ I pray, "Lét them not glóat over mé,
exúlt if my fóot should slíp."

¹⁸ For Í am on the póint of fálling,
and my páin is álways wíth me.
¹⁹ I conféss that Í am guílty;
and I am gríeved becáuse of my sín.

²⁰ My wanton énemies live ón and grow stróng,
and mány are my lýing fóes.
²¹ They repáy me évil for góod,
and attáck me for séeking what is góod.

²² Forsáke me nót, O LÓRD!
My Gód, be not fár from mé!
²³ Make háste and cóme to my hélp,
My Lórd and mý salvátion!

PRAYER

*God of hope, my Lord and my salvation, you have heard the cries of
my heart even before I can give voice to them. Amid the trials of life
keep me strong in the sure hope that my trust in you will emerge in the
victory of your grace, when I will rejoice in you to whom is due all
praise, through Christ our Lord. Amen.*

Psalm 39

AM I A STRANGER
TO YOU, O GOD?

"Hindsight is twenty/twenty," the contemporary proverb goes. One g[...]
the impression that the words of Psalm 39 might come from some[...]
looking back over life, not without regret for some bad choices along[...]
way, but confessing his guilt with the hope that God will be merc[...]
Though this psalm is not one of the official texts for Night Pray[...]

might well be read as an examination of conscience of the sort that always begins the day's last office of prayer in the Liturgy of the Hours. The psalm is a sobering reminder of the shortness of life and the need to live each day as an opportunity from God to do good, to speak kindly, and to assist others generously. It is worth noting that the Psalmist admonishes himself to watch his tongue as a potential source of sin (v. 2), particularly when coming before someone who might engender fear or threaten evil. But then the Psalmist bursts into speech, acknowledging the transitory nature of our human existence. The prayer continues with an admission that now it is late in life, and the speaker has not lived life well. He describes life as "a short span of days" (v. 6), "no more than a breath" (vv. 6, 7, 12), and "a shadow" (v. 7). Jesus, too, encouraged his disciples to reflect on the mystery of human existence and how we pass our days. In the parable of the rich man who acted rashly after a plentiful harvest, the message is plain: "But God said to him, 'You fool! This very night your life is being demanded of you. And the things you have prepared, whose will they be?' So it is with those who store up treasures for themselves but are not rich toward God" (Luke 12:20–21). As a source of reflection on the transitory nature of our human life, Psalm 38 compares well with Psalm 90. The most important lesson of both: It is never, never too late to turn to God in sincere faith and genuine trust.

PSALM 39 (38)

[1] *For the Choirmaster, for Jeduthun. A Psalm of David.*

[2] I sáid, "I will be wátchful of my wáys,
for féar I should sín with my tóngue.
I will pút a cúrb on my líps
 hen the wícked man stánds befóre me."
 was múte, sílent, very stíll,
 ny páin becáme inténse.

 héart was búrning withín me.
 thóught of it, the fíre blazed úp,
 v tóngue búrst into spéech:
 ᴅ, you have shówn me my énd,
 t is the léngth of my dáys.
 w how fléeting is my lífe.

 the span of dáys you have gíven me;
 nóthing in your síght.
 nankind stánds as but a bréath.
 rely líves as a shádow,

LMS

surely the ríches he hóards, a mere bréath;
he does not knów who will gáther thém."

⁸ And nów, Lord, whát is there to wáit for?
In yóu rests áll my hópe.
⁹ Set me frée from áll my síns,
do not máke me the táunt of the fóol.
¹⁰ I was sílent, not ópening my líps,
because thís was áll your dóing.

¹¹ Take awáy your scóurge from mé.
I am crúshed by the blóws of your hánd.
¹² With rebúkes you corréct the sínner;
like a móth you devóur all he tréasures.
All mankínd is no móre than a bréath.

¹³ O LÓRD, give héed to my práyer;
túrn your éar to my crý;
dó not be déaf to my wéeping.
Behóld, I am a stránger to yóu,
a pílgrim, like áll my fórebears.

¹⁴ Look awáy from me that Í may smíle
befóre I depárt to be no móre.

PRAYER

Lord of life and God of salvation, be close to us. Show us the way of j
tice and peace; give us hearts repentant of past failings and grant
courage to move forward in faith. Keep us mindful in the shortnes
our life that your gift of eternity awaits all who place their trust in
through Christ our Lord. Amen.

Psalm 40

I DELIGHT TO DO
YOUR WILL, O MY GOD

salm 40 is a song of persevering faith and profound gratitude. It opens
th an acknowledgment that God has already heard the Psalmist's cry,
 descended to respond, and has set him on a firm foundation. God
 dispersed the terror of "the deadly pit," and the Psalmist is ready to
 laim the story, to return thanksgiving to God, and to encourage oth-
 trust in this God who saves. God, so often represented as transcen-
 nd all powerful, is also immanent and intimately present to us,
 g our cry of need (v. 2). The "new song" (v. 4) that God puts into
 uth of the delivered one is praise—praise for an act of God never
 experienced, a redemption unlike any other. The Psalmist then
 loquently on the "wonders and designs" of God—too many to be
 never to be equaled (v. 6). We then encounter something dif-
 biblical expressions of gratitude. Normally God's goodness is
 in a sacrificial act, an offering made at the temple. Not so
 r, the Psalmist presents a new doctrine of sacrifice, an offering
 g spiritual and interior to the individual: an ear open to the
 ng (v. 7). This "open ear," receiving the word of God as read
 ll, follows that word and thus accomplishes the will of God,
 ior joy: "I delight to do your will, O my God" (v. 9a). This
 immediately followed by the assertion, "Your instruction
 me" (v. 9b). The expression "deep within" represents to
 lerstanding a literal reference to the bowels; in English
 eak analogously of a "gut feeling," an internal sensibility
 s in a specific direction. "Instruction" here refers to the
 term suggestive of divine guidance. The author of the
 rews applies this text to Jesus: "When Christ came into
 l, 'Sacrifices and offerings you have not desired, but a
 epared for me; in burnt offerings and sin offerings you
 leasure.' Then I said, 'See, God, I have come to do your
 he scroll of the book it is written of me)'" (Heb 10:5–7).
 lls God's will inspired by and fulfilling the words of the
 Psalmist describes the moment of salvation with three

MS

terms: compassion, merciful love, and faithfulness (vv. 11–12). In this wonderful experience of deliverance, an individual human person has known the hand of God; the experience brings forth deep and abiding gratitude (v. 12). While Psalm 40 begins with the repetition "I waited, I waited," it concludes with a plea, "O my God, do not delay." Once we have known God's saving help, we continue to meet each difficult situation with the firm belief that the Lord remains ever mindful of us (v. 18).

PSALM 40 (39)

1 *For the Choirmaster. Of David. A Psalm.*

2 I wáited, I wáited for the LÓRD,
and he stóoped down to mé;
he héard my crý.

3 He dréw me from the déadly pít,
from the míry cláy.
He sét my féet upon a róck,
made my fóotsteps firm.

4 He pút a new sóng into my móuth,
práise of our Gód.
Mány shall sée and féar
and shall trúst in the LÓRD.

5 Bléssed the mán who has pláced
his trúst in the LÓRD,
and has nót gone óver to the próud
who fóllow false góds.

6 How mány, O LÓRD my Gód,
are the wónders and desígns
that yóu have wórked for ús;
you háve no équal.
Should I wísh to procláim or spéak of them,
they would be móre than I can téll!

7 You delíght not in sácrifice and ófferings,
but in an ópen éar.
You do not ásk for hólocaust and víctim.

8 Then I sáid, "Sée, I have cóme."
In the scróll of the bóok it stands wrítten of mé:

⁹ "I delíght to do your wíll, O my Gód;
your instrúction lies déep withín me."

¹⁰ Your jústice I háve procláimed
in the gréat assémbly.
My líps I háve not séaled;
you knów it, O LÓRD.

¹¹ Your saving hélp I have not hídden in my héart;
of your fáithfulness and salvátion I have spóken.
I made no sécret of your mérciful lóve
ınd your fáithfulness tó the great assémbly.

O LÓRD, you will nót withhóld
ur compássion from mé.
ır mérciful lóve and your fáithfulness
álways guárd me.

r Í am besét with évils
ıány to be cóunted.
íquities have óvertáken me,
ın sée no móre.
·e móre than the háirs of my héad,
héart is sínking.

ısed, O LÓRD, to réscue me;
ke háste to hélp me.
ıre be sháme and confúsion
ho séek my lífe.

urn báck in confúsion
ın my hárm.
· appálled becáuse of their sháme,
ı and móck me.

ı rejóicing and gládness
ı you.
ıay, "The LÓRD is gréat,"
our salvátion.

ıd póor though I ám,
índful of mé.
éscuer, my hélp;
b not deláy.

9
ıs

God of compassion, mercy, and faithfulness, your justice is without measure. We turn to you in gratitude for the wonders and designs that you have worked for us, you who have no equal. Keep us mindful of your goodness, that each day we might lift up to you new songs of praise for your bountiful love, through Christ our Lord. Amen.

℘salm 41

MY FRIEND HAS LIFTED HIS HEEL AGAINST ME

To the biblical mind, sickness, disease, and misfortune come upon individuals as a result of personal sins. In the psalms, a complaint of misfortune or illness will often be accompanied by a confession of sin or guilt. Such a concept of retributive justice explains the biblical belief that evil will necessarily turn back on its perpetrator; sin begets misfortune of many varieties. Psalm 41 opens with an affirmation that divine favor comes to those who are mindful of the poor, because God will rescue such persons when they encounter difficult times themselves. When they are sick, God will bring them healing (v. 4) and free them from their foes (v. 3). Having made this general observation, the Psalmist follows with a confession of personal sin and a request for mercy (v. 5). As if the pain of illness were not enough, the Psalmist goes on to describe his foes' words against him, how they wait for his death and spread lies about him (vv. 6–9). The biblical imagination had a particularly negative view of betrayals committed by family members or friends. We expect those who are closest to us, who know our inmost thoughts, to show particular loyalty and fidelity; a betrayal of such bonds is a truly egregious offense. Verse 10 describes just such a betrayal. In Hebrew culture, eating a meal with someone was an expression of genuine alliance, the literal "companionship" of sharing "bread together." Despite the trust that had been expressed by the Psalmist in breaking bread together, betrayal is conveyed in the image of the heel of his friend having been lifted against him; we might liken it today to "a kick in the stomach." In the Gospel of

John, Jesus quotes this verse at the Last Supper when speaking of his betrayal by Judas: "It is to fulfill the scripture, 'The one who ate my bread has lifted his heel against me'" (13:18). In moving toward the conclusion of the psalm, the Psalmist reconnects his own situation to his initial assertion: as he has had "concern for the poor," he has himself been saved from his enemies. The Psalmist is among the just and upright, and God has raised him up (v. 11), freeing him from his foes, just as God was to do for Jesus at the resurrection. The doxology of verse 14 signals the end of Book One of the Psalter; similar doxologies are found at the ends of Book Two (Ps 72:18–19), Book Three (Ps 89:53); and Book Four (Ps 106:48).

PSALM 41 *(40)*

¹ *For the Choirmaster. A Psalm of David.*

² Blessed is hé who has concérn for the póor.
In time of tróuble, the LÓRD will réscue him.

³ The LÓRD will guárd him, give him lífe,
and máke him bléssed in the lánd,
not give him úp to the wíll of his fóes.
⁴ The LORD will hélp him on his béd of páin;
you will bríng him back from síckness to héalth.

⁵ As for mé, I said, "LÓRD, have mércy on mé;
héal my sóul, for I have sínned agáinst you."
⁶ My fóes are spéaking évil agáinst me:
"How lóng before he díes, and his náme be forgótten?"
⁷ When someone cómes to vísit me, he spéaks empty
wórds;
his héart stores up málice; on léaving, he spreads líes.

⁸ All my foes whísper togéther agáinst me;
they devíse evil plóts agáinst me:
⁹ "Something déadly has fástened upón him;
he will not ríse from whére he líes."

¹⁰ Thus éven my fríend, in whom I trústed,
who áte my bréad,
has lífted his héel agáinst me.

¹¹ But yóu, O LÓRD, have mércy on mé.
Raise me úp and Í will repáy them.

¹² By thís I knów your fávor:
that my fóes do not tríumph over mé.
¹³ In my intégrity yóu have uphéld me,
and have sét me in your présence foréver.

* * *

[14] Blést be the LÓRD, the Gód of Ísrael,
from áge to áge. Amén. Amén.

PRAYER

*O God, tester of mind and heart, who know our thoughts and desires,
our deeds and intentions, strengthen us by your word to do what is
right, to be faithful in our calling, and to be ever grateful for your merciful love, through Christ our Lord. Amen.*

Book Two
of the
Psalter

Psalm 42

THIRSTING FOR
THE LORD

Psalms 42 and 43 were at some time read as a single psalm; they are united by a single refrain that occurs in both of them (Pss 42:6, 12; 43:5), and Psalm 43 lacks the superscription that is found in so many other psalms, which suggests its original continuity with Psalm 42. Both psalms are about longing and yearning. The imagery here leads us to surmise that the speaker is far away from the temple in Jerusalem: Mount Hermon (v. 7) is located at the northern extreme of the kingdom, while Jerusalem is in the south. The reference in verse 5 to the house of God in Jerusalem also implies the speaker's distance from the Holy City. Israel understood God as a living God, someone with whom they had a personal relationship in covenant. Here the Psalmist expresses a longing for a deeper experience of that intimacy with God, an alliance based on mutual trust and confidence. This longing is figuratively expressed in terms of profound human need: thirst (v. 3a), presence (v. 3b), tears (v. 4), the pouring out of one's soul (v. 5), groaning (v. 6), being forgotten (v. 10a), mourning (v. 10b), and a deadly wound (v. 11). Who of us cannot empathize with the deep emotion expressed by these words? Notice how often the word *soul* appears in this psalm (vv. 2, 3, 5, 6, 7, 12). What we translate as "soul" comes from the Hebrew word *nefesh*, which means the life source within a human being; *nefesh* is what keeps us alive, vital, responsive, and active. Without the soul, we lose the source of our vitality, energy, strength, and vigor. The same longing and yearning is expressed by Jesus in the Gospels as he faces the betrayal of his disciples, the anger of the authorities, and his impending death. We read in the Gospel according to John: "Now my soul is troubled. And what should I say—'Father, save me from this hour'? No, it is for this reason that I have come to this hour" (John 12:27). We were created for union with God; when we experience personal struggles, our thirst and longing can only be fully assuaged by union with God in whose image we were made.

PSALM 42 (41)

¹ *For the Choirmaster. A* Maskil. *Of the sons of Korah.*

² Líke the déer that yéarns
for rúnning stréams,
só my sóul is yéarning
for yóu, my Gód.

³ My sóul is thírsting for Gód,
the líving Gód;
whén can I énter and appéar
before the fáce of Gód?

⁴ My téars have becóme my bréad,
by dáy, by níght,
as they sáy to me áll the day lóng,
"Whére is your Gód?"

⁵ These thíngs will Í remémber
as I póur out my sóul:
For Í would gó to the pláce
of your wóndrous tént,
all the wáy to the hóuse of Gód,
amid críes of gládness and thanksgíving,
the thróng keeping jóyful féstival.

⁶ Whý are you cast dówn, my sóul;
why gróan withín me?
Hope in Gód; I will práise him yet agáin,
my saving présence and my Gód.

⁷ My sóul is cast dówn withín me,
thérefore I remémber you
from the lánd of Jórdan and Mount Hérmon,
from the Híll of Mízar.

⁸ Déep is cálling on déep,
in the róar of your tórrents;
your bíllows and áll your wáves
swépt over mé.

⁹ By dáy the Lórd decrées
his mérciful lóve;

by níght his sóng is with mé,
prayer to the Gód of my lífe.

¹⁰ I will sáy to Gód, my róck,
"Whý have you forgótten me?
Whý do Í go móurning
oppréssed by the fóe?"

¹¹ With a déadly wóund in my bónes,
my énemies revíle me,
sáying to me áll the day lóng,
"Whére is your Gód?"

¹² Whý are you cast dówn, my sóul;
why gróan withín me?
Hope in Gód; I will práise him yet agáin,
my saving présence and my Gód.

PRAYER

*God of mercy and justice, in becoming one of us you shared fully in both
our weakness and the longing of our hearts. As we struggle to attain
deeper union with you, lead us through the challenges of our earthly
pilgrimage, those challenges that your Son Jesus Christ encountered
and overcame, and bring us to the peace you promise. To you be all
praise and honor, glory and thanksgiving, now and forever. Amen.*

Psalm 43

A REQUEST FOR GOD'S LIGHT AND TRUTH

Two things are immediately apparent in Psalm 43: the usual superscription designating dedication or authorship is not included at the opening,
and verse 5 repeats the refrain of the previous psalm. These elements
suggest that Psalms 42 and 43 were once regarded as a single psalm.

This psalm begins with expressions that intimate the poet is living away from his homeland or at least a distance from God's dwelling place (v. 3). From this distance the Psalmist decries a "nation that is faithless," comprised of "deceitful and cunning men." He develops his theme in verses 3–4, expressing the desire to return once again to God's holy mountain, where the altar of God stands in the temple at Jerusalem. The Psalmist's plea for "light and truth" in verse 3 reiterates the frequent scriptural image of "light" as bespeaking salvation, God's act of bringing redemption and deliverance into our lives. The image is beautifully expanded in Isaiah 60, a glorious and splendid description of salvation breaking into the lives of God's people, just returned from exile but finding that life in their homeland has fallen short of their hopes and expectations. Here the Psalmist is asking God for that same light of salvation, for inclusion in God's wondrous plan that promises divine fidelity, here expressed as God's "truth." These Old Testament images form our understanding of what Jesus means when he says, "I am the light of the world. Whoever follows me will never walk in darkness but will have the light of life" (John 8:12). The prophetic texts of the Old Testament also use the image of light to speak of the coming of the Messiah (see Isa 9:2–7). For us, Jesus is our salvation, our redemption, our deliverance. We look to him for the light that gives us hope in trial, strength in our struggles, and peace in our wanderings. Like the Psalmist, we are exiles longing to return to the place of God's dwelling. We look for the light of salvation, which we find in Christ.

PSALM 43 *(42)*

¹ Give me jústice, O Gód, and plead my cáuse
against a nátion that is fáithless.
From the decéitful ánd the cúnning
réscue me, O Gód.

² Yóu, O Gód, are my stréngth;
whý have you rejécted me?
Whý do Í go móurning,
oppréssed by the fóe?

³ O sénd forth your líght and your trúth;
they will guíde me ón.
They will bríng me to your hóly móuntain,
to the pláce where you dwéll.

⁴ And I will cóme to the áltar of Gód,
to God, my jóy and gládness.

To yóu will I give thánks on the hárp,
O Gód, my Gód.

5 Whý are you cast dówn, my sóul;
why gróan withín me?
Hope in Gód; I will práise him yet agáin,
my saving présence and my Gód.

PRAYER

Lord Jesus, our light and our truth, illumine for us the way to you. As we have strayed from the path of your righteousness and justice in our wanderings, bring us back again that we may declare your saving presence in our life. To you be all praise and glory, thanksgiving, honor and blessing, wisdom and might, forever and ever. Amen.

Psalm 44

WHAT HAS HAPPENED, O GOD?

Psalm 44 can be divided into two major sections: verses 2–9 enumerate the long-standing historical reasons for which the people of God have had cause to offer praise and thanks; but verses 10–22 express shock and incomprehension at the tragic situation that has befallen them. After the many blessings that have come to them as the people of God, they are stunned to have been suddenly overtaken by circumstances of defeat, disgrace, and death. The Psalmist clearly assumes that this situation has been brought about by God. As God had previously raised them up and blessed them, it can only make sense that the same God has now brought them low, lower than they had imagined was possible. Psalm 44 is an example of a Communal Lament, a prayer recalling a dark moment in Israel's history when it seemed that God had withdrawn his favor from those who had been called God's "treasured possession, a priestly kingdom, a holy nation" (Exod 19:3b–6). The words addressed to God in verses 10–14 are blunt and forthright: You have rejected us, disgraced us; you make us retreat from the foe; you make us like sheep for slaughter; you sell your own people for nothing; you make us the taunt of our neighbors. This confrontational language continues in verses 24–25, as the psalm implores God to awaken to their situation, act in their defense, and show them the divine face once more. In verse 26, the parallel assertions about "soul" and "body" imply that the whole of their being, spiritual and physical, has been brought to the lowest extreme possible—down to the dust, to the earth. The final appeal of verse 27 is to God's *hesed*, or merciful love, the love that flows from God's covenant relationship with them. God has been faithful; may that faithfulness be asserted once again on their behalf, in all its might and power. In the Gospel of Mark, toward the end of Jesus' public ministry, Jesus speaks of such wars, defeats, and disasters, only to assert that the familiar world is passing away. "When you hear of wars and rumors of wars, do not be alarmed; this must take place, but the end is still to come. For nation will rise against nation, and kingdom against kingdom; there will be earthquakes in various places; there will be famines. This is but the beginning of the birth pangs" (Mark 13:7–8). Throughout history our world has continued to experience the pangs of war. Our awareness of these pains and struggles call us to a deeper faith, to unite in prayer with those in the very midst of war or disaster, and to keep our eyes fixed on the things of heaven, our great hope.

PSALM 44 (*43*)

¹ *For the Choirmaster. Of the sons of*
  Korah. A Maskil.

² We héard with our own éars, O Gód;
  our fórebears have decláred to ús
  the thíngs you díd in their dáys,
  you yoursélf, in dáys long agó.

³ With your own hánd you dróve out the nátions,
  but thém you plánted;
  you bróught afflíction on the péoples;
  but thém you set frée.

⁴ No swórd of their ówn won the lánd;
  no árm of their ówn brought them víctory.
  It was yóur right hánd and your árm,
  and the líght of your fáce, for you lóved them.

⁵ Yóu are my kíng, O Gód;
you cómmand the víctories for Jácob.
⁶ Through yóu we béat down our fóes;
in your náme we trámpled our aggréssors.

⁷ For it was nót in my bów that I trústed,
nor yét was I sáved by my swórd:
⁸ it was yóu who sáved us from our fóes;
those who háte us, you pút to sháme.
⁹ All day lóng our bóast was in Gód,
and we will práise your náme foréver.

¹⁰ Yet nów you have rejécted us, disgráced us;
you no lónger go fórth with our ármies.
¹¹ You máke us retréat from the fóe;
those who háte us plúnder us at wíll.

¹² You máke us like shéep for the sláughter,
and scátter us amóng the nátions.
¹³ You séll your own péople for nóthing,
and máke no prófit by the sále.

¹⁴ You máke us the táunt of our néighbors,
the móckery and scórn of those aróund us.
¹⁵ Among the nátions you máke us a býword;
among the péoples they sháke their héads.

¹⁶ All day lóng my disgráce is befóre me;
my fáce is cóvered with sháme
¹⁷ at the vóice of the táunter, the scóffer,
at the síght of the fóe and avénger.

¹⁸ This beféll us though wé had not forgótten you;
wé were not fálse to your cóvenant.
¹⁹ We had nót withdráwn our héarts;
our féet had not stráyed from your páth.
²⁰ Yet you have crúshed us in a háunt of jáckals,
and cóvered us with the shádow of déath.

²¹ Had we forgótten the náme of our Gód,
or strétched out our hánds to a strange gód,
²² would not Gód have fóund this óut,
hé who knows the sécrets of the héart?
²³ It is for yóu we are sláin all day lóng,
and are cóunted as shéep for the sláughter.

²⁴ Awáke, O Lord! Whý do you sléep?
Aríse! Do not rejéct us foréver.
²⁵ Whý do you híde your fáce,
and forgét our oppréssion and mísery?

²⁶ For our sóul is brought lów to the dúst;
our bódy lies próstrate on the éarth.
²⁷ Stand úp and cóme to our hélp!
Redéem us with your mérciful lóve!

PRAYER

O God, our source of peace and our lasting hope, hear our prayer in times of trouble and touch our hearts with your healing love. Guide those who seek to establish your peace in our world, and keep us mindful of our brothers and sisters who bear the sorrows of violence, hatred, or war. In you, O God, is our sole hope for a world renewed, through Christ our Lord. Amen.

Psalm 45

A WEDDING HYMN FOR GOD'S ANOINTED

Psalm 45 is divided into two sections: verses 2–10 speak of the king, God's anointed one, and verses 11–18 present directives for the king's bride and enumerates the duties and privileges that will be hers. In its original biblical context, this hymn would have been associated with the celebration of a royal wedding in Israel. The Christian interpretation of this psalm associates those meanings with the person of Christ, in whom God's anointed king is perfectly embodied. In the associated image of the bride, Christians see both the Church and Mary. The opening chapter of the Epistle to the Hebrews cites Psalm 45:7–8 to expound the mystery of Jesus Christ as God's Anointed One, who is the Son of God: "Of the Son [God] says, 'Your throne, O God, is forever and ever, and the righteous scepter is the scepter of your kingdom. You have loved righteousness and hated wickedness; therefore God, your God, has anointed you with the oil of gladness beyond your companions'" (Heb 1:8–9). The author of Hebrews is making a point about who Jesus Christ is for the Church: the long-awaited Messiah of whom the Scriptures have spoken, and whose kingdom is built on righteous and just deeds. The Letter to the Ephesians suggests another meaning for Christians in Psalm 45 in its function as a marriage hymn: marriage is an image of the relationship between Christ and his bride, the Church. "Husbands should love their wives as they do their own bodies. He who loves his wife loves himself. For no one ever hates his own body, but he nourishes and tenderly cares for it, just as Christ does for the church, because we are members of his body (Eph 5:28–30). Finally, the liturgy for feasts of Mary makes frequent use of Psalm 45. The Responsorial Psalm for the Solemnity of the Assumption uses verses 11–17. Taken into heaven, Mary now reigns there as the Queen, and the words of Psalm 45 fittingly illustrate her royal stature and sublime beauty. This psalm thus provides three significant images for our reflection in prayer: Christ as God's Anointed, the Church as the bride of Christ, and the Virgin Mary as Queen of Heaven. Each of these images challenges us to live the will of God with openhearted fidelity and joyful surrender.

PSALM 45 (44)

¹ *For the Choirmaster. Intoned like "The Lilies." Of the sons of Korah. A Maskil. A Love Song.*

² My héart overflóws with nóble wórds.
To the kíng I addréss the sóng I have máde,
my tóngue as nímble as the pén of a scríbe.

³ Yóu are the most hándsome of the sóns of mén,
and gráciousness is póured out upón your líps,
for Gód has bléssed you forévermóre.

⁴ Gírd your swórd upon your thígh, O míghty one,
with your spléndor and your májesty.
⁵ In your májesty ríde on triúmphant
in the cáuse of trúth, méekness and jústice.
May your ríght hand shów your wóndrous déeds.

⁶ Your árrows are sharp—péoples fall benéath you—
in the héart of the fóes of the kíng.

⁷ Your thróne, O Gód, shall endúre foréver.
A scépter of jústice is the scépter of your kíngdom.
⁸ Your lóve is for jústice; your hátred for évil.

Thérefore Gód, your Gód, has anóinted you
with the óil of gládness abóve other kíngs:
⁹ your róbes are frágrant with áloes, myrrh, and cássia.

From the ívory pálace you are gláddened with músic.
¹⁰ The dáughters of kíngs are thóse whom you fávor.
On your ríght stands the quéen in góld of Óphir.

¹¹ Lísten, O dáughter; pay héed and give éar:
forgét your own péople and your fáther's hóuse.
¹² Só will the kíng desíre your béauty.
Hé is your lórd, pay hómage to hím.

¹³ And the dáughter of Týre shall cóme with gífts;
the ríchest of the péople shall séek your fávor.
¹⁴ The dáughter of the kíng is clóthed with spléndor;
her róbes are thréaded with góld.

¹⁵ In fine clóthing shé is léd to the kíng;
behínd her are her máiden compánions, brought to yóu.
¹⁶ Théy are escórted amid gládness and jóy;
they páss withín the pálace of the kíng.

¹⁷ Sóns will be yóurs to succéed your fáthers;
you will máke them rúlers over áll the éarth.
¹⁸ I will máke your náme foréver remémbered.
Thus the péoples will práise you from áge to áge.

PRAYER

O Christ, Bridegroom of the Church, strengthen us who are your Body on earth to do your will as faithful servants. Inspire us to follow you in your love of justice and in your fidelity and meekness. Increase in us the desire to praise your name in all that we say and do. In your holy name we pray. Amen.

Psalm 46

BE STILL AND KNOW

Like Psalms 42 and 43, Psalm 46 bears the distinguishing mark of a repeated refrain. "The LORD of hosts is with us: the God of Jacob is our stronghold" occurs in verses 4b, 8, and 12. The refrain suggests the heart of the psalm's meaning: God is with us, so we have no reason to fear. Earth-shattering events may come to pass, sometimes in natural calamities and sometimes through the work of human enemies; all such occasions call for confidence in God's presence as our stronghold who sustains us in all situations. The language is vivid and forceful: the earth shakes, the mountains quake, waters rage, earth melts away. And though these words speak on a literal level of natural disasters, they can well be seen as metaphors for the struggles and challenges of everyday life—responsibility for families and finances, dependence on the success of business ventures, illnesses that arise suddenly and unexpectedly. Such experiences test us; they are also an opportunity to renew our confidence in God's power to lead us in ways we may not expect or foresee. Security is certainly an issue for the Psalmist: though the presence of a river provides for this (v. 5) in some measure, it is God's presence that is the true foundation of the Holy City's safety. The command "Be still and know I am God" recalls the prophecy of Isaiah when foreign forces are arrayed for attack: "For thus said the Lord GOD, the Holy One of Israel: In returning and rest you shall be saved; in quietness and in trust shall be your strength" (Isa 30:15). The prophet's words in turn are not unlike those of Jesus on the Sea of Galilee bringing calm to threatening waters in the midst of storm: "[The disciples] went to him and woke him up, shouting, 'Master, Master, we are perishing!' And he woke up and rebuked the wind and the raging waves; they ceased, and there was a calm. [Jesus] said to them, 'Where is your faith?' They were afraid and amazed, and said to one another, 'Who then is this, that he commands even the winds and the water, and they obey him?'" (Luke 8:24–26). In the midst of the storms of our own lives, we have One who knows our struggles because he shared fully in our humanity; let us renew our confidence in Christ Jesus each day; he is the Pioneer of our salvation.

PSALM 46 (45)

¹ *For the Choirmaster. Of the sons of Korah. Intoned like "The Maidens." A Song.*

² Gód is for ús a réfuge and stréngth,
an éver-present hélp in tíme of distréss:
³ so wé shall not féar though the éarth should róck,
though the móuntains quáke to the héart of the séa;
⁴ éven though its wáters ráge and fóam,
éven though the móuntains be sháken by its túmult.

The LÓRD of hósts is wíth us:
the Gód of Jácob is our strónghold.

⁵ The wáters of a ríver give jóy to God's cíty,
the holy pláce, the dwélling of the Móst Hígh.
⁶ Gód is withín, it cánnot be sháken;
Gód will hélp it at the dáwning of the dáy.
⁷ Nátions are in túmult, kíngdoms are sháken:
he lífts his vóice, the éarth melts awáy.

⁸ The LÓRD of hósts is wíth us:,
the Gód of Jácob is our strónghold.

⁹ Cóme and behóld the wórks of the LÓRD,
the áwesome déeds he has dóne on the éarth.
¹⁰ He puts an énd to wárs over áll the éarth;
the bow he bréaks, the spear he snáps, the shíelds he burns
with fire:
¹¹ "Be stíll and knów that Í am Gód,
exálted over nátions, exálted over éarth!"

¹² The LÓRD of hósts is wíth us:
the Gód of Jácob is our strónghold.

PRAYER

O God, Creator and Master of wind and storm, bring to our turbulent hearts the peace for which we long. In the midst of life's challenges, let us be confident in your unchanging and merciful love. Teach us to be still, and to acknowledge that you are our God, forever and ever. Amen.

Psalm 47

THE KING ASCENDS

As we in our own time commemorate in the liturgy the great events of the Bible—the Passover and the Exodus of the Old Testament, the Lord's Supper and his passion, death, and resurrection from the New Testament—so also do we find psalms that reflect particular celebrations of formative importance for Israel. Some scholars suggest that ancient Israel conducted a yearly festival during which the people would symbolically acknowledge the LORD YHWH as their King, who ceremoniously ascended his throne in the presence of the people to reign over all (vv. 6, 9). Though Israel certainly had earthly kings and leaders, they affirmed this celebration that God was their true, faithful, and eternal King. Psalm 47 is an image in song of YHWH's enthronement as King. Such phrases as "great king over all the earth" (v. 3b), "God goes up" (v. 6), "God reigns," and "God sits upon his holy throne" (v. 9) are a resounding affirmation of God's universal kingship. It is easy to imagine how the early Christians came to associate this psalm with the ascension of Jesus Christ after his resurrection, as recorded in the Gospels and Acts (Mark 16:19–20; Luke 24:50–53; Acts 1:6–11). Upon his ascension, Christ takes his place at the right hand of God; from this exalted position he is able to intercede for us before the Father. He has thus entered into the sanctuary not made by human hands, bringing with him not the sacrificial blood of bulls and goats, but his own blood shed upon the cross. Christ's great act of sacrifice is not an annual ceremony like that repeated year after year by the High Priest on Yom Kippur, the Day of Atonement, to take away the sins of a single year. Rather, Christ has entered the heavenly sanctuary once and for all to bring about eternal redemption from sin for all who put their belief in him (Heb 4:14–5:10; 9:11–28). Sharing fully in our weak and fragile humanity, Jesus is the perfect High Priest who bears our sins before the Father and intercedes for us. Coming to him in faith and confidence, we can be assured of a compassionate hearing.

PSALM 47 (46)

¹ *For the Choirmaster. Of the sons of Korah. A Psalm.*

² All péoples, cláp your hánds.
Cry to Gód with shóuts of jóy!
³ For the LÓRD, the Most Hígh, is áwesome,
the great kíng over áll the éarth.

⁴ He húmbles péoples únder us
and nátions únder our féet.
⁵ Our héritage he chóse for ús,
the príde of Jácob whom he lóves.

⁶ God goes úp with shóuts of jóy.
The LORD goes úp with trúmpet blást.
⁷ Sing práise for Gód; sing práise!
Sing práise to our kíng; sing práise!

⁸ God is kíng of áll the éarth.
Sing práise with áll your skíll.
⁹ Gód reigns óver the nátions.
God síts upon his hóly thróne.

¹⁰ The prínces of the péoples are assémbled
with the péople of the Gód of Ábraham.
The rúlers of the éarth belong to Gód,
whó is gréatly exálted.

PRAYER

Lord Jesus Christ, gracious and compassionate High Priest before the heavenly throne, help us to know the depth of your care for us. As you once took on the burden of our sin, guide us now through the pilgrimage of this life, so that we may finally attain the kingdom where your righteousness, justice, and peace reign eternally. To you be all honor and glory, now and forever. Amen.

Psalm 48

WALK THROUGH SION

In the psalms, Mount Sion is another name for the city of Jerusalem. Just as Psalm 47 speaks of the enthronement of the king, so Psalm 48 speaks about the "city of the Mighty King," a further affirmation of God as Israel's true ruler (vv. 3–4). As King on Mount Sion, God manifests divine power in the fear incited in foreign rulers (vv. 5–6) and in their lasting acknowledgment of that strength and power (vv. 7–8). Verse 10 refers to the *hesed*, or merciful love of God, which is pondered in God's temple: God's covenant love is forever faithful, forever true, forever loving. Throughout Psalm 48, the enduring strength of Mount Sion is offered as proof of the divine love and mercy always present to those who turn to God in their need. It is worth noting that the Hebrew word for *city* is feminine; thus "the daughters of Judah" of verse 12 refers to Jerusalem and the surrounding cities in the territory of Judah. The people in these cities rejoice in the decrees and judgments of God; they trust that what God has declared and ordered for them is upright and will bring them blessing. The final assertion of the psalm expresses their trust in God's guidance as the people move into the future. One may recall the moving scene in the Gospel of Luke in which Jesus, coming down the Mount of Olives, looks upon Jerusalem with the temple in clear view and weeps over the city, saying, "If you, even you, had only recognized on this day the things that make for peace! But now they are hidden from your eyes" (19:41–42). Whatever praise or blessing a city or its people might merit, their hearts must be given to God's laws and decrees if they are to know true peace. His word always instructs, and his teaching brings peace.

PSALM 48 (47)

¹ *A Song. A Psalm. Of the sons of Korah.*

² Great is the LÓRD and híghly to be práised
in the cíty of our Gód.
³ His holy móuntain ríses in béauty,
the jóy of all the éarth.

Mount Síon, in the héart of the Nórth,
the cíty of the Míghty Kíng!
⁴ Gód, in the mídst of its cítadels,
has shówn himsélf its strónghold.

⁵ Behóld! the kíngs assémbled;
togéther they advánced.
⁶ They sáw; at ónce they márveled;
dismáyed, they fled in féar.

⁷ A trémbling séized them thére,
anguish, like pángs in giving bírth,
⁸ as whén the éast wind shátters
the shíps of Társhish.

⁹ As we have héard, só we have séen
in the cíty of our Gód,
in the cíty of the LÓRD of hósts,
which God estáblishes foréver.

¹⁰ Your mérciful lóve, O Gód,
we pónder in your témple.
¹¹ Your práise, O Gód, like your náme,
reaches the énds of the éarth.

Your right hánd is fílled with saving jústice.
¹² Mount Síon rejóices.
The dáughters of Júdah rejóice
at the síght of your júdgments.

¹³ Walk through Síon, wálk all aróund her;
count the númber of her tówers.
¹⁴ Consíder áll her rámparts;
exámine her cástles,

That you may téll the néxt generátion
¹⁵ that súch is our Gód,
our Gód foréver and álways.
He will guíde us foréver.

PRAYER

Your merciful love, O God, is our great and lasting hope. As we count
our many blessings, keep us mindful of our need to respond to your
goodness with thankful hearts. May we never take your gifts for

granted; may our lives be a perpetual response to your gracious love, marked by deeds of compassion, forgiveness, patience toward our neighbors, in imitation of your love to us. To you be all praise and glory, now and forever. Amen.

$\mathcal{P}$salm 49

LIFE AND DEATH
IN A BALANCE

From the beginning of human experience, people have pondered the mystery of life and death. Why are some lives filled with blessing, while others appear to be bereft of them? Why do some die young and others live into old age? Why is suffering such an overwhelming part of some lives, but less so for others? The Wisdom tradition of the Old Testament probed such questions with keen interest. Psalm 49 states in clear terms that death is as much a part of human experience as it is of any lesser creature; the refrain occurs twice (vv. 13, 21). This psalm imparts the teaching that each and every person must face death, and no mere human being can deliver another from the transience of earthly life. If someone were to try to put a price on human life as a ransom, he would be roundly mocked (vv. 8–10). The Psalmist also offers a sobering reflection on the possessions we value so much: they do not go with us to the grave (vv. 11–12), and there is no place for them in whatever follows. He exposes as a further fallacy the belief that a prominent name will endure. Like everything else, fame is left behind when the grave becomes our home (vv. 17–19). And yet verse 16 offers an intriguing ray of hope in an interjection that anticipates the Christian doctrine of eternal life: "God will ransom my soul from the grasp of hell; for he indeed will receive me." Jesus addresses this very matter of wisdom in our attitude toward the present life and the life to come in his parable of the rich man and the successful harvest, which warns against too much concern about our earthly situation. "I will say to my soul, 'Soul, you have ample goods laid up for many years; relax, eat, drink, be merry.' But God said to him, 'You fool! This very night your life is being demanded of you. And the things you have prepared, whose will they be?'" (Luke 12:19–20). Wealth is a blessing in our earthly life;

but one should never forget that all we have comes to us from the generous and gracious hands of God, and that its full realization belongs not
to this life but to the life of heaven.

PSALM 49 *(48)*

¹ *For the Choirmaster. Of the sons of Korah. A Psalm.*

² Héar this, áll you péoples,
give éar, all who dwéll in the wórld,
³ péople both hígh and lów,
rích and póor alíke!

⁴ My móuth will útter wísdom.
The refléctions of my héart offer ínsight.
⁵ I will inclíne my éar to a mýstery;
with the hárp I will sét forth my próblem.

⁶ Whý should I féar in evil dáys
the málice of the fóes who surróund me,
⁷ thóse who trúst in their wéalth,
and bóast of the vástness of their ríches?

⁸ Nó man can ránsom a bróther,
nor pay a príce to Gód for his lífe.
⁹ How hígh is the príce of his sóul!
The ránsom can néver be enoúgh!
¹⁰ Nó one can búy life unénding,
nor avóid cóming to the gráve.

¹¹ Anyone sées that the wíse will díe;
the fóolish will pérish with the sénseless,
and léave their wéalth to óthers.
¹² Their gráves are their hómes foréver,
their dwélling place from áge to áge,
though lánds were cálled by their námes.

¹³ In his ríches, mán does not endúre;
hé is like the béasts that are destróyed.

¹⁴ Thís is the wáy of the fóolish,
the óutcome of those pléased with their lót:
¹⁵ like shéep they are dríven to the gráve,
where déath shall becóme their shépherd,
and the úpright shall háve domínion.

Their outward shów wastes awáy with the mórning,
and the gráve becómes their hóme.
¹⁶ But God will ránsom my sóul from the grasp of héll;
for hé indéed will recéive me.

¹⁷ Then do not féar when a mán grows rích,
when the glóry of his hóuse incréases.
¹⁸ He takes nóthing wíth him when he díes,
his glóry does not fóllow him belów.

¹⁹ Though he fláttered himsélf while he líved,
"People will práise me for áll my succéss,"
²⁰ yet he will gó to jóin his fórebears,
and will néver see the líght any móre.

²¹ In his ríches, mán cannot discérn;
hé is like the béasts that are destróyed.

PRAYER

O Lord our God, giver of every good gift and source of all blessing, help us to use wisely the many blessings you bestow on us. May we always be grateful for the abundance of your material gifts, never allowing them to possess us, but rather employing them for your greater glory and the upbuilding of your kingdom, through Christ our Lord. Amen.

𝒫salm 50

A CALL TO HONESTY
BEFORE GOD

Every person of faith struggles with living honestly before the invisible God. While God knows all things, we are sometimes permitted to live long and confidently even amid willful blindness and self-deceit. And yet from a human perspective, who but one's own self can hope to discern whether the heart is truly set on the paths of God? Psalm 50 speaks directly to the human tendency to gloss over our own failings when evaluating our relationship with the divine. God asserts in an oracular manner, "You befriend a thief and you pretend I don't care; your mouth speaks deceit, and you presume all is well; you malign your own family and you imagine it means nothing; you recite my commandments and then throw my words behind your back—and you estimate such behavior as loyalty to me!" All such conduct bespeaks a division within the human heart; this cannot persist in an authentic relationship with God. Rather, the truths placed in the heart by God should give directions to a person's words and actions. In verse 7, the Lord calls us to consider attentively and deeply what it means to share in a covenant relationship with God, in which there are expectations on both sides. God remains faithful, but we struggle to carry out our part. The Christian, too, must consider the demands of the new law of love that Jesus taught. The Sermon on the Mount (Matt 5—7), and similarly Luke's Sermon on the Plain (Luke 6:20—49), give particular insight into this matter. The concluding words of the Sermon on the Mount sum up what this teaching is all about. "Not everyone who says to me, 'Lord, Lord,' will enter the kingdom of heaven, but only the one who does the will of my Father in heaven....Everyone then who hears these words of mine and acts on them will be like a wise man who built his house on rock. The rain fell, the floods came, and the winds blew and beat on that house, but it did not fall, because it had been founded on rock" (Matt 7:21, 24). The Psalmist speaks of our best efforts taking shape as a "sacrifice of praise," by which our lips and our deeds proclaim our deepest beliefs. Let us embrace this noble challenge.

PSALM 50 *(49)*

¹ *A Psalm of Asaph.*

The Gód of góds, the LÓRD,
has spóken and súmmoned the éarth,
from the rísing of the sún to its sétting.
² Out of Síon, the perféction of béauty,
Gód is shíning fórth.

³ Our God cómes, and does nót keep sílence.
Befóre him fíre devóurs;
aróund him témpest ráges.
⁴ He cálls on the héavens abóve,
and on the éarth, to júdge his péople.

⁵ "Gáther my hóly ones to mé,
who made cóvenant with mé by sácrifice."

⁶ The héavens procláim his jústice,
for hé, Gód, is the júdge.

⁷ "Lísten, my péople, I will spéak;
Ísrael, I will téstify agáinst you,
for Í am Gód, your Gód.

⁸ I do nót rebúke you for your sácrifices;
your ófferings are álways befóre me.
⁹ I do not táke more búllocks from your fárms,
nor góats from amóng your hérds.

¹⁰ For I ówn all the béasts of the fórest,
béasts in their thóusands on my híll s.
¹¹ I knów all the bírds on the móuntains;
all that móves in the fíeld belongs to mé.

¹² Were I húngry, Í would not téll you,
for the wórld and its fúllness is míne.
¹³ Do I éat the flésh of búlls,
or drínk the blóod of góats?

¹⁴ Give your práise as a sácrifice to Gód,
and fulfíll your vóws to the Most Hígh.
¹⁵ Then call on mé in the dáy of distréss.
I will delíver you and yóu shall hónor me."

¹⁶ But Gód will sáy to the wícked,
"Hów can you recíte my commándments,
and táke my cóvenant on your líps,
¹⁷ yóu who despíse corréction,
and cást my wórds behínd you,

¹⁸ Yóu who see a thíef and befríend him,
who thrów in your lót with adúlterers,
¹⁹ who unbrídle your móuth for évil,
and yóke your tóngue to decéit,

²⁰ You who sít and malígn your own bróther,
and slánder your own móther's són?
²¹ You do thís, and should Í keep sílence?
Do you thínk that Í am like yóu?
I accúse you, lay the chárge befóre you.

²² Mark this, yóu who are forgétful of Gód,
lest I séize you and nóne can delíver you.
²³ A sácrifice of práise gives me hónor,
and to óne whose wáy is blámeless,
I will shów the salvátion of Gód."

PRAYER

O God, ever faithful and ever just, you test the human heart and call us to integrity in word and deed. Help us to know the way we should walk, and strengthen us to follow that path with conviction and peace of heart, for only in following your ways can we discover the fullness of joy that is our goal, through Christ our Lord. Amen.

Psalm 51

MERCIFUL LOVE IN EXCHANGE FOR TRANSGRESSION

Psalm 51 is a distinguished example of the Penitential Psalms, which speak so profoundly of the experience of sin, conversion, and redemption. While most individual psalms appear in the Divine Office only once every four weeks, this psalm is prayed at Morning Prayer every Friday of the Church Year. An expression of true repentance, the psalm embodies and illustrates the human struggle with sin, locating our hope of deliverance in God who recreates us and makes us whole. Psalm 51 employs several subtly distinct terms for doing wrong: *transgression, sin, iniquity,* and *guilt*; each of these translates a different Hebrew word. The word we translate as "transgression" refers to the most serious of sins: it begins in the heart, is reflected upon, and comes to birth in one's actions. It implies deliberate wrongdoing that is thought through and performed with conscious, calculated, and intentional choice. Many times in life we sin by weak habit or a failure to respond to a situation—a sin of omission. "Transgression," as it is used here in verses 3, 5, and 15, is meant to convey the planned and purposeful intention of the heart of the offender. Transgression bespeaks a wicked and perverse heart given over to sin, and thus separates one from God and neighbor. While the Psalmist acknowledges the presence of this grievous evil within, his prayer also expresses a sincere hope that recognition and awareness of this interior disposition will reveal a path to redemption and recovery. The Psalmist acknowledges the need for a renewed and purified heart, an interior spirit restored by the touch of God's holiness, and begs for a chance to begin again as an ambassador to others of God's saving grace. Does this not illustrate perfectly the story of the gracious father and his two sons of Christ's parable in Luke 15? Throughout his life, Jesus was the Father's ambassador of mercy, reconciliation, and peace. Each week this beautiful psalm invites us to find our way to divine mercy through the hope of Jesus' resurrection.

PSALM 51 (50)

¹ *For the Choirmaster. A Psalm of David* ² *when the prophet Nathan came to him after he had gone to Bathsheba.*

³ Have mércy on mé, O Gód,
accórding to your mérciful lóve;
accórding to your gréat compássion,
blót out mý transgréssions.
⁴ Wásh me complétely from my iníquity,
and cléanse me fróm my sín.

⁵ My transgréssions, trúly I knów them;
my sín is álways befóre me.
⁶ Against yóu, you alóne, have I sínned;
what is évil in your síght I have dóne.
So yóu are júst in your séntence,
withóut repróach in your júdgment.

⁷ O sée, in guílt I was bórn,
a sínner when my móther concéived me.
⁸ Yes, you delíght in sincérity of héart;
in sécret you téach me wísdom.
⁹ Cleanse me with hýssop, and Í shall be púre;
wash me, and Í shall be whíter than snów.

¹⁰ Let me héar rejóicing and gládness,
that the bónes you have crúshed may exúlt.
¹¹ Túrn away your fáce from my síns,
and blót out áll my guílt.

¹² Creáte a pure héart for me, O Gód;
renew a stéadfast spírit withín me.
¹³ Do not cást me awáy from your présence;
take not your hóly spírit from mé.

¹⁴ Restóre in me the jóy of your salvátion;
sustáin in me a wílling spírit.
¹⁵ I will téach transgréssors your wáys,
that sínners may retúrn to yóu.

¹⁶ Réscue me from blóodshed, O Gód,
Gód of mý salvátion,
and then my tóngue shall ring óut your jústice.
¹⁷ O Lórd, ópen my líps
and my móuth shall procláim your práise.

¹⁸ For in sácrifice you táke no delíght;
burnt óffering from mé would not pléase you.
¹⁹ My sácrifice to Gód, a broken spírit:
a bróken and húmbled héart,
O Gód, you wíll not spúrn.

²⁰ In your good pléasure, show fávor to Síon;
rebuíld the wálls of Jerúsalem.
²¹ Thén you will delíght in right sácrifice,
burnt ófferings whólly consúmed.
Thén you will be óffered young búlls on your áltar.

PRAYER

God of mercy and faithfulness, whose divine goodness is manifest in
unbounded love, instill in us a knowledge of your redemption that
becomes the experience of our own lives. In knowing the depth of your
faithful love and untiring mercy, may we become ambassadors of your
reconciliation to one another, through Christ our Lord. Amen.

Psalm 52

THE SHARPENED TONGUE AND THE GROWING OLIVE TREE

The beginning and end of Psalm 52 present a sharp contrast in images: the tongue of the evildoer as a cruel instrument of deceit, and the mouth of the Psalmist given over to thanking God from a hopeful heart. This psalm instructs us in the tongue's powerful potential for evil. False and deceitful words are destructive; they tear at the very fabric of life and sow evil in hearts created for goodness and love. The Psalmist is well aware of what God's judgment on such misuse of the tongue means for the wicked: it brings about the breakdown of human life and ushers them out of the land of the living. God brings a death-dealing blow to those who employ the organ of speech for destructive evil rather than for life-affirming good. In the end, the Psalmist insists, it is all about trust: confidence in God in any and every situation. He evokes the olive tree as an image of strength and vitality. What may at first appear strange—an olive tree growing in the house of God—in fact describes something strong, deeply rooted and long lasting, that continues to produce fruit many years after it is planted. The house of God is where God's name receives its proper honor and worship; the person who trusts in God and uses the gift of speech for building up rather than tearing down is blessed with a dwelling place in God's presence. Jesus gives the image even greater depth when he says to his disciples, "Those who love me will keep my word, and my Father will love them, and we will come to them and make our home with them" (John 14:23). God comes to dwell within us when our love is manifested in our keeping of the divine word. And the divine presence within us drives out the evil that might otherwise threaten our well-being and growth as true children of God.

PSALM 52 *(51)*

> [1] *For the Choirmaster. A* Maskil *of David* [2] *after Doeg the Edomite came and told Saul, "David has gone to the house of Abimelech."*

3 Whý do you bóast of wíckedness,
you chámpion of évil?
4 Planning rúin áll day lóng,
your tóngue is like a shárpened rázor,
you who práctice déceit!

5 You love évil móre than góod,
fálsehood more than trúth.
6 You love évery destrúctive wórd,
O tóngue of decéit.

7 Then God will bréak you dówn foréver,
and he will táke you awáy.
He will snátch you from your tént, and upróot you
from the lánd of the líving.

8 The júst shall sée and féar.
They shall láugh and sáy,
9 "So thís is the chámpion who refúsed
to take Gód as a strónghold,
but trústed in the gréatness of wéalth
and grew pówerful by wíckedness."

10 But Í am like a grówing ólive tree
in the hóuse of Gód.
I trúst in the mércy of Gód,
foréver and éver.

11 I will thánk you forévermóre,
for thís is your dóing.
I will hópe in your name, for it is góod,
in the présence of your fáithful.

PRAYER

*O God, whose holy name is itself the fullness of truth and goodness,
increase our awareness of your presence within us. May the grace of
baptism, by which you made us your dwelling place, enable us to live
as the Body of your Risen Son, and so manifest your saving power to
the world. This we ask through the same Christ our Lord. Amen.*

Psalm 53

ARE ANY WISE?

If we think that the problems of materialistic culture and faithless living are new in our world, the products of contemporary secularized society, we are fooling ourselves. Psalm 53 shows that the problems of idolatry and the denial of God were already present in the cultures of the ancient Near East. The Psalmist considers this ever-present issue from the perspective of contrasting questions: What is foolishness, and what is true wisdom? In the mind of the Psalmist, the denial of God is foolishness indeed, leading as it does to corruption, depravity, and the loss of simple human goodness. We can infer from verse 3 that wisdom is to be equated with the search for God: discovering the place of God in our lives and never drawing back from that pursuit. The search for God is a lifelong endeavor leading us into a great mystery; the goal is beyond our comprehension yet continuously opens itself to us, not unlike the unfolding petals of a rose that slowly open to reveal their own beauty, shape, and order. In our quest for God, the Divine Mystery opens for us, revealing the wondrous yet unfathomable plan of salvation that is the very heart of our being. But only when God is at the center of our understanding can we hope to perceive truly. The wisdom of God is beyond the reach of human perception, and we cannot presume to say how life should play itself out. St. Paul spoke of this with remarkable insight: "Among the mature we do speak wisdom, though it is not a wisdom of this age or of the rulers of this age, who are doomed to perish. But we speak God's wisdom, secret and hidden, which God decreed before the ages for our glory" (1 Cor 2:6–7). St. Paul goes on to explain how God's wisdom is manifest most fully in the paschal mystery of Jesus: suffering and death that emerges in the glory of the resurrection. Psalm 53 invites us to keep our vision focused on precisely this kind of divine wisdom that leads to the hope of glory. The opposite, the Psalmist asserts, leads to depravity and death.

PSALM 53 *(52)*

¹ For the Choirmaster. Intoned like Mahalat. A Maskil *of David.*

² The fóol has sáid in his héart,
"There ís no Gód."
Their déeds are corrúpt, depráved;
no one dóes any góod.

³ Gód looks dówn from héaven
on the húman ráce,
to sée if ány are wíse,
if ány seek Gód.

⁴ Áll have léft the right páth,
depráved, every óne;
there is nó one who dóes any góod,
nó, not even óne.

⁵ Do nóne who do évil únderstánd?
They éat up my péople as if éating bréad;
they néver call óut to Gód.

⁶ Thére they shall trémble with féar –
without cáuse for féar –
for God scátters the bónes of your besíegers.
They are shámed; God rejécts them.

⁷ Whó will bring Ísrael salvátion from Síon?
When Gód brings abóut the retúrn of his péople,
then Jácob will be glád and Ísrael rejóice.

PRAYER

God of wisdom, who order creation in love, justice, and truth, enable us to see with eyes of faith the marvels you work in our midst. May each day reveal to us your great plan of salvation, wherein we find ourselves, our Church and our world moving toward you whose glory is our hope. We ask this through Christ our Lord. Amen.

Psalm 54

O GOD, SAVE ME
BY YOUR NAME

In the Bible, a person's name is considered the entry way to his or her deepest identity. Often a person's name is changed when that person is given a new mission. For example, Abram becomes Abraham when he is told that he is to become the father of a host of nations (Gen 17:4–5). In the Book of Exodus, we read of God's revelation of the divine name to Moses in the midst of an experience shrouded in mystery and wonder (3:13–15). YHWH, the sacred name revealed in that passage, came to be intimately associated with the saving event of the exodus from Egypt, the passage through the sea and the entry into the Promised Land. YHWH is experienced as the One whose saving strength and faithful presence accomplish great signs and wonders on behalf of the people of the covenant. Thus when the Psalmist cries out, "O God, save me by your name," it is a plea for God to put forth all that comprises his divine strength, majesty, and power to bring about salvation for the speaker in his great need. But even before he makes the specific plea that his prayer be heard, the Psalmist asks that God act in the manner in which God alone can act: with saving power and might. The Psalmist is convinced that his very life is in danger, and those who seek his ruin have no regard for God; being without regard for God, these proud individuals will stop at nothing to bring about the supplicant's ruin. But with God as his help, the Psalmist will be safe. And just as God's name had been invoked at the outset of the psalm, so it is at the end lifted again, but this time in praise (v. 8b) for the rescue that God has accomplished. Likewise, when Jesus teaches his disciples to pray, he tells them to address God saying, "Hallowed be thy name," giving glory to all that God has done as Savior, Redeemer, and Father. In Philippians 2:9–11, St. Paul attributes this divine sanctity and all it entails to the name of Jesus himself, whose name is now above all names, and whose passage through death to resurrection and glory manifests this status.

PSALM 54 (53)

¹ *For the Choirmaster. On stringed instruments. A* Maskil *of David*
² *after the Ziphites came to Saul and said, "Is not David hiding*
among us?"

³ O Gód, sáve me by your náme;
by your pówer, defénd my cáuse.
⁴ O Gód, héar my práyer;
give éar to the wórds of my móuth.

⁵ For the próud have rísen agáinst me,
and the rúthless séek my lífe.
They have nó regárd for Gód.

⁶ Sée, I have Gód for my hélp.
The Lórd sustáins my sóul.
⁷ Let évil recóil on my fóes.
In your fáithfulness, bríng them to an énd.

⁸ I will sácrifice to yóu with willing héart,
and práise your náme, for it is góod:
⁹ for it has réscued me from áll distréss,
and my éyes have gázed upon my fóes.

PRAYER

O God, whose name is holy and almighty, whose power is salvific and
redemptive, and whose mercy is unending and ever faithful, we turn
to you in our moment of need. Hear us, and in your wisdom lead us
along the ways of fidelity and peace, that we, in turn, may speak of
your faithful help to all we meet. In your holy name we pray. Amen.

Psalm 55

THE PAIN OF BETRAYAL

Three poignant motifs arise in Psalm 55 in words compelling and memorable: flight from danger, betrayal by a friend, and trust in God. In verses 7–9, the Psalmist expresses the desire to escape his present situation in the way a bird might flee from threat or terror. Images of a besieged city give shape to the experience from which the Psalmist's fear arises. His heart is overwhelmed with grief and terror; his life seems threatened. The very thought of nothing more than escape seems to become a foundation upon which he hopes to begin the rebuilding of his interior peace. But then in verses 13–15, the Psalmist reveals that the core of his terror is a painful incident of betrayal by one thought to have been a friend. Betrayal, of course, is among the most demoralizing and destructive of human experiences; valuing someone as a close and intimate friend only to discover that the relationship never had such depth or security. When the Psalmist writes, "We walked together in harmony in the house of God," he gives expression to a life-bond of shared values, hopes, and aspirations now brought to nothing. He returns to the pain of this motif in verses 21–22, a potent description of the betrayer as presenting a calm exterior and soothing words while concealing a heart at war. How can such duplicity and infidelity hope to be healed? The Psalmist's answer is unqualified: trust in God, pure and simple, challenging yet hopeful (vv. 23–24). The First Letter of Peter reiterates this message, calling for the same confidence in God. "Cast all your anxiety on [God], because he cares for you" (5:7). Such expressions are more than pious platitudes; they are the challenge of a lifetime, calling us to deep interior faith as we embrace God's mysterious plan in our lives and commit ourselves to finding our peace in God's will for us.

PSALM 55 (54)

¹ *For the Choirmaster. On stringed instruments.*
A Maskil *of David.*

² Give éar, O Gód, to my práyer;
do not híde from my pléading.

³ Atténd to mé and replý;
with my cáres, I cannot rést.

⁴ I trémble at the shóuts of the fóe,
at the críes of the wícked,
for they píle up évil upón me;
in ánger they malígn me.

⁵ My héart is strícken withín me;
death's térror falls upón me.
⁶ Trémbling and féar come óver me,
and hórror overwhélms me.

⁷ I say, "Ó that I had wíngs like a dóve,
to fly awáy and be at rést!
⁸ I would indéed escápe far awáy,
and take réfuge in the désert.
⁹ Í shall awáit him who sáves me
from the ráging wind and témpest."

¹⁰ Engúlf and confúse their speech, O Lórd,
for I see víolence and strífe in the cíty!
¹¹ Night and dáy they patról its wálls.
In its mídst are wíckedness and évil.

¹² Destrúction líes withín it.
Its stréets are néver frée
from týranny and decéit.

¹³ If an énemy made táunts agáinst me,
Í could béar it.
If my ríval had rísen agáinst me,
I could híde from hím.

¹⁴ But it is yóu, as my équal, my fríend,
whom I knéw so wéll,
¹⁵ with whóm I enjóyed friendly cóunsel!
We wálked togéther in hármony
in the hóuse of Gód.

¹⁶ May déath fall súddenly upón them!
Let them go dówn alive to the gráve,
for wíckedness dwélls in their hómes,
and déep in their héarts.

¹⁷ As for mé, I will crý to Gód,
and the LÓRD will sáve me.
¹⁸ Évening, mórning, and at nóon,
I will crý and lamént,
and he will héar my vóice.

¹⁹ He will redéem my sóul in péace
in the attáck agáinst me,
for thóse who fíght me are mány.

²⁰ Gód, who is enthróned foréver,
will héar them and húmble them.
For théy will not aménd their wáys;
they have no féar of Gód.

²¹ The tráitor has túrned against his fríends;
he has bróken his páct.
²² His spéech is sófter than bútter,
but wár is in his héart.
His wórds are smóother than óil,
but they are swórds unshéathed.

²³ Entrúst your cáres to the LÓRD,
and hé will suppórt you.
Hé will néver allów
the júst man to stúmble.

²⁴ But you will bríng them dówn, O Gód,
to the pít of déath:
the blóodthirsty ánd the líars
shall not líve even hálf their dáys.
But Í, I will trúst in you, O Lórd.

PRAYER

Ever-faithful God, who in taking on our human nature knew the pain of fear and betrayal, strengthen us to be faithful images of your Servant and Son, Jesus Christ, by whose passion and death you conquered the powers of sin that beset human weakness. He lives and reigns with you and the Holy Spirit, one God, forever and ever. Amen.

Psalm 56

MY TEARS IN GOD'S FLASK

This psalm is bracketed by expressions of trust in God in the face of difficulties. In verse 4, the Psalmist acknowledges that trust is most important when fear strikes. The motif is repeated near the end of the psalm: when foes plague the human heart, trust must be more powerful than fear (v. 12). One verse may seem at first reading surprisingly out of place, yet its message comprises a Hebraic expression of tenderness and love. Verse 9 is placed between two verses quite different from it in tone that would read perfectly well without it; in fact, verse 9 interrupts the Psalmist's comments about his foes and what he hopes God will do to them. The interruption presents an image of God's care for the Psalmist in poignant terms of loving intimacy. He speaks of God collecting his tears and placing them in a flask or bottle. So precious to God are the tears of the speaker that God saves them as a kind of remembrance of the suffering and pain that his beloved child has endured. Such an intimate portrayal of God's compassion and affection is rare in the Scriptures. This representation of a caring and gentle God stands in sharp contrast to the more frequent Old Testament image of the divine judge moved by wrath. Jesus further reveals this image of divine humility and goodness in Matthew's Gospel when he says, "Come to me, all you that are weary and are carrying heavy burdens, and I will give you rest. Take my yoke upon you, and learn from me; for I am gentle and humble in heart, and you will find rest for your souls. For my yoke is easy, and my burden is light" (11:28–30). Having reiterated the need for trust, the psalm concludes with strong assertions about God's fidelity toward those who are faithful. He commits himself to living out his vows to God (v. 13), voicing praise for the Redeemer (v. 13) in a proclamation of belief that God has rescued him from certain death and reopened his way to a life secure in the divine presence. In the midst of assailing foes, these words of faith encourage us to great confidence in the God whose love for us is beyond our comprehension.

PSALM 56 (55)

¹ *For the Choirmaster. Intoned like "The Dove of Distant Places."*
A Miktam *of David, when the Philistines seized him in Gath.*

² Have mércy on mé, O Gód,
for péople assáil me;
they fíght me all day lóng and oppréss me.
³ My fóes assáil me all day lóng:
mány fight próudly agáinst me.

⁴ On the dáy when Í shall féar,
I will trúst in yóu,
⁵ in Gód, whose wórd I práise.
In Gód I trúst; I shall not féar.
Whát can mere flésh do to mé?

⁶ All day lóng they distórt my wórds,
their évery thought agáinst me is évil.
⁷ They bánd togéther in ámbush;
they wátch my véry fóotsteps,
as they wáit to táke my life.

⁸ Repáy them, O Gód, for their crímes;
in your ánger, bríng down the péoples.
⁹ You have képt an accóunt of my wánderings;
you have pláced my téars in your flásk;
áre they not recórded in your bóok?
¹⁰ Thén my fóes will turn báck
on the dáy when I cáll to yóu.

This I knów, that Gód is on my síde.
¹¹ In Gód, whose wórd I práise,
in the LÓRD whose wórd I práise,
¹² in Gód I trúst; I shall not féar.
Whát can man dó to mé?

¹³ I am bóund by the vóws I have máde you.
O Gód, I will óffer you práise,
¹⁴ for you have réscued my sóul from déath;
you képt my féet from stúmbling,
that I may wálk in the présence of Gód,
in the líght of the líving.

God our Savior and Redeemer, how strong is the mercy, how deep the compassion, and how rich the fidelity you show us day after day. Inspire us to imitate your loving compassion to ease the suffering of all we meet along the rocky way of earthly life. We ask this through Christ our Lord. Amen.

Psalm 57

A READY HEART

The short refrain in verses 6 and 12 of Psalm 57, "Be exalted, O God, above the heavens; may your glory shine on earth!" expresses great faith in a dreadful situation. With vivid imagery he casts his foes as lions: their teeth are like spears and arrows, their tongues like a sharpened sword (v. 5). Yet even in the face of such danger, he praises God, asserting that when God's glory shines upon the earth, it will bring blessing, peace, and an end to the danger he faces (v. 6). For the Psalmist, God is life's Provider, the One who, though abiding in the heavens, is intimately bound to those upon the earth who seek refuge in divine guidance and assistance. All one need do is call out to God in faith, and the assurance of saving help from on high is readily at hand. The Psalmist offers a brief passage touching on divine retribution, explaining that when his foes take up wicked arms and plot destruction, the consequence is that their violence will rebound upon them (v. 7). In our own times, many are uncomfortable attributing such action to God, who loves all his creatures, whether just or wicked. But the ancient mind saw things differently; divine justice was naturally understood to fall thus upon the enemies of God's faithful ones. However such things might be understood, these texts give us insight into how the biblical mind conceived life and the unfolding of God's plan for the world. With such an attitude toward life, the Psalmist can only lift up enthusiastic praise. And regarding this praise, we see here how the Psalmist calls upon his own interior life and being, his very heart and soul, to awaken both himself and creation to the wonders of God's goodness. Two primary elements of divine action—mercy (*hesed*) and faithfulness (*emeth*, here rendered as "truth")—are acknowledged in verse 11 as gifts of God that come down from heaven. We find St. Paul expressing the same understanding of God's saving deeds when he proclaims, "O the depth of the riches and wisdom and knowledge of God! How unsearchable are his judgments and how inscrutable his ways!" (Rom 11:33). May our wonder and praise of God's goodness toward us be as fervent as the Psalmist's and St. Paul's!

PSALM 57 (56)

1 For the Choirmaster. Intoned like "Do not destroy." A Miktam *of David when he fled from Saul into a cave.*

2 Have mércy on me, Gód, have mércy,
for in yóu my sóul has taken réfuge.
In the shádow of your wíngs I take réfuge,
till the stórms of destrúction pass bý.

3 I cáll to you, Gód the Most Hígh,
to Gód who provídes for mé.
4 May he sénd from héaven and sáve me,
and pút to shame thóse who assáil me.
May God sénd his loving mércy and fáithfulness.

5 My sóul lies dówn among líons,
who would devóur the sons of mén.
Their téeth are spéars and árrows,
their tóngue a shárpened swórd.
6 Be exálted, O Gód, above the héavens;
may your glóry shíne on éarth!

7 They láid down a nét for my stéps;
my sóul was bowed dówn.
They dúg a pít in my páth,
but féll in it themsélves.

8 My héart is réady, O Gód;
my héart is réady.
I will síng, I will síng your práise.
9 Awáke, my sóul!
Awáke, lýre and hárp!
I will awáke the dáwn.

10 I will práise you, Lórd, among the peoples,
among the nátions sing psálms to you,

¹¹ for your mércy réaches to the héavens,
and your trúth to the skíes.
¹² Be exálted, O Gód, above the héavens;
may your glóry shine on áll the éarth!

PRAYER

God, our Creator, whose care for us is beyond what we can hope or expect, keep us always mindful of your just and loving ways. Strengthen us in faith, that we may discern your actions with trust and confidence, and so respond with ever faithful love, through Christ our Lord. Amen.

Psalm 58

BEWARE: GOD WILL JUDGE

Psalm 58 is another of those psalms that we may find difficult to pray because of its violent language and condemnatory tone. St. Paul tells us, "Bless those who persecute you; bless and do not curse them....Do not repay anyone evil for evil, but take thought for what is noble in the sight of all....Beloved, never avenge yourselves, but leave room for the wrath of God; for it is written, 'Vengeance is mine, I will repay, says the Lord.' No, 'if your enemies are hungry, feed them; if they are thirsty, give them something to drink; for by doing this you will heap burning coals on their heads.' Do not be overcome by evil, but overcome evil with good" (Rom 12:12, 14, 19–21). Putting this psalm in its biblical and historical context helps us to understand its harsh words. The psalm is addressed to unjust rulers who act as if the power they hold over others is a divine attribute that belongs to them alone, for which they answer to no one but themselves. The Psalmist classifies these rulers with the origin of all wickedness, the serpent in the Garden of Eden (vv. 5–6; cf. Gen 3:1–5, 11–14). It is clear to him that their actions and intentions are directed to the satisfaction of their own greed, without regard for those over whom they have authority—and responsibility. When their basic human rights have been disregarded or violated, people are too often inclined to assume that only one course remains open to them: anger leading to violence. How then do we pray such a psalm, while still adhering to the new law of love? One way is to pray it as the voice of those in our own world who we know must live under burdens of injustice and oppression over which they have neither power nor recourse. Though we do not seek violence or ruin for any person, we can be a voice before God for our suffering brothers and sisters, beseeching an end to any rule or regime that conspires against the freedom and hope that is the right of the children of God.

PSALM 58 (57)

¹ *For the Choirmaster. Intoned like "Do not destroy." A* Miktam *of David.*

² Do you trúly speak jústice, you who hóld divine pówer?
Do you méte out fair júdgment to the sons of mén?
³ No, in your héarts you devíse iníquities;
your hands déal out víolence to the lánd.

⁴ The wícked go astráy from the wómb;
déviant from bírth, they speak líes.
⁵ Their vénom is líke the vénom of the snáke;
they are líke a deaf víper stópping its éars,
⁶ lést it should héar the snáke-charmer's vóice,
the vóice of the skíllful déaler in spélls.

⁷ O Gód, break the téeth in their móuths;
tear out the fángs of these líons, O LORD!
⁸ Let them vánish like wáter that rúns awáy;
let them wíther like gráss that is tródden underfóot.
⁹ Let them bé like the snáil that dissólves into slíme,
like a wóman's míscarriage that néver sees the sún.

¹⁰ Before they pút forth thórns, like a brámble,
let them be swépt away, gréen wood or drý!
¹¹ The júst shall rejóice at the síght of véngeance;
they shall báthe their féet in the blóod of the wícked.
¹² People shall sáy: "Trúly, there is rewárd for the úpright.
Trúly there ís a God who júdges on éarth."

O God of justice and truth, who heard the plea of your people in slavery, hear again the cries of all who live under regimes of violence and oppression. Turn the hearts of those who have rejected your law of love, so that all people everywhere might take possession of your divine gifts of peace, hope, and freedom, through Christ our Lord. Amen.

Psalm 59

O GOD, MY STRENGTH

This psalm's refrain (v. 10, repeated with slight changes in v. 18) affirms that God is the source of strength and merciful love (*hesed*). It is clear that the Psalmist considers his enemies a deadly threat: he describes them as bloodthirsty (v. 3) and plotting against his life (v. 4). Twice he compares them to dogs that roam the city in search of prey (vv. 7, 15–16), and twice notes specifically the growling sound that comes from their mouths (vv. 6, 17). He develops this theme by describing the speech of his foes, who utter insults with lips like sharpened swords (v. 8). Again in verse 13, he casts the evil of his enemies in terms of their speech: proud words, cursing, and lies. The fear evoked by these enemies is founded on the destructive power of words. The Hebrew term for "word" is *dabar*, and it is interesting to note that this Hebrew term can also be understood to imply something tangible, physical, or material. This additional nuance underscores the effect that words can have in human experience; depending on their intent, words can cut us to the quick, or they can raise us to the heights. Unfortunately, in a society in which a glut of words flows over us from contemporary media—Internet, television, radio, or print—the true power of the word may be diminished by their sheer number. But words remain powerful. By the power of his words, Jesus brings healing and new life to the suffering. "[Jesus] went throughout Galilee, proclaiming the message in their synagogues and casting out demons" (Mark 1:39). The Psalmist uses words to lift up to God praise and gratitude for the saving help and merciful love God bestows. May our words be a source of healing and strength, joy and hope to those whose lives are interwoven with our own.

PSALM 59 (58)

¹ *For the Choirmaster. Intoned like "Do not destroy."*
A Miktam of David when Saul sent men to keep watch
on his house and kill him.

² Rescue mé from my fóes, O Gód;
protéct me from thóse who attáck me.
³ O réscue me from thóse who do évil,
and sáve me from blóodthirsty mén.

⁴ See, they líe in wáit for my lífe;
the stróng band togéther agáinst me.
For no offénse, no sín of mine, O LÓRD,
⁵ for no guílt of mine they rúsh to take their stánd.

Awáke! Come to méet me, and sée!
⁶ LORD God of hósts, you are Ísrael's Gód.
Róuse yourself and púnish the nátions;
show no mércy to évil tráitors.
⁷ Each évening théy come báck;
howling like dógs, they róam about the cíty.

⁸ Sée how their móuths utter ínsults;
their líps are like shárpened swórds.
"For whó," they sáy, "will héar us?"
⁹ But yóu, LORD, will láugh them to scórn.
You make a móckery of áll the nátions.

¹⁰ O my Stréngth, for yóu will I wátch,
for yóu, O Gód, are my strónghold,
¹¹ the God who shóws me mérciful lóve.

Now Gód will procéed befóre me;
Gód will let me lóok upon my fóes.
¹² Do not kíll them lest my péople forgét;
róut them by your pówer, lay them lów.

It is yóu, Lord Gód, who are our shíeld.
¹³ For the síns of their móuths and the wórds of their líps,
lét them be cáught in their príde;
for the cúrses and líes that they spéak.

¹⁴ Destróy them in your ánger. Destróy them
till they áre no móre.

Let them knów that Gód is the rúler
over Jácob and the énds of the éarth.

¹⁵ Each évening théy come báck;
they howl like dógs and róam about the cíty.
¹⁶ They prówl in séarch of fóod;
they grówl till they háve their fíll.

¹⁷ As for mé, I will síng of your stréngth,
and accláim your mércy in the mórning,
for yóu have béen my strónghold,
a réfuge in the dáy of my distréss.

¹⁸ O my Stréngth, to yóu I will sing práise,
for yóu, O Gód, are my strónghold,
the God who shóws me mérciful lóve.

PRAYER

God of merciful love, Lord of saving strength, let us know your near-
ness in our need, and strengthen us against fear and uncertainty.
Empower our words to build up your reign of peace and goodness, as
they bear to others your message of grace in all we say and do, through
Christ our Lord. Amen.

Psalm 60

WITH GOD, WE SHALL DO BRAVELY

The central theme of Psalm 60 is twofold: with God we can accomplish
anything, but without divine help we are destined to fail. The vocabulary
of the psalm suggests that it may have been composed as a national
prayer in the wake of some disaster, defeat, or failure of the sort that
time makes inevitable for any nation. Some social or political upheaval
has occurred, perhaps in conjunction with an earthquake (v. 4), and the

nation is dazed by the unforeseen event (v. 5), which makes them vulnerable to enemies. They ask, "Are we not God's people? Then where is the hand of the Lord, to bring us the deliverance that we have come to expect from our God? Now we face the possibility of enslavement." Clearly the Psalmist means to evoke the experience of their ancestors in Egypt, when God heard their prayer, saw their subjugation, and delivered them from oppression. The fearful lament is immediately followed by a divine oracle (vv. 8–10) in which God's own voice asserts that, now as always, God is the victor in every battle; however the prizes of war are dispersed, whatever the land (vv. 8–9a), all belongs to God, the divine warrior, the victorious champion who disposes of the spoils of war (vv. 9–10) as he sees fit. Upon hearing this oracle, the Psalmist asks rhetorically, "Why do we find ourselves without your help in a battle that seems too much for us?" And he immediately answers his own question: We must put our sole trust in God's hands—human help is of no avail (v. 13). In spite of its nationalistic fervor, this psalm speaks to each and every one of us. In those personal battles that demand of us a choice between right and wrong, between good and evil, do we place all our trust in God's help, or do we put our faith in our own ability to achieve a victory that can really be only God's? Jesus put the matter thus when describing his relationship to the Father with the image of the true vine and the vinedresser: "Those who abide in me and I in them bear much fruit, because apart from me you can do nothing" (John 15:5b). Our great hope, our sole hope, resides in a total and undivided trust in God. As the Psalmist concludes, "With God we shall do bravely, and he will trample down our foes" (60:14).

PSALM 60 (59)

[1] *For the Choirmaster. Intoned like "The Lily of Testimony." A Miktam of David for instruction when he went out against the Aram-Haharaim and Aram-Sobah, and when Joab returned to Edom and defeated twelve thousand in the Valley of Salt.*

[3] O Gód, you have rejécted us, and bróken us.
You have been ángry; come báck to ús.

[4] You have máde the earth quáke, torn it ópen.
Repáir what is sháttered, for it swáys.
[5] You have inflícted hárdships on your péople,
made us drínk a wíne that dázed us.

[6] For those who féar you, you gáve the sígnal
to flée from the fáce of the bów.

⁷ With your right hánd, grant salvátion, and give ánswer,
that thóse whom you lóve may be frée.

⁸ From his hóly place Gód has spóken:
"I will exúlt, and divíde the land of Shéchem;
I will méasure out the válley of Súccoth.

⁹ Mine is Gílead, míne is Manásseh;
Éphraim I táke for my hélmet,
Júdah ís my scépter.

¹⁰ Móab ís my wáshbowl;
on Édom I will cást my shóe.
Over Philístia I will shóut in tríumph."

¹¹ But who will léad me to the fórtified cíty?
Whó will bríng me to Édom?
¹² Have yóu, O Gód, rejécted us?
Will you márch with our ármies no lónger?

¹³ Gíve us hélp against the fóe,
for the hélp of mán is váin.
¹⁴ With Gód, wé shall do brávely,
and he will trámple down our fóes.

PRAYER

Compassionate God, who know so well our foolish inclination to put
faith in our own resources, help us to recognize that all we have or can
do is your gift; bring us by this knowledge to place all our trust in your
saving power and faithful love. We ask this through Christ our Lord.
Amen.

Psalm 61

A HEART FAINT BUT FAITHFUL

In the Roman Liturgy of the Hours, Psalm 61 appears only once in the four-week cycle. In the Monastic Liturgy of the Hours, however, Psalm 61 appears numerous times at the early morning office of Vigils, and especially on certain feast days: the commemorations of apostles, of martyrs, of pastors, and of holy men and women. What special character of Psalm 61 gives it distinction, especially in our remembrance of those saintly men and women who lived lives of such fidelity to the gospel? Psalm 61 is appropriate to any number of challenging life situations; it speaks in general terms of situations of need. The Psalmist calls out to God in prayer, having grown faint-hearted in the face of life's trials, and asks for an attentive response (v. 2). What the Psalmist needs, to his own way of thinking, is a haven of safety beyond the reach of enemies (vv. 3b–4). He seeks that sense of nearness to the divine presence afforded by nearness to the temple, God's dwelling place on earth. There the Ark of the Covenant rests, under the shelter of the cherubim's wings that mark the holy place (v. 5). The Psalmist here refers to God in terms of the divine "name," to which both reverence (v. 6) and praise (v. 9) are due. Reverence and praise for "the name" is displayed in offering respect and extolling God, whose loving mercy and fidelity have accompanied the Psalmist at all times and in all ways (v. 9). Though the Psalmist makes his prayer for personal reasons, he does not neglect to include a prayer for the king (v. 7), beseeching divine assistance for God's anointed one. We can easily see how the Church might well apply this psalm, with its many petitions for divine aid, to commemorations of apostles, martyrs, pastors, virgins, and holy men and women—those models of the faith who have stood firm in the face of opposition for the sake of the gospel. By the same token, this psalm can also be a suitable prayer for each of us as we struggle with the daily challenges of life, always striving to put our trust in the loving mercy and fidelity of God who walks with us, day in and day out, through this life.

PSALM 61 (60)

¹ *For the Choirmaster. With stringed instruments. Of David.*

² Lísten, O Gód, to my crý!
Atténd to my práyer!
³ From the énd of the éarth I cáll you;
my héart is fáint.

Sét me hígh upon the róck
too hígh for me to réach,
⁴ you, my réfuge and míghty tówer
agáinst the fóe.

⁵ Then will I dwéll in your tént foréver,
and híde in the shélter of your wíngs.
⁶ For yóu, O God, have héard my vóws;
you have gíven me the héritage of thóse
who féar your náme.

⁷ Day upon dáy you will ádd to the kíng;
his yéars as áge upon áge.
⁸ May he éver sit enthróned before Gód:
bid mércy and trúth be his protéction.
⁹ So I will síng to your náme foréver,
and dáy after dáy fulfill my vóws.

PRAYER

Merciful and faithful God, who know our needs even before our prayers are uttered, manifest to us your loving kindness, that we may glorify your name throughout the world in gratitude for the constant care and compassion you bestow upon us. We ask this through Christ our Lord. Amen.

Psalm 62

GOD ALONE

In the original oral culture of Hebrew poetry, the repetition of phrases or refrains served to highlight and emphasize significant ideas. In Psalm 62, the significance of the refrain (vv. 2, 6–7) might be summed up in the terms "God alone." Any expectation of peace, salvation, or security, any confidence, intention, or hope, must be founded on God alone. In today's Western society we are encouraged to be independent, "to burn with our own oil," to make our own path through life. Yet the person of faith acknowledges that all of life is God's gift; God's loving hand guides each of us whether we see it or not. The word *salvation* returns quite frequently to the Psalmist's lips (vv. 3, 7, 8); it is perhaps too common a convention these days to imagine salvation as some rare act of divine intervention quite beyond ordinary experience, something to be stared at in awe and wonder. But the biblical mind conceives salvation as something quite ordinary, something that comes to us each day in putting our faith in God's loving mercy. It is evident in our assurance of God's constant guidance, both by external influences and by the interior movement of the heart; we acknowledge it by our confidence in divine protection from dangers great or small. When the Psalmist asserts, "Never shall I falter," it arises in the conviction that God is always touching our life with saving power both subtle and manifest. The question is, "Can we perceive its presence all around us? Can we see with eyes of faith?" We are further instructed here not to put our hopes on the ephemeral things of life that all too suddenly may evaporate before our eyes (vv. 10–11). Jesus puts it another way in the Sermon on the Mount: "Look at the birds of the air; they neither sow nor reap nor gather into barns, and yet your heavenly Father feeds them. Are you not of more value than they?...But strive first for the kingdom of God and his righteousness, and all these things will be given to you as well" (Matt 6:26, 33). The Psalmist concludes by reminding us that merciful love and power belong to God, and it is God's to judge human actions. Is God alone our source of strength and hope?

PSALM 62 (61)

¹ *For the Choirmaster. Intoned like Jeduthun. A Psalm of David.*

² In God alóne is my sóul at rést;
my salvátion cómes from hím.
³ He alóne is my róck, my salvátion,
my fórtress; néver shall I fálter.

⁴ How lóng will you áll attack one mán
to bréak him down,
as thóugh he were a tóttering wáll,
or a túmbling fénce?

⁵ Their plán is ónly to bring dówn;
they take pléasure in líes.
With their móuth they útter bléssing,
but in their héart they cúrse.

⁶ In God alóne be at rést, my sóul,
for my hópe is from hím.
⁷ He alóne is my róck, my salvátion,
my fórtress; néver shall I fálter.

⁸ In Gód is my salvátion and glóry,
my róck of stréngth;
in Gód is my réfuge.
⁹ Trúst him at all tímes, O péople.
Póur out your héarts befóre him,
for Gód is our réfuge.

¹⁰ The sóns of mén are a bréath,
an illúsion, the sóns of mén.
Pláced in the scáles, they ríse;
they áll weigh léss than a bréath.

¹¹ Do not pút your trúst in oppréssion,
nor vain hópes on plúnder.
Éven if ríches incréase,
set not your héart on thém.

¹² For Gód has said ónly one thíng;
only twó have I héard:
that to Gód alóne belongs pówer,
¹³ and to yóu, Lord, mérciful lóve;

and that yóu repáy each mán
accórding to his déeds.

PRAYER

*O God, our source of saving power and strength: in confident assur-
ance of your everlasting love, we come before you in our need. Help us
to place all our hope in you, that we may find new determination to follow you faithfully, through Christ our Lord. Amen.*

Psalm 63

OUR DEEPEST LONGING

Psalm 63 has a long history as the preferred psalm for the Church's Morning Prayer, based on the opening line's reference to dawn. Yet this particular expression is not present in many translations of the psalm. The verb
rendered here as "seeking" has its root in the noun usually translated as
"dawn." Thus the term conveys a complex notion of an eager search early
in the morning—the objective of which, for the Psalmist, is God. His expression of desire for intimacy with God is augmented by the images of each
successive verse. To communicate the totality of his longing, a matter of
both body and spirit, the Psalmist speaks of the soul thirsting and the flesh
pining (v. 2); the desire for union with God is so great that the Psalmist
even uses a possessive pronoun: my God. A vivid image serves to illustrate
this longing: for a land that lies parched and dry for most of the year, hope
for water is eager and fervent (v. 2b); when water is scarce, life and death
hang in the balance. So too the Psalmist's life is in peril when the sense of
God's absence predominates, and anticipation of his return is all-absorbing.
When the Psalmist once again feels assured of the divine presence, he
likens the experience to a banquet that is fully satisfying (v. 6), where the
abundance of food and drink is matched by the richness of the fare. A plentiful feast naturally engenders joy and calls forth praise; it is to God that
the Psalmist's praise and joy are directed, because God himself is the source
of all this delight (v. 6). The intimacy of this relationship is further apparent
in the Psalmist's assertion that his thoughts about God persist through the
night, keeping him wakeful even as the city sentinels announce the succes-

sive watches as night progresses (v. 7). The Psalmist's words convey the depth of his love, both a fervent desire for communion and joy in the sense of closeness. The image of "the shadow of [God's] wings" refers specifically here (as elsewhere in the Psalter) to the divine presence in the temple, the dwelling place of God's holiness. The Psalmist's words in verse 9 even present the soul being held in the very embrace of God, a physical image expressing a kind of mystical communion with the One who is both creator and intimate friend. St. Paul echoes the Psalmist's assertion that God's loving mercy (hesed) is better than life (v. 4) when speaking of his own longing for such divine union: "I have suffered the loss of all things, and I regard them as rubbish, in order that I may gain Christ" (Phil 3:8b). It is of the union with God for which we were created that both saint and Psalmist speak so movingly.

PSALM 63 (62)

¹ A Psalm of David when he was in the desert of Judah.

² O Gód, you are my Gód; at dawn I séek you;
for yóu my sóul is thírsting.
For yóu my flésh is píning,
like a drý, weary lánd without wáter.
³ I have cóme before yóu in the sánctuary,
to behóld your stréngth and your glóry.

⁴ Your loving mércy is bétter than lífe;
my líps will spéak your práise.
⁵ I will bléss you áll my lífe;
in your náme I will líft up my hánds.
⁶ My sóul shall be fílled as with a bánquet;
with joyful líps, my móuth shall práise you.

⁷ When I remémber you upón my béd,
I muse on yóu through the wátches of the níght.
⁸ For yóu have béen my stréngth;
in the shádow of your wíngs I rejóice.
⁹ My sóul clings fást to yóu;
yóur right hánd uphólds me.

¹⁰ Those who séek to destróy my lífe
shall go dówn to the dépths of the éarth.
¹¹ Pút to the pówer of the swórd,
they shall be léft as préy for the jáckals.

¹² But the kíng shall rejóice in Gód;
all that swéar by hím shall exúlt,
for the móuth of líars shall be sílenced.

PRAYER

O God, who have formed in the human heart the desire for union with you, draw us ever more deeply into the great mystery that moves us to seek communion with you. Be forever our joy, our hope, our strength, and our peace, through Christ our Lord. Amen.

Psalm 64

WORDS AS BARBED ARROWS

Psalm 64 deals with the pain and sorrow felt when one is the object of vicious speech, lying tongues, and wicked plots—a theme found elsewhere among the Psalms, and frequently addressed in the Book of Proverbs: "When words are many, transgression is not lacking, but the prudent are restrained in speech" (10:19); "The words of the wicked are a deadly ambush, but the speech of the upright delivers them" (12:6); "Scoundrels concoct evil, and their speech is like a scorching fire" (16:27). Here the Psalmist seeks refuge from the weapons of evil words. The imagery employed in this psalm to describe wicked speech is potent: tongues are likened to swords (v. 4a), words are like arrows, aimed without fear at the innocent (v. 4b–5). The Psalmist asserts that the worst of this evil is that these words arise from the innermost being of those who speak them: "How profound the depths of the heart!" (v. 7d). With verse 8, the Psalmist sets up an effective rhetorical repetition by reusing the very terms and images he has just applied to the wicked to express God's just response to their evil words: God will shoot arrows at them (vv. 4b, 8a); the action will be sudden (vv. 5b, 8b); those who shot without fear will now know fear at what God is doing (vv. 5b, 10a). Thus the ruin they sought to deal out with their tongues will rebound upon them; bringing upon them the very ruin they voiced (vv. 4a, 9a). This psalm appears in the Office of Readings for the Feast of Apostles: it calls to mind the wrong inflicted on those faithful witnesses by those who opposed the gospel, and assures us that in the end, divine justice will be rendered by God for his faithful servants. Jesus himself phrases it thus: "You will be hated by all because of my name. But not a hair of your head will perish. By your endurance you will gain your souls" (Luke 21:17–19). Words are powerful, whether spoken truthfully or falsely. Let our words be few, and always spoken in truth and love.

PSALM 64 (63)

[1] *For the Choirmaster. A Psalm of David.*

[2] Hear, O Gód, the vóice of my compláint;
guard my lífe from dréad of the fóe.
[3] From the assémbly of the wícked, híde me,
from the thróng of thóse who do évil.

[4] They shárpen their tóngues like swórds.
They áim bitter wórds like árrows,
[5] to shóot at the ínnocent from ámbush,
shóoting súddenly and féarlessly.

[6] Holding fírm in their évil cóurse,
they conspíre to lay sécret snáres.
They sáy, "Whó will sée us?
[7] Whó can séarch out our crímes?"

They have hátched their wícked plóts,
and bróught them to perféction.
How profóund the dépths of the héart!

[8] Gód will shóot them with his árrow,
and déal them súdden wóunds.
[9] Their ówn tongue bríngs them to rúin;
all who sée them sháke their héads.

[10] Thén will áll be afráid;
they will téll what Gód has dóne.
Théy will pónder God's déeds.
[11] The júst one will rejóice in the LORD;
and flý to hím for réfuge.
All úpright héarts will glóry.

*O God, whose deeds of justice and mercy find their fullest expression in
the Word become flesh, grant us the strength to speak uprightly and to
act justly, that we may imitate Jesus your Son, who is Lord, forever
and ever. Amen.*

Psalm 65

OUR PROVIDENT GOD

How powerful is God's forgiveness. The Psalmist knows well the weight of
human sins, yet God simply "wipes them away." From his acknowledgment
of the power of divine forgiveness, the Psalmist passes into a hymn of
thanksgiving for the wonders of God's deliverance, a song of praise that
resounds from the nearby temple (v. 5) to the far distant isles (v. 6). From
east to west (v. 9c), from the mountains to the seas (vv. 7–8), the power of
God is manifest to the whole world, and all peoples stand in awe, rejoicing
before such marvels. The earth and all that lives or moves on it draw
strength from God; the rivers flow and the parched earth is watered by
God's will. How can the Psalmist affirm the order of the unfolding cosmos,
something so vast as to be beyond human comprehension? It is the implicit
faith, born from experience, that God is always present, giving direction at
every moment to our life and being. And it is in the recognition of a God so
infinitely wonderful that the Psalmist can see how forgiveness is poured
forth as gift, a profound spiritual insight into the love of God that surpasses
all understanding. In a similar manner, St. Paul breaks forth in a moment
of ecstasy marveling on God's goodness: "I am convinced that neither
death, nor life, nor angels, nor rulers, nor things present, nor things to
come, nor powers, nor height, nor depth, nor anything else in all creation,
will be able to separate us from the love of God in Christ Jesus our Lord"
(Rom 8:38–39). God is present to creation (v. 10), and the beauty and order
of what God has done can open the eyes of faith to see all as divine gift. God
provides for all that we have and all that we are, and it is our task, simple
yet profound, to return our praise and thanksgiving for blessings we cannot
fully comprehend.

PSALM 65 (64)

[1] *For the Choirmaster. A Psalm of David. A Song.*

[2] Práise is dúe to yóu
in Síon, O Gód.
To yóu we pay our vóws in Jerúsalem,
[3] you who héar our práyer.

To yóu all flésh will cóme.
[4] Our evil déeds are too héavy for ús,
but our transgréssions you wípe awáy.

[5] Blessed is hé whom you chóose and cáll
to dwéll in your cóurts.
We are filled with the góod things of your hóuse,
of your hóly témple.

[6] With wóndrous delíverance you ánswer us,
O Gód our sávior.
You are the hópe of áll the éarth,
and of fár distant ísles.

[7] You estáblish the móuntains with your stréngth;
you are gírded with pówer.
[8] You stíll the róaring of the séas,
the róaring of their wáves,
and the túmult of the péoples.

[9] Distant péoples stánd in áwe
at your wóndrous déeds.
The lánds of súnrise and súnset
you fill with your jóy.

[10] You vísit the éarth, give it wáter;
you fill it with ríches.
God's éver-flowing ríver brims óver
to prepáre the gráin.

And thús you províde for the éarth:
[11] you drénch its fúrrows;
you lével it, sóften it with shówers;
you bléss its grówth.

¹² You crówn the yéar with your bóunty.
Abúndance flóws in your páthways;
¹³ in pástures of the désert it flóws.

The hílls are gírded with jóy,
¹⁴ the méadows are clóthed with flócks.
The válleys are décked with whéat.
They shóut for jóy; yes, they síng!

PRAYER

O God, who created all things in love, receive our grateful praise. Help us to see with eyes of faith the beauty and wonder of the gifts you provide with each passing day. To you be all glory and praise, now and forever. Amen.

Psalm 66

THROUGH FIRE AND WATER, TO A PLACE OF PLENTY

Psalm 66 is a beautiful prayer that the Church applies to the paschal mystery on both communal (vv. 1–12) and personal (vv. 13–20) levels. The psalm dramatically recounts the Exodus event, God's deliverance of the Hebrew people from Egyptian bondage (v. 5), bringing them through the sea (v. 6), and into the Promised Land (v. 12). The paschal experience of the Jewish people was a movement from slavery to freedom, from darkness to light, from a state of having no national significance to identification as the chosen people of God. These gifts of God did not come without a price; there were tests and trials (v. 10), traps and burdens (v. 11). But their safe passage through all of them emerges in resounding praise, for God had accompanied them through it all (v. 12). Furthermore, each individual in the community is likewise called to a personal response of faith to the salvation of God, which comes both to the community as a whole and to its individual members. The Psalmist tells of his own response, bringing offerings and fulfilling personal vows to God

(vv. 13–14). Such actions bear a liturgical character and are presented a number of times in the psalms: someone who is conscious of having received a particular gift from God comes before the community to acknowledge what God has done, offering praise and thanks for the unexpected and unmerited blessing that has come into his life (v. 16). The Psalmist here asserts that God has heard and accepted a petition that has been offered in the form of a prayer. For the one who has known such blessings, this is to be recognized as God's merciful love (*hesed*) at work in one's life. In his Letter to the Ephesians, St. Paul speaks of the same kind of unexpected blessing: "Now to him who by the power at work within us is able to accomplish abundantly far more than all we can ask or imagine, to him be glory in the church and in Christ Jesus to all generations, forever and ever. Amen" (3:20–21). What a wonderful witness to God's grace. Blest be God who does not refuse the prayer we bring in faith, hope, and love!

PSALM 66 (65)

¹ *For the Choirmaster. A Song. A Psalm.*

Cry out with jóy to Gód, all the éarth;
² O síng to the glóry of his náme.
O rénder him glórious práise.
³ Say to Gód, "How áwesome your déeds!

Becáuse of the gréatness of your stréngth,
your énemies fáwn upón you.
⁴ Before yóu all the éarth shall bow dówn,
shall síng to you, síng to your náme!"

⁵ Come and sée the wórks of Gód:
awesome his déeds among the chíldren of mén.
⁶ He túrned the séa into dry lánd;
they pássed through the ríver on fóot.

Let our jóy, then, bé in hím;
⁷ he rúles foréver by his míght.
His éyes keep wátch on the nátions:
let rébels not exált themsélves.

⁸ O péoples, bléss our Gód;
let the vóice of his práise resóund,
⁹ of the Gód who gave lífe to our sóuls
and képt our féet from stúmbling.

¹⁰ For yóu, O Gód, have tésted us,
you have tríed us as sílver is tríed:
¹¹ you léd us, Gód, into the snáre,
you láid a heavy búrden on our bácks.

¹² You lét men ríde over our héads;
we wént through fíre and through wáter,
but then you bróught us to a pláce of plénty.

¹³ Burnt óffering I bríng to your hóuse;
to yóu I will páy my vóws,
¹⁴ the vóws which my líps have úttered,
which my móuth decláred in my distréss.

¹⁵ I will óffer you burnt ófferings of fátlings
with the smóke of sácrificial ráms.
I will óffer búllocks and góats.

¹⁶ Come and héar, áll who fear Gód;
I will téll what he díd for my sóul.
¹⁷ To hím I críed alóud,
with exaltátion réady on my tóngue.

¹⁸ Had I consídered évil in my héart,
the Lórd would nót have lístened.
¹⁹ But trúly Gód has lístened;
he has héeded the vóice of my práyer.
²⁰ Blest be Gód, who did nót reject my práyer,
nor withhóld from me his mérciful lóve.

PRAYER

Almighty and eternal God, who test us only to lead us to blessing, we
thank you for your boundless love and fidelity. May we give witness to
the grace at work in our lives, in our words, and especially in our deeds,
that others may come to recognize and acknowledge your provident
love, through Christ our Lord. Amen.

Psalm 67

BLESSINGS FOR US, THE NATIONS, AND THE ENDS OF THE EARTH

We encounter here another psalm with a refrain; this one thematizes Psalm 67 in an exhortation for all peoples to praise God (vv. 4, 6). The rest of the psalm makes apparent the reason for this gratitude: the divine gifts of life, justice, and abundant blessing. The opening stanza asks for God's blessing upon the community at prayer (vv. 2–3). The stanza following the first refrain calls the people to rejoice in the uprightness with which God governs the nations (v. 5). After the repetition of the refrain, the closing stanza (vv. 7–8), acknowledges the bounty God has brought forth from the earth, evoking a prayer that such harvests continue, that the whole earth might have cause to praise the God who has so favored Israel. In the tradition of the Church's liturgy, Psalm 67 is an Invitatory Psalm, one of those selected to begin the day's office of prayer with a summons to the Church to extol God, who has again brought us to a new day. The monastic Night Prayer (Compline) traditionally begins with a moment of silent recollection known as the *examen*, during which the monk may consider the thoughts and deeds of the past day. In my own spiritual observance, I have added a nuance to that moment, taking time to consider the day's blessings, not only those of my own life, but in the life of the Church and the world as well. At such moments I am aware of a powerful impulse of praise welling up in me, a sense of gratitude for so many things, great and small, and especially things that others may be unaware of. This psalm embodies that impulse. What greater motivation do we need to praise God than simply to look back over the day and see how God has been so very present—in our personal lives, in the Church, and in the world? Praise is our acknowledgment of how very blessed we know our lives to be. In the midst of disappointment, struggle, and pain, how often we can see light shining through darkness, if we just take time to look! Such a moment is apparent in the experience of Jesus, too, when he is so filled with this sense of God's goodness that all he can do is lift up his voice to bless God: "At that moment Jesus said, 'I give praise to you, Father, Lord of heaven and earth, for though you have hidden these things from the wise and the clever, you have revealed them to those who are childlike'" (Matt 11:25; translation mine). Praise and thanks come easily to children, whose freedom of heart gives them unfettered appreciation for the blessings of life. May our hearts lift up such childlike praise—for all that has been, for all that now is, and for all that is to come!

PSALM 67 (66)

¹ *For the Choirmaster. With string instruments. A Psalm. A Song.*

² O Gód, be grácious and bléss us
and let your fáce shed its líght upón us.
³ So will your wáys be knówn upon éarth
and all nátions léarn your salvátion.

⁴ Let the péoples práise you, O Gód;
let áll the péoples práise you.

⁵ Let the nátions be glád and shout for jóy;
with úprightness you rúle the peoples,
you guíde the nátions on éarth.

⁶ Let the péoples práise you, O Gód;
let áll the péoples práise you.

⁷ The éarth has yíelded its frúit
for Gód, our Gód, has bléssed us.
⁸ May Gód still gíve us his bléssing
that all the énds of the éarth may revére him.

PRAYER

O God of wonder, open our hearts to the countless ways in which you touch our lives each and every day. May we grow in gratitude for all your blessings, and may our praise be heartfelt and joyful, through Christ our Lord. Amen.

Psalm 68

FATHER OF ORPHANS, DEFENDER OF WIDOWS

Psalm 68 paints a revealing portrait of God: though mighty in battle and supreme over creation, he yet holds dear the care of orphans and widows, society's most vulnerable members. So often the powerful have little regard for the weak and the defenseless, leaving them at the mercy of unscrupulous predators. But God shows concern for the lowly and poor throughout the Old Testament. Epithets such as "Father of orphans, defender of widows" (v. 6) convey a clear understanding that the God of Israel cares in a special way for those who are at risk of exploitation. As elsewhere, the Exodus event is variously portrayed in the psalm's imagery: God leading the people through the desert (v. 8); the terror accompanying the experience at Mount Sinai (v. 9b). Such images leave the impression that the Exodus and the events that followed upon it are a long historical procession of God supplying the people's every need in his loving and ongoing providence. The terms employed here to express God's actions suggest both salvific power and intimate concern for the people in need: God gives the desolate a home (v. 7a), leads prisoners to prosperity (v. 7b), marches before them across the desert (v. 8), restores their inheritance (v. 10b), provides for the poor (v. 11b), and bears our burdens (v. 20b). All these make clear how close our God is to us. St. Paul quotes this psalm, with particular regard for the imagery of verse 19, to describe the great procession of those redeemed by the saving death and resurrection of Christ: "It is said, 'When [Christ] ascended on high he made captivity itself a captive; he gave gifts to his people'" (Eph 4:7–8). St. Paul presents the ascension of Christ as the procession of captives to freedom: it is our participation in the paschal mystery of our great pioneer, who leads us by his saving death and resurrection into the heavenly realms. It is now for us to follow him, trusting that our efforts bring us a share in the saving grace of Jesus Christ. And how full now is the hope even of sinners: the tribute of Jesus' life now includes us, for as the Psalmist tells us, "Even rebels may dwell near the LORD God" (v. 19c). With the Psalmist we also acclaim, "Blest be God!" (v. 36d).

PSALM 68 (67)

¹ *For the Choirmaster. Of David. A Psalm. A Song.*

² Let Gód aríse; let his fóes be scáttered.
Let thóse who háte him flée from his présence.
³ As smoke is dríven awáy, so dríve them awáy;
like wáx that mélts befóre the fíre,
so the wícked shall pérish at the présence of Gód.

⁴ But the júst shall rejóice at the présence of Gód;
théy shall exúlt with glád rejóicing.
⁵ O síng to Gód; make músic to his náme.
Extól the Óne who rídes on the clóuds.
The LÓRD is his náme; exúlt at his présence.

⁶ Father of órphans, defénder of wídows:
such is Gód in his hóly pláce.
⁷ God gives the désolate a hóme to dwéll in;
he leads the prísoners fórth into prospérity,
but rébels must dwéll in a parched lánd.

⁸ O Gód, when you went fórth before your péople,
when you márched acróss the désert,
⁹ the earth trémbled, heavens póured down ráin
at the présence of Gód, the God of Sínai,
at the présence of Gód, the God of Ísrael.

¹⁰ You póured down, O Gód, a génerous ráin;
when your péople lánguished, you restóred their
    inhéritance.
¹¹ It was thére that your flóck begán to dwéll.
In your góodness, O Gód, you províded for the póor.

¹² The Lórd annóunces the commánd;
a mighty thróng of maidens béars good tídings:
¹³ "Kíngs with their ármies will flée, will flée,
and at hóme the wómen alréady share the spóil,
¹⁴ though théy are at rést among the shéepfolds:

They are cóvered with sílver as the wíngs of a dóve,
its féathers brílliant with shíning góld.
¹⁵ When the Almíghty scatters kíngs on the móuntain,
it is like snów whítening Mount Zálmon."

¹⁶ You, móuntain of Báshan, are a míghty móuntain;
a mány-peaked móuntain, móuntain of Báshan!
¹⁷ Why lóok with énvy, you mány-peaked móuntain,
at the móuntain where Gód has desíred to dwéll?
It is thére that the LORD shall dwéll foréver.

¹⁸ The cháriots of Gód are thóusands upon thóusands.
The Lórd has cóme from Sínai to the hóly place.
¹⁹ You have ascénded on hígh, leading captívity cáptive;
as tríbute recéiving prísoners, O Gód,
so that éven rébels may dwéll near the LORD God.

²⁰ Dáy after dáy, may the Lórd be blést.
He béars our búrdens; Gód is our sávior.
²¹ This Gód of óurs is a Gód who sáves.
The LORD our Lórd provídes an escápe from déath.
²² And Gód will smíte the héad of his fóes,
the hairy crówn of him who wálks abóut in his guílt.

²³ The Lord sáid, "I will bríng them báck from Báshan;
I will bríng them báck from the dépth of the séa.
²⁴ Thén you will báthe your féet in their blóod,
and the tóngues of your dógs take their sháre of the fóe."

²⁵ They sée your sólemn procéssion, O Gód,
the procéssion of my Gód, of my kíng, to the hóly place:
²⁶ the síngers in the fórefront, the musícians coming lást;
betwéen them, máidens sóunding their tímbrels.

²⁷ "In the sácred assémbly, bléss God, the LÓRD,
O yóu who are fróm the fóuntain of Ísrael."
²⁸ There is Bénjamin, léast of the tríbes, at the héad;
Júdah's prínces, a míghty thróng;
Zébulun's prínces, Náphtali's prínces.

²⁹ Súmmon fórth your míght, O Gód;
your míght, O Gód, which you have shówn for ús.
³⁰ From your témple hígh in Jerúsalem,
kings will cóme to you brínging their tríbute.

³¹ Rebúke the wild béast that dwélls in the réeds,
the bánds of the míghty and rúlers of the péoples:
Scátter the péoples who delíght in wár.
³² Rich mérchants will máke their wáy from Égypt;
Ethiópia will strétch out her hánds to Gód.

³³ You kíngdoms of the éarth, sing to Gód, praise the Lórd
³⁴ who rídes on the héavens, the áncient héavens.
Behold, he thúnders his vóice, his míghty vóice.
³⁵ Cóme, acknówledge the pówer of Gód.

His glóry is on Ísrael; his míght is in the skíes.
³⁶ Áwesome is Gód in his hóly pláce.
Hé is Gód, the Gód of Ísrael.
He himsélf gives stréngth and pówer to his péople.
Blést bé Gód!

PRAYER

*Father of the orphans, Defender of widows, we bless you for your boun-
tiful devotion to all who are in need of your grace. Bestow on us the
gifts of your faithful, so that we may sing your praises in union with
the great cloud of witnesses who have preceded us and who now live
in the fullness of that kingdom where you reign, forever and ever.
Amen.*

Psalm 69

VINEGAR TO DRINK

The words of this psalm are echoed in the Gospel accounts of the passion
of Jesus. "They have hated me without cause" (v. 5; cf. John 15:25). "For
food they gave me gall" (v. 22a; cf. Matt 27:34). "In my thirst, they gave
me vinegar to drink" (v. 22b; cf. Matt 27:48; Luke 23:36). Along with
Psalm 22, Psalm 69 has a long-standing place in the liturgy of Holy Week
and the Sacred Triduum. The Psalmist movingly describes his pain in
the scorn and hatred of others (vv. 5, 11–13, 20–21, 27), rejection by family and friends (vv. 9, 13), and worst of all, the feeling of abandonment
by God (vv. 4b, 8, 10, 18, 27). He presents his personal anguish in images
and metaphors familiar from usage elsewhere in the Old Testament, particularly in other psalms. For example, the opening verses present the
peril of imminent death in an image of deep waters that threaten to
drown him (vv. 2–3); this image is reiterated later in the psalm (vv. 15–

16). Fasting and the donning of sackcloth (vv. 11–12) represent public manifestations of repentance for sin. Yet even in the midst of his pain and sorrow, the Psalmist describes himself as God's servant (v. 18). Throughout the psalm we encounter expressions of trust and confidence that God will ultimately heed the petition of his servant (vv. 6, 8, 10, 14–19). In spite of his feelings of abandonment in the delay (v. 4d), the Psalmist never ceases in his cry for help or his plea for God's presence (vv. 17–19). And like Psalm 22, this lament reaches a turning point at which languishing and sorrow are transformed into gratitude and praise (vv. 31–37): when God's saving help comes, the Psalmist confidently asserts, thanksgiving and praise will be unstinted. The Psalmist's direct linking of his lament with thanksgiving to come manifests the transformation within him from oppressive sorrow to exultant glory. The one who asked God for help in need now knows God as the One who has listened to his appeal (v. 34). The very waters that once threatened his life are now called upon to lift up praise (v. 35b). And the servant who waited upon the Lord's saving help now gives thanks for the salvation that has come not only to him, but to Sion and Judah, his people. The Psalmist has passed through the paschal mystery itself, bringing us with him in his passing: from the threat of death into new life, from sorrow into unbounded joy.

PSALM 69 (68)

¹ *For the Choirmaster. Intoned like "Lilies." Of David.*

² Sáve me, O Gód, for the wáters
have rísen to my néck.
³ I have súnk into the múd of the déep,
where there ís no fóothold.
I have éntered the wáters of the déep,
where the flóod overwhélms me.

⁴ I am wéaried with crýing alóud;
my thróat is párched.
My éyes are wásted awáy
with wáiting for my Gód.

⁵ More númerous than the háirs on my héad
are those who háte me without cáuse.
Mány are thóse who attáck me,
énemies with líes.
Whát I have néver stólen,
hów can I restóre?

⁶ O Gód, you knów my fólly;
from you my síns are not hídden.
⁷ May those who hópe in you nót be shámed
because of mé, O Lord of hósts;
may those who séek you nót be disgráced
because of mé, O God of Ísrael.

⁸ It is for yóu that I súffer táunts,
that sháme has cóvered my fáce.
⁹ To my own kín I have becóme an óutcast,
a stránger to the chíldren of my móther.
¹⁰ Zéal for your hóuse consúmes me,
and táunts against yóu fall on mé.

¹¹ When my sóul wept bítterly in fásting,
they máde it a táunt agáinst me.
¹² When I máde my clóthing sáckcloth,
I becáme a repróach to thém,
¹³ the góssip of thóse at the gátes,
the théme of drúnkards' sóngs.

¹⁴ But I práy to yóu, O LÓRD,
for a tíme of your fávor.
In your great mércy, ánswer me, O Gód.
with your salvátion that néver fáils.

¹⁵ Réscue me from sínking in the múd;
from thóse who háte me, delíver me.
Sáve me from the wáters of the déep,
¹⁶ lest the wáves overwhélm me,
Let nót the déep engúlf me,
nor the pít close its móuth on mé.

¹⁷ LORD, ánswer, for your mércy is kínd;
in your gréat compássion, turn toward mé.
¹⁸ Do not híde your fáce from your sérvant;
answer me quíckly, for Í am in distréss.
¹⁹ Come clóse to my sóul and redéem me;
ránsom me becáuse of my fóes.

²⁰ You know my táunts, my sháme, my dishónor;
my oppréssors are áll befóre you.
²¹ Táunts have bróken my héart;
hére I ám in ánguish.

I looked for sólace, but thére was nóne;
for consólers: not óne could I fínd.

²² For fóod they gáve me gáll;
in my thírst they gave me vínegar to drínk.
²³ Let their táble be a snáre to thém,
and for their fríends, a tráp.
²⁴ Let their éyes grow dím and blínd;
let their límbs contínually trémble.

²⁵ Pour óut your ánger upón them;
let your búrning fúry overtáke them.
²⁶ Lét their cámp be left désolate;
let nó one dwéll in their ténts:
²⁷ for they pérsecute óne whom you strúck;
they incréase the pain of óne whom you wóunded.

²⁸ Chárge them with guílt upon guílt;
let them háve no sháre in your jústice.
²⁹ Blot them óut from the bóok of the líving;
do not enróll them amóng the júst.
³⁰ As for mé in my póverty and páin,
let your salvátion, O Gód, raise me úp.

³¹ Then I will práise God's náme with a sóng;
I will glórify hím with thanksgíving:
³² a gíft pleasing Gód more than óxen,
more than a búll with hórns and hóofs.

³³ The póor when they sée it will be glád,
and Gód-seeking héarts will revíve;
³⁴ for the Lᴏʀᴅ lístens to the néedy,
and does not spúrn his ówn in their cháins.
³⁵ Let the héavens and the éarth give him práise,
the seas and éverything that móves in thém.

³⁶ For Gód will bring salvátion to Síon,
and rebuíld the cíties of Júdah,
and théy shall dwéll there in posséssion.
³⁷ The chíldren of his sérvants shall inhérit it;
those who lóve his náme shall dwéll there.

O God of the poor and the lowly, listen to our cry and attend to us in our need. Heal our brokenness and assuage our sorrow, for you alone can restore and make new what has been shattered by our sins. In your loving mercy and faithfulness we place all our trust, through Christ our Lord. Amen.

Psalm 70

O LORD, MAKE HASTE TO HELP ME!

The first two lines of this psalm serve as the familiar versicle that opens most choral offices of the Liturgy of the Hours. Succinct in expression, the psalm clearly conveys the speaker's pressing need for divine assistance; both the opening and the closing verses employ forms of the word *haste*, enclosing the text as an urgent plea from the midst of mortal danger (v. 3). The Psalmist confesses that God is both rescuer and helper, his only hope in this perilous situation. The last line, "do not delay," conveys a tone of anxious tension as the Psalmist awaits God's saving response. Even in its brevity this psalm expresses a fundamental posture of faith: waiting for God. Throughout the Old Testament, one encounters situations in which people are waiting for God to take action on their behalf, to demonstrate the divine favor toward them. Is this not the essential posture of all persons and peoples of faith? We know that we cannot depend on merely human resources for deliverance from the situations we face; all too often we come up against our utter inability to avoid or alter some apparent calamity that upsets our life. And then, somehow, we find that what we had seen as a calamity has somehow enabled us to understand our experience in a new light. That is the mysterious work of God. It is God alone, after all, who knows the heart of each of us, and can move our hearts to perceive with the eyes of faith. How well St. Paul knew this posture of waiting, of longing for God to bring about in his own life the mysterious working of grace. As Saul the Pharisee, he had the firm conviction that his desire to destroy the new Way of Jesus was motivated by authentic religious belief; but with many trials and much suffering, a more powerful movement of grace eventually changed his heart and his name, finally bringing the Apostle Paul to pray that God would "make haste to help him" to preach the message he had once opposed, that it might be firmly planted in the hearts of those who heard God's message of love through him.

PSALM 70 (69)

¹ *For the Choirmaster. Of David. A Memorial.*

² O Gód, cóme to my assístance;
O LÓRD, make háste to hélp me!
³ Lét there be sháme and confúsion
on thóse who séek my lífe.

O lét them turn báck in confúsion,
who delíght in my hárm;
⁴ let them retréat, cóvered with sháme,
who jéer at me and móck.

⁵ O lét there be rejóicing and gládness
for áll who séek you.
Let them sáy forever, "Gód is gréat,"
who lóve your saving hélp.

⁶ As for mé, wrétched and póor,
hasten to mé, O Gód.
Yóu are my réscuer, my hélp;
O LÓRD, do not deláy.

PRAYER

O God, whose marvels and wonders move us to place our confidence in you, hear us in our time of need. Hasten to our rescue and show us once again your merciful love that always exceeds our meager expectations, through Christ our Lord. Amen.

Psalm 71

TRUST AND CONFIDENCE
IN OLD AGE

Two points are apparent from an initial consideration of Psalm 71: first, it does not have the customary superscript; and second, verse 12b repeats verse 2b of Psalm 70. The two psalms are closely connected. Worth noting also are the number of repeated terms: save (vv. 2b, 11b, 15b); praise (vv. 6c, 8a, 14b, 16a); shame (vv. 1b, 13a, 13c, 24c). Like many other psalms, this hymn contrasts the shame of being overcome by enemies to the great exaltation of experiencing God's saving intervention in one's life. From a unique perspective, the Psalmist looks back on his life and reflects on how intimately God has been involved in it. Twice he speaks of his youth (vv. 6–7, 17), and twice of his old age (vv. 9, 18–20). His reflection moves him to effusive expressions of praise and thanksgiving. Even in the midst of threats on his life, he maintains great confidence that God, who has been with him in the past, will continue to be with him in times of trouble. The Psalmist repeatedly asserts God's justice (vv. 2a, 15a, 19a, 24b) as a source of hope and comfort. In its biblical sense, "justice" is about right relationship. With God as Creator, even of the Psalmist himself, justice is manifest as divine protection, care, and support, along with the encouragement that accompanies life's blessings. Who but God could be the source of such goodness? Any one of us, looking back on moments of uncertainty, fear or dread, can also recall those moments when prayer brought calm to our spirit, and even more important, the conviction that God would always hear our appeal—not, perhaps, in the manner we choose, but in his own way and time. Jesus expressed this kind of trust and confidence in a moment of thanksgiving: "Jesus said, 'I thank you, Father, Lord of heaven and earth, because you have hidden these things from the wise and the intelligent and have revealed them to infants; yes, Father, for such was your gracious will'" (Matt 11:25–26). May the examples of both Jesus and the Psalmist inspire us to confident prayer as we consider God's blessings in our lives.

PSALM 71 (70)

¹ In yóu, O LÓRD, I take réfuge;
let me néver be pút to sháme.
² In your jústice, réscue me, frée me;
inclíne your éar to me and sáve me.

³ Be my róck, my cónstant réfuge,
a míghty strónghold to sáve me,
for yóu are my róck, my strónghold.
⁴ My God, frée me from the hánd of the wícked,
from the gríp of the unjúst, of the oppréssor.

⁵ It is yóu, O Lórd, who are my hópe,
my trúst, O LÓRD, from my yóuth.
⁶ On yóu I have léaned from my bírth;
from my mother's wómb, you have béen my hélp.
At all tímes I gíve you práise.

⁷ My fáte has filled mány with áwe,
but yóu are my míghty réfuge.
⁸ My móuth is fílled with your práise,
with your glóry, áll the day lóng.
⁹ Do not rejéct me nów that I am óld;
when my stréngth fails dó not forsáke me.

¹⁰ For my énemies are spéaking abóut me;
those who wátch me take cóunsel togéther,
¹¹ saying: "Gód has forsáken him; fóllow him.
Séize him; there is nó one to sáve him."
¹² O Gód, do not stáy afar óff;
O my Gód, make háste to hélp me!

¹³ Let them be pút to sháme and destróyed,
thóse who séek my lífe.
Let them be cóvered with sháme and confúsion,
thóse who séek to hárm me.

¹⁴ But as for mé, I will álways hópe,
and práise you móre and móre.
¹⁵ My móuth will téll of your jústice,
and áll the day lóng of your salvátion,
though I can néver téll it áll.

¹⁶ I will cóme with práise of your míght, O Lórd;
I will cáll to mínd your jústice,
yóurs, O LÓRD, alóne.
¹⁷ O Gód, you have táught me from my yóuth,
and I procláim your wónders stíll.

¹⁸ Even tíll I am óld and gray-héaded,
dó not forsáke me, O Gód.
Let me téll of your míghty árm
to évery cóming generátion;
¹⁹ your stréngth and your justice, O Gód,
réach to the híghest héavens.
It is yóu who have wórked such wónders.
O Gód, whó is like yóu?

²⁰ You have made me wítness many tróubles and évils,
but you will gíve me báck my lífe.
You will ráise me from the dépths of the éarth;
²¹ you will exált me and consóle me agáin.

²² So I will gíve you thánks on the lýre
for your fáithfulness, Ó my Gód.
To yóu will I síng with the hárp,
to yóu, the Hóly One of Ísrael.
²³ When I síng to you, my líps shall shout for jóy,
and my sóul, which yóu have redéemed.

²⁴ And áll the day lóng my tóngue
shall téll the tále of your jústice,
for they are pút to sháme and disgráced,
thóse who séek to hárm me.

PRAYER

*O Lord our God, source of all blessing, we thank you for the wondrous
ways in which you manifest your goodness to your Church, to the
world, and to all in need of your mercy. May we see ever more clearly
the many mysterious ways in which you bring life and blessing to us.
To you be glory forever through Christ our Lord. Amen.*

Psalm 72

JUSTICE AND RIGHT JUDGMENT FOR GOD'S ANOINTED

The core of this psalm is its opening words: it is a prayer on behalf of the king for God's judgment and justice. In biblical Israel, as well as in other nations of the Ancient Near East, kings and rulers were considered God's representatives and responsible for divine order on earth. The prophets looked to God's anointed to care for the poor and needy, to deliver justice and righteous judgments, and to rule with equity and uprightness (cf. Isa 26:7–8; Jer 9:24; Amos 5:14–15; Mic 6:8). How well this psalm reflects their hopes and dreams! It was believed that when such wise governance became the order of the day, there would be peace in the land, freedom from enemies, and prosperity for all. This psalm is rightly categorized among the Messianic Psalms, expressing all that Israel hoped for in the Davidic rulers. Such hope is expressed with a degree of hyperbole here: grain waving on the mountaintops (v. 16), a population as numerous and hardy as grass (v. 16), the homage of foreign nations (vv. 10–11), and enemies put down to the ground (v. 9). All these images bespeak an enduring hope for a ruler after God's own heart. In verse 14, the Hebrew verb translated as "redeem" carries a particular meaning: it evokes familial ties requiring that the head of a clan rescue blood relatives from danger, deprivation, or captivity. This was how God's lieutenant, the king, was expected to act toward those under his charge. All of this takes on special meaning for the Christian who sees the messianic hope for the Davidic kingship fulfilled in the person of Jesus Christ, who took on our flesh and redeemed us by the shedding of his own blood (Rom 3:25; 5:9; Eph 1:7; 2:13; Col 1:20; Heb 9:22). The liturgies of Advent fittingly recall both the hopeful longing of the people of Israel and Christian anticipation of the return of Christ by the frequent use of this psalm. The Gospels are replete with examples of how Jesus' own care for the poor and the needy fulfill this psalm through teaching, healing, and caring for those in need (Matt 14:14–21). And as this psalm looks forward to one who will act as God acts, we realize that we can fulfill this psalm by our union with Christ, becoming God's eyes, hands, and words for those in need of love, kindness, mercy, or forgiveness.

PSALM 72 (71)

¹ *Of Solomon.*

O Gód, give your júdgment to the kíng,
to a king's són your jústice,
² that he may júdge your péople in jústice,
and your póor in right júdgment.

³ May the móuntains bring forth péace for the péople,
and the hílls jústice.
⁴ May he defénd the póor of the péople,
and sáve the chíldren of the néedy,
and crúsh the oppréssor.

⁵ He shall endúre like the sún and the móon
through áll generátions.
⁶ He shall descénd like ráin on the méadow,
like shówers that wáter the éarth.
⁷ In his dáys shall jústice flóurish,
and great péace till the móon is no móre.

⁸ He shall rúle from séa to séa,
from the Ríver to the bóunds of the éarth.
⁹ Let the désert-dwellers fáll befóre him,
and his énemies líck the dúst.

¹⁰ The kíngs of Társhish and the íslands
shall páy him tríbute.
The kíngs of Shéba and Séba
shall bríng him gífts.
¹¹ Before hím all kíngs shall fall próstrate,
all nátions shall sérve him.

¹² For he shall sáve the néedy when they crý,
the póor, and thóse who are hélpless.
¹³ He will have píty on the wéak and the néedy,
and save the líves of the néedy.
¹⁴ From oppréssion and víolence he redéems their sóuls;
to him their blóod is déar.

¹⁵ Lóng máy he líve!
May the góld of Shéba be gíven him.
They shall práy for hím without céasing,
and bléss him áll the dáy.

[16] May gráin be abúndant in the lánd,
wáving to the péaks of the móuntains.
May its frúit rústle like Lébanon;
may the péople flóurish in the cíties
like gráss on the éarth.

[17] May his náme endúre foréver,
his name contínue like the sún.
Every tríbe shall be blést in hím,
all nátions shall cáll him bléssed.

* * *

[18] Blést be the LÓRD, God of Ísrael,
who alóne works wónders,
[19] ever blést his glórious náme.
Let his glóry fill the éarth.
Amén! Amén!

[20] Here end the Psalms of David, son of Jesse.

PRAYER

O God of compassion, whose love and care are perfectly manifest in Christ our Redeemer, strengthen us to follow his example as instruments of your peace in a world hungering for your presence. Permit us to serve others with joy, grateful that we bear your mercy to those in need, through Christ our Lord. Amen.

BOOK THREE
OF THE
PSALTER

Psalm 73

THE VISION OF THE PURE OF HEART

Psalm 73 might rightly be called "Job's Psalm." This prayer from the Wisdom tradition struggles with the age-old question faced by Job, a question that continues to trouble us today: "Why do the just suffer while the wicked seem to prosper?" It is noteworthy that the Third Book of the Psalter begins with a Wisdom Psalm—the same category as Psalm 1, which opens the whole Psalter. Psalm 73 recapitulates the mystery of suffering in life, providing a perspective of faith and true wisdom that teaches us to accept this apparent incongruity with trust. The Psalmist begins with an acknowledgment of God's goodness for those whose hearts are pure. In Hebrew usage, the term *heart* is understood to encompass both the mind and heart in our modern sense: it is the center of the will, the locus of reasoning and discernment (cf. Ps 27). "Heart" plays a key role in this psalm (vv. 1, 7, 13, 21, 26a, 26b), both in contrasting the pure of heart with the wicked (vv. 1, 7), and in identifying the heart as that part of a human being in which God's mysterious ways are discerned (vv. 26a, 26b). The Psalmist presents a lively and vivid description of the many ways in which evildoers may appear to be blessed: untroubled by pain themselves, they have little regard for others' burdens (vv. 4–5); they are prideful and well fed; they speak with malice yet are revered by others (vv. 6–10). What sense can we make of this before a God who is just and righteous? How can one believe in a God who refuses to act in such an appalling situation? The turning point of the psalm occurs in verses 16–17: the Psalmist admits that human reasoning cannot resolve this vexing matter of life's manifest inequalities, and so the Psalmist must approach the sanctuary, the holy place of God. And now, standing before God and turning his heart to reflection, the Psalmist finds a divine response to this troubling question. The paths of wealth, prestige, and comfort invariably become a slippery slope. How easily wealth disappears, prestige vanishes, and comforts fail; such vanities are so often short-lived, and cannot be the focus of our deepest longings and hopes. In an extraordinary expression of confidence and trust, the Psalmist describes the one way by which life's richest meaning is to be found: constant belief in God's abiding presence from which comes the guidance we need to live life authentically (vv. 23–25). This path is not so much a progression from ignorance to knowledge as growth from ignorance to faith. "To be near God is my happiness; I have my hope in the Lord God" (v. 28a). Leaving aside self-centered fear, the Psalmist places all trust in God who has shown faithful love and mercy. The Epistle to the Hebrews speaks of such faith: "Now faith is the assurance of things hoped for, the conviction of things not seen" (Heb 11:1). Indeed, how good God is to us; we can draw near with certainty and conviction, knowing that God's invitation to partake fully of the wondrous journey of life is always open to us.

PSALM 73 *(72)*

¹ *A Psalm of Asaph.*

How góod is Gód to Ísrael,
to thóse who are púre of héart!
² As for mé, I came clóse to stúmbling;
my féet had álmost slípped,
³ for I was fílled with énvy of the próud,
when I sáw how the wícked prósper.

⁴ For thém there áre no páins;
their bódies are sóund and sléek.
⁵ They do not sháre in péople's búrdens;
théy are not strícken like óthers.

⁶ So they wéar their príde like a nécklace;
they clóthe themsélves with víolence.
⁷ With folds of fát, their éyes protrúde.
With imaginátion their héarts overflów.

⁸ They scóff; they spéak with málice.
From on hígh they thréaten oppréssion.
⁹ They have sét their móuths in the héavens,
and their tóngues are róaming the éarth.

¹⁰ So the péople túrn to thém
and drínk in áll their wórds.
¹¹ They sáy, "Hów can God knów?
Dóes the Most Hígh have any knówledge?"
¹² Lóok at them, súch are the wícked;
ever prósperous, they grów in wéalth.

¹³ How úseless to kéep my heart púre,
and wásh my hánds in ínnocence,

¹⁴ when I was strícken áll day lóng,
suffered púnishment with éach new mórning.
¹⁵ Then I sáid, "If I should spéak like thát,
I should betráy your chíldren's generátion."

¹⁶ I stróve to fáthom this próblem,
too hárd for my mínd to understánd,
¹⁷ until I éntered the hóly place of Gód,
and cáme to discérn their énd.

¹⁸ How slíppery the páths on which you sét them;
you máke them fáll to destrúction.
¹⁹ How súddenly they cóme to their rúin,
swept awáy, destróyed by térrors.
²⁰ Like a dréam one wákes from, O Lórd,
when you wáke you dismíss them as phántoms.

²¹ And só when my héart grew embíttered,
and I was píerced to the dépths of my béing,
²² I was stúpid and did nót understánd;
I was líke a béast in your síght.

²³ As for mé, I was álways in your présence;
you were hólding mé by my right hánd.
²⁴ By your cóunsel yóu will guíde me,
and thén you will léad me to glóry.

²⁵ What élse have I in héaven but yóu?
Apart from yóu, I want nóthing on éarth.
²⁶ My bódy and my héart waste awáy;
Gód is the stréngth of my héart;
Gód is my pórtion foréver.

²⁷ Surely, thóse who are fár from you pérish;
you destróy all thóse who are unfáithful.
²⁸ To bé near Gód is my háppiness;
I háve my hópe in the Lord Gód.
Í will procláim your wórks
at the gátes of dáughter Síon.

PRAYER

*God of wisdom and truth, who brought all creation into being and who
unfold the mysterious course of history, enlighten our hearts and show
us the way to you. Enable us to meet the movements of life with faith*

and to trust in your loving plan for each of us whom you have called to know your love. This we ask through Christ our Lord. Amen.

Psalm 74

LOOK TO YOUR COVENANT, LORD, AND ARISE

In recent decades, haunting images of destruction, devastation, and pillage have come to us through the media from such far-flung places as Sarajevo, Rwanda, and El Salvador, to name but a few. The pain implicit in such images affects the lives of so many people in so many ways; it can stagger the imagination even to reflect on it. Yet all too easily we can forget with the passage of time the pain of those directly involved, whose memories are haunted by atrocities experienced at the hands of cruel enemies. How important that we not forget these horrors, if only to preserve future generations from them. In Psalm 74, the Psalmist describes the terror and dismay that haunted the lives of those who had lived through the destruction of the temple and decimation of the people in Jerusalem at the hands of the Babylonians in 587 BC. The Psalmist asserts that future generations must never forget what happened here: how the people suffered, and how they prayed even in the midst of ruin. It all seemed impossible; how could this have fallen upon us? And that is how Psalm 74 begins: with a resounding "Why?" A significant part of the prayer calls upon God to remember how divine compassion first brought this people to birth in the Exodus—the wandering in the desert and the entry to the land of promise (vv. 12–17). It is as if the Psalmist were saying, "O God, you brought all creation into being; yours is the power. You led us through the Sea of Reeds; yours is the power. You guided us through the barren desert to the land you promised us; yours is the power. Why then has this horror befallen us, who are your people, your redeemed flock?" We note that in the concluding verses (vv. 18–23) the Psalmist addresses imperatives to God with bold assertion and hopeful conviction: Remember this; do not give us up; look to the covenant; do not let us be put to shame; arise, O God; do not forget the defiance of your foes! It is with such confidence that we also must pray, especially during those times when it seems our world is crumbling around us. Jesus tells us, "Ask, and it will be given you; search, and you will find; knock, and the door will be opened for you (Luke 11:9). One way in which we can pray this psalm today is to remember those whose lives have been turned inside out by civil strife, by unjust regimes, or by natural disasters. Our solidarity with them in prayer and mutual concern unites us with them in their suffering, reminding us that they are our brothers and sisters in the one who is God of all.

PSALM 74 (73)

¹ A Maskil *of Asaph*.

Whý, O Gód, have you cást us off foréver?
Why does your ánger bláze at the shéep of your pásture?
² Remémber your flóck which you cláimed long agó,
the tríbe you redéemed to be your ówn posséssion,
this móuntain of Síon where you máde your dwélling.

³ Turn your stéps to these pláces that are útterly rúined!
The énemy has laid wáste the whóle of the hóly place.
⁴ Your fóes have made úproar in the mídst of your assémbly;
they have sét up their émblems as tókens thére.
⁵ They have wíelded their áxes on hígh,
as at the éntrance to a gróve of trées.

⁶ Théy have bróken down áll the cárvings;
they have strúck togéther with hátchet and píckax.
⁷ O Gód, they have sét your hóly place on fíre;
they have rázed and profáned the abóde of your náme.

⁸ They sáid in their héarts, "We will útterly crúsh them;
we will búrn every shríne of Gód in the lánd."
⁹ We do not sée our émblems, nór is there a próphet;
we have nó one to téll us how lóng it will lást.

¹⁰ How lóng, O Gód, is the énemy to scóff?
Is the fóe to insúlt your náme foréver?
¹¹ Whý, O Lórd, do you hóld back your hánd?
Why do you kéep your ríght hand hídden in your clóak?

¹² Yet Gód is my kíng from time pást,
who bestóws salvátion through áll the lánd.

¹³ It was yóu who divíded the séa by your míght,
who sháttered the héads of the mónsters in the séa.

¹⁴ It was yóu who crúshed Levíathan's héads,
and gáve him as fóod to the béasts of the désert.
¹⁵ It was yóu who ópened up spríngs and tórrents;
it was yóu who dríed up éver-flowing rívers.

¹⁶ Yóurs is the dáy and yóurs is the níght;
it was yóu who estáblished the líght and the sún.
¹⁷ It was yóu who fíxed the bóunds of the éarth,
yóu who máde both súmmer and wínter.

¹⁸ Remémber this, O LÓRD: the énemy scóffed!
A sénseless péople insúlted your náme!
¹⁹ Do not gíve the sóul of your dóve to the béasts,
nor forgét the lífe of your póor ones foréver.

²⁰ Lóok to the cóvenant; each cáve in the lánd
is a pláce where víolence mákes its hóme.
²¹ Do not lét the oppréssed be pút to sháme;
let the póor and the néedy bléss your náme.

²² Aríse, O Gód, and defénd your cáuse!
Remémber how the sénseless revíle you all the dáy.
²³ Dó not forgét the clámor of your fóes,
the uncéasing úproar of thóse who defý you.

PRAYER

*Almighty and eternal God, Master of the universe and Provider in
every need, turn your ear to our appeal and remember your people
whose love for you is expressed in trust in your name. We acknowledge
that without you we are nothing; with you, we can accomplish your
will. Strengthen us to remember not only our own needs, but even more
the challenges that our brothers and sisters endure for the sake of your
name. We ask this through Christ our Lord. Amen.*

Psalm 75

DIVINE CUP OF JUDGMENT

Psalm 75 presents a different image of God as Creator. The Lord has brought the world into being, and it remains his right to judge the world according to the divine precepts established by the Most High. Judgment will come upon all, and the deciding factor, the Psalmist asserts, is one's ability to live humbly and honestly before God (in the phrase of the prophet Micah [6:8]). The psalm begins with praise to God whose deeds are wonderful and who is always near. A brief oracle follows (vv. 3–6) in which God declares his might in having established the very pillars of the earth. Then God rightly attests that there is no room for pride or boasting among human beings, for all that is comes from God and returns to God. Before such power only humility and meekness can have a place among mortals. Our strengths, our talents, our gifts—all derive from God. Life's blessings are God's gifts to us, gifts that we must acknowledge as coming from the Lord. The imagery in verse 9 may be difficult to interpret. The foaming cup of wine to be drunk by the wicked derives from the vivid language of Israel's prophets. We read in Jeremiah, "For thus the LORD, the God of Israel, said to me: Take from my hand this cup of the wine of wrath, and make all the nations to whom I send you drink it" (25:15). For the prophet, such imagery bespeaks a divine act of both judgment and destruction to be brought upon the nations. In Psalm 75, the Psalmist asserts that the proud will be given this cup of wine to drink. So abominable in the eyes of God is the pride of the wicked that they must be warned of the devastating effects this stance will bring on the day of judgment. Humility keeps us honest about who we are before God and neighbor; it is a sure path to hope on the day of judgment. Jesus himself affirms this with regard to himself: "Come to me, all you that are weary and are carrying heavy burdens, and I will give you rest. Take my yoke upon you, and learn from me; for I am gentle and humble in heart, and you will find rest for your souls" (Matt 11:28–29). Is it not true that the daily struggles of life afford us the opportunity to grow in humility? We sin again and again, often repeating the same transgression. We fall into temptation, succumb to it, and get up again to try once more to be faithful. When we see ourselves as we truly are—sinners loved but redeemed—we are on the path to humility, that noblest of virtues.

PSALM 75 (74)

¹ *For the Choirmaster. Intoned like "Do not destroy." A Psalm of Asaph. A Song.*

² We give práise to yóu, O Gód;
we give práise, for your náme is néar.
We recóunt your wónderful déeds.

³ "When I estáblish the appóinted tíme,
then I mysélf will júdge with fáirness.
⁴ Though the éarth and all who dwéll in it may róck,
it is Í who set fírm its píllars.

⁵ To the bóastful I sáy, 'Do not bóast';
to the wícked, 'Do not fláunt your stréngth,
⁶ do not fláunt your stréngth on hígh.
Do not spéak with ínsolent príde.'"

⁷ For néither from the éast nor from the wést,
nór from the désert comes hónor,
⁸ for Gód himsélf is the júdge.
One he húmbles, anóther he exálts.

⁹ For the LÓRD holds a cúp in his hánd,
full of wíne, fóaming and spíced.
He póurs it; they dráin it to the drégs;
all the wícked on the éarth must dráin it.

¹⁰ As for mé, I will rejóice foréver,
and sing psálms to the Gód of Jácob.
¹¹ I shall bréak the stréngth of the wícked,
while the stréngth of the júst will be exálted.

PRAYER

Christ Jesus, meek and humble of heart, who endured our life with all its temptations, show us in our daily living how to imitate you in seeking God above all things and in all things, growing in humility with each passing day. You live and reign forever. Amen.

𝒫salm 76

A GOD OF AWE AND DREAD

The portrait of God we encounter in Psalm 76 is distinguished by contrasting images of awe and dread. The God who is "more majestic than the everlasting mountains" (v. 5), yet comes to save the humble of the earth (v. 10b) is the One who is both transcendent and immanent. The greatness of God does not keep him from being close to those whom he loves and brought into being. This God dwells among his people, having set up a tent in Jerusalem (here called Salem) and abiding in Sion (v. 3). At the same time, this God so near us is also the Divine Warrior (vv. 6–7) who strikes terror in those who come under his scrutiny (v. 9). When God utters a verdict against the proud and arrogant, so awe inspiring and full of dread is the deed that earth itself is struck motionless. Powerful imagery expresses this effect: soldiers cannot lift their hands (v. 6b); horses and riders lay stunned (v. 7b); earth waits motionless for the divine utterance (v. 9). A similar portrait-by-contrasts is given Jesus in the Gospels. He is depicted as one whose miracles and teaching fill the people with awe, yet his force and zeal in some circumstances can also terrify. When healing the paralytic, Jesus says, "I say to you, stand up, take your mat and go to your home." The text continues, "And he stood up, and immediately took the mat and went out before all of them; so that they were all amazed and glorified God, saying, 'We have never seen anything like this!'" (Mark 2:11–12). By contrast, the imprecations of "woe" uttered against the scribes and Pharisees surprise us with the intensity of their anger and hostility: "Woe to you, scribes and Pharisees, hypocrites! For you lock people out of the kingdom of heaven. For you do not go in yourselves, and when others are going in, you stop them" (Matt 23:13–14). Both awe and dread mark our response to both the God of Psalm 76 and Jesus of the Gospels. The use of this psalm in the Christmas liturgy may thus seem in some sense incongruous. But the birth of our God as a human being is well expressed in the Psalmist's phrase: "His tent is set in Salem, and his dwelling place in Sion" (v. 3). It captures the mystery of God taking on our human flesh and dwelling among us as Immanuel, God-with-us. The same theme is potently expressed in the Prologue to John's Gospel. "And the Word became flesh and lived among us, and we have seen his glory" (John 1:14). Some translations of the phrase "lived among us" are more literally rendered "he pitched his tent among us," words that echo more directly those of verse 3 of this psalm. The presence of our astonishing and transcendent God is so immediate, so immanent, that we can only stand in wonder and awe.

PSALM 76 (75)

¹ *For the Choirmaster. With String Instruments.*
A Psalm of Asaph. A Song.

² Gód is renówned in Júdah;
in Ísrael his náme is gréat.
³ His tént is sét in Sálem,
and his dwélling pláce in Síon.
⁴ It was thére he bróke the flaming árrows,
the shíeld, the swórd, the ármor.

⁵ Respléndent are yóu, more majéstic
than the éverlásting móuntains.
⁶ The stout-héarted, despóiled, slept in déath;
none of the sóldiers could líft a hánd.
⁷ At your thréat, O Gód of Jácob,
hórse and ríder lay stúnned.

⁸ Yóu, you alóne, strike térror.
Who can stánd in your présence,
against the míght of your wráth?

⁹ You úttered your séntence from the héavens;
the éarth in térror was stíll
¹⁰ when you aróse, O Gód, to júdge,
to sáve all the húmble of the éarth.

¹¹ For the ráge of man ónly serves to práise you;
you surróund yourself with the survívors of wráth.
¹² Make vóws to the Lᴏʀᴅ your Gód and fulfíll them.
Let all aróund him pay tríbute to the Óne who strikes térror,
¹³ who cuts shórt the bréath of prínces,
who strikes térror in the kíngs of the éarth.

PRAYER

O God of power and might, be close to us in your compassion and care for your own, the poor and the needy. Grant us faith in our distress, hope in our uncertainty, and light in our fear, that we may eagerly pur-

sue your way of loving kindness. To you be all praise and glory, now and forever. Amen.

Psalm 77

THE TRACE OF YOUR STEPS WAS NOT SEEN

"I remember, I muse, and I ponder" (vv. 12–13)—such expressions convey the action of Psalm 77. This prayer-poem takes us into the heart and mind of one who broods over a situation of affliction, for himself and for the people. A clear sense of lamentation marks his words, yet strangely enough, and in contrast to so many of the psalms, no explicit request or appeal is articulated, even though the Psalmist addresses God directly and forcefully. We might call this psalm a "heart-to-heart conversation with God." The Psalmist's language gives the impression that he feels that God has not heard, or at least has not responded, to his prayers. Crying aloud day and night, he cannot rest in the absence of interior comfort, but only groan (vv. 1–4). This inner turmoil without relief raises desperate questions (vv. 8–10): Will the Lord's rejection never end? What has changed our relationship? Where are the mercy and compassion that marked the covenant communion of the past? The Psalmist reminds God of the past, when the relationship was strong. "Never have your people known any divine power other than you; you have worked great wonders and brought us redemption" (vv. 14–16). The Psalmist brings this redemption into sharp focus before God by alluding to the wonders of the saving event experienced by the children of Jacob in the Exodus, with special reference to the crossing of the Sea of Reeds (vv. 17–20). In that event, God manifested his power over nature: the winds blew; the skies pronounced God's message; the waters parted, and the people passed through on dry ground (Exod 14–15). And an important message emerges in the Psalmist's words here: the trace of God's footprints was not seen there, but his divine power was surely at work (v. 20). So often in the spiritual journey, God acts on and for us in ways that are quiet and unassuming. We might want "visible proof" of God's grace and presence in our lives. But we are reminded of that scene on Mount

Horeb when Elijah learned that the divine word was not manifest in wind, earthquake, nor fire, but in utter stillness and silence (1 Kgs 19:11–12). Our work is to be still and patient in prayer, trusting that God's word will be revealed to us; though painful at times, it is a sacred state, for God speaks profoundly there. St. Paul addresses this problem of the spiritual life. He writes, "The Spirit helps us in our weakness; for we do not know how to pray as we ought, but that very Spirit intercedes with sighs too deep for words" (Rom 8:26). Whatever path we follow in search of God, we can be assured of the divine presence that awaits us and leads us in the ways of holiness.

PSALM 77 (76)

¹ *For the Choirmaster. Intoned like "Jeduthun." Of Asaph. A Psalm.*

² I crý alóud to Gód,
cry alóud to Gód that he may héar me.

³ In the dáy of my distréss I seek the Lórd.
In the níght my hands are ráised unwéaried;
my sóul refúses cómfort.
⁴ As I remémber my Gód, I gróan.
I pónder, and my spírit fáints.

⁵ You kéep my éyes from clósing.
I am tróubled, unáble to spéak.
⁶ I thínk of the dáys of long agó,
and remémber the yéars long pást.
⁷ At níght I múse within my héart.
I pónder, and my spírit quéstions.

⁸ "Will the Lórd rejéct us foréver?
Will he shów us his fávor no móre?
⁹ Has his mércy vánished foréver?
Has his prómise cóme to an énd?
¹⁰ Has Gód forgótten his mércy,
or in ánger withdráwn his compássion?"

¹¹ I said, "Thís is what cáuses my gríef:
that the right hánd of the Most Hígh has chánged."
¹² I remémber the déeds of the LÓRD,
I remémber your wónders of óld;
¹³ I múse on áll your wórks,
and pónder your míghty déeds.

¹⁴ Your wáy, O Gód, is in the hóly place.
What gód is as gréat as our Gód?
¹⁵ Yóu are the Gód who works wónders.
Among the péoples you shówed your pówer.
¹⁶ Your strong árm redéemed your péople,
the descéndants of Jácob and Jóseph.

¹⁷ The wáters sáw you, O Gód,
the wáters sáw you and ánguished.
Yes, the dépths were móved to trémble.
¹⁸ The clóuds poured dówn with ráin.
The skíes sent fórth their vóice;
Your árrows fláshed to and fró.

¹⁹ Your thúnderous vóice was in the whírlwind;
your fláshes líghted up the wórld.
The éarth was móved and trémbled.
²⁰ Your wáy was thróugh the séa,
your páth through the míghty wáters,
but the tráce of your stéps was not séen.

²¹ You guíded your péople like a flóck
by the hánd of Móses and Áaron.

PRAYER

*O God of holiness, who beckon each of us to search for you in the depths
of our own hearts, reveal to us the path of peace. When we cannot
express our deepest needs with words, remind us that your Spirit prays
within us in utterances beyond words, expressing your message of
truth and wisdom, peace, and blessing. We ask this through Christ our
Lord. Amen.*

Psalm 78

HIDDEN LESSONS
OF THE PAST

Psalm 78, with its seventy-two verses, is distinguished as being the second longest of the Psalter. It falls into the category of Historical Psalms. It recounts in a series of vignettes the unfolding of God's loving plan of redemption—in spite of Israel's repeated infidelities. Key to Psalm 78 is the method announced in its opening verses: the Psalmist asserts in verse 2, "I will open my mouth in a parable and utter hidden lessons of the past." The psalm teaches through the stories it tells, stories that still have meaning for our lives today. It is all too easy for us to repeat our mistakes; telling stories about them can help us learn to avoid past errors. The first five books of the Bible are referred to as the Torah by the Jews. *Torah* means "instruction"; we might expect such instruction to comprise a list of things to do and not do. But the wisdom of Israel held that the best way to teach life's lessons is through stories. Chronicles, legends, and narratives implant themselves in our minds and are easily recalled. Just as the stories in the first five books of the Bible impart lessons for life, so the Historical Psalms teach by their accounts of Israel's past experiences. The Psalmist insists that these parables be passed on from parents to children (vv. 5–9), so that subsequent generations can come to know God and see how divine grace has touched the lives of their forebears. The Psalmist notes repeatedly (vv. 7–8, 10–11, 41–43) how the people's failure to remember what God had done for them constituted a violation of the covenant. His great hope was that future generations would hear these tales, remember them, and learn from them. He recalls how, in spite of the many infidelities that Israel committed against God, the One whom they had offended would invariably relent and show mercy, forgive them, and answer their needs. The stories retold in Psalm 78 remind readers to be faithful and persevering in their own calling as the people of God. Such fidelity expresses our gratitude for what God has done in the past, what God does in the present, and, we trust, will continue to do into the future. Being what it is, human nature is inclined to persist in both conscious revolt and unintentional error. The stories of our ancestors in the faith help us to look into our own lives to see the ways we have strayed from the path of true righteousness and holiness, and how God leads us back to fidelity by responding with grace and kindness to our failures of love. Like Psalm 78, the parables of Jesus unfold in stories God's gracious desire to share divine life with us. St. Matthew's great chapter on the parables of the kingdom concludes, "Every scribe who has been trained for the kingdom of heaven is like the master of a household who brings out of his treasure what is new and what is old" (Matt 13:52). What treasure of the past recounted in Psalm 78 might offer you a lesson to living life well today?

PSALM 78 (77)

¹ A Maskil *of Asaph.*

Give éar, my péople, to my téaching;
incline your éar to the wórds of my móuth.
² I will ópen my móuth in a párable
and útter hidden léssons of the pást.

³ The thíngs we have héard and understóod,
the thíngs our fáthers have tóld us,
⁴ thése we will not híde from their chíldren
but will téll them to the néxt generátion:
the glóries of the LÓRD and his míght,
and the márvelous déeds he has dóne.

⁵ He estáblished a decrée in Jácob;
in Ísrael he sét up a láw.
To our fáthers he gáve a commánd
to máke it knówn to their chíldren,
⁶ that the néxt generátion might knów it,
the chíldren yét to be bórn.

They should aríse and decláre it to their chíldren,
⁷ that they should sét their hópe in Gód,
and néver forgét God's déeds,
but kéep every óne of his commánds,

⁸ so that théy might not bé like their fáthers,
a defíant and rebéllious generátion,
a generátion whose héart was fickle,
whose spírit was not fáithful to Gód.

⁹ The sons of Éphraim, ármed with the bów,
turned báck in the dáy of báttle.

¹⁰ They fáiled to kéep God's cóvenant,
refused to wálk accórding to his láw.

¹¹ They forgót the thíngs he had dóne,
the wóndrous wórks he had shówn them.
¹² He did wónders in the síght of their fáthers,
in Égypt, in the pláins of Zóan.

¹³ He divíded the séa and led them thróugh,
and made the wáters stand úp like a wáll.
¹⁴ By dáy he léd them with a clóud;
throughout the níght, with a líght of fíre.

¹⁵ He splít the rócks in the désert.
He gave them pléntiful drínk, as from the déep.
¹⁶ He made stréams flow óut from the róck,
and made wáters run dówn like rívers.

¹⁷ Yet stíll they sínned agáinst him,
rebelled agáinst the Most Hígh in the désert.
¹⁸ In their héart they put Gód to the tést
by demánding the fóod they cráved.

¹⁹ They spóke against Gód and sáid:
"Can Gód spread a táble in the wílderness?
²⁰ Sée, he strúck the róck:
water gushed fórth and swept dówn in tórrents.
But can he álso gíve us bréad?
Can hé provide méat for his péople?"

²¹ When he héard this, the LÓRD was ángry.
A fíre was kíndled against Jácob;
his ánger róse against Ísrael.
²² For they hád no fáith in Gód,
and did not trúst his sáving pówer.

²³ Yet he commánded the clóuds abóve,
and ópened the gátes of héaven.
²⁴ He ráined down mánna to éat,
and gáve them bréad from héaven.

²⁵ Mán ate the bréad of ángels.
He sént them abúndance of fóod;
²⁶ the east wínd he stirred úp in the héavens,
the south wínd he dirécted by his míght.

²⁷ He rained flésh upón them like dúst,
winged fówl like the sánds of the séa.
²⁸ He let it fáll in the mídst of their cámp,
and áll aróund their ténts.

²⁹ So they áte and hád their fíll,
whát they cráved, he gáve them.

³⁰ But befóre they had sáted their húnger,
while the fóod was stíll in their móuths,
³¹ God's ánger róse agáinst them.
He sléw the stróngest amóng them,
struck dówn the flówer of Ísrael.

³² Despíte all this, they képt on sínning;
they fáiled to belíeve in his wónders.
³³ So he énded their dáys like a bréath,
and their yéars in súdden térror.

³⁴ When he sléw them, thén they sóught him,
repénted and éarnestly sought Gód.
³⁵ They would remémber that Gód was their róck,
Gód the Most Hígh their redéemer.

³⁶ Yét they decéived him with their móuths;
they líed to hím with their tóngues.
³⁷ For their héarts were not stéadfast toward hím;
théy were not fáithful to his cóvenant.

³⁸ Yet hé who is fúll of compássion
forgáve them their sín and spáred them.
So óften he héld back his ánger,
and did not stír up áll his ráge.

³⁹ He remémbered they were ónly flésh,
a breath that pásses, néver to retúrn.
⁴⁰ They rebélled against him óften in the désert,
and cáused him páin in the wásteland!

⁴¹ Yet agáin they túrned and tested Gód;
they provóked the Hóly One of Ísrael.
⁴² They fáiled to remémber his déeds
on the dáy he sáved them from the fóe,
⁴³ when he wórked his sígns in Égypt,
his wónders in the pláins of Zóan.

⁴⁴ He túrned their rívers into blóod;
they cóuld not drínk from their stréams.
⁴⁵ He sent swárms of ínsects to devóur them,
and frógs to destróy them.
⁴⁶ He gáve their cróps to ínsects,
the frúit of their lábor to the lócust.

⁴⁷ He destróyed their vínes with háil,
their sýcamore trées with fróst.
⁴⁸ He gáve up their cáttle to háil,
their hérds to dárts of líghtning.

⁴⁹ He unléashed on them the héat of his ánger,
fúry, ráge and hávoc,
a tróop of destróying ángels.

⁵⁰ He léveled a páth for his ánger.
He did not spáre their líves from déath,
but gáve their lívestock to the plágue.
⁵¹ He strúck all the fírstborn in Égypt,
the first vígor of yóuth from the dwéllings of Hám.

⁵² Then he bróught forth his péople like shéep;
like a flóck he léd them in the désert.
⁵³ He led them sáfely with nóthing to féar,
while the séa engúlfed their fóes.

⁵⁴ So he bróught them to his hóly lánd,
to the móuntain his right hánd had wón.
⁵⁵ He dróve out the nátions befóre them,
and appórtioned to éach their héritage.
The tribes of Ísrael he séttled in their ténts.

⁵⁶ With defíance they tésted God Most Hígh;
they refúsed to obéy his decrées.
⁵⁷ They stráyed, fáithless like their fáthers;
they betráyed him like a tréacherous bów.
⁵⁸ They provóked God to wráth with their hígh
    places,
made him jéalous with the ídols they sérved.

⁵⁹ God héard this and was fílled with fúry;
he útterly rejécted Ísrael.
⁶⁰ He forsóok his dwélling place in Shíloh,
the tént where he dwélt with mán.

⁶¹ He gáve his stréngth into captívity,
his spléndor to the hánds of the fóe.
⁶² He gáve up his péople to the swórd,
and showed his ánger agáinst his héritage.

⁶³ So fíre devóured their young mén,
their máidens had no wédding sóngs;
⁶⁴ their príests féll by the swórd,
and their wídows máde no lamént.

⁶⁵ Then the Lórd awóke as if from sléep,
like a wárrior máddened by wíne.
⁶⁶ He strúck his fóes from behínd,
and pút them to sháme foréver.

⁶⁷ He rejécted the tént of Jóseph.
He did not chóose the tríbe of Éphraim,
⁶⁸ but he chóse the tríbe of Júdah,
the móuntain of Síon which he lóves.
⁶⁹ He búilt his shríne like the héavens,
or like the éarth which he fóunded foréver.

⁷⁰ And he chóse his sérvant Dávid,
and tóok him awáy from the shéepfolds.
⁷¹ From the cáre of the éwes he bróught him
to be shépherd of Jácob his péople,
of Ísrael his ówn posséssion.
⁷² He ténded them with blámeless héart;
with his skíllful hánds he léd them.

PRAYER

God ever faithful and true, guide us through life's journey by your word of life. May the stories of our ancestors in the faith teach us the straight path that leads to you and keep us ever grateful for your abundant compassion and mercy. We ask this through Christ our Lord. Amen.

Psalm 79

BROUGHT VERY LOW

Psalm 79 resembles Psalm 74 in that both describe the destruction of the temple in Jerusalem and its surrounding areas by the Babylonians in 587 BC. What is distinctive about Psalm 79 is its portrayal of that devastating experience in terms of a personal relationship. From beginning to end, the pronouns *you* and *your* indicate the closeness between God and the people. Expressions like "your heritage, your holy temple, your servants, your faithful, your compassion, your people, the flock of your pasture" are evidence of how deeply the Psalmist feels these bonds with God, who called them into being as a people but now seems to have handed them over to foreign enemies. In the Psalmist's eyes, the only remedy for this situation of pain, struggle, humiliation, and fear is for God to bring about a reversal of fortune for Israel. Even in his preferred terms of closeness and endearment, the Psalmist asks, "Why has this happened, and how long will the outburst of divine anger against us last?" (vv. 3–5). In a way distinctively defensive and self-preservational, the Psalmist suggests that God's wrath be turned in the other direction, against the faithless neighboring nations (vv. 6–7). These foreigners do not know God's name—that is, they have no experiential knowledge of God's identity or providential care. Had they known the God of Israel, they would never have laid waste the holy place, God's dwelling among the people. So the question remains: Why is God's anger toward us so severe, why has God allowed this to happen? Anticipating God's reversal of this catastrophe, the Psalmist asserts that the people will then be able to lift up thanks and praise for God's fidelity toward them (vv. 12–13). While this situation seems far from our own experience, we have only to think of places like the Balkans or the Middle East, where either internal civil strife or external war have shattered the lives of people of good will; innocent people have died and homes have been devastated. Their lives have been upended, their hope reduced to ashes. This is one way to pray Psalm 79—in solidarity with people who can hardly know what to say to God from the midst of such horror. We can pray these words for them, trusting that in time, they will find God's sustaining power in the midst of their sorrow and pain. Jesus knew that this fate would come again one day upon the city of God's temple: "As [Jesus] came near and saw the city (Jerusalem), he wept over it, saying, 'If you, even you, had only recognized on this day the things that make for peace! But now they are hidden from your eyes'" (Luke 19:41–42). The pleas for divine assistance provided by Psalm 79 can lead us to pray for our brothers and sisters throughout the world who live amid the ravages of war and who depend upon our solidarity in faith with them.

PSALM 79 (78)

[1] *A Psalm of Asaph.*

O Gód, the nátions have inváded your héritage;
théy have profáned your hóly témple.
They have máde Jerúsalem a héap of rúins.
[2] They have hánded óver the bódies of your sérvants
as fóod to féed the bírds of héaven,
and the flésh of your fáithful to the béasts of the éarth.

[3] They have póured out their blóod like wáter round Jerúsalem;
nó one is léft to búry the déad.
[4] Wé have becóme the táunt of our néighbors,
the móckery and scórn of thóse aróund us.
[5] How lóng, O LÓRD? Will you be ángry foréver?
Will your jéalous ánger búrn like fíre?

[6] Póur out your ráge on the nátions,
thóse that dó not knów you,
kingdoms that dó not cáll upon your náme.
[7] For théy have devóured Jácob
and laid wáste the pláce where he dwélls.

[8] Do nót remémber agáinst us
the guílt of fórmer tímes.
Let your compássion hásten to méet us;
for wé have been bróught very lów.

[9] Hélp us, O Gód our sávior,
for the sáke of the glóry of your náme.
Frée us and forgíve us our síns,
becáuse of your náme.

[10] Whý should the nátions say, "Whére is their Gód?"
Before our éyes make it knówn amóng the nátions
that you avénge the blóod of your sérvants that was shéd!
[11] Let the gróans of the prísoners cóme befóre you,
your strong árm repríeve those condémned to díe.

¹² Pay báck to our néighbors séven times óver
the táunts with whích they táunted you, O Lórd.
¹³ Then we, your péople, the flóck of your pásture,
will give you thánks foréver and éver.
From age to áge we will recóunt your práise.

PRAYER

*God and Savior of us all, look kindly on those who bear the wounds of
your Son through the shock and ruin of war. Bring hope to those who
have lost sight of your loving mercy; restore faith to those whose lives
have been torn asunder. Keep us ever mindful of our brothers and sisters who walk the upward road of the cross with grief so much heavier
than our own. We ask this through Christ our Lord. Amen.*

Psalm 80

BRING US BACK

Three times Psalm 80 repeats its refrain (vv. 4, 8, 20), providing the key
to its central theme: the grace of conversion. This psalm represents a
communal Lament, giving utterance both to the pain of separation from
God felt by the people (vv. 5–7) and their plea for divine help (vv. 2–3).
The Psalmist's "bring us back" derives from a Hebrew verb meaning
"turn us in another direction," "direct us down other paths." This is what
conversion is really about—taking hold of the grace from God that
enables us to live differently, to think in new ways, and to act with new
purpose. Conversion does not come easily; it requires human will and
action, but most important, God's gracious strength that can accomplish
the change we know to be necessary. Two images in this refrain capture
the work of grace in the act of conversion. First, we ask that God "bring
us back"; that is, deliver us from where we are or have been: we need
God's help to accomplish this, for we know we can't achieve it by ourselves. Second, in pleading, "Let your face shine on us," we invoke the
image of light as a symbol of salvation, in contrast to the shadows of sin—
a frequent scriptural trope. Where darkness and failure are foremost,
God's light transforms that which is in need of healing. This is salvation;

thus the addition of "and we shall be saved" (vv. 4, 8, 20). Too often our idea of salvation involves an epic gesture of divine intervention; but in the Scriptures, salvation is the hand of God touching our lives in such a way as to ward off the self-destruction attending the short-sighted attitude of "doing what we want." In verses 9–12, the Psalmist recalls the central act of redemption, the Exodus from Egypt. Israel is imagined as a vine that God has taken up, transplanted, and nurtured. After all that effort, why does it seem that God has now abandoned the vine and left it to be devoured by the beasts of the field (vv. 13–14)? Early Christian interpreters understood "the son of man" (vv. 16, 18) as referring to Christ, whom God had anointed and sent to lead the people to a new conversion of heart. Such a conversion would usher in the reign of God, where righteousness, care for the poor, and authentic love of neighbor would have sovereignty. "Jesus came to Galilee, proclaiming the good news of God, and saying, 'The time is fulfilled, and the kingdom of God has come near; repent, and believe in the good news'" (Mark 1:14–15). For the whole people of God, conversion constitutes our lifelong journey into the wonder of God's grace, forming us in its power, beauty, and mystery.

PSALM 80 (79)

¹ *For the Choirmaster. Intoned like "Lilies of Testimony."*
Of Asaph. A Psalm.

² O shépherd of Ísrael, héar us,
yóu who lead Jóseph like a flóck:
enthróned on the chérubim, shine fórth
³ upon Éphraim, Bénjamin, Manásseh.
Rouse up your míght and cóme to sáve us.

⁴ O Gód, bríng us báck;
let your face shíne on us, and wé shall be sáved.

⁵ How lóng, O LÓRD, God of hósts,
will you be ángry at the práyer of your péople?
⁶ You have féd them with téars for their bréad,
an abúndance of téars for their drínk.
⁷ You have máde us the táunt of our néighbors;
our foes móck us amóng themsélves.

⁸ O Gód of hósts, bríng us báck;
let your fáce shine fórth, and wé shall be sáved.

⁹ You bróught a víne out of Égypt;
you dróve out the nátions and plánted it.
¹⁰ Befóre it you cléared the gróund;
it took róot and fílled the lánd.

¹¹ The móuntains were cóvered with its shádow,
the cédars of Gód with its bóughs.
¹² It strétched out its bránches to the séa;
to the Ríver it strétched out its shóots.

¹³ Then whý have you bróken down its wálls?
It is plúcked by all who páss by the wáy.
¹⁴ It is rávaged by the bóar of the fórest,
devóured by the béasts of the fíeld.

¹⁵ God of hósts, turn agáin, we implóre;
look dówn from héaven and sée.

Vísit this víne and protéct it,
¹⁶ the víne your right hánd has plánted,
the son of mán you have cláimed for yoursélf.
¹⁷ They have búrnt it with fíre and cut it dówn.
May they pérish at the frówn of your fáce.

¹⁸ May your hánd be on the mán at your right hánd,
the son of mán you have confírmed as your ówn.
¹⁹ And we shall néver forsáke you agáin;
give us lífe that we may cáll upon your náme.

²⁰ O LÓRD God of hósts, bríng us báck;
let your fáce shine fórth, and wé shall be sáved.

PRAYER

O Lord, God of hosts, bring us back; show us the power of your grace at work in our lives, that we in turn may praise and thank you for the wonders of your providential care. We need your guidance and strength; let us see your salvation at work in our lives each day in our joyful service as ambassadors of your reign. To you be praise and glory, now and forever. Amen.

Psalm 81

IF ONLY YOU WOULD HEED

Psalm 81 comprises two sections: verses 2–6b present an invitation to praise God according to the divine commands, and verses 6c–17 form an impassioned oracle of God for the people. The psalm opens with a jubilant summons for the people to lift up voices and instrumental music in praise of God; this answers the divine statute that such be done for the commemoration of the Exodus feast. This marvelous and life-altering account of God on behalf of the children of Jacob demands appropriate acclamation and exaltation. God is called "our strength," having accomplished for the descendants of Jacob and Joseph what no human being could have done. But the psalm shifts suddenly in both structure and tenor: now the voice of God speaks fervently of his love for his people, once a motley group of slaves, and his desire that they who are now his own return that love. God recounts having freed this people from the burdens that bound them as slaves. All they had to do was ask, call out in need, and God readily responded with what they had asked for and more. The single stipulation was that they acknowledge no other god but God, certainly a fitting response to the divine favor. Only the God who had brought them out of Egypt could be their God. Do this, God says, and I will provide for you: "Open wide your mouth, and I will fill it." But as was so frequently the case, the people did not heed God's call; thus they were left "to follow their own designs." We hear how disheartened God is, who gave so much yet received so little in return. The Psalmist's presentation emphasizes how just God is, always true to the word given and the promise made, pointing out to the people their wandering paths away from the divine presence. But God's final word is full of grace and tender mercy, forgetting wrath and bestowing forgiveness in providing sustenance for the people: the finest of wheat and honey from the rock. Both substantial to the body and sweet to the taste is the nourishment offered by God. This oracle evinces God's overflowing love, unending forgiveness, and ready compassion for his people. In the New Testament, Jesus frequently expresses the same goodness and love toward those whom he encounters, despite their wayward and unfaithful course. One scene in particular holds a note of special warmth and affection: "Jerusalem, Jerusalem, the city that kills the prophets and stones those who are sent to it! How often have I desired to gather your children together as a hen gathers her brood under her wings, and you were not willing!" (Matt 23:37). We live under the expansive umbrella of divine love and kindness, a love older than creation itself. Let us take hold of that love and embrace it as our own.

PSALM 81 *(80)*

¹ *For the Choirmaster. Upon the gittith. Of Asaph.*

² Sing jóyfully to Gód our stréngth,
shout in tríumph to the Gód of Jácob.
³ Raise a sóng and sóund the tímbrel,
the swéet-sounding hárp and the lúte;
⁴ blów the trúmpet at the néw moon,
when the móon is fúll, on our féast.

⁵ For thís is a státute in Ísrael,
a commánd of the Gód of Jácob.
⁶ He máde it a decrée for Jóseph,
when he went óut from the lánd of Égypt.

A vóice I did not knów said to mé:
⁷ "I fréed your shóulder from the búrden;
your hands were fréed from the buílder's básket.
⁸ You cálled in distréss and I delívered you.

I ánswered, concéaled in the thúnder;
at the wáters of Méribah I tésted you.
⁹ Lísten, my péople, as I wárn you.
O Ísrael, if ónly you would héed!

¹⁰ Let there bé no strange gód amóng you,
nor shall you wórship a fóreign gód.
¹¹ Í am the LÓRD your Gód,
who brought you úp from the lánd of Égypt.
Ópen wide your móuth, and I will fill it.

¹² But my péople did not héed my vóice,
and Ísrael would nót obéy me.
¹³ So I léft them in their stúbbornness of héart,
to fóllow their ówn desígns.

¹⁴ Ó that my péople would héed me,
that Ísrael would wálk in my wáys!

¹⁵ At ónce I would subdúe their fóes,
turn my hánd agáinst their énemies.

¹⁶ Those who háte the LORD would crínge befóre him,
and their subjéction would lást foréver.
¹⁷ But Ísrael I would féed with finest whéat,
and sátisfy with hóney from the róck."

PRAYER

O God, faithful and true, forgiving and compassionate, all that you
have done from the beginning of time manifests your goodness to us.
In your loyal and steadfast devotion, teach us the way of fidelity; may
we embody your faithfulness in our own lives, especially toward those
who are most in need. In Jesus' name we pray. Amen.

Psalm 82

FALLEN GODS

Understanding Psalm 82 in its original context of Ancient Near Eastern
culture is essential for appreciating its message for both the past and the
present. Recall the opening chapters of the Book of Job: in the heavenly
court, beings of divine nature pose questions to God about the righteousness of Job. Similarly, the opening verse of Psalm 29 ("Ascribe to the
LORD, you heavenly powers") paints a scene of the heavenly court in
which God-like creatures are called to praise God's glory and power. And
as we will see in Psalm 89, a rhetorical question is posed: "Who is like
the LORD among the heavenly powers?" (v. 7b), which expects the
answer, "The only true God, the God of Israel." All of these passages help
us to imagine the scene for Psalm 82. Here God assembles these divine
beings who have responsibility for exercising power and judgment in
line with the principles God has established for his reign in Israel. They
have been found wanting in the exercise of their power. These "gods"
have failed miserably in their responsibility, and are now being "called
on the carpet" to face judgment themselves. All those for whom God has
special concern—the weak and orphaned, the afflicted, the needy and

the poor—have been neglected and uncared for by those who could make a difference in their well-being. These "gods" whom God reprimands are expected to bring light to situations of darkness and to help others see the ways of God in the manner in which they exercise their power. Psalm 82 presents us with a model of how the reign of God is to be exercised by those who are closest to the Divine Judge. While the culture of the Ancient Near East may be unfamiliar to our present circumstances, the message of the supremacy of the meaning of God's reign is relevant for us today. We know that there will be a day of judgment, and Jesus tells us how that judgment will take place. "The king will say to those at his right hand, 'Come, you that are blessed by my Father, inherit the kingdom prepared for you from the foundation of the world; for I was hungry and you gave me food, I was thirsty and you gave me something to drink, I was a stranger and you welcomed me" (Matt 25:34–35). The great and awesome God is a Judge whose reign is built on genuine love: God's love for us, and our love for God and neighbor. How will we fare before the Judge on that final day?

PSALM 82 *(81)*

[1] *A Psalm of Asaph.*

God stánds in the divíne assémbly.
In the mídst of the góds, he gives júdgment.

[2] "How lóng will you júdge unjústly,
and fávor the cáuse of the wícked?
[3] Do jústice for the wéak and the órphan;
give jústice to the póor and afflícted.
[4] Réscue the wéak and the néedy;
set them frée from the hánd of the wícked."

[5] They néither knów nor understánd;
they wálk abóut in dárkness,
and all the éarth's foundátions are sháken.

[6] I have sáid to you, "Yóu are góds,
and áll of you, sóns of the Most Hígh.
[7] And yét, like mén you shall díe;
you shall fáll, like ány of the prínces."

[8] Aríse, O Gód; judge the éarth!
For áll the nátions are yóurs.

O God, Judge of the living and the dead, whose reign is eternal and whose mercy is endless: continue to show us the way to justice and righteousness in our day, so that we may proclaim you and your reign in word and especially in deed. We ask this through Christ our Lord. Amen.

Psalm 83

O GOD, DO NOT BE SILENT

Psalm 83 gives utterance to the fear that the dominion of God may be under threat from the nations surrounding Israel. The perception of God's silence and apparent abandonment of guardianship over Israel has precipitated a moment of crisis. For when the people of God are threatened, God is also threatened. The expectation of the covenant is that God protect Israel; the honor, power, and nobility of God stand exposed and vulnerable before the nations of the world when it appears that God is not acting on Israel's behalf. The nations are arrogant toward God, "lifting up their heads" and raising a tumult (v. 3). When the very name of Israel is in danger of extinction, the covenant requires that God intervene on their behalf (vv. 4–6). In verses 7–12, a litany of nations presents the foes surrounding Israel on every side, a virtual enclosure with Israel at its center. Israel is besieged by enemies, yet God is silent, unmoved. Why was Israel, a small territory physically, continually beset by foes through the course of its history? The territory that makes up Israel (about the size of New Jersey) occupied a strategic topographical position in the Ancient Near East, standing at the crossroads between the dominant world powers: Assyria and Babylon to the north and east, Egypt to the south and west. Thus Israel's neighbors repeatedly sought to gain control over this strategic territory; control of trade routes would secure greater power for whoever controlled them. Possession of this land was key to trade and wealth. Israel's hope and confidence could remain strong as long as their covenant with YHWH, the one true God, endured. Yet the situation addressed in this psalm appears utterly different. Had God withdrawn support and care for the people he called into being? (v. 2). Words of petition in verses 10–18 might equally be seen as curses invoked upon enemies. Such vindictive and aggressive language is thorny and difficult for modern sensitivities. Why does Israel make such harsh and hostile pleas? The answer resides in verse 19: if the nations experience such destructive power at the hand of the God of Israel, they will surely know that there is only one God in this world, and that YHWH, God of Israel, Most High over all the earth, is a deity to be respected. In our own day and age, we know of situations when people of faith are threatened by others whose words echo the threats attributed to the Psalmist's foes: "Come, let us destroy them as a nation; let not their name be remembered" (v. 5). While we might not subscribe to such a violent idiom, the language of Psalm 83 reminds us that people of faith throughout the world still suffer threats of hatred, violence, and destruction. Our prayer for them beseeches God to bring justice where discrimination and intolerance hold sway.

PSALM 83 *(82)*

¹ *A Song. A Psalm of Asaph.*

² O Gód, do nót be sílent;
do not be stíll and unmóved, O Gód.
³ For your énemies ráise a túmult;
those who háte you líft up their héads.

⁴ They plót agáinst your péople,
conspíre against thóse you chérish.
⁵ They say, "Cóme, let us destróy them as a nátion;
let not the náme of Ísrael be remémbered."

⁶ They conspíre with a síngle mínd;
against yóu they máke a cóvenant:
⁷ the cámps of Édom and of Íshmael,
of Móab and Hágar,

⁸ Gébal and Ámmon and Ámalek,
Philístia, with the péople of Týre.
⁹ Assýria, tóo, is their álly,
and joins hánds with the chíldren of Lót.

¹⁰ Tréat them like Mídian, like Sísera,
like Jábin at the Ríver Kíshon,
¹¹ thóse who were destróyed at Éndor,
whose bódies rótted on the gróund.

¹² Make their cáptains like Óreb and Zéeb,
all their prínces like Zébah and Zalmúnna,
¹³ the mén who sáid, "Let us táke
the fíelds of Gód for oursélvés."

¹⁴ My God, scátter them líke the whírlwind,
dríve them like cháff in the wínd!
¹⁵ As fíre that búrns away the fórest,
as the fláme that sets the móuntains abláze,
¹⁶ dríve them awáy with your témpest,
and fill them with térror at your stórm.

¹⁷ Cóver their fáces with sháme,
so that they séek your náme, O LÓRD.
¹⁸ Shame and térror be théirs foréver.
Lét them be disgráced; let them pérish!

¹⁹ Let them knów that yóu alóne,
yóu whose náme is the LÓRD,
are the Most Hígh over áll the éarth.

PRAYER

O righteous and just Lord, who stand victorious over the powers of death and destruction, hear our plea for peace in the world. Raise up leaders who will do battle with the forces of injustice and fear, that the power of your grace may live in the hearts of all people everywhere, through Christ our Lord. Amen.

𝒫salm 84

HOW BLESSED TO DWELL IN YOUR HOUSE

We can imagine the great joy and eager anticipation in the hearts of the Jewish people as they went to Jerusalem three times each year for the three pilgrim festivals (Passover, Pentecost, and Tents). Psalm 84 gives heartfelt expression to this pilgrim spirit. The opening verses employ several varying images of God. "Lord of hosts" implies God's mighty power as commander of the armies of heaven. Immediately following in the next verse is the epithet "the living God," meaning that our immanent God is not derived from a limited understanding of nature but has manifested himself as living in the hearts of those who yearn to enter the divine presence. In verse 4, the possessive pronoun *my* suggests an intimacy we might not usually associate with such magnificent titles as *king* and *God*. It is this closeness to God that enables the Psalmist to assert how even the sparrow and the swallow have a place in God's providence, here signified by the courts of the temple, the place of divine dwelling (v. 4). These pilgrims can expect blessings in abundance; in the approach to Sion, strength grows within them in having known divine protection along the way, and now their longing and yearning is to be fulfilled within the courts of the temple, God's abode on earth (vv. 3, 7–8). "One day within your courts," they proclaim, "is better than a thousand elsewhere" (v. 11). What a powerful statement! The desire to be in God's presence, to live under the divine rule, and to experience God fully and intimately are the very heart of this psalm. Three times the Psalmist repeats the word *blessed* (vv. 5, 6, 13), that momentous term that begins the whole Psalter. Psalm 1 calls the just person "blessed." Here it affirms the Psalmist's conviction that God's favor and blessing come upon the pilgrim. Those numbered among the blessed thus include the people singing praise in the courts of the temple, making pilgrimage with an open heart, and trusting in God. Some commentators suggest that the love of the Psalmist is here focused on the temple courts themselves. But such love must be predicated upon love for the Holy One who dwells there. We have been created for union with God. Human experience is so often characterized by an enduring and inexplicable ache. That interior hunger and yearning has often led to the insight that the distance between us and our Creator God is greater than it perhaps should be. If our appetites are focused on possessions, power, or prestige, on objects or even persons, a mysterious inner mechanism reminds us that we were created for God: as St. Augustine writes, we are restless until we rest in God alone. Jesus himself puts it thus in the Last Supper Discourse of John's Gospel: "This is eternal life, that they may know you, the only true God, and Jesus Christ whom you have sent" (John 17:3). To know, to experience God, the living God, brings vitality and joy to our existence; such delight is a foretaste of eternity. Until then, we long and yearn for a relationship with God that will feed our deepest hunger and assuage our most intense thirst—such intimacy with God is the purpose for which we were created.

PSALM 84 (83)

For the Choirmaster. Upon the gittith. Of the sons of Korah. A Psalm.

2 How lóvely is your dwélling pláce,
O LÓRD of hósts.
3 My sóul is lónging and yéarning
for the cóurts of the LÓRD.
My héart and my flésh cry óut
to the líving Gód.

4 Éven the spárrow finds a hóme,
and the swállow a nést for hersélf
in which she séts her yóung, at your áltars,
O LORD of hósts, my kíng and my Gód.

5 Blessed are théy who dwéll in your hóuse,
foréver sínging your práise.
6 Blessed the péople whose stréngth is in yóu,
whose héart is sét on pilgrim wáys.

7 As they gó through the Báca Válley,
they máke it a pláce of spríngs;
the áutumn rain cóvers it with póols.
8 They wálk with éver-growing stréngth;
the God of góds will appéar in Síon.

9 O LORD Gód of hósts, hear my práyer;
give éar, O Gód of Jácob.
10 Turn your éyes, O Gód, our shíeld;
lóok on the fáce of your anóinted.

11 One dáy withín your cóurts
is bétter than a thóusand élsewhere.
The thréshold of the hóuse of Gód
I prefér to the dwéllings of the wícked.

12 For the LORD Gód is a sún, a shíeld;
the LORD will gíve us his fávor and glóry.
he will nót withhóld any góod
to thóse who wálk without bláme.
13 O LÓRD of hósts, how bléssed
is the mán who trústs in yóu!

O God, our living God, hear our earnest prayer as we seek you in the winding paths of our lives. When we are borne down by distance from you, help us to know that our yearning has been planted by you in our hearts, and that you will fulfill our longing even as we journey toward eternity. Blessing and thanksgiving be yours, with praise and glory, now and forever. Amen.

Psalm 85

PEACE FOR THOSE
WHO TURN TO GOD

Psalm 85 brings the season of Advent to mind. Acknowledging past experience of God's salvation, the people adopt a posture of waiting—waiting in the hope that God will act again on their behalf. Expectant waiting is the hallmark of Advent; in Psalm 85 we wait with the Psalmist for God's act of restoration (vv. 5, 7, 8), a sign that God is with us as we make our way on the pilgrimage of life. The Psalmist's words seem to ask God to repent for having withdrawn from them, yet the people cannot deny their own need to return to God. The biblical mindset often understands Israel's periods of misery and grief as signs of God's withdrawal: God has turned his back on their sinfulness and withdrawn divine protection, a fundamental expectation of the covenant relationship. Yet the firm hope remains that God will again bestow covenant blessings upon those who wait for the blessings that manifest the divine presence among them. Initially the Psalmist speaks of "your" land (v. 2), reminding God that the territory in which his people dwell is God's own property, bestowed upon them long ago in their ancestor Abraham. But as the psalm progresses, a transition from "your" land to "our" land, "our" earth (vv. 10, 13; "land" and "earth" are represented by the same Hebrew term) indicates that God's land is indeed "our" land, our inheritance of old enduring into the present. The situation set forth here reflects that peace that flows from living out the covenant with God. In the biblical mind, "peace" is not merely an absence of anxiety; rather, it is a sense of total well-being—physical, spiritual, emotional. The early Christians understood that the Psalmist's hoped-for salvation and redemption had been fulfilled in Jesus. Thus we can see how this psalm, appropriate to Advent, also might articulate our response to the great mystery of the incarnation. For those who turn to Christ in their hearts (v. 9c), his assumption of our fragile flesh has brought divinity closer to humanity than could possibly have been imagined (v. 10). "We have seen his glory, the glory as of a father's only son, full of grace and truth," says John's Gospel (1:14); his words echo those of the Psalmist: "His glory will dwell in our land" (v. 10b). "Merciful love and faithfulness have met" in the coming of Jesus Christ, who has shown the world how God's steadfast mercy and faithfulness to his promise are to be united in the living of our lives. Likewise, Jesus has shown the world how "justice and peace have kissed" (v. 11b) in binding his love for the poor and needy with genuine acts of care for them. Psalm 85 begins with the spirit of Advent and concludes with images that resonate with the Christmas mystery. Though specific liturgical seasons provide for celebration of these mysteries of Christ, each day can have room for waiting in faith and pondering the incarnation; our lives are rightly centered on Christ who has come among us to free us for living the paschal mystery.

PSALM 85 *(84)*

¹ *For the Choirmaster. Of the sons of Korah. A Psalm.*

² O Lᴏʀᴅ, you have fávored your lánd,
and brought báck the cáptives of Jácob.
³ You forgáve the guílt of your péople,
and cóvered áll their síns.
⁴ You avérted áll your ráge;
you turned báck the héat of your ánger.

⁵ Bring us báck, O Gód, our sávior!
Put an énd to your gríevance agáinst us.
⁶ Will you be ángry with ús foréver?
Will your ánger last from áge to áge?

⁷ Will you nót restóre again our lífe,
that your péople may rejóice in yóu?
⁸ Let us sée, O Lᴏʀᴅ, your mércy,
and gránt us yóur salvátion.

⁹ I will héar what the Lᴏʀᴅ God spéaks;
he speaks of péace for his péople and his fáithful,

and those who túrn their héarts to hím.
¹⁰ His salvátion is néar for those who féar him,
and his glóry will dwéll in our lánd.

¹¹ Merciful lóve and fáithfulness have mét;
jústice and péace have kíssed.
¹² Fáithfulness shall spríng from the éarth,
and jústice look dówn from héaven.

¹³ Also the Lórd will bestów his bóunty,
and our éarth shall yíeld its íncrease.
¹⁴ Jústice will márch befóre him,
and gúide his stéps on the wáy.

PRAYER

O God, our Savior and Redeemer, who have shown us great favor in generous mercy and loving fidelity, grant us the vision to see your hand at work in things subtle and hidden, profound and life-altering, so that we may wait in confidence for the great day when the fullness of your kingdom is revealed among us, through Christ our Lord. Amen.

Psalm 86

SHOW REDEMPTION TO YOUR SERVANT

A clear sense of the Psalmist's relationship to God emerges in the terms addressed to the Almighty One: "You alone are God" (v. 10); "You have saved me from the depths of the grave" (v. 13); "You are compassionate and gracious, abundant in mercy and fidelity" (v. 15). The speaker has unmistakably experienced firsthand the loving kindness of God, and has derived from his encounter the strength and conviction necessary for living life according to the Lord's way. Likewise, the Psalmist is transparent regarding his utter need for God's support in meeting the challenges of life: "I am poor and needy" (v. 1b); "I cry to you all the day long"

(v. 3b); "I lift up my soul to you" (v. 4b); "Surely you will answer me" (v. 7b); "Teach me, Lord, your way" (v. 11). Twice he refers to himself as "servant" (vv. 2b, 16b), an infrequent self-designation among the writers of the psalms. In its biblical sense, a servant is one who stands at the beck and call of the One who directs all the things of life, from words and deeds to desires and wishes, to hopes and expectations. As noted elsewhere, the use of personal pronouns in Hebrew (rather than employing particles attached to nouns and verbs) indicates a particularly emphatic form of expression. This usage is frequent in Psalm 86: "who trust in you, my God" (v .2b); "you are good and forgiving" (v. 5a); "you are great and do marvelous deeds, you who alone are God" (vv. 10a, 10b); "I will praise you" (v. 12a); "But you, O God, are compassionate and gracious" (v. 15a); "you, O LORD, give me comfort and help" (v. 17c). In the New Testament, Jesus himself speaks of servanthood in words both noble and challenging: "Whoever wants to be first must be last of all and servant of all" (Mark 9:35). "The Son of Man came not to be served but to serve, and to give his life as a ransom for many" (Mark 10:45). St. Paul takes up the theme in describing the extent to which Jesus had gone in becoming God's servant. "Though [Jesus] was in the form of God,...he emptied himself,...he humbled himself and became obedient to the point of death—even death on a cross" (Phil 2:6–8). How could Jesus so completely empty himself, manifest obedience even to the point of death, and allow himself to become our ransom—how could he have done this, had he not shared such a profound and personal relationship with the One he called Abba? True servanthood begins with a personal relationship with God, a relationship that is open, loving, trusting, persevering, and confident of God's direction for our lives. Jesus has shown us both the origin and path to genuine service—it begins and proceeds in oneness with the God who brought us into being and leads us to eternal joy.

PSALM 86 *(85)*

¹ *A Prayer of David.*

Turn your éar, O LÓRD, and ánswer me,
for Í am póor and néedy.
² Presérve my sóul, for I am fáithful;
save the sérvant who trústs in you, my Gód.

³ Have mércy on mé, O Lórd,
for I crý to you áll the day lóng.
⁴ Gládden the sóul of your sérvant,
for I líft up my sóul to you, O Lórd.

⁵ O Lórd, you are góod and forgíving,
full of mércy to áll who call to yóu.
⁶ Give éar, O Lᴏ́ʀᴅ, to my práyer,
and atténd to my vóice in supplicátion.

⁷ In the dáy of distréss, I will cáll to you,
and súrely yóu will ánswer me.
⁸ Among the góds there is nóne like you, O Lórd,
nor wórks to compáre with yóurs.

⁹ All the nátions you have máde shall cóme;
they will bow dówn befóre you, O Lórd,
and glórify your náme,
¹⁰ for you are gréat and do márvelous déeds,
yóu who alóne are Gód.

¹¹ Téach me, O Lᴏ́ʀᴅ, your wáy,
so that Í may wálk in your trúth,
single-héarted to féar your náme.

¹² I will práise you, Lord my Gód, with all my héart,
and glórify your náme foréver.
¹³ Your mércy to mé has been gréat;
you have sáved me from the dépths of the gráve.

¹⁴ The proud have rísen agáinst me, O Gód;
a bánd of the rúthless seeks my lífe.
To yóu they páy no héed.

¹⁵ But you, O Gód, are compássionate and grácious,
slów to ánger, O Lórd,
abúndant in mércy and fidélity;
¹⁶ túrn and take píty on mé.

O gíve your stréngth to your sérvant,
and sáve the són of your hándmaid.
¹⁷ Shów me the sígn of your fávor,
that my fóes may sée to their sháme
that you, O Lᴏ́ʀᴅ, give me cómfort and hélp.

PRAYER

O God, whose mercy is eternal and whose wisdom is unsearchable,
guide us in the paths that lead to you; make us confident that by our
openness to your wondrous and inscrutable ways, you will transform

us into servants who mirror the goodness and compassion of your Son and Servant Jesus, who lives and reigns, forever and ever. Amen.

Psalm 87

GLORIOUS CITY OF GOD

A visionary assertion of divine love is the subject of Psalm 87—love poured out on Jerusalem and the whole world. Mount Sion (the height within the city's precincts that sometimes meant the whole of Jerusalem and Israel) is acclaimed as the place God has selected as an abiding place on earth. Out of all the nations in the world, God has chosen to dwell on Mount Sion, with humble and insignificant Israel. The theology of election, God's selection of Israel as his chosen people, is a frequent theme of Old Testament writings. Broadly speaking, God chooses some person or place of no particular dignity or importance, and by this divine election raises that person or place to great significance. Such actions provide an insight into the character of the God as depicted in the Old Testament: God is compassionate and good, manifesting to the world that divine election is not to be understood on merely human standards. Similarly, such actions demonstrate that God, Creator of this vast cosmos and all its marvels, is yet concerned for each and every creature, great and small alike. Regardless of our standing in human estimation, each of us enjoys God's favor—much like Sion, which in spite of impressive natural fortifications, is a minor and even insignificant place in worldly terms. The psalm goes on to bring forth another important theological motif: universalism. God invites the whole world to share in the divine gift of the covenant. In any other context, verse 4 would amount to a list of Israel's historical enemies. Rahab, another name for Egypt, was the place of Israel's former slavery, out of which God had led them to the Promised Land. Babylon was the place of Israel's later exile; that people had pillaged Jerusalem, destroyed the temple, and left the land desolate while taking the people captive. Tyre (to the north), Philistia (to the west), and Ethiopia (to the southwest) were nations against whom the people of Israel struggled in disputes over foreign domination and the introduction of idol worship. In this psalm, however, God's oracle asserts that these nations have come to know the true God; their "birth" to this knowledge of God comes through association with Sion, God's city (v. 4d). God has made Sion the means by which the nations come to know and experience the Creator of the world, the true God who has made Sion the divine abode, where all will find a home. Isaiah 60 provides a full expression of God's universal salvation: all the nations stream toward daughter Jerusalem, once desolate and forgotten but now the site upon which God's glory rests. When Jesus encounters the centurion whose great faith so impresses him, he attests to the same universalism when he says, "I tell you, many will come from east and west and will eat with Abraham and Isaac and Jacob in the kingdom of heaven" (Matt 8:11). Our God calls all people to experience the joy of the divine reign by accepting God's covenant with faith, trust, and perseverance.

PSALM 87 *(86)*

¹ *Of the sons of Korah. A Psalm. A Song.*

Founded by hím on the hóly móuntain,
² the LÓRD loves the gátes of Síon,
more than áll the dwéllings of Jácob.
³ Of yóu are told glórious thíngs,
yóu, O cíty of Gód!

⁴ "Rahab and Bábylon Í will cóunt
among thóse who knów me;
of Tyre, Philístia, Ethiópia, it is tóld,
'There was thís one bórn.'
⁵ But of Síon it sháll be sáid,
'Each one was bórn in hér.'"

Hé, the Most Hígh, estáblished it.
⁶ In his régister of péoples the LORD wrítes,
"Hére was thís one bórn."
⁷ The síngers cry óut in chórus,
"In yóu, all fínd their hóme."

PRAYER

God Most High, great Creator in whom all nations find their home: grant us the faith to acknowledge your will; give us hope for the things of heaven, and stir up in us the charity to accept all people as our brothers and sisters, through Christ our Lord. Amen.

Psalm 88

MY ONE COMPANION
IS DARKNESS

Psalm 88 is an intense reflection on a period of emotional darkness and interior suffering undergone by a person of faith. Every line bespeaks unbearable spiritual torment, yet the psalm is a masterpiece of poetic imagery and rhetorical power. The reader is drawn into the speaker's seemingly unending affliction; the language burns with the fires of inner anguish and fearful threats to life itself. The reader is drawn into this experience by repeated images evoking death: grave (vv. 4b, 12a), tomb (v. 5a), slain (v. 6b), the pit (v. 7a), regions dark and deep (v. 7b), the place of perdition (v. 12b), land of oblivion (v. 13b), closeness to death (v. 16a). This progressive buildup of images underscores the extent to which the Psalmist has endured the diminishment of life, with the concurrent threat that the grave will be his only home. The Psalmist poses a series of rhetorical questions, an oblique plea for God to address this life-threatening situation: "Will you work your wonders for the dead?... Will your mercy be told in the grave?...Will your justice be known in the land of oblivion?" (vv. 11–13). The questions are a clever and pointed way of suggesting to God, "If I am deprived of life, there will be no one to make your mercy and faithfulness known." Clearly the Psalmist has brought these matters before God in a prayerful spirit; to "stretch out one's hands" (v. 10c) is a Hebraic gesture of supplication, a bodily posture in tune with verbal petitions ascending to the throne of God, begging for a hearing (v. 3). Despite the pervasive tone of fear and anguish, an unmistakable stance of faith also characterizes the Psalmist's words. The first line invokes the "God of my salvation": the Psalmist turns to the One who alone can transform his situation into a redemptive experience—the God who has always sustained the Psalmist in a communion of trust and confidence. Longing to be remembered (v. 15), the Psalmist remains faithful in prayer: he calls out day and night (v. 2b); as a new day dawns, his first thoughts return to God (v. 14b). The language and imagery of the psalm gives a precise portrait of Jesus in Gethsemane. That scene recounts the agitation Jesus felt at that moment of profound anguish: "He threw himself on the ground and prayed, 'My Father, if it is possible, let this cup pass from me; yet not what I want but what you want'" (Matt 26:39). Having shared so fully in our humanity makes Jesus a perfect High Priest for us before God: he experienced the torment and uncertainty of what all human beings face on life's pilgrimage (Heb 2:18—3:2). Praying Psalm 87 can unite us with many people of faith who struggle through life's most difficult situations; we turn to Christ as the pioneer of our salvation who knows our burdens. In our communion with Christ, we are not alone even in the most difficult circumstances.

PSALM 88 (87)

¹ *A Song. A Psalm. Of the sons of Korah. For the Choirmaster. Intoned like* Mahalat Leannoth. *A Maskil. For Heman the Ezrahite.*

² O LÓRD and Gód of my salvátion,
I crý before you dáy and níght.
³ Let my práyer cóme into your présence.
Inclíne your éar to my crý.
⁴ For my sóul is fílled with évils;
my lífe is on the brínk of the gráve.

⁵ I am réckoned as óne in the tómb;
Í am like a wárrior without stréngth,
⁶ like one róaming amóng the déad,
like the sláin lýing in their gráves,
like thóse you remémber no móre,
cut óff, as they áre, from your hánd.

⁷ You have láid me in the dépths of the pít,
in régions that are dárk and déep.
⁸ Your ánger wéighs down upón me;
I am drówned benéath your wáves.
⁹ You have táken awáy my fríends;
to thém you have máde me háteful.

Imprísoned, I cannót escápe;
¹⁰ my éyes are súnken with gríef.
I cáll to you, LÓRD, all day lóng;
to yóu I strétch out my hánds.

¹¹ Will you wórk your wónders for the déad?
Will the shádes rise úp to práise you?
¹² Will your mércy be tóld in the gráve,
or your fáithfulness in the pláce of perdítion?

¹³ Will your wónders be knówn in the dárk,
your jústice in the lánd of oblívion?

¹⁴ But Í, O Lᴏʀᴅ, crý out to yóu;
in the mórning my práyer comes befóre you.
¹⁵ Whý do you rejéct me, O Lóʀᴅ?
Why do you híde your fáce from mé?

¹⁶ I am wrétched, close to déath from my yóuth.
I have bórne your tríals; I am númb.
¹⁷ Your fúry has swept dówn upón me;
your térrors have útterly destróyed me.

¹⁸ They surróund me all the dáy like a flóod;
togéther they close ín agáinst me.
¹⁹ Friend and néighbor you have táken awáy:
my óne compánion is dárkness.

PRAYER

Lord Jesus Christ, Pioneer of our salvation and High Priest of the good things to come, grant us strength and perseverance to face life's difficulties with faith and courage. May we fix our hearts on you, never forgetting your promise of eternal life for all who hold fast to you, who live and reign, forever and ever. Amen.

Psalm 89

COVENANT GIVEN, COVENANT BROKEN

Psalm 89 begins and ends with contrasting experiences of God's presence. The opening verses extol God's faithful mercy: "I will sing forever of your mercies, O Lᴏʀᴅ; through all ages my mouth will proclaim your fidelity. I have declared your mercy is established forever; your fidelity stands firm as the heavens." But the same terms are transformed into questions of anguished desolation at the end of the psalm: "Where are your mercies of the past, O LORD, which you swore in your faithfulness to David?" (v. 50). The psalm thus moves from covenant celebrated to covenant broken. The story of David's covenant is retold twice in the Psalter (here and in Ps 132); the earlier narratives (2 Sam 7, 1 Chr 17) begin with David's intention to build a house for the LORD. But that God's intention is otherwise: "I will establish a house for you and your descendants; from them will come my Anointed" (2 Sam 7:10–16; 1 Chr 17:10–14). Its formulation of the great Davidic promise gives Psalm 89 a prominent place in the Church's liturgy. It provides the responsorial psalm on December 24, in anticipation of the birth of Jesus, in whom that promise is fulfilled. "I have found my servant David, and with my holy oil anointed him. My hand shall always be with him, and my arm shall make him strong....He will call out to me, 'You are my father, my God, the rock of my salvation'....I will keep my faithful love for him always; with him my covenant shall last" (vv. 21–22, 27, 29). The psalm's powerful expression of divine commitment becomes a word of hope for Israel later in their history, when circumstances seem to have alienated them from the blessings of the covenant. The final passages of the psalm, painful in their sense of loss and fearful of impending annihilation, demonstrate nonetheless a firm faith in God, whose intention for them is not destruction and death. The Psalmist persists in his conviction that God, who could "crush Rahab underfoot like a corpse," and "scatter foes with a mighty arm," could meet whatever circumstance confronted them and bring them through to victory and success. The Christian cherishes the same confidence in the person of Jesus Christ, God incarnate in human flesh. We say with the Psalmist, "You are mighty, O LORD, and fidelity surrounds you....Merciful love and fidelity walk in your presence....How blessed the people who know your praise...who make your justice their joyful acclaim" (vv. 9b, 15b, 16a, 17b). When Israel proved unable to live out the covenant in its fullness, God's response was to become one of us in Jesus Christ, in whom the covenant is perfectly fulfilled. Jesus Christ is the ultimate Word uttered by the One who is Father; Jesus now walks with us in our efforts to be faithful to the covenant of love, having come among us "to save us from our sins" (Matt 1:21).

PSALM 89 *(88)*

[1] *A Maskil. For Ethan the Ezrahite.*

[2] I will síng foréver of your mércies, O LÓRD;
through all áges my móuth will procláim your fidélity.
[3] I have decláred your mércy is estáblished foréver;
your fidélity stands fírm as the héavens.

⁴ "With my chósen one Í have made a cóvenant;
I have swórn to Dávid my sérvant:
⁵ I will estáblish your descéndants foréver,
and sét up your thróne through all áges."

⁶ The héavens práise your wónders, O LÓRD,
your fidélity ín the assémbly of your hóly ones.
⁷ For whó in the skíes can compáre with the LÓRD,
or whó is like the LÓRD among the héavenly pówers?
⁸ A Gód to be féared in the cóuncil of the hóly ones,
gréat and áwesome to áll aróund him.

⁹ O LÓRD God of hósts, whó is your équal?
You are míghty, O LÓRD, and fidélity surróunds you.
¹⁰ It is yóu who rúle the ráging of the séa;
it is yóu who stíll the súrging of its wáves.
¹¹ It is yóu who crush Ráhab underfóot like a córpse;
you scátter your fóes with your míghty árm.

¹² The héavens are yóurs, the éarth is yóurs;
yóu have fóunded the wórld and its fúllness;
¹³ it is yóu who creáted the Nórth and the Sóuth.
Tábor and Hérmon shout for jóy at your náme.

¹⁴ Yóurs is a míghty árm.
Your hánd is stróng; your right hánd is exálted.
¹⁵ Jústice and right júdgment are the píllars of your
        thróne;
merciful lóve and fidélity wálk in your présence.

¹⁶ How bléssed the péople who knów your práise,
who wálk, O LÓRD, in the líght of your fáce,
¹⁷ who fínd their jóy every dáy in your náme,
who máke your jústice their jóyful accláim.

¹⁸ For yóu are the glóry of their stréngth;
by your fávor it ís that our míght is exalted.
¹⁹ Behóld, the LÓRD is our shíeld;
he is the Hóly One of Ísrael, our kíng.

²⁰ Thén you spóke in a vísion.
To your fáithful ónes you sáid,
"I have sét the crówn on a wárrior,
I have exálted one chósen from the péople.

²¹ I have fóund my sérvant Dávid,
and with my hóly óil anóinted him.
²² My hánd shall álways be with hím,
and my árm shall máke him stróng.

²³ The énemy shall néver outwít him,
nor shall the són of iníquity húmble him.
²⁴ I will béat down his fóes befóre him,
and thóse who háte him I will stríke.

²⁵ My mércy and my fáithfulness shall bé with hím;
by my náme his míght shall bé exálted.
²⁶ I will strétch out his hánd to the Séa,
and his right hánd upón the Rívers.

²⁷ He will call óut to me, 'Yóu are my fáther,
my Gód, the róck of my salvátion.'
²⁸ I for my párt will máke him my fírstborn,
the híghest of the kíngs of the éarth.

²⁹ I will kéep my faithful lóve for him álways;
with hím my cóvenant shall lást.
³⁰ I will estáblish his descéndants foréver,
and his thróne as lásting as the dáys of héaven.

³¹ If his descéndants forsáke my láw
and refúse to wálk as I decrée,
³² and if éver they víolate my státutes,
fáiling to kéep my commánds:

³³ Then I will púnish their offénses with the ród;
then I will scóurge them on accóunt of their guílt.
³⁴ But I will néver take báck my mércy;
my fidélity will néver fáil.
³⁵ I will néver víolate my cóvenant,
nor go báck on the prómise of my líps.

³⁶ Once for áll, I have swórn by my hóliness.
'I will néver líe to Dávid.
³⁷ His descéndants shall contínue foréver.
In my síght his thróne is like the sún;
³⁸ like the móon, it shall endúre foréver,
a fáithful wítness in the héavens.'"

³⁹ But yet yóu have spúrned and rejécted,
you are ángry with the óne you have anóinted.
⁴⁰ You have renóunced your cóvenant with your sérvant,
and dishónored his crówn in the dúst.

⁴¹ You have bróken down áll his wálls,
and redúced his fórtresses to rúins.
⁴² Áll who pass bý despóil him;
he has becóme the táunt of his néighbors.

⁴³ You have exálted the right hánd of his fóes;
you have máde all his énemies rejóice.
⁴⁴ You have turned báck the édge of his swórd;
you have nót uphéld him in báttle.

⁴⁵ You have bróught his glóry to an énd;
you have húrled his thróne to the gróund.
⁴⁶ You have cut shórt the dáys of his yóuth;
you have héaped disgráce upon hím.

⁴⁷ How lóng, O LÓRD? Will you híde yourself foréver?
How lóng will your ánger búrn like a fíre?
⁴⁸ Remémber the shórtness of my lífe,
and how fráil you have máde the children of mén.
⁴⁹ What mán can líve and néver see déath?
Who can sáve himsélf from the grásp of the tómb?

⁵⁰ Where are your mércies of the pást, O Lórd,
which you swóre in your fáithfulness to Dávid?
⁵¹ Remémber, O Lórd, the táunts to your sérvant,
how I háve to béar all the ínsults of the péoples.
⁵² Thus your énemies líft up a táunt, O LÓRD,
táunting your anóinted at évery stép.

* * *

[53] Blést be the LÓRD foréver.
Amén and amén!

PRAYER

O God, faithful and true, who in fulfilling your promise to David have given us Christ Jesus as perfect Mediator and High Priest: grant that we may grow in understanding of the price paid for our salvation, and respond to your merciful love and compassion with ever-greater faith, through the same Christ our Lord. Amen.

BOOK FOUR
OF THE
PSALTER

Psalm 90

THE BREVITY OF LIFE

The Psalmist here speaks from a situation in which the people, shattered by divine anger (vv. 7, 9, 11), acknowledge the shortness of life and call out for mercy. The specific language of the request in verse 14, that they be filled with "merciful love," signals a plea for renewal of the covenant promises. God's merciful love is the sign of a living and active covenant, but now divine care and protection seems to have been withdrawn, the covenant annulled. The text of the psalm begins with an affirmation of the eternal power and might of God, who brought the world into being and sustains it even to the present moment. God's immortality is contrasted with human mortality (vv. 3–4), fragile and short-lived as grass, springing up only to wither almost immediately. Human life passes quickly, no more than a sigh (vv. 9–10), yet it bears the weight of grief and anguish, drudgery and toil. How can a mere mortal stand this uncertainty and ambiguity, this desperation and doubt? The Psalmist begs for wisdom—that profound insight and understanding that transcends mere education, that "life learning" that probes the meaning of human existence and finds a way through the labyrinth of human experience. The Wisdom tradition of the Scriptures provides a helpful way to face such probing questions. In the minds of the Wisdom authors, real answers to these perplexing questions could be found embedded in creation itself. Everything God has created provides a potential gateway into wisdom: the transition of night into day, the regular change of seasons, the alternation of sowing and reaping, the care of animals for their young followed by their timely leaving of the nest—the constant yet ever-varied cycles of all God's creation. Jesus himself refers to this fundamental character of God's creation when he says, "Can any of you by worrying add a single hour to your span of life? And why do you worry about clothing? Consider the lilies of the field, how they grow; they neither toil nor spin, yet I tell you, even Solomon in all his glory was not clothed like one of these. But if God so clothes the grass of the field, which is alive today and tomorrow is thrown into the oven, will he not much more clothe you—you of little faith?" (Matt 6:27–30). Wisdom comes in knowing our place in the universe, using the gifts God has given us, and knowing ourselves in relationship to God, our source of blessing, our hope in time of need. It is for us to work with what we have been given, and to ask God to bring blessing to our efforts.

PSALM 90 *(89)*

¹ *Prayer of Moses, the man of God.*

O Lórd, yóu have been our réfuge,
from generátion tó generátion.
² Befóre the móuntains were bórn,
or the éarth or the wórld were brought fórth,
you are Gód, from áge to áge.

³ You túrn man báck to dúst,
and say, "Retúrn, O chíldren of mén."
⁴ To your éyes a thóusand yéars
are like yésterday, cóme and góne,
or líke a wátch in the níght.

⁵ You swéep them awáy like a dréam,
like gráss which is frésh in the mórning.
⁶ In the mórning it spróuts and is frésh;
by évening it wíthers and fádes.

⁷ Indéed, we are consúmed by your ánger;
we are strúck with térror at your fúry.
⁸ You have sét our guílt befóre you,
our sécrets in the líght of your fáce.

⁹ All our dáys pass awáy in your ánger.
Our yéars are consúmed like a sígh.
¹⁰ Seventy yéars is the spán of our dáys,
or éighty if wé are stróng.
And móst of these are tóil and páin.
They pass swíftly and wé are góne.

¹¹ Who understánds the pówer of your ánger?
Your fúry mátches the féar of you.
¹² Then téach us to númber our dáys,
that wé may gain wísdom of héart.

¹³ Turn báck, O LÓRD! How lóng?
Show píty tó your sérvants.
¹⁴ At dawn, fill us with your mérciful lóve;
we shall exúlt and rejóice all our dáys.

¹⁵ Give us jóy for the dáys of our afflíction,
for the yéars when we lóoked upon évil.

¹⁶ Let your déed be séen by your sérvants,
and your glórious pówer by their chíldren.
¹⁷ Let the fávor of the Lórd our Gód be upón us;
give succéss to the wórk of our hánds.
O give succéss to the wórk of our hánds.

PRAYER

O God, source of blessing and hope in time of trouble, we acknowledge before you our weak and mortal nature. As we can accomplish nothing of value without you, we beg that you grant us wisdom to use well your gifts, that we may praise you who are their origin and ours. We ask this through Christ our Lord. Amen.

Psalm 91

MY GOD, IN WHOM I TRUST

One technique for reading a psalm is to look at its opening and closing: a linking idea, phrase, or image may reveal the psalm's theme. This is true of Psalm 91, which begins with a strong affirmation of trust in God (vv. 1–2) and concludes with God's promise to the one who has trusted (vv. 14–16). When someone in need prays with confident trust in God's ways, divine love inevitably responds, bringing a sense of salvation and protection to the one who prays. We may too often imagine salvation as an act of God that turns the world upside down, an earth-shattering response to a suppliant word. But in the biblical mind, especially in the Psalms, salvation is often more apparent in the daily events of life in which God acts on our behalf. It can be as ordinary as the return to health after a prayer in sickness or as quiet as the return to peace of mind after an upsetting incident. God is wonderfully close to us in every act of faith, each time we acknowledge his awareness of and power over the challenges, great and small, that confront us in life. A key to unlocking this truth is found in God's own expression "for he knows my name"

(v. 14). To know the name of God is to have experienced the wonder and mystery of all that God is. The concept of "name" in the Scriptures is intimately connected with "identity." This is evident in stories of characters whose names are changed or on whom a particular name is bestowed. Jesus himself is a prime example: the angel of the Lord speaks to Joseph in a dream, saying, "You are to name him Jesus, for he will save his people from their sins" (Matt 1:21). Here the Psalmist confesses unshakable trust in God: whether it be night's terrors (v. 5), a wasting scourge (v. 6), or a band of ten thousand that comes against him (v. 7), God's fidelity continues to be his protection (v. 4b). Several images associate this safety and security with the temple, the place where one encounters the divine presence. "The shelter of the Most High," "the shade of the Almighty (v. 1), "pinions" and "wings" (v. 4), all call to mind the Ark of the Covenant, presenting the outspread wings of the cherubim as a manifestation of the invisible presence of God in the temple sanctuary. The ark was imagined as the earthly footstool of God, sitting on his throne in the heavens (cf. 1 Chr 28:2; also Pss 99:2, 5; 132:7). God says to the Psalmist, "I will be with [you] in distress; I will deliver [you] and give [you] glory" (v. 15). The Church gives this psalm a special place in its liturgy at Night Prayer, the Church's final words as the day ends, expressing our trust in God and the divine protection we so sorely need.

PSALM 91 *(90)*

¹ He who dwélls in the shélter of the Most Hígh,
and abídes in the sháde of the Almíghty,
² sáys to the LÓRD, "My réfuge,
my strónghold, my Gód in whom I trúst!"

³ He will frée you from the snáre of the fówler,
from the destrúctive plágue;
⁴ hé will concéal you with his pínions,
and únder his wíngs you will find réfuge.
His fáithfulness is búckler and shíeld.

⁵ You will not féar the térror of the níght,
nor the árrow that flíes by dáy,
⁶ nor the plágue that prówls in the dárkness,
nor the scóurge that lays wáste at nóon.

⁷ A thóusand may fáll at your síde,
ten thóusand fáll at your ríght:
yóu it will néver appróach.

⁸ Your éyes have ónly to lóok
to sée how the wícked are repáid.
⁹ For yóu, O LÓRD, are my réfuge.
You have máde the Most Hígh your dwélling.

¹⁰ Upon yóu no évil shall fáll,
no plágue appróach your tént.
¹¹ For yóu has he commánded his ángels
to kéep you in áll your wáys.

¹² They shall béar you upón their hánds,
lest you stríke your fóot against a stóne.
¹³ On the líon and the víper you will tréad,
and trámple the young líon and the sérpent.

¹⁴ Since he clíngs to me in lóve, I will frée him,
protéct him, for he knóws my náme.
¹⁵ When he cálls on mé, I will ánswer him;
I will bé with hím in distréss;
I will delíver him, and gíve him glóry.

¹⁶ With léngth of dáys I will contént him;
I will shów him my sáving pówer.

PRAYER

Almighty and Most High God, dwelling both in the highest heavens and in the lowly hearts of your people: deepen our trust in you, we pray, that we may recognize the power of your love and compassion in our lives, and so offer you all glory and praise forever. Amen.

Psalm 92

STILL FULL OF SAP, STILL GREEN

As the Psalmist here praises God for the wondrous works and intricate design of creation (v. 6), we can understand why Jewish synagogues assigned this prayer to the Sabbath, God's day of rest after the creation of the world. The Church continues to pray this psalm on Saturday mornings at the Liturgy of the Hours, acknowledging its original use in Judaism. The Psalmist begins by encouraging us to give thanks—both at the outset of the day (for God's loving mercy) and in the watches of the night (for God's faithfulness; v. 3), thus enclosing the waking day with words of gratitude to God. The Psalmist acknowledges that the experience of God's deeds is the source of joy and gladness (v. 5), asserting that it is only with spiritual insight, with wisdom, that one sees how the mysterious and surprising plan of God unfolds in human history (vv. 6–7). This wisdom is far deeper than what may be learned from books; such wisdom arises in reflecting upon the knowledge that our lives are lived always in the hands of our loving Creator. Having seen how wickedness recoils on those who bring forth evil (vv. 8–10), the Psalmist raises a personal confession of the marvelous ways God has touched his own experience, giving him a sense of personal strength in God's presence. The description of the just in verses 13–15 employs two familiar biblical images of beauty and strength: the palm tree and the cedar of Lebanon. On the one hand, the cedar of Lebanon recurs in the Scriptures as an icon of strength: its wood is solid, stable, and resistant to changes in humidity and temperature; it was used for many kinds of construction. Solomon built both his palace and the temple itself of Lebanon cedar. The palm tree, on the other hand, symbolized beauty with its sinuous trunk topped by a spray of large, symmetrical leaves. Palms maintain their splendor even in the hottest temperatures, when other plants begin to wither and die. The cedar of Lebanon and the palm tree are emblems of the strength and beauty of the just. Planted in God's temple (vv. 14–15), these people are outstanding among God's people; the wisdom God has given them manifests the path of blessing and peace. Even in old age, they are "still full of sap, still green" (v. 15). St. Paul encouraged his beloved Church at Philippi to live justly and righteously, as witnesses to others; his message still heartens us today. "Do all things without murmuring and arguing, so that you may be blameless and innocent, children of God without blemish in the midst of a crooked and perverse generation, in which you shine like stars in the world" (Phil 2:14–15).

PSALM 92 (91)

¹ A Psalm. A Song for the Sabbath.

² It is góod to give thánks to the LÓRD,
to make músic to your náme, O Most Hígh,
³ to procláim your loving mércy in the mórning,
and your trúth in the wátches of the níght,

⁴ on the tén-stringed lýre and the lúte,
with the sóund of sóng on the hárp.

⁵ You have gláddened me, O LORD, by your déeds;
for the wórk of your hánds I shout with jóy.
⁶ O LORD, how gréat are your wórks!
How déep are yóur desígns!
⁷ The sénseless cánnot knów this,
and the fóol cannót understánd.

⁸ Though the wícked spring úp like gráss,
and áll who do évil thríve,
they are dóomed to be etérnally destróyed.
⁹ But you, O LORD, are etérnally on hígh.

¹⁰ Sée, your énemies, O LORD,
sée, your énemies will pérish;
áll who do évil will be scáttered.

¹¹ To mé you give the wíld ox's stréngth;
you have poured óut on me púrest óil.
¹² My éyes looked in tríumph on my fóes;
my éars heard gládly of their fáll.
¹³ The júst will flóurish like the pálm tree,
and grów like a Lébanon cédar.

¹⁴ Plánted in the hóuse of the LORD,
they will flóurish in the cóurts of our Gód,
¹⁵ stíll bearing frúit when they are óld,
stíll full of sáp, still gréen,
¹⁶ to procláim that the LORD is úpright.
In hím, my róck, there is no wróng.

PRAYER

*LORD Most High, we offer you gratitude and praise for your provident
and loving presence, today and throughout our lives. Grant that we
may be counted among your just ones, so that in the strength and
beauty of your grace we may witness the wisdom of your saving plan
to the whole world. We ask this through Christ our Lord. Amen.*

Psalm 93

GREATER THAN MIGHTY WATERS

Psalm 93 might best be thought of as an acclamation of God's majesty, because of its brevity and the repeated rhetorical elements focused on God's divine and royal attributes. The text presents several repetitions: The LORD, The LORD (v. 1); enrobed, has robed (v. 1); made firm, stood firm (vv. 1d, 2); The floods have lifted up (v. 3); mighty waters, the sea (v. 4); more glorious, glorious (v. 4). These repetitions create a sense of shouted acclaim, much like a sporting event or political rally. They are addressed here to the LORD, whose power is endless (v. 5c) and whose might subdues the surging waters (v. 3). God's power over the flooding waters acclaimed here evokes the opening verses of the Book of Genesis that tell of the ancient and mythic waters of chaos, devoid of life, order, and harmony, possessing neither light nor beauty (1:1–2). Then God speaks a word and the darkness and disorder of chaos is banished (Gen 1:3). In the writings of the Ancient Near East, water has singular significance in that it both gives life and growth (as rain for crops or as drinking water for man and beast) and deals death (in floods, storms, or the raging of the oceans). This psalm praises the Lord God of Israel, Creator of the universe, for the mastery that the Almighty One exercises even over the waters of life and death. Their natural power, so threatening to us, presents no such threat to God. On the contrary, they only "lift up their thunder" at the will and decree of the One who brought them into being. It is significant for us to see that Jesus himself in his baptism enters the waters that represent for us the destructive power of sin and death but emerges to the sound of a heavenly voice "lifting up" a proclamation, "You are my Son, the Beloved; with you I am well pleased" (Mark 1:11). Jesus shows us that the chaos of darkness and sin in our lives is conquered through the grace of baptism. Our baptism draws us into the waters of sin and death, and we emerge cleansed, made whole, and formed into children of God. "Baptism...now saves you—not as a removal of dirt from the body, but as an appeal to God for a good conscience, through the resurrection of Jesus Christ, who has gone into heaven and is at the right hand of God, with angels, authorities, and powers made subject to him" (1 Pet 3:21–22). The waters thunder forth, acclaiming the power of Christ over sin and death and ushering us into the light and glory of God's reign in our world.

PSALM 93 (92)

¹ The LORD is kíng, with májesty enróbed.
The LORD has róbed himsélf with míght;
he has gírded himsélf with pówer.

The wórld you made fírm, not to be móved;
² your thróne has stood fírm from of óld.
From all etérnity, O LÓRD, you áre.

³ The flóods have lífted up, O LÓRD,
the flóods have lífted up their vóice;
the flóods have lífted up their thúnder.

⁴ Gréater than the róar of mighty wáters,
more glórious than the súrgings of the séa,
the LÓRD is glórious on hígh

⁵ Trúly your decrées are to be trústed.
Hóliness is fítting to your hóuse,
O LÓRD, until the énd of tíme.

PRAYER

O Lord, whose reign calls us to holiness of life, preserve us from the dark waters of sin and selfishness, and by the refreshing waters of baptism empower us to announce the message of your love and compassion to all who would follow the teaching of your Son, Jesus Christ, who is Lord, forever and ever. Amen.

Psalm 94

PEACE IN EVIL DAYS

To understand this psalm, the reader must imagine a courtroom scene. The Psalmist approaches God as Judge, repeatedly employing a title that helps to establish the theme of his suit: avenging God! (v. 1). The language of the psalm is harsh, judgmental, and tinged with anger: "Judge of the earth, give the proud what they deserve" (v. 2). The genuine frustration of the Psalmist with his situation is apparent in his rhetorically repetitive question, "How long, O LORD, shall the wicked, how long shall the wicked triumph?" (v. 3). Such repetitions are a common feature of Hebrew poetry, giving emphasis to the point at hand. In verses 5–8, he outlines the crimes of the wicked that God should scrutinize: they crush and humble God's people (v. 5), they murder widows, strangers, and orphans. To add force to his argument, he recounts the enemy's assumption of impunity: "God pays no attention, and will not interfere with our deeds" (v. 7). In verses 9–10, the Psalmist points out the folly of their attitude in a series of rhetorical questions about the God of Israel who sees all, hears all, and knows all; he rounds his argument with the assertion that not a single plan of anyone on earth goes unnoticed by the One who created and sustains all creation. In verse 12, the psalm changes perspective with "Blessed," pointing out by this term of beatitude where God's favor really falls—on the one who lives by the divine law and puts it into practice. The life of such an individual is marked by peace (v. 13), implying the Hebrew sense of the word, entailing well-being of body, mind, and spirit. This second half of the psalm is marked by statements of confidence, trust, and faith in the care that God gives to those who remain loyal to the divine law. The second half of the psalm also employs a series of rhetorical questions: "Who will stand up for me, defend me against those who do evil?" (v. 16). God, of course! "Can judges who do evil be counted among your friends?" (v. 20). Of course not! In verses 17–19, the Psalmist voices a tender expression of personal faith, describing how close and intimate his relationship with God continues to be. "When I lose my foothold, your mercy holds me up; when cares increase, your consolation is a balm for my soul" (vv. 18–19). The Psalmist's remark about "go[ing] down to the silence" (v. 17) is a reference to Sheol, the abode of the dead: without God's help, he is as good as dead. In

2 Corinthians 11–12, St. Paul recounts his personal trials in bringing the gospel message to others—beatings, shipwreck, stoning, and betrayals. Yet, like the Psalmist, he concludes with a declaration of utter trust and confidence in God's guidance, help, and protection. "I am content with weaknesses, insults, hardships, persecutions, and calamities for the sake of Christ; for whenever I am weak, then I am strong" (2 Cor 12:10). Trust and confidence in God lead us to experience the richest of God's saving grace.

PSALM 94 (93)

¹ O LÓRD, avénging Gód,
avénging Gód, shine fórth!
² Júdge of the éarth, aríse;
gíve the próud what they desérve!

³ How lóng, O LÓRD, shall the wícked,
how lóng shall the wícked tríumph?
⁴ They blúster with árrogant spéech;
those who do évil bóast to each óther.

⁵ They crúsh your péople, LÓRD;
and they húmble yóur inhéritance.
⁶ They kíll the wídow and the stránger,
and múrder the fátherless chíld.

⁷ And they sáy, "The LÓRD does not sée;
the God of Jácob páys no héed."
⁸ Mark thís, you sénseless péople;
fóols, when wíll you understánd?

⁹ Can he who plánted the éar not héar?
Can he who fórmed the éye not sée?
¹⁰ Will he who tráins the nátions not púnish?
Will he who téaches mán not have knówledge?
¹¹ The LÓRD knows the pláns of mán.
He knóws they are no móre than a bréath.

¹² Blessed the mán whom you díscipline, O LÓRD,
whom you tráin by méans of your láw;
¹³ to whóm you give péace in evil dáys,
while the pít is being dúg for the wícked.

¹⁴ The LÓRD will not abándon his péople,
nor forsáke thóse who are his héritage;

¹⁵ for júdgment shall agáin be júst,
and áll true héarts shall uphóld it.

¹⁶ Who will stand úp for me agáinst the wícked?
Who will defénd me from thóse who do évil?
¹⁷ If the LORD were nót to hélp me,
my soul would sóon go dówn to the sílence.

¹⁸ When I thínk, "I have lóst my fóothold,"
your mércy, O LORD, holds me úp.
¹⁹ When cáres incréase in my héart,
your consolátion cálms my sóul.

²⁰ Can júdges who do évil be your fríends?
They do injústice under cóver of láw;
²¹ they attáck the lífe of the júst,
and condémn the ínnocent to déath.

²² As for mé, the LORD will be a strónghold;
my Gód will be the róck where I take réfuge.
²³ Hé will repáy them for their wíckedness,
destróy them for their évil déeds.
The LORD, our Gód, will destróy them.

PRAYER

O God, rock of refuge and stronghold in times of distress, continue to manifest your unending compassion for all your creatures. Banish injustice among us, and strengthen us to be instruments of your righteousness, compassion, mercy, and kindness, to friend and enemy alike. In your holy name we pray. Amen.

Psalm 95

WORSHIP WITH
A WARNING

Psalm 95 holds a special place in the Church's tradition; it is the Invitatory Psalm for morning celebrations of the Liturgy of the Hours. The imperative "Come," appearing twice in the opening verses, serves as a call to worship. The Psalmist envisions a festive celebration marked by songs of joy and hymns of praise and thanksgiving, hailing the "rock who saves us" (v. 1). This image evokes the Exodus event, recalling the rock that provided sustenance and refreshment for the people in their desert journey to the land of promise (cf. Exod 17). The text then presents a series of images of God as Creator and ruler over all the gods. From the heights to the depths, God has brought all things into being: whether in the sea or on the dry land, all are creatures shaped by the divine hands (vv. 3–5). In verses 6–7, the Psalmist unites the themes of Creation and the Exodus. He first calls us once again to "come," to "bow and bend low" in an act of homage to the God who brought us into being. The subsequent reference to the "flock led by [God's] hand" draws us back into the whole Exodus experience, the wandering in the desert, the pilgrim journey to the land of promise. But in the next stanza, beginning at verse 7d, the mood changes from joyous acclamations of praise and thanks to serious words of warning and counsel about the future, not without an implicit threat of what will happen to those who stray. The Psalmist's earlier reference in verse 1 to the "rock" that saved the people now leads into a warning: despite having been saved in the desert by God's saving power, the people failed to respond in faith and neglected their responsibilities to the covenant relationship. God had protected and cared for them; they were expected to follow faithfully the Law that God had given them. But they didn't, and God's justice forbade the faithless generation to enter the land of promise: they died in the desert. The "hardening of the hearts" in verse 8 recalls their lack of faith in the midst of the journey. At Rephidim (Meribah and Massah), they thirsted for water and turned against the Lord; they complained against Moses and tested God's patience. In justice God punished them; this was to be a warning to later generations to stand firm in the faith, whatever the situation. The author of the Epistle to the Hebrews quotes this passage from Psalm 95, warning the early Christians about this outcome, calling them to greater faith in the midst of their trials. "Take care, brothers and sisters, that none of you may have an evil, unbelieving heart that turns away from the living God" (Heb 3:12). The second half of Psalm 95 warns that if we lift up worship to God, we must do so with the kind of living faith that springs from trust in God who created us and leads us, even as he led our ancestors in the faith, on the pilgrimage to the promised kingdom.

PSALM 95 (94)

¹ Come, let us ríng out our jóy to the LÓRD;
háil the róck who sáves us.
² Let us cóme into his présence, giving thánks;
let us háil him with a sóng of práise.

³ A míghty Gód is the LÓRD,
a great kíng abóve all góds.
⁴ In his hánds are the dépths of the éarth;
the héights of the móuntains are hís.
⁵ To hím belongs the séa, for he máde it,
and the dry lánd that he sháped by his hánds.

⁶ O cóme; let us bów and bend lów.
Let us knéel before the Gód who máde us,
⁷ for hé is our Gód and wé
the péople who belóng to his pásture,
the flóck that is léd by his hánd.

O that todáy you would lísten to his vóice!
⁸ "Hárden not your héarts as at Méribah,
as on that dáy at Mássah in the désert
⁹ when your fórebears pút me to the tést;
when they tríed me, though they sáw my wórk.

¹⁰ For forty yéars I wéaried of that generátion,
and I sáid, 'Their héarts are astráy;
this péople does not knów my wáys.'
¹¹ Thén I took an óath in my ánger,
'Néver shall they énter my rést.'"

PRAYER

God, our Creator and Guide, whose justice is eternal and whose mercy is everlasting, keep us always faithful to your covenant of love. Show us the way through the desert of our present existence, that we may one day enter the realm of your heavenly reign, where compassion and goodness hold sway. We ask this through Christ our Lord. Amen.

Psalm 96

THE LORD REIGNS WITH JUSTICE AND TRUTH

In an age when political situations and government actions dominate the news from all parts of the world, we hear too often of human fear, frustration, and dissatisfaction; such accounts often elicit the same feelings in us. Psalm 96 presents an approach to this endemic human experience that offers us a contrasting perspective of joy, hope, and fidelity; its message envisions a world governed on the basis of God's justice, equity, fairness, and truth. The psalm embodies the rhetoric and style of Hebrew poetry, communicating and highlighting the message through a particular rhetorical form: each stanza comprises three lines of text—a tricolon—rather than the more familiar two lines, or bicolon. These expanded stanzas enlarge and enhance the text, increasing the significance of the message and developing it thematically. What the Psalmist has to say about how wonderful the world is when governed by God is thus greatly increased. Three times at the outset we are told to "sing a new song to the LORD"; the second line adds the information that those called to sing include the whole world; the third expands their action to include "bless[ing] his name" in addition to singing. Then we are three times commanded to proclaim this wonder, "day after day," "among the nations," and "to all the peoples" (vv. 2b–3). This expanded style is employed through the entire psalm, up to a climactic five-line final stanza that fixes God's governance on divine principles of justice and truth. The phrase "all the gods" in verse 4 refers to the idea of a court of heavenly or angelic powers believed by the ancients to give direction to the movements of the world. But the God of Israel stands above these heavenly beings as the One who made the heavens and all they contain (v. 5b); this is why the heavens, the seas, and the land must rejoice (vv. 11–12a), for God's rule will bring justice and peace to all who follow the divine bidding. The Church uses this psalm at both Christmas and Easter, when the liturgy unfolds the mystery of the coming of Christ, whose rule embodies the new law of love and transcends all previous regulations and stipulations. The psalm announces the coming of God to judge the world in truth (v. 13); the advent of Christ ushers in the final age of the world, when Christ teaches both by word and example how God's law is to be lived, transforming the world by compassion, goodness, and charity toward all peoples—this is the message of Christmas hope. At Easter, the Church turns to verse 12b, which describes the "trees of the wood" shouting for joy at what has been accomplished through the wood of a tree. The wood of the cross brings an end to death and sin; from the cross Christ judges the world, showing that divine justice transcends human understandings of judgment and righteousness. The experience of suffering and death has become the pathway to eternal life. Psalm 96 beckons all creation to "sing a new song" of God's unspeakable love, which has brought about our redemption in a wondrous and mysterious way—through the resurrection accomplished in the victory of the cross.

PSALM 96 (95)

¹ O síng a new sóng to the LÓRD;
síng to the LÓRD, all the éarth.
² O síng to the LÓRD; bless his náme.

Procláim his salvátion day by dáy.
³ Téll among the nátions his glóry,
and his wónders amóng all the péoples.

⁴ For the LÓRD is great and híghly to be práised,
to be féared abóve all góds.
⁵ For the góds of the nátions are náught.

It was the LÓRD who máde the héavens.
⁶ In his présence are májesty and spléndor,
stréngth and hónor in his hóly place.

⁷ Give the LÓRD, you fámilies of péoples,
gíve the LORD glóry and pówer;
⁸ give the LÓRD the glóry of his náme.

Bring an óffering and énter his cóurts;
⁹ wórship the LÓRD in holy spléndor.
O trémble befóre him, all the éarth.

¹⁰ Say to the nátions, "The Lórd is kíng."
The wórld he made fírm in its pláce;
he will júdge the péoples in fáirness.

¹¹ Let the héavens rejóice and earth be glád;
let the séa and all withín it thunder práise.
¹² Let the lánd and all it béars rejoice.

Then will all the trées of the wóod shout for jóy
¹³ at the présence of the Lórd, for he cómes,
he cómes to júdge the éarth.
He will júdge the wórld with jústice;
he will góvern the péoples with his trúth.

PRAYER

*Lord of majesty and splendor, justice and truth, we praise you for your
salvation, wondrous and mysterious, poured out on the whole world.
Grant that our worship may always arise from sincere hearts. May we
witness it by our lives, and so give glory to your holy name. We ask this
through Christ our Lord. Amen.*

Psalm 97

THE JOY AND BLESSING
OF JUSTICE

Psalm 97 is bracketed by rejoicing: it begins with a call for the whole earth
to rejoice (v. 1), and concludes with a command for the just to rejoice in
the Lord, who reigns over heaven and earth (v. 12). Three themes unfold
as we read through this psalm: the theophany of God's majesty (vv. 2–6),
the contrast of those who serve idols to faithful Judah (vv. 6–9), and the
blessings of the just (vv. 10–12). The opening verses evoke the people's
experience at Sinai, when God entered into covenant with Moses and the
Israelites. In the Book of Exodus, we read, "On the morning of the third
day there was thunder and lightning, as well as a thick cloud on the moun-

tain, and a blast of a trumpet so loud that all the people who were in the camp trembled....Now Mount Sinai was wrapped in smoke, because the LORD had descended upon it in fire; the smoke went up like the smoke of a kiln, while the whole mountain shook violently. As the blast of the trumpet grew louder and louder, Moses would speak and God would answer him in thunder" (19:16–17, 19). This language depicts a divine event; God's presence calls forth a forceful response from nature, so the natural world erupts in violent acclaim, as if to sweep away any act of worship not directed to the one true God. Yet such a reaction comes not merely because the God of Israel is great, but even more because God's *deeds* are great: God acts always in justice and uprightness (vv. 2, 6, 8, 11, 12). When the Psalmist says that "justice and right are the foundation of [God's] throne" (v. 2), he declares the manner of rule that is the hallmark of the Lord's reign. The One who is justice and righteousness itself, eternally upright and sound in judgment, carries out that which is inherent in the divine nature. Thus, acts on behalf of the poor and the needy, the creation of just laws, and equity of judgment all manifest how God reigns, and furthermore establish the expectation of similar deeds from those who are God's chosen people. Thus the reason for rejoicing on the part of the just is made clear, for the One whom they imitate is the One who protects and frees them (v. 10), granting them joy and the light of salvation (v. 11). Jesus says the same thing in the Sermon on the Mount (though without the accompanying natural fireworks) when he gives us the invitation, "Strive first for the kingdom of God and his righteousness, and all these things will be given to you as well" (Matt 6:33). The foundation of God's kingdom demands justice and righteousness, and invites us, God's people, to participate in the building up of God's reign upon earth.

PSALM 97 (96)

¹ The LORD is kíng, let éarth rejóice;
let the mány íslands be glád.
² Clóud and dárkness surróund him;
justice and ríght are the foundátion of his thróne.

³ A fíre prepáres his páth;
it búrns up his fóes on every síde.
⁴ His líghtnings líght up the wórld;
the éarth looks ón and trémbles.

⁵ The móuntains mélt like wáx
befóre the fáce of the LÓRD,
before the fáce of the Lórd of all the éarth.

⁶ The skíes procláim his jústice;
all péoples sée his glóry.

⁷ Let thóse who serve ídols be ashámed,
those who bóast of their wórthless góds.
All you ángels, wórship hím.

⁸ Síon héars and is glád;
the dáughters of Júdah rejóice
becáuse of your júdgments, O LÓRD.

⁹ For yóu indéed are the LÓRD,
most hígh above áll the éarth,
exálted fár above all góds.

¹⁰ The LÓRD loves thóse who hate évil;
he guárds the sóuls of his fáithful;
he séts them frée from the wícked.

¹¹ Líght shines fórth for the júst one,
and jóy for the úpright of héart.
¹² Rejóice in the LÓRD, you júst;
to the mémory of his hóliness give thánks.

PRAYER

*O just and righteous Lord, who bestow a father's care for each and
every creature you have made, increase in us the sincere desire to imitate your goodness and to witness to the true joy that comes with
uprightness of heart, through Christ our Lord. Amen.*

Psalm 98

A NEW SONG OF PRAISE

Almost everyone is familiar with the Christmas carol, "Joy to the World."
Psalm 98 served as the inspiration for the text; its closing verses speak

of God's coming (v. 9), making "heaven and nature sing" with joy at this glorious event (vv. 7–8). At the same time, the deepest meaning of the psalm is salvation itself; three times the Psalmist explicitly remarks on God's salvation breaking into our world (vv. 1, 2, 3), an unmatchable occasion for joy. While we often think of salvation in terms of life-altering events, the biblical mind also appreciates salvation in the less spectacular ways that characterize God's continual care, protection, and fidelity toward his chosen ones. In verse 3, the Psalmist indicates that merciful love (*hesed*) and truth/faithfulness (*emeth*) constitute our reason for the kind of joy that is manifested in songs (v. 4), psalms on the harp (v. 5), and the blare of trumpets (v. 6). Whether this praise emerges as a consequence of rescue from the nations in their very sight (vv. 2, 3cd), or as an experience of God's justice (v. 9cd) toward an individual or the house of Israel (v. 3), such an encounter with God always changes life for the better. Though not readily apparent in English translation, the terminology indicates that this particular event deserves more than mere mention. The "horn" of verse 6a is the Hebrew *shofar*, the instrument used to announce great feasts or other important events. This, then, is the reason the psalm begins with the expression "Sing a new song": a fresh and original act of God has taken place. The event calls for a new song, a new account of God's faithful and compassionate love. The situation is not locked in the past; it can be true for us also. Whether it be healing from a serious illness, the end of a long conflict in our lives, the long-awaited answer to a prayer, an unexpected and life-altering blessing—any or all of these experiences call forth from us a response to God's grace in the events of our lives. St. Paul's words about his experience on the road to Damascus and the consequences of that event fit the circumstances: "When God, who had set me apart before I was born and called me through his grace, was pleased to reveal his Son to me, so that I might proclaim him among the Gentiles....[The people] only heard it said, 'The one who formerly was persecuting us is now proclaiming the faith he once tried to destroy.' And they glorified God because of me" (Gal 1:15–16, 23–24). St. Paul never stopped singing the "new song" of God's marvelous love for him. Let us look deep into our own hearts to find there the faithful love of God, that we may sing our own "new song" of praise, thanksgiving, and joy.

PSALM 98 *(97)*

[1] *A Psalm.*

O síng a new sóng to the LÓRD,
for hé has worked wónders.
His right hánd and his hóly árm
have bróught salvátion.

² The LORD has made knówn his salvátion,
has shówn his delíverance to the nátions.
³ He has remémbered his mérciful lóve
and his trúth for the hóuse of Ísrael.

All the énds of the éarth have séen
the salvátion of our Gód.
⁴ Shóut to the LORD, all the éarth;
break fórth into jóyous sóng,
and síng out your práise.

⁵ Sing psálms to the LORD with the hárp,
with the hárp and the sóund of sóng.
⁶ With trúmpets and the sóund of the hórn,
raise a shóut before the Kíng, the LORD.

⁷ Let the séa and all withín it thúnder;
the wórld, and thóse who dwéll in it.
⁸ Let the rívers cláp their hánds,
and the hílls ring out their jóy
⁹ at the présence of the LORD, for he cómes,
he comes to júdge the éarth.

He will júdge the wórld with jústice,
and the péoples with fáirness.

PRAYER

O God, eternal and true, whose faithful love is without end, help us always to sing a new song of your compassion, fidelity, and wisdom, so that we might unite with all creation in joyous and grateful acclamation of your salvation, through Christ our Lord. Amen.

Psalm 99

HOLY IS THE LORD OUR GOD

The word *holy* connotes a sense of awe, mystery, and wonder, especially in the Scriptures. Holiness (*qadosh* in Hebrew) is a quality of something or someone who is wholly other in nature, set apart from other things or beings. In the Eucharistic Prayer, the community acclaims, "Holy, holy, holy Lord God of hosts," singing at that sacred moment the words of the seraphim recorded in the Book of Isaiah: finding himself in the presence of the Most Holy LORD, the prophet hears this angelic chant as God calls him to become the mouthpiece of the Holy One to a people blind in faith (cf. Isa 6). Three times Psalm 99 attests God's holiness (vv. 3, 5, 9), each time presenting a distinct perspective on this divine attribute. The first acclamation of God's holiness (v. 3b) is presented in language bespeaking majesty and fear: peoples tremble and the earth quakes as God is enthroned on the angelic cherubim. God rules as King over peoples and nations, bringing order and harmony to the whole created world. The great God who at Sinai revealed to Moses the divine name YHWH is acclaimed and honored in Sion by all the people (v. 2). This praise of God's name as great and awesome leads to the first affirmation: Holy is he! (v. 3). In verses 4–5, holiness is presented under a different aspect. Here God is described as a lover of justice, foundation of all that is upright, source of righteousness among his people, the descendants of Jacob (v. 4). God's holiness is rendered tangible and distinct in his relationship to the people he has chosen as his own: God acts toward them with righteousness, uprightness, and justice, so they are called to act thus toward one another. God's justice is present in the world through all who are in truth the people of God. The third account of the divine holiness (vv. 6–8) casts it in God's relationship with significant leaders (Aaron, Moses, and Samuel) who had mediated between God and the people. To "invoke the name" of the LORD (v. 6) means to speak to God in prayer; to share a direct communion with the God who is wholly other (v. 6ab). Forgiveness is here recognized as a constituent of divine holiness (v. 8). A God who forgives is merciful and compassionate; yet, the text reminds us, God is also just, and sin calls for punishment. In the Canticle of Zechariah, we are reminded that as God has rescued us, saved us, and freed us in Christ—who bore our punishment—

so we are called to a life of godly holiness (Luke 1:74–75). Psalm 99 tells us that such holiness is founded in the practice of justice and forgiveness. As God has shown us the way in Jesus Christ, so we are to follow the path of holiness—praising God with lives characterized by merciful love and faithful righteousness.

PSALM 99 *(98)*

¹ The LORD is kíng; the péoples trémble.
He is enthróned on the chérubim; earth quákes.
² The LÓRD is gréat in Síon.
He is exálted over áll the péoples.

³ Let them práise your gréat and awesome náme.
Hóly ís hé!
⁴ O mighty Kíng, lóver of jústice,
you have estáblished whát is úpright;
you have made jústice and ríght in Jácob.

⁵ Exált the LÓRD our Gód;
bow dówn befóre his fóotstool.
Hóly ís hé!

⁶ Amóng his príests were Áaron and Móses;
among thóse who invóked his náme was Sámuel.
They cried óut to the LÓRD and he ánswered.

⁷ To them he spóke in the píllar of clóud.
They obéyed his decrées and the státutes
which hé had gíven thém.

⁸ O LÓRD our Gód, you ánswered them.
For thém you were a Gód who forgíves,
and yét you púnished their offénses.

⁹ Exált the LÓRD our Gód;
bow dówn before his hóly móuntain,
for the LÓRD our Gód is hóly.

PRAYER

Holy God, holy and immortal One, to you be praise and glory, honor and thanksgiving, wisdom, power, and all blessing; for in knowing your holiness we have known your goodness and mercy, compassion and peace. To you we lift up our grateful hearts, acclaiming you through Christ, your Son and our Lord, for ever and ever. Amen.

Psalm 100

FAITHFUL FROM AGE TO AGE

This is another psalm that has become an English hymn: Psalm 100 is the basis for "Praise God from Whom All Blessings Flow," which draws even the name of its familiar tune ("The Old One Hundredth") from the psalm. As short as it is, there is much contained in the few verses of this psalm. We have noted before that the number seven has a particular significance in the Scriptures. Psalm 100 contains seven imperative verbal phrases: Cry out with joy (v. 1), Serve the LORD (v. 2a), Come before him, singing for joy (v. 2b), Know the LORD is God (v. 3a), Enter his gates (v. 4a), Give thanks (v. 4c), and Bless his name (v. 4c). Each of these presents a different way of coming into the divine presence for proper worship. As noted previously, Psalms 93 and 95—99 focus on the reign of God as King: King of his people, King over the nations, King over all the heavenly powers. Here in Psalm 100, the kingship of God is presented in a subtle yet singularly important metaphor: God's people are the sheep of his flock (v. 3c). In the Scriptures, the image of the shepherd is applied to kingship numerous times. From the beginning of the monarchy, when David came forth from his task as keeper of flocks, the kingship modeled by God for his earthly rulers was likened to the immediate and personal care a shepherd gives his flock. In verse 5, God's goodness is communicated in the words "merciful love" (*hesed*) and "faithfulness": these terms are understood to refer to a covenant relationship. God's eternal and faithful love demands a similar response from those who would be his people. This understanding remains an important truth of our own worship, our praise and thanksgiving to God. How often the prophets reminded the people that when they come to the temple to offer gratitude and honor to God, their acts of worship must arise from hearts given over to the following of God's commands. Their worship is to be an external sign of the disposition of their hearts, formed in love of God and neighbor. To know "how good is the LORD" (v. 5) calls for a response, and words of praise are not sufficient in themselves. Jesus makes this quite explicit in the Sermon on the Mount: "When you are offering your gift at the altar, if you remember that your brother or sister has something against you, leave your gift there before the altar and go; first be reconciled to your brother or sister, and then come and offer your gift" (Matt 5:23–24). Our truest praise and thanksgiving to God comes from a pure heart coupled with kind and loving deeds.

PSALM 100 (99)

¹ *A Psalm of Thanksgiving.*

Cry out with jóy to the LÓRD, all the éarth.
² Sérve the LÓRD with gládness.
Come befóre him, sínging for jóy.

³ Know that hé, the LÓRD, is Gód.
He máde us; we belóng to hím.
We are his péople, the shéep of his flóck.

⁴ Énter his gátes with thanksgíving
and his cóurts with sóngs of práise.
Give thánks to him, and bléss his náme.

⁵ Indéed, how góod is the LÓRD,
etérnal his mérciful lóve.
He is fáithful from áge to áge.

PRAYER

O God, who in merciful love and fidelity nourish the hearts of your people, show us the way to worship in spirit and in truth, that all we say and do may be fitting praise and gratitude to your most holy name. We ask this through Christ our Lord. Amen.

Psalm 101

THE WAY OF INTEGRITY

Psalm 101 is both a prayer and a statement of purpose by someone (probably a king or other leader in Israel) whose responsibilities extend beyond his own home to include both the people of the land (v. 6) and Jerusalem, the city of the LORD (v. 8c). In the opening stanza, the Psalmist sets the stage for what is to follow by acclaiming merciful love (Hebrew *hesed*) and justice (Hebrew *mishpat*) as foundations for a life of integrity. In verse 2b, the enigmatic question is put forth: "O when will you come to me?" Several interpretations are possible, but it seems most likely that the poet expresses here that he needs God's help to live a life of justice, mercy, and integrity; any frail human who claims to walk with a blameless heart does so only by a power beyond his own. How is this to be done? Note that the word *heart* appears three times in this psalm: a blameless heart (v. 2c), the false-hearted (v. 4a) and haughty heart (v. 5c). In the biblical world, the heart was not usually seen as the seat of emotions, as it is today. Rather, "heart" is a combination of intellect, will, and desire. So what the Psalmist sees as important is interior truthfulness, honor, and uprightness. If one's heart is lacking in truth (v. 4a) and is steeped in haughtiness (v. 5c), there is no way for the virtues of justice and mercy to guide one's decisions and actions. The Psalmist expresses this forcefully in the contrasting terms that follow each of the "heart" statements. To walk with a blameless heart (v. 2c) means that you cannot be preoccupied with base things (v. 3ab); similarly, the false-hearted person (v. 4) who slanders another will be silenced (v. 5). And again, the person who walks in the way of the blameless shall find a place in his house as a servant (v. 6cd) because his heart is not haughty (v. 5c). Many of us might admit a twinge of conscience reading this psalm, knowing that we often fail to put into deeds the kind of justice and mercy that we see exemplified in the person of Jesus, whose deeds flowed from a rightly disposed heart. Yet this psalm might be taken as a goad to keep us attentive to the ways we think and act, and perhaps even more important, how we listen to the Spirit that dwells within us, inviting us to become living examples of the gospel. St. Paul writes of this inner conflict in his letter to the Romans: "I do not understand my own actions. For I do not do what I want, but I do the very thing I hate" (7:15). Each decision we make continues to form us as a person. Let us work to see the gospel come to life in us by the grace of the risen Christ, given each of us in our baptism.

PSALM 101 *(100)*

¹ *Of David. A Psalm.*

I sing of mérciful lóve and jústice;
I raise a psálm to yóu, O LÓRD.
² I will pónder the wáy of the blámeless.
O whén will you cóme to mé?

I will wálk with blámeless héart
withín my hóuse;
³ I will not sét befóre my éyes
whatéver is báse.

I háte the déeds of the cróoked;
Í will have nóne of it.
⁴ The false-héarted must kéep far awáy;
I will knów no évil.

⁵ Whoever slánders a néighbor in sécret
I will bríng to sílence.
Proud éyes and háughty héart
I will néver endúre.

⁶ My éyes are on the fáithful of the lánd,
that they may dwéll with mé.
The one who wálks in the wáy of the blámeless
shall bé my sérvant.

⁷ Nó one who práctices decéit
shall líve within my hóuse.
Óne who útters líes
shall not stánd before my éyes.

⁸ Morning by mórning Í will destróy
all the wícked in the lánd,
upróoting from the cíty of the LÓRD
áll who do évil.

PRAYER

*Lord of truth and justice, who by your Holy Spirit guide us in the ways
of uprightness and mercy, strengthen us in our journey, that we may
walk in the paths of humility and integrity as authentic witnesses to
the power of the gospel of your Son, Jesus Christ, who is Lord, forever
and ever. Amen.*

Psalm 102
A HEART, DRIED UP
LIKE THE GRASS

The Hebrew poetry of this psalm draws upon images of ordinary life to
give shape to a personal experience of suffering, a sense of divine
absence, and long-enduring misery. Expressions like "My heart is with-
ered like the grass" (v. 5) reveal the depth of the speaker's distress; the
plea for God "not to hide his face" bespeaks the longing for closeness
with the One who alone can alleviate the present sorrow (v. 3). The
image of a bird alone and moaning on a roof (v. 8) suggests a personal
anguish so deep that the cry for relief is beyond the power of words to
express. In addition to these illustrative figures, the Psalmist draws on
notions of time to demonstrate how utterly different is his situation
from that of God's. The Psalmist writes about "the day of my distress"
(v. 3), "my days are vanishing like smoke" (v. 4), "my days are like a fading shadow" (v. 12). In contrast to this, God dwells in eternity, beyond
the limits of time and place that define the Psalmist's distress: "But you,
O Lord, are enthroned forever, and your renown is from age to age" (v.
13). From the stooped posture of pain and grief, the Psalmist implores
God, almost as if to ask that some measure of eternity's bliss might be
spared to give him the comfort that will reverse his woeful condition.
His pain is chronic, unrelenting; the multiplicity of images itself
becomes a cry to God for relief. And while the opening verses (2–12)
focus on an expression of an individual's torment, they are followed by
a representation of a like situation for daughter Sion, the whole people
(vv. 14–23). The Psalmist has a close relationship with the Holy City,

Sion or Jerusalem. Sion's circumstances of distress and anguish are identical to the Psalmist's own. The very stones and dust move the speaker to pity, so great is the city's need for divine healing and comfort (v. 15). We can speculate about whether this psalm might have originated in a period of enemy occupation or exile, considering its reference to prisoners and those condemned to die (v. 21), or to the helpless whose prayers God alone can answer (v. 18). How might we pray this psalm today? Certainly its words can draw us into prayer for the many people in our world today whose lives are burdened by war, captivity, exile, poverty, or disease—ills that they themselves have no power to change. In verse 23, the Psalmist looks to that day when those dispersed by such suffering will be gathered again as one people, joyful in their praise to God for rescue and liberation; what gratitude will then burst forth from those who know the saving hand of our good and merciful God. Let us unite ourselves in solidarity with those who suffer: our brothers and sisters in the human family, all children of one God. In our world today, innumerable people have legitimate reasons to pray these words of sorrow, but cannot; we can be their voice before God, who, we trust, will hear and answer.

PSALM 102 (101)

¹ *Prayer of someone afflicted who is weary and pours out his trouble to the Lord.*

² O LÓRD, héar my práyer,
and let my crý come to yóu.
³ Do not híde your fáce from mé
in the dáy of my distréss.
Túrn your éar towards mé;
on the dáy when I cáll,
spéedily ánswer me.

⁴ For my dáys are vánishing like smóke;
my bónes burn awáy like a fúrnace.
⁵ My heart is wíthered and dried úp like the gráss.
I forgét to éat my bréad.
⁶ Becáuse of the sóund of my gróaning,
my skín clíngs to my bónes.

⁷ I have becóme like a vúlture in the désert,
like an ówl amóng the rúins.
⁸ I líe awáke and I móan,
like a bírd alóne on a róof.

⁹ All day lóng my fóes revíle me;
those who deríde me use my náme as a cúrse.

¹⁰ I have éaten áshes like bréad,
and míngled téars with my drínk.
¹¹ Becáuse of your ánger and fúry,
you have lífted me úp and thrown me dówn.
¹² My dáys are like a fáding shádow,
and I wíther awáy like the gráss.

¹³ But you, O LÓRD, are enthróned foréver,
and your renówn is from áge to áge.

¹⁴ You will aríse and take píty on Síon,
for thís is the tíme to have mércy;
yes, the tíme appóinted has cóme.
¹⁵ Behold, your sérvants lóve her very stónes,
are móved to píty for her dúst.

¹⁶ The nátions shall féar the náme of the LÓRD,
and áll the earth's kíngs your glóry.
¹⁷ When the LÓRD shall buíld up Síon,
he will appéar in áll his glóry.
¹⁸ Then he will túrn to the práyers of the hélpless;
he will nót despíse their práyers.

¹⁹ Let this be wrítten for áges to cóme,
that a péople yet unbórn may praise the LÓRD;
²⁰ The LORD looked dówn from his hóly place on hígh,
looked dówn from héaven to the éarth,
²¹ to héar the gróans of the prísoners,
and frée those condémned to díe.

²² May the náme of the LÓRD be procláimed in Síon,
and his práise in Jerúsalem,
²³ when péoples and kíngdoms are gáthered as óne
to óffer their wórship to the LÓRD.

²⁴ He has bróken my stréngth in midcóurse;
he has shórtened my dáys.
²⁵ I say: "My Gód, do not táke me awáy
before hálf of my dáys are compléte,
you, whose dáys last from áge to áge.

²⁶ Long agó you fóunded the éarth,
and the héavens are the wórk of your hánds.
²⁷ They will pérish but yóu will remáin.
They will áll wear óut like a gárment.
You will chánge them like clóthes, and they chánge.
²⁸ But yóu are the sáme, and your yéars do not énd."

²⁹ The chíldren of your sérvants shall dwéll untróubled,
and their descéndants estáblished befóre you.

PRAYER

O God, whose years are endless and whose goodness is unchanging, be mindful of all who call out to you from lives broken by sorrow. Help us, too, to be mindful of these, our brothers and sisters in Christ, who lives and reigns with you and the Holy Spirit, one God, forever and ever. Amen.

Psalm 103

HEALER OF EVERY ILL

What an unimaginable thought: God does not treat us according to our faults! All too often our notions reduce God to the role of divine Judge whose stern and exacting justice fills us with dread. Psalm 103 lauds our God as the One who forgives, heals, and redeems, whose justice is tempered by compassion and mercy (vv. 3–6). This psalm begins and concludes with the command to "bless the LORD," which means to offer praise in the understanding of the Hebrew term. The opening stanza of Psalm 103 conveys a very personal sense of profound gratitude and praise: the word *soul* (in Hebrew, *nephesh*) refers to a human being's vital element, that inner force that sustains one's life and energy. The Psalmist calls on that vital source within, and expands his summons to include "all within me," commanding his whole being to "bless [God's] holy name." The previous psalm (Psalm 102) clearly expressed the biblical awareness of both the frailty of the human person and the power and strength of God. This psalm, too, employs the image of fragile and insubstantial grass as an image of our human condition before God, standing against the wind only briefly before disappearing (vv. 15–16). What saves us in our weakness is God's enduring mercy (v. 17). The frequent repetition of the term *mercy* (in Hebrew, *hesed*) throughout the psalm (vv. 4b, 8b, 11b, 17a) is noteworthy. The term specifically signifies God's covenant love, faithful and enduring. The Psalmist describes God's loving mercy in terms of spatial expansiveness: "As the heavens are high above the earth, so strong his mercy for those who fear him. As far as the east is from the west, so far from us does he remove our transgressions" (vv. 11–12). The Psalmist's paean to God's mercy climaxes in the image of a father's care for his child (v. 13); the word translated here as "compassion" derives from a Hebrew root referring to the inner organs, the bowels, which were held to be the seat of human emotions. The English word *visceral* and the informal idiom, "He feels it in his guts," convey the same sense: these feelings and affections arise from deep within. This divine mercy flows from the covenant relationship we share with God (v. 18); our willingness to follow the divine teaching manifests our response to God's loving care for us. As this psalm comes to a close, what began with an individual call to the self now becomes a summons to all creation, all God's works, and even the heavenly host: "Bless the LORD" (vv. 21–22). Jesus knew fully the meaning of his Father's mercy and compassion: in the parable of the father and his two sons (Luke 15), the father's response to his wayward son—quite atypical of Middle Eastern culture, by the way—is the image of God's fatherly care: "While he was still far off, his father saw him and was filled with compassion; he ran and put his arms around him and kissed him" (Luke 15:20). Psalm 103 is an apt and sensitive prayer to accompany our reading of Luke 15.

PSALM 103 *(102)*

¹ *Of David.*

Bléss the LÓRD, O my sóul,
and all withín me, his hóly náme.
² Bléss the LÓRD, O my sóul,
and néver forgét all his bénefits.

³ It is the Lórd who forgíves all your síns,
who héals every óne of your ílls,
⁴ who redéems your lífe from the gráve,
who crówns you with mércy and compássion,
⁵ who fílls your lífe with good thíngs,
renéwing your yóuth like an éagle's.

⁶ The LÓRD does júst déeds,
gives full jústice to áll who are oppréssed.
⁷ He made knówn his wáys to Móses,
and his déeds to the chíldren of Ísrael.

⁸ The LÓRD is compássionate and grácious,
slow to ánger and rích in mércy.
⁹ Hé will not álways find fault,
nor persíst in his ánger foréver.
¹⁰ He does not tréat us accórding to our síns,
nor repáy us accórding to our fáults.

¹¹ For as the héavens are hígh above the éarth,
so strong his mércy for thóse who féar him.
¹² As fár as the éast is from the wést,
so far from ús does he remóve our transgréssions.

¹³ As a fáther has compássion on his chíldren,
the LORD's compássion is on thóse who féar him.
¹⁴ For he knóws of whát we are máde;
he remémbers that wé are dúst.

¹⁵ Mán, his dáys are like gráss;
he flówers like the flówer of the fíeld.
¹⁶ The wind blóws, and it ís no móre,
and its pláce never sées it agáin.

¹⁷ But the mércy of the LÓRD is everlásting
upon thóse who hóld him in féar,
upon chíldren's chíldren his jústice,
¹⁸ for thóse who kéep his cóvenant,
and remémber to fulfíll his commánds.

¹⁹ The LORD has fíxed his thróne in héaven,
and his kíngdom is rúling over áll.
²⁰ Bless the LÓRD, all yóu his ángels,
mighty in pówer, fulfílling his wórd,
who héed the vóice of his wórd.

²¹ Bléss the LÓRD, all his hósts,
his sérvants, who dó his wíll.
²² Bléss the LÓRD, all his wórks,
in évery pláce where he rúles.
Bléss the LÓRD, O my sóul!

God of infinite mercy and compassion, who never fail to extend to us a love beyond what we can expect or merit, enable us in faith to discern and acknowledge your loving kindness, so that we, in turn, may be instruments of that same mercy to others. We ask this through Christ our Lord. Amen.

Psalm 104

THE PROVIDENT CREATOR

In only two places in the Psalms does the expression "Bless the LORD, O my soul" appear: in the previous psalm (Ps 103:1, 22) and in this one (104:1, 35). With these words the speaker directs the deepest recesses of his own being to lift up fitting praise and thanks to God, first for the compassionate mercy that God pours forth on all creation (Ps 103), and then in this psalm for the wonders of creation itself. Here the Psalmist acknowledges the marvelous order and harmony in creation, surveying the innumerable wonders that manifested the stability of the universe to the ancients. God has orchestrated this in all its beauty and wonder, first having brought it into being and now sustaining it with supreme wisdom. From the perspective of the Psalmist, there is nothing in our created world that has not been given its proper place and purpose. Springs of water provide drink for animals (vv. 10–11); green plants nourish both cattle and human beings (v. 14), providing for the latter the means to produce bread, wine, and oil as well (vv. 14–15). All this comes from the one Lord of creation, whose glory is vividly recounted (vv. 1–2). Even the most expansive components of nature—mountains, valleys, seas—are situated and directed by God (vv. 5–9); they take their place and fulfill their purpose at the divine command. And the great luminaries of the sky, the sun and the moon themselves, are fitted to God's design: they give light and warmth for growth, and they mark out the days and seasons, telling beasts of prey when to hunt and human beings when to labor (vv. 19–23). Then, as if in acclamation of all he has contemplated, the Psalmist's words burst forth: "How many are your works, O LORD! In wisdom you have made them all. The earth is full of your creatures" (v. 24). God's wisdom is apparent in all creation, and we are called to ponder ever more deeply the world around, absorbing the wisdom it presents and responding with both awe and gratitude for what we daily encounter. The Psalmist affirms that everything comes from God who is the source of life, goodness, hope, and looks to God for its ongoing sustenance and support (vv. 27–32); only thus may God's will for the human family be carried out in peace and harmony. Finding an even fuller meaning for such an outlook, St. Paul witnesses in a profound expression of faith to the wonder of the new creation accomplished in Christ: "I pray that you may have the power to comprehend, with all the saints, what is the breadth and length and height and depth, and to know the love of Christ that surpasses knowledge, so that you may be filled with all the fullness of God" (Eph 3:14–19). May we possess the wisdom to look upon God's creation with such wonder, awe, and faith!

PSALM 104 *(103)*

¹ Bléss the LÓRD, O my sóul!
O LORD my Gód, how gréat you áre,
clóthed in májesty and hónor,
² wrápped in líght as with a róbe!

You strétch out the héavens like a tént.
³ On the wáters you estáblish your dwélling.
You máke the clóuds your cháriot;
you ríde on the wíngs of the wínd.
⁴ You máke the wínds your méssengers,
fláme and fíre your sérvants.

⁵ You sét the éarth on its foundátion,
immóvable from áge to áge.
⁶ You wrápped it with the dépths like a clóak;
the wáters stood hígher than the móuntains.
⁷ At your thréat they tóok to flíght;
at the vóice of your thúnder they fléd.

⁸ The mountains róse, the válleys descénded,
to the pláce which yóu had appóinted them.
⁹ You set límits they míght not páss,
lest they retúrn to cóver the éarth.

¹⁰ You make spríngs gush fórth in the válleys;
they flów in betwéen the hílls.

¹¹ They give drínk to all the béasts of the field;
the wild ásses quénch their thírst.
¹² There the bírds of héaven build their nésts;
from the bránches they síng their sóng.

¹³ From your dwélling you wáter the hílls;
by your wórks the éarth has its fíll.

¹⁴ You máke the grass grów for the cáttle
and plánts to sérve mankind's need,
That he may bríng forth bréad from the éarth
¹⁵ and wíne to chéer the héart;
óil, to máke faces shíne,
and bread to stréngthen the héart of mán.

¹⁶ The trées of the LÓRD drink their fíll,
the cédars he plánted on Lébanon;
¹⁷ thére the bírds build their nésts;
on the tréetop the stórk has her hóme.
¹⁸ For the góats the lófty móuntains,
for the rábbits the rócks are a réfuge.

¹⁹ You made the móon to márk the mónths;
the sún knows the tíme for its sétting.
²⁰ You spréad the dárkness, it is níght,
and all the béasts of the fórest creep fórth.
²¹ The young líons róar for their préy,
and séek their fóod from Gód.

²² At the rísing of the sún they gáther;
and they gó to lie dówn in their déns.
²³ Mán goes fórth to his wórk,
to lábor till évening fálls.

²⁴ How mány are your wórks, O LÓRD!
In wísdom you have máde them áll.
The éarth is fúll of your créatures.

²⁵ Vast and wíde is the spán of the séa,
with its créeping thíngs past cóunting,
líving things gréat and smáll.
²⁶ The shíps are móving thére,
and Levíathan you máde to pláy with.

²⁷ Áll of these lóok to yóu
to gíve them their fóod in due séason.
²⁸ You gíve it, they gáther it úp;
you ópen wide your hánd, they are well fílled.

²⁹ You híde your fáce, they are dismáyed;
you táke away their bréath, they díe,
retúrning to the dúst from which they cáme.
³⁰ You sénd forth your spírit, and théy are creáted,
and you renéw the fáce of the éarth.

³¹ May the glóry of the LORD last foréver!
May the LORD rejóice in his wórks!
³² He lóoks on the éarth and it trémbles;
he tóuches the móuntains and they smóke.

³³ I will síng to the LORD all my lífe,
sing psálms to my Gód while I líve.
³⁴ May my thóughts be pléasing to hím.
Í will rejóice in the LORD.

³⁵ Let sínners vánish from the éarth,
and the wícked exíst no móre.
Bléss the LORD, O my sóul.

Alleluia!

PRAYER

O God, our Creator and Redeemer, wondrous are your works, mar-
velous your deeds, and awesome your plan for our salvation. Enliven
our faith, that with the eyes of our heart we may gaze upon the marvels
of creation, and fittingly respond by lives of goodness and compassion.
Through Christ our Lord. Amen.

Psalm 105

THE FAITHFUL GOD WHO
REMEMBERS HIS PROMISE

Following upon the inspired description of creation in Psalm 104, Psalms 105 and 106 offer the story of salvation history in poetic form. At the heart of this account is a sense of God's fidelity to those chosen as the people of God. God is mindful of the covenant initiated with Abraham (v. 8), a promise that the people have not forgotten. The Psalmist thus begins with a call for the people of Israel to offer thanksgiving to God and also to make it known to the nations what God has done for them (v. 1). Israel's recollection is not to be a boast but rather an occasion for calling to mind all that God has done in the past, is doing now, and will continue to do in the future for the chosen people. A large segment of Psalm 105 is found in 1 Chronicles 16, where David leads the congregation in praising God on the occasion of the return of the Ark of the Covenant to its tent in the city of David after having rested for a time in the house of Obed Edom. Just as in the past, God's favor once again rests upon Israel, which is reason for celebration. From the time of Abraham to that of Joseph, from Joseph to Moses, to the moment when Israel was to take possession of the Promised Land, God has been with them (v. 44). As the psalm concludes, the Psalmist reiterates his earlier point: God remembers his covenant with Abraham (v. 42). God's undiminished fidelity constitutes their reason for praise and gratitude. In this particular account of God's fidelity, the person of Joseph has special prominence. Joseph, who had been sold by his brothers into slavery and then imprisoned on the basis of a lie, became by God's design the catalyst for a blessing that changed the status of God's people. By interpreting the troublesome dreams of Pharaoh, he who had been weighed down in chains (v. 18) was released, becoming a wisdom figure and a leader among the people of Egypt (vv. 20–22). Though Joseph had suffered the envy and spite of others, God would raise him from slavery to leadership in the land; from that eminent position he would save the brothers who had betrayed him (cf. Gen 45). In the New Testament, Joseph the foster father of Jesus bears notable similarities to his Old Testament namesake. Both are associated with the interpretation and understanding of dreams (Gen 41:37–45; Matt 1:18–25; 2:13–15), and both have significant roles in the unfolding of salvation history (Gen 50:22–26; Matt 2:21–23). These two figures manifest for us the wondrous way in which any of us may become instruments of God's salvation—if we are open to a call that promises suffering along the way, and for which the final results may long remain hidden.

PSALM 105 *(104)*

¹ Give thánks to the LÓRD; proclaim his náme.
Make knówn his déeds among the péoples.

² O síng to him, síng his práise;
téll all his wónderful wórks!
³ Glóry in his hóly náme;
let the héarts that seek the LÓRD rejóice.

⁴ Túrn to the LÓRD and his stréngth;
cónstantly séek his fáce.
⁵ Remémber the wónders he has dóne,
his márvels and his wórds of júdgment.

⁶ O chíldren of Ábraham, his sérvant,
O descéndants of the Jácob he chóse,
⁷ hé, the LÓRD, is our Gód;
his júdgments are in áll the éarth.

⁸ He remémbers his cóvenant foréver:
the prómise he ordáined for a thóusand generátions,
⁹ the cóvenant he máde with Ábraham,
the óath he swóre to Ísaac.

¹⁰ He confírmed it for Jácob as a láw,
for Ísrael as a cóvenant foréver,
¹¹ saying, "I will gíve you the lánd of Cánaan
to bé your allótted inhéritance."

¹² When théy were féw in númber,
a hándful of strángers in the lánd,
¹³ when they wándered from nátion to nátion,
from one kíngdom and péople to anóther,

¹⁴ He allówed nó one to oppréss them;
he admónished kíngs on their accóunt,
¹⁵ saying, "Thóse I have anóinted, do not tóuch;
do no hárm to ány of my próphets."

¹⁶ But he cálled down a fámine on the lánd;
he bróke their stáff of bréad.
¹⁷ He had sént a mán ahéad of them,
Jóseph, sóld as a sláve.

¹⁸ His féet were wéighed down in cháins,
his néck was bóund with íron,
¹⁹ untíl what he sáid came to páss,
and the wórd of the LÓRD proved him trúe.

²⁰ Then the kíng sent órders and reléased him;
the rúler of the péoples set him frée.
²¹ He máde him máster of his hóuse
and rúler of áll his posséssions,
²² to instrúct his prínces from his héart,
and to téach his élders wísdom.

²³ So Ísrael cáme into Égypt;
Jacob dwélt in the lánd of Hám.
²⁴ He gáve his péople great íncrease;
he máde them strónger than their fóes,
²⁵ whose héarts he turned to háte his péople,
and to déal decéitfully with his sérvants.

²⁶ Thén he sent Móses his sérvant,
and Áaron whóm he had chósen.
²⁷ They perfórmed God's sígns amóng them,
and his wónders in the lánd of Hám.

²⁸ He sent dárkness, and dárk was máde,
but they rebélled agáinst his wórds.
²⁹ He túrned their wáters into blóod,
and cáused their físh to díe.

³⁰ Their lánd was overrún by frógs,
éven to the hálls of their kíngs.
³¹ He spóke; there came swárms of flíes,
and gnáts covered áll the cóuntry.

³² He sent háilstones in pláce of the ráin,
and líghtning fláshing in their lánd.
³³ He strúck their vínes and fíg trees;
he sháttered the trées through their cóuntry.

³⁴ He spóke; the lócusts came fórth,
young lócusts, too mány to be cóunted.
³⁵ They áte up every plánt in the lánd;
they áte up all the frúit of their fíelds.

³⁶ He strúck all the fírstborn in their lánd,
the first frúit of áll their stréngth.
³⁷ He led out Ísrael with sílver and góld.
In his tríbes were nóne who stúmbled.

³⁸ Égypt rejóiced when they léft,
for dréad had fállen upón them.
³⁹ He spréad a clóud as a scréen,
and fire to illúmine the níght.

⁴⁰ When they ásked he sént them quáils;
he fílled them with bréad from héaven.
⁴¹ He pierced the róck and wáter gushed fórth;
it flówed as a ríver in the désert.

⁴² For he remémbered his hóly wórd,
spóken to Ábraham his sérvant.
⁴³ So he bróught out his péople with jóy,
his chósen ones with shóuts of rejóicing.

⁴⁴ And he gáve them the lánds of the nátions.
Of other péoples they posséssed the tóil,
⁴⁵ that thús they might kéep his précepts,
that thús they might obsérve his láws.

Alleluia!

PRAYER

God of our ancestors, God of our faith, whose provident grace emerges
in ways we cannot foresee: strengthen our trust and confidence in your
mysterious plan. May we hear your voice and follow your holy bidding
with conviction and perseverance. Through Christ our Lord. Amen.

Psalm 106

A HISTORY OF
HUMAN FAILURES

A clue to the historical context of this psalm and the dating of its original composition is provided in the closing stanzas. There the text reads, "[God] let them be treated with compassion by all who held them captive. Save us, O Lord our God! And gather us from the nations" (vv. 46–47). Reference to being held "captive" and the petition that God gather the people from among the nations suggest that the psalm comes from the period of the Babylonian exile. Further evidence for this hypothesis is discernible in the frequent references to past sinful behavior, both in the desert (vv. 6–33) and in the Promised Land (vv. 34–46)—behavior that is the presumptive cause of their exile. The divine response to their infidelity—the withdrawal of God's merciful love and compassion—had made clear that their repeated breaches of the covenant could not in justice be overlooked by God. Although the psalm opens with an expression of thanksgiving for God's mercy, it quickly moves to the presentation of a people coming forward to acknowledge their sins and their need of repentance (v. 6). The confession of sin, beginning in verse 6, asserts that Israel has failed to comprehend or respond to the divine intervention in their lives as a people even as far back as their experience of slavery in Egypt. An interesting contrast between Psalm 105 and Psalm 106 may be drawn: in Psalm 105, Israel rejoices in the fact that God remembers his promise to Abraham and remains faithful to his covenant, but in Psalm 106 we are told three times (vv. 7c, 13, 21) that the people did not remember, but rather had forgotten the meaning of their commitment to God and failed to live according to the covenant. They even scorned God's promise by their ingratitude for the Lord's gift of the land (v. 24); they took up the worship practices of their neighbors (vv. 34–39) and by this idolatry insulted and rejected God, who had given them all they had and were as a people. Yet in spite of the fact that Israel had forgotten God's goodness, the Psalmist tells, God was faithful, and, remembering the covenant once made with a motley group of slaves, came to save them (v. 45). The same goodness of God comes to us at the end of the ages in the sacrificial and redemptive death of Christ, God's ultimate act of love and remembrance toward his people. "You know that you were ransomed from the futile ways inherited from your ancestors, not with perishable things like silver or gold, but with the precious blood of Christ, like that of a lamb without defect or blemish" (1 Pet 1:18–19). With its concluding doxology, this psalm brings the fourth book of the Psalter to its end.

PSALM 106 (105)

¹ *Alleluia!*

O give thánks to the LÓRD, for he is góod;
for his mércy endúres foréver.
² Who can téll the LÓRD's mighty déeds,
or recóunt in fúll his práise?

³ Blessed are théy who obsérve what is júst,
who at áll times dó what is ríght.
⁴ O LÓRD, remémber mé
with the fávor you shów to your péople.

Visit mé with your sáving pówer,
⁵ that I may sée the ríches of your chósen ones,
and may rejóice in the gládness of your nátion,
bóasting in the glóry of your héritage.

⁶ Like our fáthers, wé have sínned.
We have done wróng; our déeds have been évil.
⁷ Our fórebears, when théy were in Égypt,
did not grásp the méaning of your wónders.

They forgót the great númber of your mércies,
at the Réd Sea defíed the Most Hígh.
⁸ Yet he sáved them for the sáke of his náme,
in órder to make knówn his pówer.

⁹ He rebúked the Red Séa; it dried úp,
and he léd them through the déep as through the désert.
¹⁰ He sáved them from the hánd of the fóe;
he fréed them from the gríp of the énemy.

¹¹ The wáters cóvered their oppréssors;
not óne of thém was léft.
¹² Thén they belíeved in his wórds;
thén they sáng his práises.

¹³ But they sóon forgót his déeds,
and wóuld not wáit upon his cóunsel.
¹⁴ They yíelded to their crávings in the désert,
and put Gód to the tést in the wílderness.

¹⁵ He gránted them the fávor they ásked,
but strúck them with a wásting diséase.
¹⁶ In the cámp, they were jéalous of Móses,
and also Áaron, who was hóly to the LÓRD.

¹⁷ The earth ópened and swállowed up Dáthan,
and búried the clán of Abíram.
¹⁸ Fíre blazed úp against their clán,
and flámes devóured the wícked.

¹⁹ They fáshioned a cálf at Hóreb
and wórshiped an ímage of metal;
²⁰ théy exchánged their glóry
for the ímage of a búll that eats gráss.

²¹ They forgót the Gód who was their sávior,
who had dóne such gréat things in Égypt,
²² such wónders in the lánd of Hám,
such márvels at the Réd Séa.

²³ For thís he sáid he would destróy them,
but Móses, the mán he had chósen,
stóod in the bréach befóre him,
to túrn back his ánger from destrúction.

²⁴ Then they scórned the desírable lánd;
they hád no fáith in his wórd.
²⁵ They compláined insíde their ténts,
and did not lísten to the vóice of the LÓRD.

²⁶ So he ráised his hánd to them and swóre
that he would láy them lów in the désert,
²⁷ would dispérse their descéndants through the nátions
and scátter them throughóut the lánds.

²⁸ They bówed before the Báal of Péor,
ate ófferings made to lífeless góds.
²⁹ They róused the LORD to ánger with their déeds,
and a plágue broke óut amóng them.

³⁰ Then Phínehas stood úp and intervéned.
Thús the plágue was énded,
³¹ and this was cóunted to hím as ríghteous
from áge to áge foréver.

³² They provóked him at the wáters of Méribah.
Through their fáult it went íll with Móses,
³³ for they máde his spírit grow bítter,
and he úttered wórds that were rásh.

³⁴ They fáiled to destróy the péoples,
as the LÓRD had commánded thém;
³⁵ instéad they míngled with the nátions,
and léarned to áct as théy did.

³⁶ They álso sérved their ídols,
and thése became a snáre to entráp them.
³⁷ They éven óffered their sóns
and their dáughters in sácrifice to démons.

³⁸ They póured out ínnocent blóod,
the blóod of their sóns and dáughters,
whom they óffered to the ídols of Cánaan.
The lánd was pollúted with blóod.

³⁹ So they defíled themsélves by their áctions;
their déeds were thóse of a hárlot.
⁴⁰ Then God's ánger blázed against his péople;
he was fílled with hórror at his héritage.

⁴¹ So he hánded them óver to the nátions,
and their fóes becáme their rúlers.
⁴² Their énemies álso oppréssed them;
they were subdúed benéath their hánd.

⁴³ Tíme after tíme he réscued them,
but in their málice they dáred to defý him
and were wéakened even móre by their guílt.
⁴⁴ In spite of thís he paid héed to their distréss,
so óften as he héard their crý.

⁴⁵ For their sáke he remémbered his cóvenant.
In the gréatness of his mércy, he relénted,
⁴⁶ and he lét them be tréated with compássion
by áll who héld them cáptive.

⁴⁷ Sáve us, O Lórd our Gód!
And gáther ús from the nátions,
to give thánks to your hóly náme,
and máke it our glóry to práise you.

* * *

[48] Blést be the Lórd, God of Ísrael,
foréver, from áge to áge.
Let áll the péople sáy,
"Amén! Amén! Allelúia!"

PRAYER

All-faithful and compassionate God, who time after time have shown us your forgiveness and mercy, help us to acknowledge the great price of our redemption, that we might fittingly respond to the sacred covenant you have established by the blood of your Son, Jesus Christ, who is Lord, forever and ever. Amen.

BOOK FIVE
OF THE
PSALTER

𝒫salm 107

GOD'S FAITHFUL LOVE
ENDURES FOREVER

Jewish tradition recommends the thankful recitation of Psalm 107 to four situations, each associated with specific sections of the psalm: (1) crossing the sea successfully (vv. 23–32); (2) traversing the desert in safety (vv. 4–9); (3) healing from an illness (vv. 17–22); and (4) release from imprisonment (vv. 10–16) (cf. Talmud; Berachos 54). Deliverance from these four terrifying situations provides the story line of Psalm 107; unifying the psalm as a whole are two recurrent refrains: first, "Then they cried to the LORD in their need, / and he rescued them from their distress (vv. 6, 13, 19, 28); and second, "Let them thank the LORD for his mercy, / his wonders for the children of men" (vv. 8, 15, 21, 31). At the heart of these refrains is the recollection of how true God is to the people of the covenant, consistently coming to their rescue with merciful love. The Hebrew term translated here as "merciful love" is *hesed*, the word used throughout the Old Testament to describe the love of God that flows from the covenant relationship; it conveys God's faithfulness, loyalty, steadfastness, trustworthiness, reliability, devotion, commitment. Psalm 106 asserts that Israel's unfaithful behavior is no better than a harlot's (v. 39); yet God in his goodness cannot but be faithful, returning time and time again to forgive wayward Israel. To make this point, the Psalmist presents contrasting reflections that counter the persistence of divine love to human weakness and inconstancy. For example, those who are lost in the barren desert, fainting from hunger and thirst (vv. 4–5), the LORD "satisfies" and "fills with good things" (v. 9). And again, those imprisoned in dark dungeons, bearing the chains of their punishment, the LORD "[leads] out of darkness and the shadow of death, [breaking] their chains to pieces" (v. 14). By such contrasts the Psalmist shows the gracious and loving hand of God at work in our world. This technique culminates as the psalm draws to a close (vv. 33–42): while God "pours contempt upon princes, makes them wander in trackless wastes" (v. 40), he "raises the needy from distress; makes families numerous as a flock" (v. 41). Similar contrasts appear in the Canticle of Mary: she proclaims, the Lord "has brought down the powerful from their thrones, and lifted up the lowly; he has filled the hungry with good things, and sent the rich away empty" (Luke 1:52–53). The opening verse encapsulates the message of the entire psalm: "O give thanks to the LORD for he is good; for his mercy endures forever."

PSALM 107 *(106)*

¹ "O give thánks to the LÓRD for he is góod;
for his mércy endúres foréver."
² Let the redéemed of the LÓRD say thís,
those he redéemed from the hánd of the fóe,
³ and gáthered from fár-off lánds,
from éast and wést, north and sóuth.

⁴ They wándered in a bárren désert,
finding no wáy to a cíty they could dwéll in.
⁵ Húngry they wére and thírsty;
their sóul was fáinting withín them.

⁶ Then they críed to the LÓRD in their néed,
and he réscued thém from their distréss,
⁷ and he guíded them alóng a straight páth,
to réach a cíty they could dwéll in.

⁸ Let them thánk the LÓRD for his mércy,
his wónders for the chíldren of mén;
⁹ for he sátisfies the thírsty sóul,
and the húngry he fílls with good thíngs.

¹⁰ Some dwelt in dárkness and the shádow of déath,
prísoners in mísery and cháins,
¹¹ having rebélled against the wórds of Gód,
and spúrned the plán of the Most Hígh.
¹² He húmbled their héart with tóil.
They stúmbled; there was nó one to hélp.

¹³ Then they críed to the LÓRD in their néed,
and he réscued thém from their distréss.
¹⁴ He léd them out of dárkness and the shádow of déath,
and bróke their cháins to píeces.

¹⁵ Let them thánk the LÓRD for his mércy,
his wónders for the chíldren of mén;
¹⁶ for he búrsts the gátes of brónze,
and cúts through the íron bárs.

¹⁷ Some fell síck on accóunt of their síns,
and were afflícted on accóunt of their guílt.
¹⁸ They had a lóathing for évery fóod;
they drew néar to the gátes of déath.

¹⁹ Then they críed to the LÓRD in their néed,
and he réscued thém from their distréss.
²⁰ He sént forth his wórd to héal them,
and sáved their lífe from destrúction.

²¹ Let them thánk the LÓRD for his mércy,
his wónders for the chíldren of mén.
²² Let them óffer a sácrifice of thánks,
and téll of his déeds with rejóicing.

²³ Some went dówn to the séa in shíps,
to tráde on the míghty wáters.
²⁴ These have séen the déeds of the LÓRD,
the wónders he dóes in the déep.

²⁵ For he spóke and ráised up the stórm-wind,
tóssing high the wáves of the séa
²⁶ that surged to héaven and drópped to the dépths.
Their souls mélted awáy in their distréss.

²⁷ They stággered and réeled like drúnkards,
for áll their skíll was góne.
²⁸ Then they críed to the LÓRD in their néed,
and he réscued thém from their distréss.

²⁹ He stílled the stórm to a whísper,
and the wáves of the séa were húshed.
³⁰ They rejóiced becáuse of the cálm,
and he léd them to the háven they desíred.

³¹ Let them thánk the LÓRD for his mércy,
his wónders for the chíldren of mén.
³² Let them exált him in the assémbly of the péople,
and práise him in the méeting of the élders.

³³ He chánges rívers into désert,
springs of wáter into thírsty gróund,   `
³⁴ fruitful lánd into a sálty wáste,
for the wíckedness of thóse who líve there.

³⁵ He changes désert into póols of wáter,
thirsty gróund into spríngs of wáter.
³⁶ Thére he séttles the húngry,
and they estáblish a cíty to dwéll in.

³⁷ They sow fíelds and plánt their vínes,
which yíeld an abúndant hárvest.
³⁸ He blésses them; they grów in númbers.
He does nót let their cáttle decréase.

⁴⁰ He póurs contémpt upon prínces,
makes them wánder in tráckless wástes.
³⁹ Théy are dimínished and brought lów
by oppréssion, évil and sórrow.

⁴¹ But he ráises the néedy from distréss;
makes fámilies númerous as a flóck.
⁴² The úpright sée it and rejóice,
while all the wícked clóse their móuths.

⁴³ Should nót one who is wíse recall these thíngs,
and understánd the merciful déeds of the LÓRD?

PRAYER

Lord God of heaven and earth, who remain forever constant in love and mercy despite our countless infidelities: grant us vision to see with eyes of faith how you touch our lives each day, freeing us from the powers of darkness and guiding us into the light of your risen Son, Jesus Christ, who is Lord, forever and ever. Amen.

Psalm 108

COME AND DELIVER
YOUR FRIENDS

Psalm 108 will sound familiar to anyone reading the Psalter straight through. It is largely composed of texts taken from two previous psalms: the opening verses (vv. 2–6) repeat Psalm 57:8–12, and the concluding verses (8–14) are from Psalm 60:8–14. Though the alterations in these borrowed texts are minor, their new combination and arrangement in Psalm 108 gives the words a very different sense. This psalm begins with a declaration of readiness to acclaim God with voice and music such as will awaken the dawn (vv. 1–3). Once again, the paired terms *mercy* and *truth* form the basis for gratitude to God; these blessings reach in their expansiveness to the limits of the universe (v. 5), calling forth from the Psalmist a glorious exaltation that all peoples and nations of the earth will witness. The Psalmist petitions for salvation, imploring that all those who are friends of God be delivered by his powerful hand (v. 7), but the mood shifts in verse 8 as the Psalmist recollects the promise of God, distinguishing among the nations whether they will know divine blessing or divine wrath; the litany of names in the oracle is an assertion that all of them, and by extension all created things, are under God's dominion. God is the One who divides lands and distributes portions, making use of them as he will, giving the portions of some away and retaining others as his own. All belongs to God, who ultimately retains as a divine right the power to decide matters that we are inclined to see as the prerogatives of earthly rulers. After the oracle, the Psalmist anxiously poses the question, "But who will lead me to the fortified city?" (v. 11). By this he means "Who will bring me to safety from present dangers?" The right and simple answer conveys a sense of heartfelt contentment: "Human aid is vain," but "with God, we shall do bravely, and he will trample down our foes" (vv. 13b–14). Truly, our greatest help and hope rests in the God who created us and who continues to watch over us. How well St. Paul expressed this when he said, "The God who made the world and everything in it, he who is Lord of heaven and earth, does not live in shrines made by human hands, nor is he served by human hands, as though he needed anything, since he himself gives to all mortals life and breath and all things. For 'In him we live and move and have our being'" (Acts 17:24–25, 28). Glory, praise, and honor to our God, who gives us strength, wisdom, and love through Jesus Christ, our risen Lord.

PSALM 108 (107)

¹ *A Song. A Psalm of David.*

² My héart is réady, O Gód;
my héart is réady.
I will síng, I will síng your práise.
Awáke, my sóul;
³ Awáke, O lýre and hárp.
I will awáke the dáwn.

⁴ I will práise you, LÓRD, among the péoples;
I will sing psálms to yóu among the nátions,
⁵ for your mércy réaches to the héavens,
and your trúth to the skíes.

⁶ O Gód, be exálted above the héavens;
may your glóry shine on áll the éarth!
⁷ With your right hánd, grant salvátion and give ánswer;
O cóme and delíver your fríends.

⁸ From his hóly place Gód has made this prómise:
"I will exúlt, and divíde the land of Shéchem;
I will méasure out the válley of Súccoth.

⁹ Gílead is míne, as is Manásseh;
Éphraim I táke for my hélmet,
Júdah ís my scépter.
¹⁰ Móab ís my wáshbowl;
on Édom I will tóss my shóe.
Over Philístia I will shóut in tríumph."

¹¹ But who will léad me to the fórtified cíty?
Whó will bríng me to Édom?
¹² Have you not cást us óff, O Gód?
Will you márch with our ármies no lónger?

¹³ Give us réscue agáinst the fóe,
for húman áid is váin.
¹⁴ With Gód, wé shall do brávely,
and he will trámple dówn our fóes.

O God our strength, who guide us through the passages of life and keep our feet from stumbling: May your strong right hand lead us in ways of faith, hope, and love, that we might share the victory of the risen Christ, who lives and reigns, forever and ever. Amen.

Psalm 109

O GOD, DO NOT BE SILENT

Psalm 109 is distinguished by the fact that it is not used in the liturgy: neither as a Responsorial Psalm at Mass nor in the Roman Liturgy of the Hours is the psalm employed as an element of the Church's official prayer. (Many monastic communities that retain the tradition of praying all 150 psalms do, of course, give this psalm a place in their local celebrations of the Liturgy of the Hours.) As Christian spirituality and practice developed over the centuries, many became uncomfortable attempting to pray this psalm with its vindictive language and images of retributive assault against others. Even more difficult for some is the fact that these spiteful and malicious words are bracketed by expressions of praise to God (vv. 1, 30). An examination of the psalm reveals a situation that has generated such highly charged expressions: falsehoods have been leveled against the Psalmist; his own loving deeds for others have been scorned, repaid with wickedness and hate (vv. 2–3). In what follows (vv. 6–20), the Psalmist lashes out at what he rightly conceives to be the very foundation of human life, including that of his enemies: the family. From his embittered heart a stream of invective against parents, wife, and children of his opponent spews forth (vv. 9–10, 12–14). To support his diatribe he expounds on the offenses of his enemy with accusations of ill treatment of the poor and the needy (v. 16). It is from all of this that the Psalmist asks to be saved by God's merciful love, or *hesed* (v. 26). Though the language and tone employed in this psalm may grate against Christian sensibilities, we nonetheless acknowledge its inclusion among the divinely inspired Scriptures. How can we in our contemporary context pray a psalm like this? Every day the news media report acts of hatred and violence that human beings have unjustly perpetrated against other human beings. We cannot condone brutality returned for brutality. But we can find in the words of Psalm 109 a witness to the pain and anguish of those innocent persons who suffer hatred, scorn, or violence from their fellow human beings. These bitter words, fraught with dark but genuine human emotion, can when we recite them serve to unite us in solidarity with those who have no one to stand up for them, those whose innocent voices will never be heard. We can become the voice of prayer for those who are so deeply wounded that they are unable even to find words to express their agonized grief. In faith, we unite ourselves with them, and willingly pray for the deliverance that will ease their burdens and give them new hope. We cannot allow our prayer to become so elevated or antiseptic that we fail to take account of the pain and suffering endured by our brothers and sisters in the human family, those who with us form the very Body of Christ.

PSALM 109 (108)

1 *For the Choirmaster. Of David. A Psalm.*

O Gód whom I práise, do not be sílent,
2 for the móuths of decéit and wíckedness
are ópened agáinst me.

3 They spéak to me with lýing tóngues;
they besét me with wórds of háte,
and attáck me without cáuse.

4 In retúrn for my lóve, they accúse me,
while Í am at práyer.
5 They repáy me évil for góod,
hátred for lóve.

* * *

6 Appóint someone wícked over hím;
let an accúser stánd at his ríght.
7 When he is júdged, let him cóme out condémned;
let his práyer be consídered as sín.

8 Let the dáys of his lífe be féw;
let anóther assúme his óffice.
9 Let his chíldren be fátherless órphans,
and his wífe becóme a wídow.

¹⁰ Let his chíldren be wánderers and béggars,
dríven from the rúins of their hóme.
¹¹ Let the créditor séize all his góods;
let strángers take the frúit of his wórk.

¹² Let nó one shów him any mércy,
nor píty his fátherless chíldren.
¹³ Let his postérity bé destróyed,
in a generátion his náme blotted óut.

¹⁴ Let his fáther's guílt be remémbered to the LÓRD,
his móther's sín be retáined.
¹⁵ Let it álways stánd before the LÓRD,
that their mémory be cut óff from the éarth.

¹⁶ For hé did not thínk of showing mércy,
but pursúed the póor and the néedy,
hóunding to déath the brokenhéarted.
¹⁷ He loved cúrsing; let cúrses fall on hím.
He scorned bléssing; let bléssing pass him bý.

¹⁸ He pút on cúrsing like his cóat:
let it sínk into his bódy like wáter;
let it sínk like óil into his bónes.
¹⁹ Let it bé like the clóthes that cóver him,
like a bélt he wéars all the tíme.

²⁰ Let the LÓRD thus repáy my accúsers,
all thóse who speak évil agáinst me.
²¹ But yóu, O LÓRD, my Lórd,
do with mé as befíts your náme.
How good your mérciful lóve! Delíver me.

²² For Í am póor and néedy,
and my héart is píerced withín me.
²³ I fáde like an évening shádow;
I am sháken óff like a lócust.

²⁴ My knées are wéak from fásting;
my bódy is thín and gáunt.
²⁵ I have becóme an óbject of scórn;
when they sée me they sháke their héads.

²⁶ Hélp me, LÓRD my Gód;
sáve me with your mérciful lóve.

²⁷ Let them knów that thís is your hánd,
that thís is your dóing, O LÓRD.

²⁸ They may cúrse, but yóu will bléss.
Let my attáckers be pút to sháme,
but lét your sérvant rejóice.
²⁹ Let my accúsers be clóthed with dishónor,
cóvered with sháme as with a clóak.

³⁰ Loud thánks to the LÓRD are on my líps.
I will práise him in the mídst of the thróng,
³¹ for he stánds at the right hánd of the póor,
to sáve his soul from thóse who condémn him.

PRAYER

God of justice and mercy, who heed the cry of the poor and afflicted: keep us ever mindful of our brothers and sisters whose pain exceeds the limits of human endurance. Make us bearers of your strength for them in their time of need, and awaken in us the desire to support all who yearn for your compassion. We ask this through Christ our Lord. Amen.

Psalm 110

THE VICTORIOUS MESSIAH

Psalm 110 is more frequently quoted in the New Testament than any other psalm. The opening line's reference to the Lord "seated at the right hand" of God came to be associated in the minds of the New Testament authors with both the divinity of Jesus and the fulfillment of his mission. Individual instances in which this line is linked directly to Jesus are numerous (Matt 22:44; Mark 14:62; 16:19; Luke 22:69; Acts 2:34–35; 7:55; Rom 8:34; Eph 1:20; Col 3:1; Heb 1:3, 13; 8:1; 10:12; 1 Pet 3:22). Furthermore, the early Christians incorporated the phrase directly into both the Apostles' and Nicene Creeds. Christian tradition understands this psalm in relation to Jesus' threefold mission: as priest ("You are a priest forever in the line of Melchizedek" v. 4); as prophet ("The LORD's revelation to my Lord" v. 1); and as king ("The LORD will send from Sion your scepter of power" v. 2). These three roles demonstrate that Jesus is the fulfillment of all that had preceded him in the Old Testament. As priest, he is both offerer and offering, presenting himself to the Father as the perfect paschal lamb. As prophet, he is the mouthpiece of God who both announces the reign of divine love and lives it to perfection. As king, he mandates a new rule of life within the scope of God's divine law, judging the world of sin yet proclaiming forgiveness for all who will follow God's commands. For many, the closing verse of the psalm is full of mysterious portent: "He shall drink from the stream by the wayside, and therefore he shall lift up his head" (v. 7). With the preceding verses, this closing line depicts the climax of a battle scene in which the victorious Lord brings judgment upon the nations and subdues those who will not submit to the divine rule. Having brought about the defeat of the enemy, he can now pause to refresh himself from the waters of the stream, after which he rises to gaze over the powers that had threatened his people. This becomes for the Church an image of Jesus, who claims the palm of victory in his paschal mystery, triumphant over the powers of sin and death. He has won for us the freedom of the children of God (Rom 8:21); we are no longer slaves to the power of Satan, but free to live in joy as Spirit-filled members of the household of God (Gal 5:1, 13–14). The Book of Revelation adopts similar imagery in speaking of the battle that Christ has won for us: through the shedding of his blood he has cleansed us for our own living out of the paschal mystery. "It is done! I am the Alpha and the Omega, the beginning and the end. To the thirsty I will give water as a gift from the spring of the water of life. Those who conquer will inherit these things, and I will be their God and they will be my children" (Rev 21:6–7). We cannot wonder that the early Church saw such hope in this psalm; Christ's victory over sin and death is also ours in all its abundance.

PSALM 110 *(109)*

[1] *Of David. A Psalm.*

The LÓRD's revelátion to my lórd:
"Sít at my right hánd,
until I máke your fóes your fóotstool."

[2] The LÓRD will sénd from Síon
your scépter of pówer:
rúle in the mídst of your fóes.

³ With yóu is príncely rúle
on the dáy of your pówer.
In holy spléndor, from the wómb before the dáwn,
I have begótten yóu.

⁴ The LÓRD has sworn an óath he will not chánge:
"Yóu are a príest foréver,
in the líne of Melchízedek."

⁵ The LÓRD, stánding at your ríght,
shatters kíngs in the dáy of his wráth.

⁶ He brings a júdgment amóng the nátions,
and héaps the bódies hígh;
he shatters héads throughóut the wide éarth.

⁷ He shall drínk from the stréam by the wáyside,
and thérefore he shall líft up his héad.

PRAYER

*Lord Jesus Christ, Alpha and Omega, First and Last, we acclaim your
wondrous victory over sin and death, lifting up to you our prayers of
gratitude for all you have accomplished. Strengthen us in our battle
against sin and temptation, that we may experience the fullness of your
grace at work in our lives. In your holy name we pray. Amen.*

Psalm lll

A FULL HEART'S THANKS

In a brief ten verses, the Psalmist presents a rich collection of biblically
nuanced terms that pay tribute to the God who alone works wonders.
The Psalmist's acclamations of gratitude arise from a full heart (v. 1),
knowing as he does the bounty with which the Lord has enriched both
the people of Israel and its individual members (v. 2). To underscore the
idea of fullness, the Psalmist employs a literary technique called "acros-

tic," in which successive lines of the psalm begin with consecutive letters of the Hebrew alphabet. Notice how descriptive terms and expressions build up as the psalm progresses. The attributes of God are designated by terms such as *majestic* and *glorious, gracious* and *merciful, just* and *true, upright* and *holy*. Such freighted terms expand the Psalmist's portrayal of God's fidelity to Israel that flows from the covenant relationship: even when the newly freed Hebrews fashion a molten calf in the desert and worship it in God's place, God forgives them. In conversation with Moses, God had revealed the extent of his mercy and graciousness (cf. Exod 34:5–7); as covenant mediator, Moses had made plain to the people their wrongdoing so that they might turn their hearts back to God. Another important image employed by the Psalmist is the "wondrous memorial of food" that God provided for those who fear him (vv. 4–5). The manna in the desert, a unique and unprecedented form of nourishment, was available to the people through their entire desert trek. The Church sees in this image a type of the Eucharistic food that Christ gives to his Church as a memorial of his own reconciling love and faithful promise to remain with his followers. From the beginning of the psalm to its end, we discern a sense of wonder at the marvelous ways in which God has been faithful to the people—those first redeemed in covenant, and now us who abide beneath the outspread mantle of our Savior. To know God's ways—that is, to experience the greatness of his faithful love—is to find the peace for which we were created. How forcefully the Psalmist presents the manner by which God's holiness stirs up in us a sense of awe and overwhelming gratitude before the power that sustains us through each passing day. The one who knows the ways of God's redeeming love will have wisdom as a companion in life (v. 10). The author of the Book of Revelation expresses this profoundly in the acclamations: "Great and amazing are your deeds, Lord God the Almighty! Just and true are your ways, King of the nations! Lord, who will not fear and glorify your name? For you alone are holy" (15:3–4a). All glory be to God, who still works wonders among us!

PSALM 111 *(110)*

¹ *Alleluia!*

I will práise the LÓRD with all my héart,
in the méeting of the júst and the assémbly.
² Gréat are the wórks of the LÓRD,
to be póndered by áll who delíght in them.

³ Majéstic and glórious his wórk;
his jústice stands fírm foréver.

⁴ He has gíven us a memórial of his wónders.
The LÓRD is grácious and mérciful.

⁵ He gives fóod to thóse who féar him;
keeps his cóvenant éver in mínd.
⁶ His mighty wórks he has shówn to his péople
by gíving them the héritage of nátions.

⁷ His hándiwork is jústice and trúth;
his précepts are áll of them súre,
⁸ standing fírm foréver and éver,
wróught in úprightness and trúth.

⁹ He has sént redémption to his péople,
and estáblished his cóvenant foréver.
Hóly his náme, to be féared.

¹⁰ The fear of the LÓRD is the begínning of wísdom;
understánding marks áll who attáin it.
His práise endúres foréver!

PRAYER

Majestic and glorious LORD, whose ways are just and true, upright and holy: we give you thanks for the wondrous ways by which you bring perpetual blessings to our world and to the lives of each of us. Receive our humble offering and uphold us in fidelity to your holy name, who live and reign, forever and ever. Amen.

Psalm 112

THE WAY OF THE JUST

Psalms 111 and 112 are directly linked. "The fear of the Lord" is a singularly important concept in biblical Wisdom literature; Psalm 111 concludes with a reference to it, and Psalm 112 opens with a similar assertion. As Psalm 111 recounts the wondrous deeds of God that flow from the relationship established in the covenant, Psalm 112 enumerates the blessings that come to those who live justly and uprightly as their part of the covenant. We know that God's covenant promises divine blessing and protection if we adhere to it; Psalm 112 begins by listing those blessings that come to all who "delight in [God's] commandments" (v. 1). Some readers of the Old Testament have difficulty with the expression "the fear of the Lord," because Jesus so frequently admonishes his followers in the New Testament, "Do not fear." But an authentic understanding of this Old Testament expression recognizes a spiritual nuance beyond the ordinary sense of the English word *fear* as a negative emotional state. "Fear of the LORD" implies rather a sense of awe, reverence, and wonder at the majesty and power of God, who yet always treats his creatures with kindness and compassion. Yes, God is Judge, but a judge whose loving mercy triumphs over the power of justice that punishes sin. One need only reflect momentarily on the blessings of creation that we witness each day to bring forth this sense of awe and wonder at God's almighty power. To experience both the compassion and the majesty of God leads us to the kind of reverence and delight that are conveyed in the biblical expression "fear of the LORD." Another likeness between Psalms 111 and 112 encourages us to ponder deeply: the actions of God in Psalm 111 are recounted in the same terms that are employed in Psalm 112 to describe the person who acts in accord with the covenant. For example, Psalm 111:3 tells us that "[God's] justice stands firm forever;" Psalm 112:3b applies precisely the same terms to the person who abides by the covenant. God's just ways are seen to be the model of our own way of living. And though the translation here varies slightly, the Hebrew terms of Psalm 111:4b are repeated in Psalm 112:4b: God, who is gracious (Hebrew *chanan*) and merciful (Hebrew *racham*), expects those who live by the covenant likewise to manifest lives that are generous (Hebrew *chanan*) and merciful (Hebrew *racham*). Our understanding of the witness we give and the commitment we maintain in our relationship with God should fill us with awe: we are to be agents and instruments of God's own just and merciful ways in our world today. As Jesus witnessed so profoundly after washing his disciples' feet: "I have set you an example, that you also should do as I have done to you" (John 13:15). May it be our joy and glory to be the loving hands and heart of the Lord to our brothers and sisters each day.

PSALM 112 *(111)*

¹ *Alleluia!*

Bléssed the mán who fears the LÓRD,
who tákes great delíght in his commándments.

² His descéndants shall be pówerful on éarth;
the generátion of the úpright will be blést.

³ Ríches and wéalth are in his hóuse;
his jústice stands firm foréver.

⁴ A light ríses in the dárkness for the úpright;
he is génerous, mérciful and júst.

⁵ It goes wéll for the mán who deals génerously and lénds,
who condúcts his affáirs with jústice.

⁶ Hé will néver be móved;
foréver shall the júst be remémbered.

⁷ He hás no féar of evil néws;
with a firm héart, he trústs in the LÓRD.

⁸ With a stéadfast héart he will not féar;
he will sée the dównfall of his fóes.

⁹ Openhánded, he gíves to the póor;
his jústice stands firm foréver.
His míght shall be exálted in glóry.

¹⁰ The wícked sées and is ángry,
grinds his téeth and fádes awáy;
the desíre of the wícked leads to dóom.

PRAYER

All merciful and gracious God, who reveal to us the way of holiness in the example of your son Jesus: strengthen our wills and confirm us in our resolve to be your servants in thought, word, and deed, through the same Christ our Lord. Amen.

Psalm 113

THE EXALTED NAME

Psalm 113 is the first in a group commonly known as the Hallel Psalms. The designation derives from the word that opens each of them: *Halleluiah* (or *Alleluia*), which is translated literally as "Praise the Lord." The Psalms of Praise (from Psalm 113 to Psalm 118) recall the great event of Israel's salvation, beginning with the Exodus from Egypt; they extol the Lord who mercifully rescues his chosen ones from difficult situations. These psalms would have been sung at particular Jewish festivals of the year, especially Passover. In this first of the Hallel Psalms, the word *hallel* (praise) is associated with the name of the Lord three times in the opening three verses. As previously noted, "name" is associated in Scripture with identity and mission; this is true especially of the name of God. In Exodus 3:14–15, God reveals to Moses the divine name YHWH, a word so sacred to Jews that it is not spoken aloud when it occurs in a reading during a synagogue service, and a euphemism such as "Adonay" (my Lord), or occasionally "The Sovereign One," is substituted. In this psalm, blessing and praise are lifted up to the "name" for the marvelous salvation God has accomplished for the people of Israel throughout history. Expressions of fullness, totality, or completeness characterize praise that is befitting of God: now and forevermore (v. 2), from the rising of the sun to its setting (v. 3). But in expressing that exaltation proper to God, the Psalmist here focuses not on God's spectacular deeds as the reason for his words, but rather on God's care for the poor and the lowly. God "lifts up the lowly and raises the poor from the ash heap" (v. 7); "to the childless wife he gives a home as a joyful mother of children" (v. 9). We can hear in the tone of this psalm an echo of Moses's encounter with God on Sinai: "The Lord said, 'I have observed the misery of my people who are in Egypt; I have heard their cry on account of their taskmasters. Indeed, I know their sufferings, and I have come down to deliver them from the Egyptians, and to bring them up out of that land to a good and broad land'" (Exod 3:7–8a). Thus begins the history of God's merciful and compassionate dealings with those he first rescued from slavery and whom he continues to succor in time of need. Mary proclaims the same loving mercy in her Magnificat, affirming to her cousin Elizabeth—and to us—that God overturns the world of the rich and powerful but brings the poor and the needy to a place of blessing: "[The Lord] has brought down the powerful from their thrones, and lifted up the lowly; he has filled the hungry with good things, and sent the rich away empty" (Luke 1:52, 53). Our God, exalted in majestic power, descends from above to lift up those who call out to him in faith and confidence.

PSALM 113 *(112)*

¹ *Alleluia!*

Práise, O sérvants of the LÓRD,
práise the náme of the LÓRD!
² May the náme of the LÓRD be blést
both nów and forévermóre!
³ From the rísing of the sún to its sétting,
práised be the náme of the LÓRD!

⁴ Hígh above all nátions is the LÓRD,
above the héavens his glóry.
⁵ Whó is like the LÓRD, our Gód,
who dwélls on hígh,
⁶ who lówers himsélf to look dówn
upon héaven and éarth?

⁷ From the dúst he lífts up the lówly,
from the ásh heap he ráises the póor,
⁸ to sét them in the cómpany of prínces,
yés, with the prínces of his péople.
⁹ To the chíldless wífe he gives a hóme
as a jóyful móther of chíldren.

PRAYER

O God of power and might, ever close to those who call to you in their need: Guide us in the ways of lowliness and humility, so that, numbered among your poor in spirit, we may offer fitting praise for the blessings of your merciful love. We ask this through Christ our Lord. Amen.

Psalm 114

TREMBLING JORDAN, LEAPING MOUNTAINS

This short psalm covers a vast history—from the Exodus out of Egypt to the crossing of the Jordan into the land of promise, and even up to the present. Although we might expect a solemn tone in the account of such a significant series of events, the Psalmist sometimes describes these events playfully, with seas fleeing and rivers changing course (v. 3), with leaping mountains and hills (v. 4). Knowing this second of the Hallel Psalms was to be sung at Passover, we can perhaps appreciate how such lively imagery might well bring joy to the annual celebration of liberation and freedom. Yet even amid such lighthearted imagery, this psalm opens with a profound teaching: the covenant people is itself the very dwelling place of God. Among Ancient Near Eastern peoples, mountains or other special sanctuaries were commonly represented as the dwelling places of their gods. So there is something radically new and spiritually provocative about the way the Psalmist recognizes the people as God's dwelling place: "Judah became his temple, Israel became his domain" (v. 2). One way of understanding this tradition in the Scriptures is to recall the account of God's revelation of the divine name in Exodus 3. The text there further asserts, "God also said to Moses, 'Thus you shall say to the Israelites, "The LORD, the God of your ancestors, the God of Abraham, the God of Isaac, and the God of Jacob, has sent me to you:" This is my name forever, and this my title for all generations'" (Exod 3:15). We see how God directly identifies himself with the people, affirming in sum, "Where you find my people, there will you find me." Such a concept is unprecedented among the people of the Ancient Near East, showing the depth of YHWH's commitment to the covenant he has made with his people Israel. How appropriate, then, the Psalmist's joy in describing the Exodus event as creation reversing its ordinary patterns of behavior when confronted with the presence of the Lord! A God who turns a rock into a spring of water to refresh his people must surely be close to them, whom he has created in his own image and sustains in a covenanted relationship. But such blessing is no longer limited to the people of Israel alone; God's great gifts are now available to us in the new covenant of Christ. The First Letter of Peter affirms to those who follow the new way: "You are a chosen race, a royal priesthood, a holy nation, God's own people, in order that you may proclaim the mighty acts of him who called you out of darkness into his marvelous light" (1 Pet 2:9). The joy of this psalm resounds in the hearts of all who know the wondrous grace of Christ's resurrection in their lives.

PSALM 114 *(113A)*

¹ *Alleluia!*

When Ísrael came fórth from Égypt,
the house of Jácob from a fóreign péople,
² Júdah becáme his témple,
Ísrael becáme his domáin.

³ The séa behéld them and fléd;
the Jórdan turned báck on its cóurse.
⁴ The móuntains léapt like ráms,
and the hílls like yéarling shéep.

⁵ Whý was it, séa, that you fléd;
that you túrned back, Jórdan, on your cóurse?
⁶ O móuntains, that you léapt like ráms;
O hílls, like yéarling shéep?

⁷ Trémble, O éarth, before the Lórd,
in the présence of the Gód of Jácob,
⁸ who túrns the róck into a póol,
and flínt into a spríng of wáter.

PRAYER

Almighty and ever-living God, who in merciful love once freed an enslaved people and brought them to the land of promise: Grant that we, your new people redeemed by the precious blood of Christ, may rejoice in the wondrous ways you manifest your glory among us even to this day. Through Christ our Lord. Amen.

Psalm 115

TO YOU ALONE, LORD, ALL GLORY

Several times the Psalter sounds forth a clarion call, summoning the people to put their faith in the God of Israel and to reject the gods of other nations (consider Pss 9:17, "the work of their hands"; 42:4, "where is your God?"; and 86:8, with its references to "the gods"). Psalm 115 expresses this concern at the outset: "Why should the nations say, 'Where is their God?'" (v. 2). The Psalmist here proceeds to mock the gods of the nations that, as mere images formed of metal or wood, are the work of human hands (v. 4); while these have mouths, eyes, ears, and nostrils, none of these body parts function (vv. 5–7). He foresees a dire fate for those who put their faith in such idols: those who worship such empty beings will become as useless and impotent as they are! (v. 8). There follows a short litany (vv. 9–11), calling all to trust in the Lord—the house of Israel, the House of Aaron, and all who "fear" God in that particular biblical sense (cf. Ps 112 previous). Verse 12 offers a strong affirmation of the value of faith: the Psalmist reminds us that when we make God our "help and our shield," he will "remember us." In biblical theology, the notion of "remembrance" bears a strong sense of intimacy, care, and protection. For God to "remember" us means that we have a place in his mind and heart, that we will never lack the divine care and support necessary for our pilgrimage in life. God's remembrance of us, both individual and communal, assures us that the loving kindness (Hebrew *hesed*) springing from God's covenant love for those who put their trust in him is ours, as long as we persevere in confident hope of that love. We may be inclined to smile at the primitive quality of a faith that insists upon such a literal notion of idolatry. But we do well to remember that every generation creates new idols particular to itself—possessions, celebrities, ideologies, even opinions and attitudes. Psalm 115 invites the people of every age to look carefully into their hearts to assess whether they put their greatest confidence in themselves or in God, in their own powers or in divine grace, in their own sense of self or in the name of the Lord. Too often we do not even recognize that we have created such "gods," because they seem to meet a need in our drive for self-sufficiency or self-preservation:

"If I don't work hard, I won't achieve what I feel is essential for my well-being." The Epistle to the Hebrews offers a profound commentary on this human situation: "Faith is the assurance of things hoped for, the conviction of things not seen....By faith we understand that the worlds were prepared by the word of God, so that what is seen was made from things that are not visible" (Heb 11:1, 3). Our God is a God who acts: God's acts are manifest, but God himself remains invisible, thus calling us to a persevering faith in what we cannot see.

PSALM 115 *(113B)*

¹ Not to ús, O LÓRD, not to ús,
but to your náme give the glóry,
for your mérciful lóve and fidélity.
² Whý should the nátions sáy:
"Whére is their Gód?"

³ But our Gód is ín the héavens;
he dóes whatéver he wílls.
⁴ Their ídols are sílver and góld,
the wórk of húman hánds.

⁵ They have móuths but they cánnot spéak;
they have éyes but they cánnot sée.
⁶ They have éars but they cánnot héar;
they have nóstrils but they cánnot sméll.

⁷ They have hánds but they cánnot féel;
they have féet but they cánnot wálk.
They máke no sóund from their thróats.
⁸ Their mákers will cóme to be líke them,
as will áll who trúst in thém.

⁹ House of Ísrael, trúst in the LÓRD;
hé is their hélp and their shíeld.
¹⁰ House of Áaron, trúst in the LÓRD;
hé is their hélp and their shíeld.
¹¹ Those who féar the LORD, trúst in the LÓRD;
hé is their hélp and their shíeld.

¹² The LORD remémbers us, and hé will bléss us;
he will bléss the hóuse of Ísrael.
He will bléss the hóuse of Áaron.

¹³ He will bléss those who féar the LᴏRD,
the líttle no léss than the gréat.
¹⁴ To yóu may the LᴏRD grant íncrease,
to yóu and áll your chíldren.

¹⁵ Máy you be blést by the LᴏRD,
the máker of héaven and éarth.
¹⁶ The héavens, the héavens belóng to the LᴏRD,
but to the chíldren of mén, he has gíven the éarth.

¹⁷ The déad shall not práise the LᴏRD,
nor thóse who go dówn into the sílence.
¹⁸ But wé who líve bless the LᴏRD
both nów and forévermóre.

Alleluia!

PRAYER

All-powerful and all-knowing God, who dwell in the heavens and yet abide too among the people of the covenant: Guide us in the ways of faith, so that we may prefer nothing to you, who are our help and our shield, living and reigning forever and ever. Amen.

𝒫salm 116

I WILL CALL UPON THE NAME OF THE LORD

Psalm 116 has an interesting history as well as a significant place in the liturgy. The Greek and Latin traditions have divided this psalm into two (as designated following), so it becomes Psalms 114 and 115, yet the numeration of the verses remains continuous. As one of the Hallel Psalms, it speaks cogently about the Passover experience: when Israel was oppressed by the snares of death (v. 3), the LᴏRD came to their rescue and saved them (v. 6); for this reason, the cup of salvation (v. 13), identified with the Kiddush cup of the Jewish Passover meal, is raised in praise of the name of the Lord. A refrain "I will call on the name of the LORD" is repeated three times (vv. 4, 13b, 17b). In the Christian tradition, the Holy Thursday Mass of the Lord's Supper uses this psalm as the response to the reading from the Book of Exodus, recounting the story of Israel's departure from Egypt. The frequent references to death (vv. 3, 8, 15), with vivid images of death's finality ("anguish of the grave," "deliver my soul"), reveal how close the Psalmist feels he has come to death. But having been snatched from imminent destruction, the Psalmist lifts up ringing words of gratitude for God's attentive response (v. 2), compassion (v. 5), and saving help (v. 6b). In contrast to the three repetitions of the word *death*, the Psalmist joyfully acclaims, "I will walk in the presence of the LORD in the land of the living" (v. 9). In the biblical mind, "to walk" means more than mere progress on foot; it also entails "to live, to act, to direct one's life" (cf. Ps 1). Thus the Psalmist is saying that God's saving action has given direction to his way of life, now lived in accord with God's covenant. His assertion conveys both gratitude to God and the desire to live in a way that is life-giving before God and neighbor. A distinguishing mark of this psalm is its opening phrase: "I love the LORD" (v. 1a). Psalm 18 begins in a similar way, but it uses a different verb for the word *love*. Such a uniquely forceful expression raises the question, "How is such love for God manifested in practice?" The Psalmist answers the question in a number of ways that speak to a life lived with a spiritual focus. First, we find here the recognition of what God has done for him: God has heard his appeal (v. 1), has turned his ear whenever the Psalmist has called (v. 2), has shown compassion when the Psalmist was brought low (vv. 5–6), and has saved him from stumbling and death (v. 8). Second, the Psalmist affirms trust and confidence in God's help even in the midst of suffering (v. 10). Third, in the triple repetition, "I called upon the name of the LORD," the Psalmist affirms the source of his hope, confidence, and reliance—the foundation of his inner strength. Fourth, in acknowledging that God has "loosened the bonds" that held him captive (v. 16c), he now assumes a posture of being bound to God as a servant (v. 16a). And fifth, in the presence of the Jerusalem congregation, he offers a public sacrifice of thanksgiving as a way of fulfilling his vow before the Lord (vv. 17–19). In moving from suffering to deliverance, from oppression to freedom, the Psalmist draws greater trust and faith in God's goodness. His experience gives witness to the power of paschal living. The author of the Epistle to the Hebrews expounds on the similar experience of Jesus himself: "Although he was a Son, he learned obedience through what he suffered; and having been made perfect, he became the source of eternal salvation for all who obey him" (Heb 5:8–9). As the pioneer of our faith, Jesus points out to us the path to fullness of eternal life, a path the Psalmist had anticipated in earthly life centuries before.

PSALM 116A *(114:10–19; 115)*

¹ I lóve the LORD, for he has héard
my vóice, my appéal;
² for he has túrned his éar to mé
whenéver I cáll.

³ They surróunded me, the snáres of déath;
the ánguish of the gráve has fóund me;
ánguish and sórrow I fóund.
⁴ I cálled on the náme of the LORD:
"Delíver my sóul, O LORD!"

⁵ How grácious is the LORD, and júst;
our Gód has compássion.
⁶ The LORD protécts the símple;
I was brought lów, and he sáved me.

⁷ Turn báck, my sóul, to your rést,
for the LORD has been góod to yóu;
⁸ he has képt my sóul from déath,
my eyes from téars, and my féet from stúmbling.
⁹ I will wálk in the présence of the LORD
in the lánd of the líving.

PSALM 116B *(115:10–19)*

¹⁰ I trústed, éven when I sáid,
"I am sórely afflícted,"
¹¹ and whén I sáid in my alárm,
"These péople are all líars."

¹² Hów can I repáy the LORD
for áll his góodness to mé?
¹³ The cúp of salvátion I will ráise;
I will cáll on the náme of the LORD.

¹⁴ My vóws to the LORD I will fulfíll
before áll his péople.
¹⁵ How précious in the éyes of the LORD
is the déath of his fáithful.

¹⁶ Your sérvant, LORD, your sérvant am Í,
the són of your hándmaid;
you have lóosened my bónds.

¹⁷ A thánksgiving sácrifice I máke;
I will cáll on the náme of the LÓRD.

¹⁸ My vóws to the LÓRD I will fulfíll
before áll his péople,
¹⁹ in the cóurts of the hóuse of the LÓRD,
in your mídst, O Jerúsalem.

Alleluia!

PRAYER

Lord God, Deliverer and Redeemer, we come before you as your servants who have experienced your saving grace in our lives. In your loving kindness, enable us to walk in your truth and fidelity as we witness to the power of your salvation, calling always upon your name with trust and confidence. We ask this through Christ our Lord. Amen.

Psalm 117

ALL PEOPLES, PRAISE THE LORD

At a mere two verses, Psalm 117 is the shortest in the Psalter. Yet we know that at times a brief text may bear a powerful message; this is especially true of Psalm 117. First, the text presents a call for all nations and peoples to praise the LORD (v. 1). This stands out as a significant point among the Hallel Psalms: these psalms are often prayed in the context of Israel's great festivals, in which God's saving deeds for the children of Abraham are recalled, but here we encounter a universal call for all nations and peoples to acclaim the One Lord, the God of Israel. The universality of God's grace is echoed in the second Servant Song of the prophet Isaiah: "It is too light a thing that you should be my servant to raise up the tribes of Jacob and to restore the survivors of Israel; I will give you as a light to the nations, that my salvation may reach to the end of the earth" (Isa 49:6). The Babylonian captivity was a traumatic event for Israel, but the task of restoring the faith of those who survived was only part of what God was to bring about from that whole experience. Rather, Israel was to become a light to guide others to an experience of salvation in the One God of Israel. Nearer the end of the Isaiah's writings we read, "From new moon to new moon, and from sabbath to sabbath, all flesh shall come to worship before me, says the LORD" (Isa 66:23). The prophet offers a vision of all humanity coming before the Lord to worship the God who had entered into covenant with the people of Israel and revealed the holy name YHWH to them. Here in Psalm 117, the Psalmist takes up this vision, bringing the whole human race into the act of praising the One God. The second point (v. 2) links the Hebrew words *hesed* ("merciful love") and *emeth* ("faithfulness"). As previously noted (cf. Ps 89), these two words are often used in tandem to express the particular character of God's loyalty, steadfastness, and fidelity to the covenant relationship. The Psalmist here proclaims God's trustworthiness in upholding his part of the divine–human relationship. The expression "has prevailed over us" derives from a Hebrew noun meaning a strong man, a warrior, one who triumphs and overcomes difficult situations. Despite Israel's infidelities, God remains faithful; despite Israel's lack of loyalty, God is always steadfast in fulfilling his part of the covenant relationship. Writing to his disciple Timothy, St. Paul, the apostle to the Gentiles, reaffirms the message of Psalm 117: "The saying is sure: If we have died with him, we will also live with him; if we endure, we will also reign with him; if we deny him, he will also deny us; if we are faithless, he remains faithful—for he cannot deny himself" (2 Tim 2:11–13). For Christians, the covenant offered us in baptism, sealed by the blood of Christ, invites us too to experience the merciful love and fidelity of the Lord. And by the terms of that covenant, we are commanded to be a light for others, by which they too may come to know the goodness of our God.

PSALM 117 *(116)*

¹ O práise the LÓRD, all you nátions;
acclátim him, all you péoples!

² For his mérciful lóve has prevátiled over ús;
and the LÓRD's fátithfulness endútires forétver.

Alleluia!

PRAYER

Faithful and merciful God, whose steadfast loyalty manifests to us both our origin and our destiny in you: Transform us by your grace that we may respond to your covenant with that faithful love so perfectly mod-

eled in your Son. May his goodness draw all peoples to praise you with one accord. We ask this through Christ our Lord. Amen.

Psalm 118

THE STONE REJECTED BY THE BUILDERS

In both Jewish and Christian traditions, Psalm 118 is rich with meaning and matter for profound reflection. Psalm 118 concludes the collection of the great Hallel Psalms (113–18), those community prayers recited at the major Jewish festivals each year. In particular, Psalm 118 is associated with the Jewish feast of Sukkoth, or Tabernacles, the closing feast of the harvest season, when the people gave glad voice to their joy for God's blessings (Lev 23:33–36). In this psalm we find all the motifs of the preceding Hallel Psalms, those phrases and images repeated throughout the psalm to emphasize their significance. This psalm speaks of God's help and deliverance for those who put their trust in his holy name. In a frequent rhetorical device of Hebrew poetry, the opening verse is repeated as the closing of the psalm (v. 29); here the refrain repeats the word *mercy* (Hebrew, *hesed*), evoking God's covenant love and grounding this Thanksgiving Hymn in the theme of God's steadfast and faithful goodness. Finally, it is of interest to note that in the organization of the Psalter, the Hymn Book of the Second Temple, this psalm is placed between the shortest (Ps 117) and the longest (Ps 119) psalms of the Psalter. From the Christian perspective, Psalm 118 is often called "The Easter Psalm," as it provides texts that the early authors of the New Testament saw fulfilled in the person of Jesus Christ. The imagery of the paschal mystery, the movement from death to life, weaves its way through this psalm; for example, in verse 5, the simple text "He answered and freed me" is understood to refer to the passage of Jesus from death to life, freed from the bonds that sin had brought upon our race. This motif of liberation is echoed several times throughout the psalm (vv. 10–14, 17–18). Furthermore, the victorious hand of God is presented as transforming potentially fatal situations into moments of divine glory. For example, the confident assertion of faith that God stands at the side of the Psalmist allows him to look in triumph on his foes (v. 7). This motif of God's saving might also recurs several times throughout the psalm (vv. 11, 12, 14, 15b–16, 17–18, 22–23). Finally, the phrase "The stone which the builders rejected has become the cornerstone" (v. 22) is instantly recognizable for its many recurrences in the Easter liturgy. For the Jewish people, the "stone rejected" refers to Israel itself, while the "builders" are those larger and more powerful nations surrounding that small territory and people known by their ancestor's name. For Christians, the "stone rejected" comes to be identified with Jesus the Christ, the Messiah, whom the leaders of the people had refused to accept. In the mysterious unfolding of God's plan, Jesus is raised from the tomb, victorious over death and sin, and "opens the gates of justice" (v. 19) for all held captive by that enslaving power. Though no individual is named in the text itself, the Church naturally came to see Jesus as the one spoken of in the phrase "Blest is he who comes in the name of the LORD" (v. 26). He came among us to turn the engulfing tide of sin flowing from the Fall, creating us anew in the divine image originally intended for Adam and Eve and their descendants. We acclaim this phrase daily in the "Holy, Holy, Holy" following the preface to the Eucharistic Prayer. Addressing the Jerusalem leaders after Pentecost, the Apostle Peter explicitly affirms, "This Jesus is 'the stone that was rejected by you, the builders; it has become the cornerstone.' There is salvation in no one else, for there is no other name under heaven given among mortals by which we must be saved" (Acts 4:11–12). Thus does each day of the Easter season resound with the acclamation, "This is the day the LORD has made; let us rejoice in it and be glad" (v. 24)!

PSALM 118 (117)

¹ Give práise to the LÓRD, for he is góod;
his mércy endúres foréver.

² Let the hóuse of Ísrael sáy,
"His mércy endúres foréver."
³ Let the hóuse of Áaron sáy,
"His mércy endúres foréver."
⁴ Let thóse who féar the LORD sáy,
"His mércy endúres foréver."

⁵ I cálled to the LÓRD in my distréss;
he has ánswered and fréed me.
⁶ The LÓRD is at my síde; I do not féar.
Whát can mankínd do agáinst me?

⁷ The LORD is at my síde as my hélper;
I shall lóok in tríumph on my fóes.

⁸ It is bétter to take réfuge in the LORD
than to trúst in mán;
⁹ it is bétter to take réfuge in the LORD
than to trúst in prínces.

¹⁰ The nátions all encírcled mé;
in the náme of the LORD I cut them óff.
¹¹ They encírcled me áll aróund;
in the náme of the LORD I cut them óff.

¹² They encírcled me abóut like bées;
they blázed like a fíre among thórns.
In the náme of the LORD I cut them óff.

¹³ I was thrust dówn, thrust dówn and fálling,
but the LORD was my hélper.
¹⁴ The LORD is my stréngth and my sóng;
hé was my sávior.

¹⁵ There are shóuts of jóy and salvátion
in the ténts of the júst.
"The LORD's right hánd has done míghty déeds;
¹⁶ his ríght hand is exálted.
The LORD's right hánd has done míghty déeds."

¹⁷ I shall not díe, Í shall líve
and recóunt the déeds of the LORD.
¹⁸ The LORD púnished me, púnished me sevérely,
but did not hánd me óver to déath.

¹⁹ Open to mé the gátes of jústice:
I will énter and thánk the LORD.
²⁰ Thís is the LORD's own gáte,
where the júst énter.
²¹ I will thánk you, for yóu have ánswered,
and yóu are my sávior.

²² The stóne that the búilders rejécted
has becóme the córnerstone.
²³ By the LORD has thís been dóne,
a márvel in our éyes.

²⁴ This is the dáy the LÓRD has máde;
let us rejóice in ít and be glád.

²⁵ O LÓRD, gránt salvátion;
O LÓRD, gránt succéss.
²⁶ Blést is hé who cómes
in the náme of the LÓRD.
We bléss you from the hóuse of the LÓRD;
²⁷ the LORD is Gód, and has gíven us líght.

Go fórward in procéssion with bránches,
as fár as the hórns of the áltar.
²⁸ Yóu are my Gód, I práise you.
My Gód, I exált you.
²⁹ Give práise to the LÓRD, for he is góod;
his mércy endúres foréver.

PRAYER

O Christ, victorious over sin and death, we lift up praise and thanks-giving to your holy name, acknowledging you as the Pioneer of our sal-vation. Help us to walk the path of paschal victory in imitation of you, who are Lord, forever and ever. Amen.

Psalm 119

TREASURING GOD'S WORD
IN MY HEART

At 176 verses, Psalm 119 bears the distinction of being the longest in the Psalter. In addition to this, Psalm 119 is an extended acrostic, meaning that the opening word of each verse in a section begins with a consecutive letter of the Hebrew alphabet. Thus the first eight verses all begin with the letter aleph, the second eight verses with the letter beth, and so forth. As with other acrostic psalms we have encountered (Pss 9–10, 25, 34, 37, 111, 112, and 145), Psalm 119 belongs to that genre known as Wisdom Psalms. Like biblical proverbs, the Wisdom Psalms address the matter of living life well and in full accord with divine teachings. This understanding accords with the further classification of Psalm 119 as a Torah Psalm. The Hebrew word *torah* immediately brings the English word *law* to mind. But to appreciate the biblical sense of torah, we have to put aside any facile suggestions of speed limits or stop signs. Rather, the Hebrew sense of torah more broadly encompasses an understanding of a word like *instruction*. One way to appreciate this idea is to remind ourselves that the first five books of the Bible are called the Torah in the Jewish tradition; and though they contain sections and even books (Leviticus and parts of Deuteronomy) about laws in the plain sense of the word, most of the Torah is made up of narrative stories. These stories describe the way people live their lives in relation to God's teachings and guidance. Living the Torah means living according to the spirit of God's will and plan for the human race. The opening two verses of Psalm 119 express these ideas very well: Blessings will come upon those who walk in (that is, who live in accord with) the way that is blameless. As mentioned previously, the biblical mind conceives "walking" as living, and "the way" in which we walk is the path of life before us (v. 1). Walking thus under the guidance of God's plan will bring divine favor. Setting out to do this wholeheartedly charts a course by which we seek and find God in the midst of ordinary human experience (v. 2). As the text proceeds, we see how avoiding evil (v. 3), staying on the straight and narrow (v. 4), pondering the meaning of God's plan (v. 15), choosing to be faithful (v. 30), and bending one's heart to instruction (v. 36) constitute the path of the blameless. The Psalmist uses simple, homespun language to get across the idea that living God's law is something practical in ordinary terms, yet demanding our daily attention. Without a sense of focus or discipline, the daily matters of life fall into bad patterns and eventually wither and die. Psalm 119 reminds us that divine instruction must find an abiding place in the human heart if we are to persevere in seeking and eventually finding God in the human sphere. The Letter of James says it well: "Those who look into the perfect law, the law of liberty, and persevere, being not hearers who forget but doers who act—they will be blessed in their doing" (Jas 1:25). Holding God's instruction deep in our hearts brings us the wholeness that is true holiness.

PSALM 119 *(118)*:1–8

ALEPH

> ¹ Blessed are thóse whose wáy is blámeless,
> who wálk in the láw of the LÓRD!

² Blessed are thóse who kéep his decrées!
With áll their héarts they séek him.
³ They néver do ánything évil,
but wálk in his wáys.
⁴ Yóu have láid down your précepts
to be cárefully képt.

⁵ Máy my wáys be fírm
in kéeping your státutes.
⁶ Thén I shall nót be put to sháme
as I obsérve all your commánds.

⁷ I will thánk you with an úpright héart,
as I léarn your just júdgments.
⁸ Í will kéep your státutes;
do not éver forsáke me.

PSALM 119 *(118)*:9–16

BETH

⁹ How shall a yóuth remain púre on his wáy?
By obéying your wórd.
¹⁰ I have sóught you with áll my héart;
let me not stráy from your commánds.

¹¹ I tréasure your wórd in my héart,
lest I sín agáinst you.
¹² Blést are yóu, O Lᴏʀᴅ;
téach me your státutes.

¹³ With my líps have Í recóunted
all the decrées of your móuth.
¹⁴ I rejóice in the wáy of your précepts,
as though all ríches were míne.

¹⁵ Í will pónder your précepts,
and consíder your páths.
¹⁶ I táke delíght in your státutes;
I will nót forget your wórd.

PSALM 119 *(118)*:17–24

GIMEL

^{17.}Deal bóuntifully wíth your sérvant,
that I may líve and keep your wórd.
¹⁸ Ópen my éyes, that I may sée
the wónders of your láw.

¹⁹ Í am a pílgrim in the lánd;
híde not your commánds from mé.
²⁰ My sóul is consúmed with lónging
at all tímes for yóur decrées.

²¹ You thréaten the próud, the accúrsed,
who stráy from your commánds.
²² Frée me from scórn and contémpt,
for I obsérve your decrées.

²³ Though prínces sit plótting agáinst me,
your servant pónders your státutes.
²⁴ Sée, your decrées are my delíght;
your státutes are my cóunselors.

PSALM 119 *(118)*:25–32

DALETH

²⁵ My sóul holds fást to the dúst;
revíve me by your wórd.
²⁶ I declóred my wáys and you ánswered me;
téach me your státutes.

²⁷ Make me grásp the wáy of your précepts,
and I will pónder your wónders.
²⁸ My sóul pines awáy with gríef;
by your wórd raise me úp.

²⁹ Kéep me from the wáy of fálsehood;
grant me mércy by your láw.
³⁰ I have chósen the wáy of fáithfulness;
your decrées I have uphéld.

³¹ I clíng to your decrées, O LÓRD;
let me nót be put to sháme.

³² I will rún the wáy of your commánds;
you open wíde my héart.

PSALM 119 *(118)*:33–40

HE

³³ LORD, téach me the wáy of your státutes,
and I will kéep them to the énd.
³⁴ Grant me ínsight that Í may keep your láw,
and obsérve it wholehéartedly.

³⁵ Guíde me in the páth of your commands,
for in thém is my delíght.
³⁶ Bénd my héart to your decrées,
and not to wróngful gáin.

³⁷ Turn my éyes from gázing on vánities;
in your wáy, give me lífe.
³⁸ Fulfíll your prómise to your sérvant,
that yóu may be revéred.

³⁹ Túrn away the táunts I dréad,
for your decrées are góod.
⁴⁰ Sée, I lóng for your précepts;
give me lífe by your jústice.

PSALM 119 *(118)*:41–48

VAU

⁴¹ LÓRD, let your mércy come upón me,
the salvátion you have prómised.
⁴² I shall ánswer thóse who táunt me,
for I trúst in your wórd.

⁴³ Never táke the word of trúth from my móuth,
for I hópe in your decrées.
⁴⁴ I shall álways kéep your láw,
foréver and éver.

⁴⁵ I shall wálk on a spácious pláin,
for I séek your précepts.
⁴⁶ I will spéak of your decrées before kíngs,
and nót be abáshed.

⁴⁷ In your commánds I have fóund my delíght;
thése I have lóved.
⁴⁸ I reach óut to your commánds, which I lóve,
and pónder your státutes.

PSALM 119 *(118)*:49–56

ZAYIN

⁴⁹ Remémber your wórd to your sérvant,
by which you máde me hópe.
⁵⁰ Thís is my cómfort in sórrow:
that your prómise gives me lífe.

⁵¹ Though the próud may útterly deríde me,
I do not túrn from your láw.
⁵² When I remémber your júdgments of óld,
these, O Lórd, consóle me.

⁵³ I am séized with indignátion at the wícked
who forsáke your láw.
⁵⁴ Your státutes have becóme my sóng
wheréver I dwéll.

⁵⁵ I remémber your náme in the níghttime,
and I kéep your láw.
⁵⁶ Thís has béen my lót,
for I have képt your précepts.

PSALM 119 *(118)*:57–64

HETH

⁵⁷ I have sáid, "O Lórd, my pórtion
is to obéy your wórds."
⁵⁸ With all my héart I implóre your fávor;
as with your prómise, have mércy.

⁵⁹ Í have póndered my wáys,
and turned my stéps to your decrées.
⁶⁰ I made háste; I did nót deláy
to obéy your commánds.

⁶¹ Though the néts of the wícked ensnáre me,
your láw I did nót forgét.

⁶² At mídnight I will ríse and thánk you
for your júst decrées.
⁶³ I am a fríend of áll who revére you,
who kéep your précepts.
⁶⁴ O LORD, your mérciful lóve fills the éarth.
Téach me your státutes.

PSALM 119 *(118)*:65–72

TETH

⁶⁵ O LÓRD, you have been góod to your sérvant,
accórding to your wórd.
⁶⁶ Téach me good júdgment and knówledge,
for I trúst in your commánds.

⁶⁷ Befóre I was húmbled, I stráyed,
but nów I keep your wórd.
⁶⁸ You are góod, and you dó what is góod;
téach me your státutes.

⁶⁹ The árrogant sméar me with líes;
with all my héart I keep your précepts.
⁷⁰ Their héart is dénse like fát,
but your láw is my delíght.

⁷¹ It was góod for mé to be húmbled,
that I might léarn your státutes.
⁷² The láw from your móuth means móre to me
than large qúantities of sílver and góld.

PSALM 119 *(118)*:73–80

YOD

⁷³ It was your hánds that máde me and sháped me;
grant me ínsight to léarn your commánds.
⁷⁴ Those who revére you sée me and rejóice,
for I trúst in your wórd.

⁷⁵ O LORD, I knów that your decrées are ríght;
though I am húmbled, you are júst.
⁷⁶ Let your mérciful lóve consóle me
by your prómise to your sérvant.

⁷⁷ Show me compássion, that Í may líve,
for your láw is my delíght.
⁷⁸ Let the árrogant be shámed who defléct me with líes;
as for mé, I will pónder your précepts.

⁷⁹ Let those who féar you túrn to mé,
that they may knów your decrées.
⁸⁰ Let my héart be blámeless in your státutes,
that I may nót be put to sháme.

PSALM 119 *(118)*:81–88

CAPH

⁸¹ My soul yéarns for yóur salvátion;
I hópe in your wórd.
⁸² My eyes yéarn to sée your prómise.
I ask, "Whén will you cómfort me?"

⁸³ I am like a wíneskin shríveled by smóke,
yet I remémber your státutes.
⁸⁴ How lóng must your sérvant endúre?
Whén will you bring júdgment on my fóes?

⁸⁵ For mé the próud have dug pítfalls;
they defý your láw.
⁸⁶ Your commánds are all trúe; then hélp me
when líes oppréss me.

⁸⁷ They have álmost made an énd of me on éarth,
yet I forsáke not your précepts.
⁸⁸ In your mérciful lóve, give me lífe;
I will obéy the decrées of your líps.

PSALM 119 *(118)*:89–96

LAMED

⁸⁹ Foréver is your wórd, O LÓRD,
standing fírm in the héavens.
⁹⁰ From áge to áge is your trúth;
like the éarth, it stands fírm.

⁹¹ Your júdgments endúre to this dáy,
for áll things are your sérvants.

⁹² Had your láw not béen my delíght,
I would have díed in my afflíction.
⁹³ I will néver forgét your précepts,
for with thém you give me lífe.
⁹⁴ Sáve me, Í am yóurs,
for I séek your précepts.

⁹⁵ Though the wícked lie in wáit to destróy me,
yet I pónder your decrées.
⁹⁶ I have séen that all perféction has an énd,
but your commánd is bóundless.

PSALM 119 *(118)*:97–104

MEM

⁹⁷ O Lórd, how I lóve your láw:
my meditátion all the dáy!
⁹⁸ Your commánd makes me wíser than my fóes,
for it is wíth me álways.

⁹⁹ I have more ínsight than áll who téach me,
for I pónder your decrées.
¹⁰⁰ I have gáined more understánding than my élders,
for I kéep your précepts.

¹⁰¹ I keep my féet from évery evil páth,
to obéy your wórd.
¹⁰² I have nót turned awáy from your decrees,
which you yoursélf have táught me.

¹⁰³ How swéet is your prómise to my tóngue,
more than hóney in the móuth.
¹⁰⁴ I gáin understánding from your précepts,
and so I háte all false wáys.

PSALM 119 *(118)*:105–112

NUN

¹⁰⁵ Your wórd is a lámp for my féet,
and a líght for my páth.
¹⁰⁶ I have swórn an óath and affirmed it,
to obéy your just júdgments.

¹⁰⁷ I am déeply afflícted, O LÓRD;
by your wórd, give me lífe.
¹⁰⁸ Accépt, LORD, my fréely offered hómage,
and téach me your decrées.

¹⁰⁹ My lífe is in my hánds at all tímes;
I do nót forget your láw.
¹¹⁰ For me the wícked have sét a snáre;
yet I do not stráy from your précepts.

¹¹¹ Your decrées are my héritage foréver,
the jóy of my héart.
¹¹² I inclíne my heart to cárry out your státutes
foréver, to the énd.

PSALM 119 *(118)*:113–120

SAMECH

¹¹³ I detest thóse with a divíded héart,
but I lóve your láw.
¹¹⁴ Yóu are my híding place, my shíeld;
I hópe in your wórd.

¹¹⁵ Depárt from me, yóu who do évil;
I will kéep my God's commánds.
¹¹⁶ Uphóld me by your prómise; I shall líve.
Let my hópes not be in váin.

¹¹⁷ Bear me úp and Í shall be sáved,
and ever múse on your státutes.
¹¹⁸ You spúrn all who stráy from your státutes;
their cúnning is in váin.

¹¹⁹ You regárd the wícked like dróss,
so I lóve your decrées.
¹²⁰ My flesh trémbles in térror befóre you;
I féar your júdgments.

PSALM 119 *(118)*:121–128

AYIN

¹²¹ I have dóne what is júst and ríght;
do not léave me to my fóes.

¹²² Guarantée the well-béing of your sérvant;
let not the próud oppréss me.
¹²³ My eyes grow wéary as I wátch for your salvátion,
and for your prómise of jústice.
¹²⁴ Treat your sérvant with mérciful lóve,
and téach me your státutes.

¹²⁵ I am your sérvant; gíve me understánding:
then I shall knów your decrées.
¹²⁶ It is tíme for the LÓRD to áct,
for your láw has been bróken.

¹²⁷ That is whý I lóve your commánds
more than fínest góld,
¹²⁸ why I rúle my lífe by your précepts,
and háte false wáys.

PSALM 119 *(118)*:129–136

PE

¹²⁹ Your decrées are wónderful indéed;
therefore my sóul obéys them.
¹³⁰ The unfólding of your wórd gives líght,
and understánding to the símple.

¹³¹ I have ópened my móuth and I sígh,
for I yéarn for your commánds.
¹³² Túrn and have mércy on mé,
as is your rúle for those who lóve your náme.

¹³³ Let my stéps be guíded by your prómise;
may évil never rúle me.
¹³⁴ Redéem me from mán's oppréssion,
and I will kéep your précepts.

¹³⁵ Let your fáce shine fórth on your sérvant,
and téach me your decrées.
¹³⁶ My éyes shed stréams of téars,
because of thóse who have not képt your láw.

PSALM 119 *(118)*:137–144

TSADE

¹³⁷ Yóu are júst, O LÓRD;
your júdgments are úpright.
¹³⁸ You have impósed your decrées with jústice,
and with útter fidélity.

¹³⁹ Í am consúmed with zéal,
for my fóes forget your wórd.
¹⁴⁰ Your prómise has been thóroughly tésted,
and it is chérished by your sérvant.

¹⁴¹ Although Í am yóung and despísed,
I do nót forget your précepts.
¹⁴² Your jústice is jústice foréver,
and your láw is trúth.

¹⁴³ Though ánguish and distréss have fóund me,
your commánds are my delíght.
¹⁴⁴ Your decrées are foréver júst;
give me ínsight, and Í shall líve.

PSALM 119 *(118)*:145–152

KOPH

¹⁴⁵ I cáll with all my héart; LORD, ánswer me.
I will obsérve your státutes.
¹⁴⁶ I cáll upón you; sáve me,
and I will kéep your decrées.

¹⁴⁷ I ríse before dáwn and cry for hélp;
I have hóped in your wórd.
¹⁴⁸ My éyes awáken before dáwn,
to pónder your prómise.

¹⁴⁹ In your mércy, héar my voice, O LÓRD;
give me lífe by your decrées.
¹⁵⁰ Those who pursúe me with malíce draw néar;
they are fár from your láw.

¹⁵¹ But yóu, O LÓRD, are clóse;
all your commánds are trúth.

¹⁵² From of óld I have knówn that your decrées
are estáblished foréver.

PSALM 119 *(118)*:153–160

RESH

¹⁵³ Sée my afflíction and delíver me,
for I do nót forget your láw.
¹⁵⁴ Uphóld my cáuse and defénd me;
by your prómise, give me lífe.

¹⁵⁵ Salvátion is fár from the wícked,
who are héedless of your státutes.
¹⁵⁶ Númberless, LÓRD, are your mércies;
in your jústice, give me lífe.

¹⁵⁷ Though my fóes and oppréssors are cóuntless,
I have not swérved from your decrées.
¹⁵⁸ I lóok at the fáithless with disgúst;
they have not képt your wórd.

¹⁵⁹ See how I lóve your précepts, O LÓRD!
In your mércy, give me lífe.
¹⁶⁰ Trúth is the súm of your wórd;
all your just júdgments are etérnal.

PSALM 119 *(118)*:161–168

SHIN

¹⁶¹ Though prínces oppréss me without cáuse,
my heart revéres your wórd.
¹⁶² Í rejóice at your prómise,
like one who fínds a great tréasure.

¹⁶³ Fálsehood I háte and detést,
but I lóve your láw.
¹⁶⁴ Séven times a dáy I práise you
for your júst decrées.

¹⁶⁵ The lóvers of your láw have great péace;
no stúmbling block for thém.
¹⁶⁶ I awáit your salvátion, O LÓRD;
I fulfíll your commánds.

¹⁶⁷ My sóul obéys your decrées,
and lóves them déarly.
¹⁶⁸ I obéy your précepts and decrées;
all my wáys are befóre you.

PSALM 119 *(118)*:169–176

TAU

¹⁶⁹ Let my crý come befóre you, O LÓRD;
give me ínsight by your wórd.
¹⁷⁰ Let my pléading cóme befóre you;
rescue me accórding to your prómise.

¹⁷¹ My líps shall procláim your práise,
because you téach me your státutes.
¹⁷² My tóngue will síng of your prómise,
for your commánds are júst.

¹⁷³ Let your hánd be réady to hélp me,
for I have chósen your précepts.
¹⁷⁴ I have lónged for your salvátion, O LÓRD,
and your láw is my delíght.

¹⁷⁵ My sóul shall líve and práise you.
Your júdgments give me hélp.
¹⁷⁶ I have stráyed like a shéep; seek your servant,
for I dó not forgét your commánds.

PRAYER

Lord Jesus, Eternal Word, who perfectly fulfilled the Father's plan by which human nature is renewed and set upon the ways of peace: transform our hearts' longing into deeds that give witness to the law of love, so that we may more fittingly glorify God and more truly love our neighbor. You live and reign as Lord, forever and ever. Amen.

Psalm 120

I AM FOR PEACE

Psalms 120–34 present another unified group of psalms that are collectively designated the Psalms of Ascent. Some theories hold that these songs were sung by people making a pilgrimage to Jerusalem for any of the great festivals; it has further been suggested that the fifteen psalms may have been sung successively on each of the fifteen steps up to the temple. The topography of the Holy Land means that any trip to Jerusalem demands that one ascend; hence the superscription "A Song of Ascent" common to all of these psalms. Most of these (apart from Psalm 132) are short and repetitious, making them easy to memorize. These psalms employ language and imagery evoking both the city of Jerusalem and the rural agricultural areas distant from the Holy City. Though many of the psalms represent the various literary genres of laments, complaints, hymns, and songs of confidence, their unity is manifest in the repeated motifs of peace, the city of Jerusalem, the hope for blessing, and trust in God's providential care for Israel. In Psalm 120, we encounter an interesting pair of images that appears elsewhere in the Psalter: lying lips, deceitful tongue (v. 2; cf. Pss 10, 31, 36, 50, 52, 101, 109). For the Psalmist, a deceitful tongue is a weapon for a kind of war: a personal war waged against another individual. The deceitful tongue is likened to sharp arrows and red-hot coals (v. 4), weapons with potential to inflict serious and even mortal injury. Such powerful language demonstrates how seriously a moral flaw deceitfulness was held to be. Duplicity and dishonesty destroy the peace of anyone they are employed against—the peace that comprises personal well-being, encompassing physical, emotional and spiritual security and health. Faced with the distress arising from being the victim of deceit, the Psalmist turns to prayer, with the assurance of God's response (v. 1). In the pilgrimage of life, too many are subjected to the pain of deceit and dishonesty. Early Christians witnessed this very situation in the experience of St. Paul, who struggled with various communities to whom he preached the gospel message, where his teaching was misinterpreted, misrepresented, or misunderstood. His sorrow at the situation is poignantly brought out in his Letter to the Galatians. Dealing with the falsehood spoken against him and his message, Paul is blunt in his efforts to set things right and restore peace among his converts. "Have I now become your enemy by telling you the truth? My little children, for whom I am again in the pain of childbirth until Christ is formed in you, I wish I were present with you now and could change my tone, for I am perplexed about you" (Gal 4:16, 19–20). St. Paul affirms the lengths to which he would go in order to correct the situation, to form the truth aright in the lives of his converts. The powerful effect of the tongue can also be employed for good, when the truth is offered in charity and gentleness.

PSALM 120 *(119)*

¹ *A Song of Ascents.*

To the LÓRD in the hóur of my distréss
I cáll: and he ánswers me.
² "O LÓRD, save my sóul from lying líps,
from the tóngue of the decéitful."

³ What should he gíve you, whát repáy you,
O decéitful tóngue?
⁴ The wárrior's árrows shárpened,
with red-hot cóals from the bróom tree!

⁵ Alás, that I líve in Méshech,
dwell among the ténts of Kédar!
⁶ Í have had enóugh of dwélling
with thóse who hate péace.
⁷ Í am for péace, but when I spéak,
théy are for wár.

PRAYER

Lord God, whose truth and wisdom guide us on our pilgrim way to you: Give us the words that will bring healing and hope to others, that we may be formed in your truth as a community of love. Through Christ our Lord. Amen.

Psalm 121

THE LORD YOUR GUARD, YOUR SHIELD

Our world today seems beset by a widespread failure of trust. The confidence that most people want to have—in governments, in businesses, and in other ordinary people—has too often been betrayed, broken, or compromised. As an alternative to such an unsatisfactory outlook, Psalm 121 presents a powerful expression of trust in God, whose divine deeds sustain and move the entire universe, yet also influence our individual lives in personal and intimate ways. In the opening two verses the Psalmist affirms his confidence in God in several ways. First, by the phrase "I lift up my eyes to the mountains," the Psalmist indicates the divine nature of the object of his gaze. Among many peoples of the Ancient Near East, mountains were held to be the homes of the gods. Rising toward the heavens, the dwelling place of the divine, mountains were themselves places of holiness. Second, the first person singular employed in these verses communicates the personal character of the speaker's relationship to God. By applying the possessive *my* to God, the Psalmist shows that in having passed through some unspecified life experiences, he has found the LORD (he uses here the divine name that God revealed at Sinai in Exod 3) to be the sure source of help (v. 2a). Our own experience of knowing the presence and aid of God in challenging circumstances similarly bolsters and confirms our own trust. Third, the Psalmist knows that the God who has been "my help" also remains the One who brought into being the heavens and the earth (v. 2b). The omnipotent and infinite Creator remains close to these small, insignificant creatures he has set upon the earth. Our God is a figure of both power and compassion—at once both transcendent and immanent. In the transition from the first person singular "I" (vv. 1–2) to the second person singular "you" (vv. 3–8), the Psalmist modifies his remarks to speak of God in relation to the whole of Israel (v. 4b); that is, to all who would believe. This section of the psalm comprises a series of images representing situations in which God has proven to be worthy of human trust. To "keep your foot from stumbling" is a Hebraic metaphor for the grace that prevents us from falling into moral error: our God is ever awake to the dangers that beset our path (vv. 3–4). As the guardian of Israel, the Lord watches over its ways and guides its steps. The Hebrew syntax leaves ambiguous whether these references are to the corporate Israel or to individuals; perhaps this rhetorical device is meant to let us have it both ways—God is the guardian both of the people of the covenant and of each of its members. The closing verse is a sweeping blessing on the whole of our earthly journey, both literal and figurative; we are assured that God guards us at each step. The Psalmist's deep trust in God is manifest in the expression. In much the same terms, Jesus reveals the depth of his own trust and confidence in the One whom he calls Abba. The Gospel of John reiterates over and over the manner by which Christ invites his followers to share in this unique relationship: "Holy Father, protect them in your name that you have given me, so that they may be one, as we are one" (John 17:11b). Jesus' own experience of God fills him with an unshakable trust and confidence; thus is he able to accomplish the Father's will—which is to bring about our eternal salvation through the paschal mystery. Jesus himself shows us the way to unshakable trust and absolute peace.

PSALM 121 *(120)*

¹ *A Song of Ascents.*

I líft up my éyes to the móuntains;
from whére shall come my hélp?
² My hélp shall cóme from the LÓRD,
who made héaven and éarth.

³ He will kéep your fóot from stúmbling.
Your guárd will never slúmber.
⁴ Nó, he sléeps not nor slúmbers,
Ísrael's guárd.

⁵ The LORD your guárd, the LÓRD your sháde
at yóur right hánd.
⁶ By dáy the sún shall not smíte you,
nor the móon in the níght.

⁷ The LÓRD will guárd you from évil;
he will guárd your sóul.
⁸ The LORD will guárd your góing and cóming,
both nów and foréver.

Lord God, our guardian and our help in life's journey: open our hearts to know the wondrous love and protection you extend to us as your children. May our confidence in your constant guidance deepen our faith, so that we may profess your holy name as the source of all blessings. We ask this through Christ our Lord. Amen.

Psalm 122

THE PEACE OF JERUSALEM

Upon a pilgrim's arriving in Jerusalem, Psalm 122 would have provided suitable words for celebrating all the things that Jerusalem represented for ancient Israel: the dwelling place of the Lord, the seat of government, the place of pilgrimage, the "city of peace" (the literal meaning of "Jerusalem"). References to the "house of the Lord" in its opening and closing verses bracket this psalm. The temple in Jerusalem was understood to house the divine presence—within the Holy of Holies (the inner sanctuary), in the mercy seat above the Ark of the Covenant. The long history of Jerusalem back to the kingship of David recounts God's many deeds on their behalf. The city represented the unity of the covenant people, called to be one people under one God and one law (v. 3). The peace and well-being of Jerusalem became a symbol of the state of being of the whole people. Peace, so dear to the hearts of the people of Israel, is here spoken of as if it were a person: "May peace abide in your walls, and security be in your towers" (v. 7). And always coupled with peace is praise for God, whose marvelous deeds of salvation were recalled at the great festivals of the year. Israel gave witness to its deepest identity in praising the name of the Lord (v. 4cd). Israel had been called into existence for the very purpose of giving glory to God, and in so doing, witnessed to God's invitation to them to enter into a covenant relationship. As the Book of Deuteronomy puts it, "It was not because you were more numerous than any other people that the Lord set his heart on you and chose you—for you were the fewest of all peoples. It was because the Lord loved you and kept the oath that he swore to your ancestors, that the Lord has brought you out with a mighty hand, and redeemed you from the house of slavery, from the hand of Pharaoh king of Egypt" (7:7–8). The sense of well-being—of having been chosen, loved, protected, and cared for—pervades this psalm and gives reason for the joy that it exudes. "Peace upon you"— *Shalom* (v. 8)—manifests a blessing that to this day is a familiar way of greeting friends and wishing them well. For Christians who seek the new Jerusalem promised to those who love God and remain faithful to the new law of love, the closing chapter of the Book of Revelation sums up our hopes: "I saw the holy city, the new Jerusalem, coming down out of heaven from God, prepared as a bride adorned for her husband. [God] will dwell with them; they will be his peoples, and God himself will be with them; he will wipe every tear from their eyes. Death will be no more; mourning and crying and pain will be no more, for the first things have passed away" (Rev 21:2, 3b–4). We continue to pray for the peace of Jerusalem, divided and war weary; and we look forward to a new Jerusalem, where our God will be all in all. Psalm 122 still encompasses our hope.

PSALM 122 *(121)*

¹ *A Song of Ascents. Of David.*

I rejóiced when they sáid to mé,
"Let us gó to the hóuse of the LÓRD."
² And nów our féet are stánding
withín your gátes, O Jerúsalem.

³ Jerúsalem is buílt as a cíty
bonded as óne togéther.
⁴ It is thére that the tríbes go úp,
the tríbes of the LÓRD.

For Ísrael's wítness it ís
to práise the náme of the LÓRD.
⁵ Thére were set the thrónes for júdgment,
the thrónes of the hóuse of Dávid.

⁶ For the péace of Jerúsalem práy,
"May they prósper, thóse who lóve you."
⁷ May péace abíde in your wálls,
and secúrity bé in your tówers.

⁸ For the sáke of my fámily and fríends,
let me sáy, "Péace upon yóu."
⁹ For the sáke of the hóuse of the LÓRD, our Gód,
Í will séek good thíngs for yóu.

Almighty and ever-living God, bestower of every good gift and source of all blessing, may the joy of your peace abide in our hearts as we look to the day when Jerusalem will be truly a city of peace, and where all may dwell in the harmony and concord to which you call us. We ask this through Christ our Lord. Amen.

Psalm 123

OUR EYES LOOK TO THE HEAVENS

This short psalm of only four verses offers at its outset a resemblance to an earlier psalm. In Psalm 121, the Psalmist "lifts up [his] eyes to the mountains"; here in Psalm 123, the Psalmist has "lifted up [his] eyes" to God "who dwell[s] in the heavens." Media specialists have long known that a person's eyes are a powerful indicator of his or her emotional or spiritual outlook. Eyes welling with tears, eyes bright with joy, eyes eager for an answer, eyes grateful for a response—all of these tell us how we "speak" with our eyes. Four times in this brief psalm we encounter the word *eyes* (vv. 1b, 2a, 2c, 2e). Psalm 145:15 says of the LORD, "The eyes of all look to you, and you give them their food in due season." The words of that psalm express both expectant hope and secure satisfaction; eyes eager with anticipation become eyes that recognize fulfillment. A similar posture is presented in this psalm: the eyes of slaves look upon their lord or mistress in anticipation of a gracious response, just as we look to the Lord our God for mercy. The Hebrew word translated here as "mercy" (v. 2f) bears a sense of graciousness, a sign of divine favor. 1 Samuel 1–2 provides an account of the mother of the young prophet Samuel. Her name is "Hannah," which derives from the same Hebrew word under consideration. This story begins with a paradox: Hannah, who was barren, bore a name indicating the favor of God; only as the story develops and she gives birth to Samuel does her name become appropriate to her situation. The text tells us, "Elkanah knew his wife Hannah, and the LORD remembered her" (1 Sam 1:19c). In the Lord's remembrance, gracious mercy was extended to Hannah. The final verse of this psalm similarly asks for gracious favor from God that the speaker be freed from contempt for the proud and arrogant. The message of both story and psalm? The One who dwells in the heavens is sought out by the humble servant, who looks toward the divine dwelling place with confidence and trust. In the Sermon on the Mount, Jesus too speaks about the eye of a person: "The eye is the lamp of the body. So, if your eye is healthy, your whole body will be full of light; but if your eye is unhealthy, your whole body will be full of darkness. If then the light in you is darkness, how great is the darkness!" (Matt 6:22–23). May we keep our eyes fixed on the Lord, that the light of Jesus' own vision may enable us to see and know the gracious mercy our God wishes to bestow on us.

PSALM 123 (122)

¹ *A Song of Ascents.*

To yóu have I lífted up my éyes,
you who dwéll in the héavens.

² Behóld, like the éyes of sláves
on the hánd of their lórds,
líke the éyes of a sérvant
on the hánd of her místress,
so our éyes are on the LÓRD our Gód,
till he shów us his mércy.

³ Have mércy on us, LÓRD, have mércy.
We are fílled with contémpt.
⁴ Indéed, all too fúll is our sóul
with the scórn of the árrogant,
the disdáin of the próud.

PRAYER

O God, who dwell in the heavens yet show mercy to those who look to you with faith, enliven our trust, that in all of life's challenges we may seek your guidance and find the path to truth and joy. Through Christ our Lord. Amen.

Psalm 124

A DANGEROUS FLOOD
AND A SNARE

In the biblical outlook, water was seen to possess the opposed characteristics of both blessing and danger. In Psalm 124, the many images of dangerous flood waters create a sense of potential disaster and imminent death. Yet the Psalmist's opening words offer heartfelt thanksgiving, for the Lord, he asserts, truly stands with the chosen people and protects them from harm. Had the Lord not been with them, the Psalmist insists, utter ruin and tragedy would surely have befallen them. How difficult it is for modern minds to make such a profound faith their own! In our world today, where emphasis is laid on one's individual ability to overcome, accomplish, succeed, and achieve, the placing of one's total trust in God's grace at work in us becomes an act of extraordinary faith. The Psalmist's words are indeed extreme: "swallowed alive" (v. 3), "engulfed " (v. 4a), "over our heads...raging waters" (v. 5). All these expressions are suggestive of a near-death experience. It has been said that only by passing through the very jaws of death and coming out alive is one able to appreciate life fully. This seems to be the kind of experience the Psalmist speaks of here: he employs communitarian terms (v. 1), but the immediacy of the experience is personally and individually intense. Words of praise burst forth from one who has been personally ransomed from death by the intervention of God's saving hand (v. 6). To "bless the LORD" (v. 6) is to offer a proclamation of praise and thanksgiving to the One who has accomplished what would otherwise have been impossible; having been subjected to danger like prey to a predator's teeth, but now having come to know the joyous relief of rescue and peace, is more than sufficient reason for the Psalmist's heartfelt gratitude. Many religious communities begin meetings with a brief prayer comprising a versicle and response taken from the final lines of this psalm: the superior recites, "Our help is in the name of the LORD," and those gathered respond, "Who made heaven and earth." The words bear a much deeper significance than we might give them in such ordinary circumstances, for with them we affirm with the Psalmist that "God alone, the God of heaven and earth, is our help, our refuge, our stronghold, our safety, our protection, our hope." In the Gospels, Jesus had clearly personalized this sense of God as the One who provides all things: "Do not worry, saying, 'What will we eat?' or 'What will we drink?' or 'What will we wear?' For it is the Gentiles who strive for all these things; and indeed your heavenly Father knows that you need all these things. But strive first for the kingdom of God and his righteousness, and all these things will be given to you as well. So do not worry about tomorrow, for tomorrow will bring worries of its own. Today's trouble is enough for today" (Matt 6:31–34). Each day does indeed have its troubles, but God is with us to bring us through them, as long as we place our faith firmly in his steadfast love.

PSALM 124 (123)

¹ *A Song of Ascents. Of David.*

"If the LORD had not béen on our síde,"
let Ísrael sáy –
² "If the LORD had not béen on our síde
when péople rose agáinst us,
³ thén would they have swállowed us alíve
when their ánger was kíndled.

⁴ Thén would the wáters have engúlfed us,
the tórrent gone óver us;
⁵ óver our héad would have swépt
the ráging wáters."

⁶ Blést be the LORD who did not gíve us
a préy to their téeth!
⁷ Our lífe, like a bírd, has escáped
from the snáre of the fówler.

Indéed, the snáre has been bróken,
and wé have escáped.
⁸ Our hélp is in the náme of the LORD,
who made héaven and éarth.

PRAYER

Lord our God, source of blessing and giver of every good gift, open in us the eyes of faith, so that, confident of your provision for all our needs, we might walk the ways of peace in the presence of your Word, Jesus Christ, who is Lord, forever and ever. Amen.

Psalm 125

THE LORD SURROUNDS HIS PEOPLE

Anyone who has approached Jerusalem from the Jericho Road will have a special appreciation for this psalm. Only ten miles from the Dead Sea, Jericho is approximately 800 feet below sea level. And though Jerusalem is only 15 miles from Jericho, the land rises some 3,400 feet in that short distance; it is a steep climb. But when you reach the point where Jerusalem comes into view, you see the city from a unique perspective. The words of this psalm capture the particular thrill of that moment: "Jerusalem! The mountains surround her; so the LORD surrounds his people, both now and forever" (v. 2). Jerusalem stands there, a mountaintop stronghold protectively surrounded by other mountains. The meaning of the Psalmist's image is readily apparent: the encircling mountains are like the arms of God embracing Sion, daughter Jerusalem, his chosen city (cf. Ps 132:13–14). This wonderful image of divine love and protection evokes Israel's trust in God who created and chose this place as a unique dwelling for the divine presence on earth. Yet close upon this reassuring image of God's protective love there follows a warning about those who might choose to do evil in the land. The wicked will not be permitted to dwell with the faithful, lest their bad influence lead the just astray (v. 3). Certainly the teaching and example of others has an impact on those with whom they live, work, and do business; intimate family connections and those whom we choose as friends have an incalculable influence. Thus the wise advise us to choose friends carefully and associate with good people; we will come to be like them, and they like us. The Psalmist concludes with a petition that the LORD bestow blessings on those who act in accord with his ways: living uprightly and doing good (v. 4). These two courses of action represent a way of life that includes the whole person, exterior and interior. The desired result is that true peace—well-being of mind, heart, and body— will come to rest upon the people of Israel. In his Letter to the Galatians, St. Paul bemoans the negative influence that has hindered them from living authentically "in Christ." He writes, "You were running well; who prevented you from obeying the truth? Such persuasion does not come from the one who calls you" (5:7–8). The One who calls us is God, who invites us to be ambassadors of goodness, truth, and righteousness, of justice, mercy, and peace, that we might be the very "aroma of Christ" in our world today (2 Cor 2:15).

PSALM 125 *(124)*

¹ *A Song of Ascents.*

Thóse who put their trúst in the LÓRD
are like Mount Síon, that cánnot be sháken,
that stánds foréver.
² Jerúsalem! The móuntains surróund her;
so the LÓRD surróunds his péople,
both nów and foréver.

³ For the scépter of the wícked shall not rést
over the lánd allótted to the júst,
for féar that the hánds of the júst
should túrn to évil.

⁴ Do góod, LORD, to thóse who are góod,
to the úpright of héart;
⁵ but thóse who túrn to crooked wáys –
the LÓRD will drive awáy with the wícked!
On Ísrael, péace!

PRAYER

Almighty and ever-living God, whose merciful providence for us over-flows in abundance: May our confidence in your love and compassion strengthen us to choose the paths of justice and peace, so becoming instruments of your infinite good, through Christ our Lord. Amen.

Psalm 126

SOWING IN TEARS

Certain historical moments have significance for both communities and individuals. In the Bible, the return from the Babylonian exile (c. 539 BC) had an overwhelming influence on Israel's national identity and how they understood their relationship with God. In an earlier era, they had experienced liberation from oppression in Egypt as an act of God's power and love for them, and centuries later, the mighty arm of their compassionate God again came to their rescue in bringing back the people of Judah from captivity in Babylon. Small and insignificant, Judah had been largely integrated into the life and culture of Babylon, and the apparent hopelessness of their situation seemed to leave no future for the identity of God's people as an independent community. Only a miracle of divine love could bring about the reversal of fortunes that the faithful among the captives hoped for. And that is what happened: the impossible occurred. Stunned by the event, the people "thought [they] were dreaming" (v. 1). Here we encounter an important truth about how God's actions are presented in Scripture. The Exodus from Egypt does not represent a one-time experience; the movement from oppression to freedom is brought about again and again in the life of the people of Israel. The word *exodus*, from the Greek *ex hodos*, means, quite literally, "a way out." Think of the many ways such a concept of liberation can be applied to human experience, individually or in community. When war or civil strife breaks out (such as we have seen so often in the Middle East and Africa recently), the true "way out" must include taking hold of the grace that God provides (v. 3) and putting forth the best human efforts to bring about situations of justice and equity. On an individual level, when two people experience a rupture in relationship, the way out must involve the grace of forgiveness and understanding, moving forward with a new perspective, each allowing the other the space to grow and mature. In both situations, seeds sown in the tears of forgiveness and relinquishing of past hurts will flow naturally into a song of grace, giving voice to joy of heart and praise for God's reconciling love. Such experiences enjoin us to open our hearts to the newness of God's Spirit, who invites us to find a way out of life's hurts and misunderstandings; each time we are freed of our subjugation (too often self-imposed), we are strengthened in our witness to the transforming power of the gospel. St. Paul borrows this image from Psalm 126 when he writes, "The one who sows sparingly will also reap sparingly, and the one who sows bountifully will also reap bountifully....The One who supplies seed to the sower and bread for food will supply and multiply your seed for sowing and increase the harvest of your righteousness" (2 Cor 9:6, 10). Let us assert with the Psalmist: "What great deeds the LORD works for us in this our day; indeed, we are glad" (v. 3).

PSALM 126 *(125)*

¹ *A Song of Ascents.*

When the LÓRD brought back the éxiles of Síon,
we thóught we were dréaming.
² Thén was our móuth filled with láughter;
on our tóngues, songs of jóy.

Then the nátions themselves sáid, "What great déeds
the LÓRD worked for thém!"
³ What great déeds the LÓRD worked for ús!
Indéed, we were glád.

⁴ Bring báck our éxiles, O LÓRD,
as stréams in the sóuth.
⁵ Thóse who are sówing in téars
will síng when they réap.

⁶ They go óut, they go óut, full of téars,
bearing séed for the sówing;
they come báck, they come báck with a sóng,
béaring their shéaves.

PRAYER

God of the Harvest, who have sown among us seeds of divine compassion and mercy: Open our hearts to know your guidance as we journey from oppression to freedom, from sadness to joy, so that at all times and in all things we may praise you for your bountiful love. We ask this through Christ our Lord. Amen.

Psalm 127

IF THE LORD BUILDS THE HOUSE

Intentional double meaning is occasionally found in biblical poetry, such as in the opening lines of this psalm. We are accustomed today to assume that "building a house" means the construction of a physical edifice. In the biblical mind, a "house" can also mean a family lineage or dynasty. Recall the passage in 2 Samuel 7 that is constructed on a pun regarding the word *house*. David tells the prophet Nathan that he wishes to build a temple, a "house" worthy to be the dwelling of the Lord, but God reverses David's good intention: God will build from David's line a "house" from which the Messiah, the Anointed One, is to be born. The annunciation of the Davidic Messiah is the main thrust of the story. In Psalm 127, we can see how "building a house" may refer to the erection of an edifice, the establishment of a family lineage, or both. First, when one sets out to construct a building, planning and execution demand much toil; working late and rising early are fundamental requisites (v. 2). Second—and this was especially so in the ancient world—fostering a family required a concerted effort among many to assure the well-being of all; strong and youthful helpers in the form of many children would help to assure success (v. 4). For both meanings of "building a house," Psalm 127 acknowledges that such an undertaking will come to fruition only under the watchful eye and loving care of God. Behind all our labors there abides the mysterious unfolding of God's wondrous plan for the salvation and redemption of the world; in that plan, we all have a part to play. Learning our part in God's plan can be a challenging task: we must strive for that delicate sense of balance between our total dependence upon God and our own decisions to make good use of the talents God gives us. It is in the living of life, in our own human experiences, that each of us comes to know and appreciate the gifts God has given us, as well as those He has given to others. Finding our place in God's plan and putting our confidence in God's grace is the path to salvation. We come to recognize blessings more easily when we can manage that delicate balance of trusting in God while making the best use of what we have been given—and then simply waiting to see what emerges from God's grace and our efforts. Jesus, we may say, achieved a perfect balance: in the Gospel of John, he asserts, "When you have lifted up the Son of Man, then you will realize that I am he, and that I do nothing on my own, but I speak these things as the Father instructed me. And the one who sent me is with me; he has not left me alone, for I always do what is pleasing to him" (8:28–29). All that we have and do are gifts, gifts to be used to the best of our ability, for the glory of God and the good of our neighbor.

PSALM 127 (126)

¹ *A Song of Ascents. Of Solomon.*

If the Lᴏʀᴅ does not build the house,
in váin do its buílders lábor;
if the Lᴏʀᴅ does not guárd the cíty,
in váin does the guárd keep wátch.

² In váin is your éarlier rísing,
your góing láter to rést,
you who tóil for the bréad you éat,
when he pours gífts on his belóved while they slúmber.

³ Yes, chíldren are a gíft from the Lᴏʀᴅ;
a bléssing, the frúit of the wómb.
⁴ Indéed, the sóns of yóuth
are like árrows in the hánd of a wárrior.

⁵ Bléssed ís the wárrior
who has fílled his quíver with these árrows!
He will háve no cáuse for sháme,
when he dispútes with his fóes in the gáteways.

PRAYER

Lord of heaven and earth, who provide for all our needs and whose loving fidelity is boundless: Help us to use wisely the gifts that you have given us, that in the name of Christ we might be true builders on earth of your heavenly kingdom, where you live and reign forever. Amen.

Psalm 128

BLESSINGS UPON LABOR, FAMILY, AND SION

Here we have yet another psalm that commences with the announcement that blessings come upon those "who fear the LORD." Reflection upon the wonders of creation, the movements of history, and the experiences of our personal lives stir in us a sense of awe before the mysterious ways of God. While such contemplation may indeed inspire a sort of fear in us, we might more appropriately say that it enables us to recognize in our lives and our world the workings of our faithful and loving God. Psalm 128 emphasizes three areas in which such blessings come upon those who fear the LORD: in their labors, in their families, and in the Holy City Sion. Let us first consider labor. Work has an eminent place in the Scriptures. The Book of Genesis declares that God labored six days in the creation of the world and rested on the seventh; thus for human beings, labor is holy, the means by which we participate in the very endeavors of God. Work confers divine dignity, involving our efforts with those of God himself. The Psalmist tells us that when we labor, we can expect both "blessings and prosperity" to result from our efforts (v. 2). Second, when we "walk in God's ways" (v. 1), we can expect the blessing of a substantial family. In the Hebrew mind, large numbers ensured a family's well-being. Children would naturally be expected to work with their parents to support the family's needs. It is important for us today to understand the biblical concept of the family. Many of these same values continue to be recognized and affirmed, perhaps especially in cultures not overcome by technology or industrialization. However a culture or society views the family, the Scriptures remind us that it represents the basic unit in which a person becomes a person—where one is cared for and learns to care for others. It is a simple but essential doctrine. The Psalmist's third emphasis reaffirms the biblical insistence that Jerusalem, Sion, has been since the time of David a place of peace and a point of pride in the traditions of Israel (vv. 5–6). Messianic writings portray Jerusalem as the place God has chosen as his dwelling; it comes to stand for all that the people of God can hope for—unity, justice, strength, safety, well-being. God's blessing coming from Sion to rest upon the person of faith "all the days of [his] life"—this image encapsulates everything that is good, holy, and upright. It is the vision of peace. And it is certainly significant that the last chapters of the Bible in the Book of Revelation recapture this image of Jerusalem, emphasizing the joy associated with this city, the end of suffering and the promise of eternal life that it portends: "I saw the holy city, the new Jerusalem....And I heard a loud voice from the throne saying, 'See, the home of God is [with the human race]. He will dwell with them as their God; they will be his peoples, and God himself will be with them; he will wipe every tear from their eyes. Death will be no more; mourning and crying and pain will be no more, for the first things have passed away'" (Rev 21:2a, 3–4). Our God is a God of blessings, wondrous blessings that will never end. Let us walk always in the ways of the Lord, that we may know the divine favor of our gracious God.

PSALM 128 (127)

¹ *A Song of Ascents.*

Blessed are áll who féar the LÓRD,
and wálk in his wáys!
² By the lábor of your hánds you shall éat.
You will be bléssed and prósper.

³ Your wífe like a frúitful víne
in the héart of your hóuse;
your chíldren like shóots of the ólive
aróund your táble.
⁴ Indéed thus shand be bléssed
the man who féars the LÓRD.

⁵ May the LÓRD bléss you from Síon.
May you sée Jerúsalem prósper
all the dáys of your lífe!
⁶ May you sée your chíldren's chíldren.
On Ísrael, péace!

PRAYER

O God our Savior, who bestow blessing and lead us to holiness: Enlighten our understanding, that we may come to know the share our labors have in your holy endeavors, and so work to build up your kingdom here on earth. Through Christ our Lord. Amen.

Psalm 129

GOD'S VICTORY IN US

In the Psalms of Ascent, the speaking voice of the text often exhibits a shifting perspective: sometimes the words are those of a single first-person speaker expressing personal concerns and experiences, sometimes they represent a voice exhorting the community, and sometimes they appear to be the voice of the community speaking collectively. In Psalm 129, we encounter the exhortation for Israel to sing (v. 1c), which they do collectively as a single first-person speaker (vv. 1–4); verses 5–8b present a singular first-person voice that might be either individual or collective; and in verse 8c, we hear the voice of the entire community in the plural. Old Testament writers often make use of a rhetorical trope commonly known as the "corporate personality," in which an individual speaks on behalf of the community, implying the speaker's identification with the whole people of God. In Psalm 129, the Psalmist recounts a long history of God's people suffering at the hands of others. "They have pressed me hard from my youth" (v. 1); that is to say, from our earliest days as a people we have known cruelty and mistreatment at the hands of others. The historical psalms tell this story in a variety of ways (see Pss 78, 105–7, 135–36); these consistently acknowledge that God has been with Israel through it all, despite Israel's own repeated infidelities. Verse 4 tellingly relates this truth as referring not only to Israel's enemies, but also for the people of God themselves: "The LORD, who is just, has destroyed the yoke of the wicked." "Justice" characterizes all God's dealings with all people at all times. The image of "plowmen plow[ing] my back" presents the idea that the oppression of Israel has been vigorously prosecuted, yet they have survived. How have they been able to endure? The answer appears at the end of the psalm: their continued existence is a "blessing of the LORD." Underlying the Psalmist's confession that their surprising victory over forces more powerful than they is the belief that God alone is victorious in all things, at all times, and in all places. Thus the Psalmist confidently consigns their enemies to the hands of God, asking only that God act justly toward them (v. 4). Implicit in this attitude is the belief that God is the origin of every victory we experience in life. We can do nothing without the gifts God has given us, gifts that are manifested sometimes in quiet ways, sometimes overpoweringly. Divine victory is the center of our lives. How well St. Paul knew this. In his First Letter to the Corinthians, he quells an inappropriate partisanship among them, insisting that neither he nor his coworker Apollos is to be credited for their conversion: "I have applied these things to myself and Apollos for your benefit, brothers [and sisters], so that none of you will be inflated with pride in favor of one person over against another. Who confers distinction upon you? What do you possess that you have not received? But if you have received it, why are you boasting as if you did not receive it?" (1 Cor 4:6–7). All that we have, all that we are, stands as signs of God's love and mercy for us. Let our boast be in our God, who is the source of all blessing.

PSALM 129 *(128)*

¹ *A Song of Ascents.*

"They have préssed me hárd from my yóuth,"
let Ísrael síng.
² "They have préssed me hárd from my yóuth,
but could néver overcóme me.

³ The plówmen plówed my báck,
dráwing long fúrrows.
⁴ Yet the LÓRD, who is júst, has destróyed
the yóke of the wícked."

⁵ Lét them be shámed and róuted,
all thóse who hate Síon!
⁶ Lét them be like gráss on the roof,
that wíthers befóre it flówers.

⁷ With thát no réaper fills his hánds,
no bínder of shéaves his árms.
⁸ And thóse passing bý will not sáy,
"The bléssing of the LÓRD be upón you!"
We bléss you in the náme of the LÓRD!

PRAYER

God of mercy and compassion, who stand with those who follow the ways of your justice: Keep us mindful of your wondrous gifts, that gratitude may be our daily song to you, who live and reign as one God, forever and ever. Amen.

Psalm 130

WITH YOU IS FOUND FORGIVENESS

Numbered among the seven Penitential Psalms (6, 32, 38, 51, 102, 130, and 143), Psalm 130 is familiar both for its striking imagery and its frequent use in the liturgy. The Penitential Psalms, designated thus by the Christian Church from the time of St. Augustine, are powerful expressions of contrition, in which the speaker resolves to reject the ways of sin in order to follow the paths of God with greater constancy. Christian culture often refers to Psalm 130 as *De Profundis*, the Latin title formed from the opening phrase of the psalm. And while these words may indeed symbolize the deadly waters of chaos and destruction, the image also evokes the destructive power of sin in the life of the Psalmist. Sin has brought the speaker to the depth of misery and anguish, and escape is quite beyond his own power. Three times the Psalmist reiterates his supplication: "I cry to you," "Hear my voice," "Be attentive to my pleadings." In utter humility, the Psalmist acknowledges his complete inability to free himself from the influence of sin. The Hebrew word translated here as "iniquities" (v. 3) is understood to imply the mysterious inclination of the human heart to seek out paths that separate us from God and neighbor. The Psalmist immediately acknowledges that ours is a God of forgiveness, and it is in the apparent hopelessness of our situation that we come to know the love and compassion of God most surely. Even in these earliest expressions of Israel's faith, forgiveness is recognized as a characteristic attribute of God, for which we must revere him. The old adage, "To err is human, to forgive divine," is a folksy expression of this profound theological insight. Longing and waiting (vv. 5–7a) mark the posture of faith assumed by the one who knows this. The Psalmist waits for the word of the LORD that will signal the end of his desolation and the beginning of a renewed relationship with God. Here the image of the "watchmen" creates an expectant tone. Some scholars see these watchmen as representing the priestly guardians of the temple precincts: after long night watches over the holy places, their exultant joy at the first signs of dawn signaled the coming day and the new beginning it meant. Forgiveness is the foundation of God's covenant love, always offering the hope of redemption, freedom from past failings, and anticipation of a new beginning. Who can fail to feel a surge of joy at the parable of the father who welcomes with prodigal love his wayward son? "Quickly," he says, "bring out a robe—the best one—and put it on him; put a ring on his finger and sandals on his feet. And get the fatted calf and kill it, and let us eat and celebrate; for this son of mine was dead and is alive again; he was lost and is found!" (Luke 15:22–24). For your forgiving love, O Lord, we revere you.

PSALM 130 *(129)*

¹ *A Song of Ascents.*

Out of the dépths I crý to you, O LÓRD;
² Lórd, hear my vóice!
O lét your éars be atténtive
to the sóund of my pléadings.

³ If you, O LÓRD, should márk iníquities,
Lórd, who could stánd?
⁴ But with yóu is fóund forgíveness,
that yóu may be revéred.

⁵ I lóng for yóu, O LÓRD,
my soul lóngs for his wórd.
⁶ My sóul hópes in the Lórd
more than wátchmen for dáybreak.

Móre than wátchmen for dáybreak,
⁷ let Ísrael hópe for the LÓRD.
For wíth the LÓRD there is mércy,
in hím is pléntiful redémption.
⁸ It is hé who will redéem Ísrael
from áll its iníquities.

PRAYER

Almighty and ever-living God, in your boundless forgiveness hear our pleas and bestow on us your reconciling love; for without your pardon, our journey is aimless, and only by your grace may we come to know the true meaning of our life. Through Christ our Lord. Amen.

Psalm 131

AS A WEANED CHILD

A profound humility emerges from this short Psalm of Ascent; genuine self-knowledge is evident in the Psalmist's posture before God. Authentic evaluation of both our abilities and our limitations engenders gratitude combined with diffidence: we count our blessings as we admit our shortcomings. The term "soul" (v. 2a) is used here to translate the Hebrew *nefesh*, that internal entity or quality that keeps one alive, vital, and active. Here the Psalmist humbly admits that the soul within him is as helpless and dependent before God as a child resting against his mother, the source of his nourishment and security. Coming from an adult as they do, the words describe a particular sort of relationship: God treats us with gentleness, understanding, and kindness, and we respond with unwavering trust—just as we might expect between a loving mother and her child. When we reach the profound realization that everything we are, all we have been given, comes from God, we advance to the realm of utter and unconditional gratitude. People who have experienced such gratitude are humbled by the goodness extended to them by others. Every act of kindness is recognized as an unmerited gesture of love, and all of life is seen as God's gracious gift. Even a brief musing on the course of our life can lead us to see more clearly that God has stood with us at each crossroad or juncture, quietly guiding us in ways of peace and blessing. As a child waits upon a loving mother to meet whatever needs might arise, so Israel must do with regard to the Lord, adopting a child's posture of dependence, hope, and trust. The evangelist Matthew presents just such an attitude as the heart of Jesus' message to his disciples: "He called a child, whom he put among them, and said, 'Truly I tell you, unless you change and become like children, you will never enter the kingdom of heaven. Whoever becomes humble like this child is the greatest in the kingdom of heaven. Whoever welcomes one such child in my name welcomes me'" (Matt 18:2–5). Jesus teaches us that true greatness resides in the unassuming ways of children; in this attitude we discover the One whose new law of love guides us in the ways of the kingdom. In both the Old and New Testaments, we discover a God who identifies himself with the poor and the lowly, the needy and the childlike. Following such an example will form us as true disciples.

PSALM 131 *(130)*

¹ *A Song of Ascents. Of David.*

O LÓRD, my héart is not próud,
nor háughty my éyes.
I have not góne after thíngs too gréat,
nor márvels beyónd me.

² Trúly, I have sét my sóul
in tranquílity and sílence.
As a wéaned chíld on its móther,
as a weaned chíld is my sóul withín me.

³ O Ísrael, wáit for the LÓRD,
both nów and foréver.

PRAYER

Lord Jesus Christ, who in taking on human flesh and becoming a little child manifested the way of true humility: Strengthen us in your love, that we might in childlike trust follow you upon the path of the meek and lowly. You live and reign, forever and ever. Amen.

Psalm 132

AN OATH TO DAVID

The Second Book of Samuel tells the story of King David's recovery of the Ark of the Covenant and the joyous celebration upon its return to Jerusalem. David genuinely desires to build a proper dwelling place for the Lord, but the Lord's response is surprising. At David's wish to build a house for God, God says, "No, I will build a 'house' for you." From David's lineage will come God's Anointed One, the Messiah, and God will remain faithful to this descendant of David. Psalm 132 recounts the same story poetically. The primary motif of this psalm is the fidelity of God; both David and his people are to share in the blessings of God's steadfast love for them. Verses 3–5 tell of David's desire to build this dwelling worthy of God's presence (cf. 2 Sam 7:1–3). Subsequent verses (8–10) tell of the great procession to Jerusalem, bearing the ark to its new resting place with joyful songs of praise (cf. 2 Sam 6:1–5). Verses 11–18 reiterate in brief the Lord's promise to David made through the Prophet Nathan (cf. 2 Sam 7:8–17). The text thus presents an example of what is termed "election theology": it refers to the Lord's choice, first of David as his Anointed, and then of Sion as his earthly dwelling place. Among most Ancient Near Eastern peoples, it was commonplace that a people would choose a god or gods who were equipped to meet their needs and bring blessing upon them. In stark contrast, the biblical accounts affirm that it is God who has chosen Israel, rather than the reverse, and in spite of the fact that Israel is "the smallest among the nations" (Deut 7:7; author's translation). And now, repeating the pattern, God chooses David, the youngest son of Jesse, as king and ancestor of the Messiah; and furthermore, God chooses Sion—one mountain among many—as the place of divine dwelling. These divine choices make it clear that God's favor is not with the powerful and mighty, but rather with the small and weak; it is they who are to be "the apple of God's eye" (cf. Ps 17:8). And to those whom God has chosen, God remains always faithful. In this truth we find both a hope and an invitation. The hope is that despite our infidelities God is always faithful; we can count on divine care to attend to us each day if we are willing to wait upon the Lord, whose ways are sometimes mysterious. The invitation is to imitate God's faithfulness in our own lives in whatever path we follow; our fidelity in return should be our ready response to God's fidelity toward us. Jesus restates and reinforces this theology of election in immediate terms for his disciples at the Last Supper: "You did not choose me but I chose you. And I appointed you to go and bear fruit, fruit that will last, so that the Father will give you whatever you ask him in my name. I am giving you these commands so that you may love one another" (John 15:16–17). How wonderful to be among God's chosen! In God's choice of us, we are called to respond in love—love that springs from the love we have ourselves received from our Father.

PSALM 132 (131)

[1] *A Song of Ascents.*

O LORD, remémber Dávid
and áll the hárdships he endúred,
[2] the óath he swóre to the LORD,
his vów to the Stróng One of Jácob.

3 "Í will not énter my hóuse,
nor gó to the béd where I rést;
4 I will gíve no sléep to my éyes,
to my éyelids I will gíve no slúmber,
5 till I fínd a pláce for the LÓRD,
a dwélling for the Stróng One of Jácob."

6 At Éphrata we héard of it;
we fóund it in the pláins of Yéarim.
7 "Let us gó to the pláce of his dwélling;
lét us bow dówn at his fóotstool."

8 Go úp, LORD, to the pláce of your rést,
yóu and the árk of your stréngth.
9 Your príests shall be clóthed with jústice;
your fáithful shall ríng out their jóy.
10 For the sáke of Dávid your sérvant,
dó not rejéct your anóinted.

11 The LÓRD swore an óath to Dávid;
he will nót go báck on his wórd:
"A són, the frúit of your bódy,
will I sét upón your thróne.

12 If your sóns hold fást to my cóvenant,
and my láws that Í have táught them,
their sóns, in túrn, shall sít
on your thróne from áge to áge."

13 For the LÓRD has chósen Síon;
hé has desíred it for his dwélling:
14 "This is my résting place from áge to áge;
hére have I chósen to dwéll.

15 I will gréatly bléss her próduce;
I will fill her póor with bréad.
16 I will clóthe her príests with salvátion,
and her fáithful shall ríng out their jóy.

17 I will máke a stock spróut up for Dávid;
I will prepáre a lámp for my anóinted.
18 I will cóver his énemies with sháme,
but on hím my crówn shall shíne."

God ever faithful, whose steadfast love is eternal and unbounded, help us to fix our eyes upon your Anointed Son, Jesus Christ, in whose humble response to your gifts of love we find our perfect model. All praise and thanksgiving be to you, now and for ever. Amen.

Psalm 133

LIVING IN UNITY

Brief as it is, Psalm 133 proclaims an all-inclusive message. In family, in community, at work; in a neighborhood, in the Church, or even in the world as a whole—unity bestows profound blessings. This psalm opens with the forceful assertion: "How good and how pleasant it is when brothers live in unity." While the Hebrew term is translated here as "brothers," its fuller meaning is as a metaphor for many different relational situations. The most important relationships are those in the family; in the Psalms of Ascent we encounter several references to family connections—consistently positive and instructive expressions linked to the growth, well-being, care, and honor of the family (Pss 122:3–4, 8–9; 127:3–5; 128:3, 6; 131:2). We know that the family is the primary locus of learning in a child's life: growth in faith, the formation of values, the creation of self-image. It is from the family that one launches into life in a challenging and sometimes dangerous world. For the biblical mind, "oil" (v. 2) represents something both essential for life (cooking and eating, lighting the home) and sacred for its ritual usage (anointing of kings, priests and sacred objects, a healing remedy). With so many useful and meaningful purposes, oil comes to be associated with joy and gladness, as evinced especially in this psalm. Oil has significance beyond its physical being; a brief lesson in the geography of the Holy Land will help to illustrate this. Notice that the phrase "running down" appears three times in the psalm, the last usage describing the dew of Mount Hermon running down on the mountains of Sion. Mount Hermon is at the northernmost reach of Israel, while Sion is located in the south. So abundant is the oil of unity in the Psalmist's conception that it is imagined to cascade from the northern to southern extremity, a symbol of superabundant joy and blessing for the family that is truly united. From such unity flows abundant love, protection, and compassion—all so essential to true comfort and peace. To strive for unity is thus a noble effort indeed; such unity comes as God's gift to those who seek to live in accord with the divine word, from the precepts of the old covenant to the teachings of Jesus. St. Paul knew well the challenge of establishing and maintaining unity as he strove to form the communities to which he had preached. His closing words in the Second Letter to the Corinthians express his hope that the blessing of unity could become a reality for them. "Finally, brothers and sisters, farewell. Be restored, encourage one another, agree with one another, live in peace; and the God of love and peace will be with you" (2 Cor 13:11; translation mine). Similarly, the final words of Jesus's prayer at the Last Supper embody the same motif: unity among us is a blessing that unites us with God: "Holy Father, protect them in your name that you have given me, so that they may be one, as we are one" (John 17:11b). How good and how pleasant indeed is the blessing of unity!

PSALM 133 (132)

¹ *A Song of Ascents. Of David.*

How góod and how pléasant it ís,
when bróthers líve in únity!

² It is like précious óil upon the héad,
running dówn upon the béard,
running dówn upon Áaron's béard,
upon the cóllar of his róbes;

³ like the déw of Hérmon, which runs dówn
on the móuntains of Síon.
For thére the LÓRD bestows his bléssing:
lífe foréver.

PRAYER

Triune God, Father, Son, and Holy Spirit, united in bonds of love that encompass all creation, help us to strive for unity of mind and heart, that your Church may ever be the sacrament of true hope and peace for the world. To you all praise and glory, honor and thanksgiving, forever and ever. Amen.

Psalm 134

BY NIGHT IN GOD'S COURT

Psalm 134, the last of the Psalms of Ascent, holds the distinction of being the shortest of the collection. In the Church's tradition this psalm is associated with Compline or Night Prayer. It tells of standing by night in the courts of the LORD (v. 1d–e). Abiding in the holy place of God brings a blessing, simply by spending a few quiet hours in the divine presence. The opening is phrased as an imperative: O come, bless the LORD. The Hebrew verb *baruk*, translated here as "bless," means to praise God specifically, to acclaim his wondrous deeds. God is identified here as the Maker of heaven and earth (v. 3b), the One who brought all things into being, and through whom all things exist. The command to bless the LORD is repeated in verse 2b; the phrase thus frames this opening passage. In such a brief psalm, the triple repetition of *bless* (vv. 1b, 2b, 3a) brings out its significance as the key motif of the psalm. Giving glory to God, lifting up praise and acclaiming God's wonders, is the heart of biblical prayer, constantly directing all one's attention toward God. In the biblical tradition, God is often invoked while standing upright (v. 1d), with one's hands raised upward in an image suggesting both supplication and the ascent of the prayer to God in the heavens; Psalm 141:2 makes this clear: "Let my prayer be accepted as incense before you, the raising of my hands like an evening oblation." The final verse of Psalm 134 shifts from the plural (v. 1c, 2a) to the singular (3a): what had been addressed to servants now turns to address an individual. One might imagine a priestly blessing in the temple precincts turning to one of the servants there, as if to bestow a "blessed good night" and a wish for sleep in the Lord's peace. St. Paul gives this idea of prayer and blessing a somewhat different yet equally authentic application. In acknowledging all that God has done through him and in his ministry, he says, "Let the one who boasts, boast in the Lord" (2 Cor 10:17). In other words, any apparent achievement on our part must be credited to God, who provides the strength by which we accomplish anything at all, and who thus merits our praise. The beautiful union of prayer, blessing, and praise is bound up in this notion, for all who recognize that God is the source of all good gifts.

PSALM 134 *(133)*

¹ *A Song of Ascents.*

O cóme, bléss the LÓRD,
áll you sérvants of the LÓRD,
who stánd by níght in the cóurts
of the hóuse of the LÓRD.
² Lift up your hánds to the hóly pláce,
and bléss the LÓRD.

³ May the LÓRD bléss you from Síon,
he who máde both héaven and éarth.

PRAYER

O God, Creator of heaven and earth, receive our words of praise as the humble acknowledgment that all blessing comes from you. Deepen our awareness of your presence in our lives, so that all our words and deeds may return to you the gifts you have first bestowed upon us. Through Christ our Lord. Amen.

Psalm 135

SIGNS AND WONDERS

The opening verses of Psalm 135 echo much of the vocabulary of the short psalm preceding it. One might thus expect Psalm 135 to include words of praise and blessing similar to the ones commanded in Psalm 134. These phrases evoke the opening of the Book of Genesis, as well as the accounts in Exodus of the marvelous deeds God has wrought for the children of Israel, here referred to as "his treasured possession" (v. 4b). The cosmic imagery—the heavens, the earth, the seas, the depths—reminds us of the various elements of the creation story. Verbal phrases like "summons the clouds," "brings forth rain," and "sends the wind" bespeak the wondrous choreography of the creation of the universe, assuring the well-being and blessing of God's creatures (v. 7). In verses

8–12, the Psalmist presents a précis of the saving acts of God on behalf of Israel, rescuing them from slavery and bringing them into the Promised Land, as he had promised on oath to Abraham, father of Israel's faith. Following this narrative of wonders, the Psalmist commences a diatribe against the pagan gods of the Ancient Near Eastern peoples. These are lifeless idols, created by human hands, which do not possess the power to speak, see, hear, or even breathe. The psalm concludes with a call for praise from the various families in the Israelite community, which expands into a universal call to all who would regard God with an attitude of awe and reverence (v. 20b). Despite the recitation of historical events long past, it nonetheless bears signal relevance for our prayer today. First, how important it is for us to look back on the history of our nation, our own family, our community of faith, and our individual experience. From such recollections we might well be moved to announce our personal history of God's blessing upon us, and rightly return blessing and thanksgiving to God. Second, in our world today are many idols—false gods that are too often seen as necessary achievements in life: prestige, wealth, rank, power. Unless we first acknowledge that God is the source of all blessings and the giver of every good gift we have, we will have turned God's very blessing itself into a false idol, turning what was given as a precious gift into a quickly fading possession. Let our praise of God be given readily and joyfully to the One who gives us, while yet on our earthly pilgrimage, a foretaste of divine life. Let us acclaim with St. Paul, "Now to him who by the power at work within us is able to accomplish abundantly far more than all we can ask or imagine, to him be glory in the church and in Christ Jesus to all generations, forever and ever. Amen" (Eph 3:20–21).

PSALM 135 (134)

¹ *Alleluia!*

Práise the náme of the LÓRD;
práise him, sérvants of the LÓRD,
² who stánd in the hóuse of the LÓRD,
in the cóurts of the hóuse of our GÓd.

³ Praise the LÓRD, for the LÓRD is góod.
Sing a psálm to his náme, for this is our delíght.
⁴ For the LÓRD has chosen Jácob for himsélf,
and Ísrael as his tréasured posséssion.

⁵ For I knów that the LÓRD is gréat,
that our Lórd is hígh above all góds.

⁶ The LORD dóes whatéver he wílls,
in héaven, ánd on éarth,
in the séas, and in áll the dépths.

⁷ He summons clóuds from the énds of the éarth,
makes líghtning prodúce the ráin;
from his tréasuries he sénds forth the wínd.

⁸ The firstbórn of the Egýptians he smóte,
of mán and béast alíke.

⁹ He sent sígns and wónders in your mídst, O Égypt,
against Pháraoh and áll his sérvants.

¹⁰ Nátions in great númbers he strúck,
and kíngs in their míght he sléw:

¹¹ Síhon, kíng of the Ámorites,
Óg, the kíng of Báshan,
and áll the kíngdoms of Cánaan.

¹² Their lánd he gáve as a héritage,
a héritage to Ísrael, his péople.

¹³ LÓRD, your náme stands foréver,
your renówn, LORD, from áge to áge.

¹⁴ For the LÓRD does jústice for his péople
and takes píty on his sérvants.

¹⁵ Pagan ídols are sílver and góld,
the wórk of húman hánds.

¹⁶ They have móuths but they dó not spéak;
they have éyes but they dó not sée.

¹⁷ They have éars but they dó not héar;
there is néver a bréath on their líps.

¹⁸ Their mákers will cóme to be like thém,
and só will áll who trúst in them!

¹⁹ House of Ísrael, bléss the LÓRD!
House of Áaron, bléss the LÓRD!

²⁰ House of Lévi, bléss the LÓRD!
You who féar the LORD, bléss the LÓRD!

²¹ From Síon may the LÓRD be blést,
hé who dwélls in Jerúsalem!

Alleluia!

God our Creator and Redeemer, who manifest your power and com-
passion in the progress of our lives, open our eyes to the many gifts that
daily come to us, so that in all things and at all times we may offer you
fitting praise. We ask this through Christ our Lord. Amen.

Psalm 136

A HISTORICAL LITANY

The Litany of the Saints is a prayer familiar to many Catholics; at bap-
tisms, ordinations, or the profession of religious vows, the listing by
name of holy men and women who have preceded us in the faith reminds
us of their sanctity and good works. A litany may be said to walk us
through the history of the Church; it allows us to see how God has raised
up individuals—some prominent and well known, others whose lives
were hidden from the public eye—to accomplish great deeds for the good
of the Church and the world. Psalm 136 is a litany of such deeds, but
these are deeds accomplished by God himself. Punctuating each item on
the list is the repeated refrain, "for his mercy endures forever." The
psalm is an acclamatory account of the wondrous works of God from the
beginning of creation through the life-altering experience of the Exodus,
when the people of Israel end their trek through the desert and enter
the Promised Land. The deeds recounted are marvels quite beyond the
capacity of the human beings who have benefitted from them; thus the
Psalmist provides a context for the opening verses, calling for thanksgiving to the Lord—the God of gods and Lord of lords, as the Psalmist
refers to him (vv. 2–3). The psalm similarly concludes by reiterating the
call for gratitude for the loving mercy God has shown us. The Hebrew
word *hesed*, here translated as "mercy," appears in each repetition of the
refrain. The word conveys the distinguishing mark of God's covenant
love, love that is faithful, loyal, and steadfast. Historical Psalms such as
this are public acts of remembering and celebrating God's love, care, and
protection for the people. "Remembering," as discussed in the comments
on Psalms 105 and 106, becomes the collective way of keeping alive the
many past experiences of God's saving deeds; it is engaged with consid-

eration of how that salvation continues to function in the present moment, and it includes an expression of hope that God's favor will continue unwavering into the future. Each of us might do well to take the time to compose a "Personal Historical Litany Psalm," a sacred moment in which we remind ourselves of the many amazing ways God has guided and directed our lives—sometimes through suffering and pain, but always to new life and inner strength. In his Letter to the Philippians, St. Paul does precisely this as he recalls the course of his own life and its many unexpected turns. "If anyone else has reason to be confident in the flesh, I have more: circumcised on the eighth day, a member of the people of Israel, of the tribe of Benjamin, a Hebrew born of Hebrews; as to the law, a Pharisee; as to zeal, a persecutor of the church; as to righteousness under the law, blameless. Yet whatever gains I had, these I have come to regard as loss because of Christ" (Phil 3:4b–7a). The faithful love and compassion of God remains our eternal hope!

PSALM 136 (135)

1 O give thánks to the LÓRD, for he is góod,
for his mércy endúres foréver.
2 Give thánks to the Gód of góds,
for his mércy endúres foréver.
3 Give thánks to the Lórd of lórds,
for his mércy endúres foréver;

4 Who alóne has wrought márvelous wórks,
for his mércy endúres foréver;
5 who in wísdom máde the héavens,
for his mércy endúres foréver;
6 who spréad the éarth on the wáters,
for his mércy endúres foréver.

7 It was hé who máde the great líghts,
for his mércy endúres foréver;
8 the sún to rúle in the dáy,
for his mércy endúres foréver;
9 the móon and the stárs in the níght,
for his mércy endúres foréver.

10 The firstbórn of the Egýptians he smóte,
for his mércy endúres foréver.
11 He brought Ísrael óut from their mídst,
for his mércy endúres foréver;

¹² with mighty hánd and óutstretched árm,
for his mércy endúres foréver.

¹³ The Réd Sea he divíded in twó,
for his mércy endúres foréver;
¹⁴ he made Ísrael páss through the mídst,
for his mércy endúres foréver;
¹⁵ he flung Pháraoh and his fórce in the Réd Sea,
for his mércy endúres foréver.

¹⁶ Through the désert his péople he léd,
for his mércy endúres foréver.
¹⁷ Nátions in their gréatness he strúck,
for his mércy endúres foréver.
¹⁸ Kíngs in their spléndor he sléw,
for his mércy endúres foréver:

¹⁹ Síhon, kíng of the Ámorites,
for his mércy endúres foréver;
²⁰ and Óg, the kíng of Báshan,
for his mércy endúres foréver.

²¹ He gáve their lánd as a héritage,
for his mércy endúres foréver;
²² A héritage for Ísrael, his sérvant,
for his mércy endúres foréver.
²³ He remémbered us in óur distréss,
for his mércy endúres foréver.

²⁴ And he snátched us awáy from our fóes,
for his mércy endúres foréver.
²⁵ He gives fóod to áll living créatures,
for his mércy endúres foréver.
²⁶ To the Gód of héaven give thánks,
for his mércy endúres foréver.

PRAYER

O God ever faithful and true, who come in ways we cannot imagine or foresee: Open our hearts to your wondrous and mysterious presence in our lives. Remain close to us, your children; may our gratitude never falter, but grow always in depth and devotion. Through Christ our Lord. Amen.

Psalm 137

BY THE RIVERS OF BABYLON

God had once promised to Abraham and his descendants a land that would be their own possession (Gen 12:7). God would make them a great nation on this land, possessed of a great name and many blessings, and they would become a blessing to others (Gen 12:2–3). But in Psalm 137, that promise has apparently been turned on its head: the people of God are living in exile, deprived of their land; their temple lies in ruins and they are enslaved by foreigners who do not know God. What had happened? Israel had been unfaithful, to God and to the covenant, and their infidelity had necessarily called forth God's justice. In rupturing the covenant, in their disobedience to God's law, the people had fallen prey to their own sinfulness and lost God's protection; the Babylonians had conquered them. This psalm recalls one of the saddest moments of Israel's history, yet they recognized that the event had to be included among their sung prayers: it was to become both a reminder of past failure and a continuing call to fidelity. A distinctive element of this psalm is its authentic grasp of our emotional response to difficult situations: we don't want to sing when we are in pain. "We hung up our harps" is another way of saying "We simply could not sing." When asked to do so (v. 3de), the exiles were emphatic: "O how could we sing the song of the LORD on foreign soil?...O let my tongue cleave to my palate" (vv. 4, 6ab). It is virtually impossible to sing when engulfed by grief and sorrow; such grief must be given voice by someone else, at a distance from the immediate experience. The choppy lines and almost erratic syntax are themselves structured in such a way as to suggest a tearful attempt to get out words too difficult to utter. So how can we pray Psalm 137 today? We may do so on behalf of others deprived of their human dignity, living as exiles, oppressed by enemies, and no longer in control of their own lives—too downtrodden and broken, perhaps, to pray for themselves. We can be their voice before God. We pray for them in their darkness, and we consciously voice their cry before the One who alone can reverse such tragic situations. Contemporary readers may find the shockingly violent curse with which this psalm ends difficult even to put on their lips. This is understandable, but it may help our understanding of the situation that the Psalmist seeks to create if we consider the structure of the last two verses. The Psalmist's invocation of the curse on the Babylonian children in verse 9 is a textual parallel to the situation implicit in verse 8—it is an anguished recollection that precisely the destructive violence had been perpetrated on their own children. In other words, "Let what they did to our children be done to their own: let them know the grief they have inflicted upon us." The psalm simply cannot proceed beyond this cry of profound emotional pain. Jesus, too, clearly knew just such anguish when he foresaw the loss of his beloved Jerusalem: weeping over the city, he laments: "[Your enemies] will crush you to the ground, you and your children within you, and they will not leave within you one stone upon another; because you did not recognize the time of your visitation from God" (Luke 19:44). Let us pray the psalms not only for ourselves, but for the downtrodden and poor whose sorrow is so deep that they cannot pray on their own behalf.

PSALM 137 *(136)*

¹ By the rívers of Bábylon
thére we sat and wépt,
remémbering Síon;
² on the póplars that gréw there
we húng up our hárps.

³ For it was thére that they ásked us,
our cáptors, for sóngs,
our oppréssors, for jóy.
"Síng to us," they sáid,
"one of Síon's sóngs."

⁴ O hów could we síng
the sóng of the LÓRD
on fóreign sóil?
⁵ If I forgét you, Jerúsalem,
let my ríght hand wíther!

⁶ O lét my tóngue
cléave to my pálate
if I remémber you nót,
if I príze not Jerúsalem
as the fírst of my jóys!

⁷ Remémber, O LÓRD,
against the chíldren of Édom

the dáy of Jerúsalem,
when they sáid, "Tear it dówn!
Tear it dówn to its foundátions!"

⁸ O dáughter Bábylon, destróyer,
bléssed whoéver repáys you
the páyment you páid to ús!
⁹ Blessed whoéver grásps and shátters
your chíldren on the róck!

PRAYER

Lord our God, we acclaim your compassion for the weak and suffering.
Keep us mindful of the many in our world who, tormented by pain and
grief, are unable to sing. Make of us the instruments by which you
change their sorrow to joy, manifesting to them the power of your love.
We ask this through Christ our Lord. Amen.

Psalm 138

WHOLEHEARTED THANKS

Many times in the Psalter, we encounter verbal or thematic links
between sequences of psalms. Psalm 138 in this way takes its cue from
Psalm 137. Psalm 137 lamented the people's exile, far from the land of
promise and the temple where God dwelt. In Psalm 138, the Psalmist
gives thanks to God by bowing toward the temple (v. 2a) and offering
praise "in the presence of the angels" (v. 1d). Such a gesture is a bodily
expression of gratitude and praise for the One God who alone is sovereign and mighty. The opening line of the psalm, "I thank you, LORD, with
all my heart," is meant to bring the whole person into the gesture. The
biblical image of "all [one's] heart" includes both the rational mind that
confesses belief and the emotional will that directs our desires. The
united images of the "whole heart" and the bow toward the temple present an acknowledgment of God that is both interior and exterior. As
God has heard his entreaty (v. 1c), so the Psalmist is confirmed in his
belief that God is indeed a "living God" who sees into the hearts of his

people, knows their needs, and provides for them. Yet it is significant that after the initial expression of thanks, the text implies that perhaps the speaker's difficulty has not been fully overcome (vv. 7–8). One might legitimately suppose that the Psalmist is still waiting upon God for a "complete" answer to his prayer. Clearly the speaker wants to affirm his faith that "the LORD will accomplish this" for him (v. 8a). So perhaps the full meaning of this psalm presents someone who comes to "give thanks to [God's] name" both for what has been accomplished and for what yet remains to be realized. Confidence in God's merciful love and faithfulness is sufficient reason for this exuberant gratitude; three times the Psalmist addresses thanks to God (vv. 1b, 2b, 4a). The idols of the nations are lifeless things, crafted by human hands; but the God of Israel behaves as a God who is very much alive, active, and ever close to the chosen people (vv. 6–7). The Psalmist affirms God's preference for the lowly and the corresponding rejection of the haughty; in the midst of their afflictions, God's hand stretches out to the lowly to save and strengthen them (v. 7). When we come to know at first hand God's saving action in our lives, we grow in trust. Nothing can compare with having experienced the immediate threat of death, loss, or affliction, and then being snatched away into blessing and new life. To know that God has led us through a painful desert to an oasis of new life builds up and fortifies our faith. St. Paul knew well how faith had to inform all experience, even our anxiety and fear: "Rejoice always, pray without ceasing, give thanks in all circumstances" (1 Thess 5:16–18a). With the Psalmist, we thank our living and faithful God for the merciful love poured out on us, always and everywhere, even when we are unaware of it!

PSALM 138 (137)

¹ *Of David.*

I thánk you, LÓRD, with all my héart;
you have héard the wórds of my móuth.
In the présence of the ángels I práise you.
² I bow dówn toward your hóly témple.

Í give thánks to your náme
for your mérciful lóve and your fáithfulness.
You have exálted your náme over áll.
³ On the dáy I cálled, you ánswered me;
you incréased the stréngth of my sóul.

⁴ All earth's kíngs shall thánk you, O LÓRD,
when they héar the wórds of your móuth.

⁵ They shall síng of the wáys of the LÓRD,
"How gréat is the glóry of the LÓRD!"

⁶ The LORD is hígh, yet he lóoks on the lówly,
and the háughty he knóws from afár.

⁷ You give me lífe though I wálk amid afflíction;
you strétch out your hánd against the ánger of my fóes.

With yóur right hánd you sáve me;
⁸ the LÓRD will accómplish this for mé.
O LORD, your mérciful lóve is etérnal;
discárd not the wórk of your hánds.

PRAYER

Almighty and ever-living God, whose merciful love and faithfulness is manifest amid both our fears and our hopes: Strengthen our faith, that we may readily acclaim your steadfast kindness with our whole heart. Through Christ our Lord. Amen.

Psalm 139

KNOW MY HEART, O GOD

As a prayer, Psalm 139 articulates with profound beauty how powerful and permeating our relationship with God can be. The Psalmist asserts that God is present everywhere and in all situations (v. 3). He begins by saying, "O LORD, you search me and you know me." The nuance of the phrase in Hebrew is intensely personal. "To know" someone is to have direct and immediate experience of that person, to possess an intimate and pene-trating understanding. When the prophet Hosea exhorts his people to con-version, he says with emphatic reiteration, "Let us know, let us press on to know the LORD; his appearing is as sure as the dawn; he will come to us like the showers, like the spring rains that water the earth" (Hos 6:3). Until one comes to know God in just such a manner, conversion remains little more than a mental exercise, far short of a life-altering encounter with the living God. From beginning to end, Psalm 139 throbs with the spiritual intensity of knowing and being known by God. "Too wonderful for me, this knowledge," the Psalmist says, "too high, beyond my reach" (v. 6). Such an experience of the living God is inexhaustible in its potential; our understanding can only grow with each new experience; an unfolding revelation at one and the same time mysterious and enthralling. In a series of contrasted images the poet shows how God is present always and everywhere: in the heavens or the grave (v. 8), at dawn or dusk (v. 9), in darkness or light (vv. 11–12). God is with us as surely as the immutable elements of creation that surround us. In verses 13–16, this all-pervasive presence is expressed in intimate terms of God's loving kindness in having brought each of us into being, having formed us from our very beginning in the womb; from this recognition a deep sense of gratitude naturally flows. Having considered the wonderful manner by which he was formed, the Psalmist is able to consider the wonder of creation as a whole (v. 14). The abrupt shift in tone that follows is perhaps surprising: from a prayer of profound faith the Psalmist leaps to expressions of violence and vengeance against his foes (vv. 19–22). But having quickly spent his anger, the Psalmist reverts to his original theme, the genuine desire to be fully known by God: "Search me...know my heart...test me" (v. 23). The psalm concludes with these expressions of longing for union with God, including the hope that these bonds will sustain an everlasting communion with God (vv. 23–24). Psalm 139 opens to us the great mystery of our being: though we imagine ourselves to be searching for God, our experience reveals that God is forever in search of us!

PSALM 139 *(138)*

¹ *For the Choirmaster. Of David. A Psalm.*

O Lᴏ́ʀᴅ, you séarch me and you knów me.
² You yoursélf know my résting and my rísing;
you discérn my thóughts from afár.
³ You márk when I wálk or lie dówn;
you knów all my wáys through and thróugh.

⁴ Before éver a wórd is on my tóngue,
you knów it, O Lᴏ́ʀᴅ, through and thróugh.
⁵ Behínd and befóre, you besíege me,
your hánd ever láid upón me.
⁶ Too wónderful for mé, this knówledge;
too hígh, beyónd my réach.

⁷ O whére can I gó from your spírit,
or whére can I flée from your fáce?

⁸ If I clímb the héavens, you are thére.
If I líe in the gráve, you are thére.

⁹ If I táke the wíngs of the dáwn
or dwéll at the séa's furthest énd,
¹⁰ even thére your hánd would léad me;
your right hánd would hóld me fást.

¹¹ If I sáy, "Let the dárkness híde me
and the líght aróund me be níght,"
¹² even dárkness is not dárk to yóu,
the níght shall be as bríght as dáy,
and dárkness the sáme as the líght.

¹³ For it was yóu who fórmed my inmost béing,
knit me togéther in my móther's wómb.
¹⁴ I thánk you who wónderfully máde me;
how wónderful áre your wórks,
which my sóul knows wéll!

¹⁵ My fráme was not hídden from yóu,
when Í was being fáshioned in sécret
and mólded in the dépths of the éarth.

¹⁶ Your éyes saw me yét unfórmed;
and all dáys are recórded in your bóok,
formed before óne of them cáme into béing.

¹⁷ To me how précious your thóughts, O Gód;
how gréat is the súm of thém!
¹⁸ If I cóunt them, they are móre than the sánd;
at the énd I am stíll at your síde.

¹⁹ O Gód, that you would sláy the wícked,
that men of blóod would depárt from mé!
²⁰ With decéit they rebél agáinst you,
and sét your desígns at náught.

²¹ Do Í not hate thóse who hate yóu,
abhor thóse who ríse against yóu?
²² I háte them with a pérfect háte,
and théy are fóes to mé.

²³ O séarch me, Gód, and know my héart.
O tést me, and knów my thóughts.

²⁴ Sée that my páth is not wícked,
and léad me in the wáy everlásting.

℘salm 140

LORD, GUARD ME

The Psalms present familiar patterns. Psalm 140 makes use of one such pattern: it opens with an emphatic expression of mortal fear, but it concludes with an affirmation of faith. The Psalmist's initial plea, "Rescue me,...keep me safe" includes vivid images of his enemies' tactics: they "plan evil in their hearts...stir up strife...sharpen their tongues" to spread poison like venomous snakes (vv. 3–4). The Psalmist's images suggest that he is being treated as a beast: his prideful adversaries have hidden traps, nets, and snares (v. 6), all of which are intended to make him stumble and fall (v. 5c). The language clearly presents the speaker's fear of collapse, ruin, and disgrace at an enemy's hand. But in verse 7, the prayer shifts dramatically to terms of personal intimacy and familiarity with God. Expressions like "my God" and "my Lord" demonstrate that even in the midst of the assault the Psalmist knows that God will provide the strength and courage necessary to meet the challenges that beset him. God is not presented as a figure of distant transcendence, but rather as "my" God and "my" Lord, with whom the Psalmist enjoys a personal and close bond of faith, hope, and love. The Psalmist adopts the language of warfare to show how "my" God will combat the evil and strife brought against him by his foes. Who does the Psalmist see God to be? God is "my mighty help," who "shields my head in the battle" and who will bring the plots of the wicked to nothing. A Christian reader may see the violent expressions of verses 10–12 as inimical to the gospel, in which Jesus encourages his followers to "turn the other cheek," adopting a stance of meekness in the face of such threats. Indeed, the Psalmist's words are more emotional than reasonable. And yet all too often today we hear how wars turn neighbor against neighbor in acts of violence and hatred that result in injury and even death for innocent people. It is significant that St. Paul quotes from the Psalms (14:1–3) when he writes about the culture of sin so prevalent in our world. "What then? Are we any better off? No, not at all; for we have already charged that all, both Jews and Greeks, are under the power of sin, as it is written: 'There is no one who is righteous, not even one'" (Rom 3:9–10). The Psalmist's last word on the matter here (vv. 13–14) affirms his belief that God will intervene in a world marred by human sin, establishing justice, caring for the poor, and securing a place for the upright. Until then, when we encounter violent emotional outbursts and harsh language in a psalm, they can serve as a reminder that in our own small part of the world, whatever we can do to act with justice and nonviolence enables us to be part of a world that is being renewed and recreated in the power of God and by the teachings of the gospel.

PSALM 140 *(139)*

¹ *For the Choirmaster. A Psalm of David.*

² Réscue me, LÓRD, from evil mán;
from the víolent man kéep me sáfe,
³ from thóse who plan évil in their héarts,
and stír up strífe every dáy;
⁴ who shárpen their tóngue like an ádder's,
with the póison of víper on their líps.

⁵ LORD, guárd me from the hánds of the wícked;
from the víolent kéep me sáfe;
they plán to máke me stúmble.
⁶ The próud have hídden a tráp,
have spréad out línes in a nét,
set snáres acróss my páth.

⁷ I have sáid to the LÓRD, "You are my Gód."
Give ear, O LÓRD, to the crý of my appéal!
⁸ LORD, my Lórd, my míghty hélp,
you shíeld my héad in the báttle.
⁹ Do not gránt, O LORD, the wícked their desíre,
nor lét their plóts succéed.

¹⁰ Those surróunding me líft up their héads.
Let the málice of their spéech overwhélm them.

¹¹ Let cóals of fíre rain upón them.
Let them be flúng in the abýss, no more to ríse.
¹² Let the slánderer not endúre upon the éarth.
Let évil quickly tráp the víolent!

¹³ I know the LÓRD will avénge the póor,
that hé will do jústice for the néedy.
¹⁴ Truly the júst will give thánks to your náme;
the úpright shall líve in your présence.

PRAYER

My Lord and my God, who extend to the poor of this world a Father's
love and care, guard and strengthen all who suffer injustice and hatred
at the hands of the wicked. Increase in us the desire to build up in our
world the reign of your Son, who lives and reigns, forever and ever.
Amen.

Psalm 141

MY PRAYER AS
INCENSE BEFORE YOU

From the earliest centuries of its use in the Church, Psalm 141 has held
a place of special importance. It became "the" psalm of Vespers, the
Church's evening prayer. The image in verse 2 of prayer rising to God
like incense offered at an evening sacrifice made this psalm the epitome
of all prayer—the lifting up to God of our praise and gratitude for all the
gifts we receive from him. This image is followed by what sounds like an
examination of conscience: the Psalmist asks God to "set a guard" at "the
door of [his] lips" (v. 3) that his speech might not be marked by sin; to
keep his heart from evil intentions (v. 4a); to keep him from joining with
sinners in wicked deeds (v. 4b); to stop him from feasting with them (vv.
4c, 5b); to help him recognize authentic concern in others, whatever
form it takes (v. 5a); and to sustain his prayer in opposition to their malice (v. 5c). The Psalmist knows that God has accepted our prayer (v. 1)

when our lives come to reflect both divine law and God's goodness. Thus may we rightly examine our thoughts and actions to be sure they conform to God's call to righteousness. All of us have experienced that quiet interior voice that suggests to us "Do this," or "Don't do that," or "This is the right way to go in this situation." Whether we call that our conscience or the voice of the Holy Spirit within us, its quiet and unassuming influence leads us to compassion, understanding, and kindness in our actions, if we but listen attentively. But when we turn our hearts to the Lord and truly take refuge in him (cf. v. 8), nothing can turn us from that path, even in the midst of trial and tribulation. Julian of Norwich, the fourteenth-century English mystic, writes succinctly and powerfully of such trust: "[God] did not say 'You shall not be tempest-tossed, you shall not be work-weary, you shall not be discomforted.' But he did say, 'You shall not be overcome.' God wants us to heed these words so that we shall always be strong in trust, both in sorrow and in joy." Indeed, trust can be a fragile virtue. All seems to be going smoothly, but suddenly some unforeseen disaster throws us off track, and we wonder, "Why me?... How could God let this happen?...What did I do wrong?" Such situations truly put our trust to the test. But when we strive to believe that God will be with us through these trials, we find ourselves able to return to the path of peaceful trust. St. Paul remained confident through trials and disappointments that God would not fail to assist him in whatever situation he encountered. "For this gospel I was appointed a herald and an apostle and a teacher, and for this reason I suffer as I do. But I am not ashamed, for I know the one in whom I have put my trust, and I am sure that he is able to guard until that day what I have entrusted to him" (2 Tim 1:11–12).

PSALM 141 (140)

¹ *A Psalm of David.*

I have cálled to you, LÓRD; hásten to hélp me!
Héar my vóice when I crý to yóu.
² Let my práyer be accépted as íncense befóre you,
the ráising of my hánds like an évening oblátion.

³ Sét, O LÓRD, a guárd on my móuth;
keep wátch at the dóor of my líps!
⁴ Do not túrn my héart to thíngs that are évil,
to wícked déeds with thóse who are sínners.

Néver allów me to sháre in their féasting.
⁵ If a góod man stríkes me it is kíndness;

but let the óil of the wícked not anóint my héad.
Let my práyer be éver agáinst their málice.

⁶ If they fáll into the mérciless hánds of their júdges,
théy will grásp how kínd are my wórds.
⁷ As clóds of éarth plowed úp on the gróund,
so their bónes were stréwn at the móuth of the gráve.

⁸ To you my éyes are túrned, O Lᴏʀᴅ, my Lórd.
In yóu I take réfuge; spáre my sóul!
⁹ From the tráp they have láid for me, kéep me sáfe;
kéep me from the snáres of thóse who do évil.

¹⁰ Let the wícked togéther fáll into their tráps,
while Í pursúe my wáy unhármed.

PRAYER

*Lord God, whose ear is ever attentive to the prayers of the upright,
watch over us, your children and servants, that we may faithfully walk
the paths of righteousness, confident of your loving care. We ask this
through Christ our Lord. Amen.*

Psalm 142

BRING MY SOUL OUT OF PRISON

The authors of the Psalms pour out their hearts in prayerful expressions
of need, often from desperate circumstances. Notice here how the
Psalmist formulates his entreaty in four distinct phrases, all having a
single intent: "I cry to the Lᴏʀᴅ," "I entreat the Lᴏʀᴅ," "I pour out my
troubles," "I tell all my distress" (vv. 2–3). The cumulative effect of these
petitionary phrases makes it clear that the speaker is calling out to God
from a situation of significant stress; the fourfold supplication heightens
the sense of significance about what is at stake. And as if that were not
enough, the Psalmist further asserts that his "spirit faints within" him,
indicating that his very life-breath, the vital principle within, is draining

away, and he is drawing closer and closer to the end of his rope. The Psalmist describes how, in the midst of these troubles, others are watching him: enemies who seek to snare him and thus bring about his downfall (vv. 4cd–5ab). As if to crown his grievous situation, he asserts that "no one cares for my soul" (v. 5cd); standing alone, unsure of when or where his enemies will strike, he sees no way out; he is trapped on every side. Yet from the very midst of such straits he makes a powerful confession of faith, saying to God, "You are my refuge, my portion in the land of the living" (v. 6bc). Life for the Psalmist has become a kind of death-in-life, a prison from which there is no apparent way of escape (v. 8); he knows there is but one hope left, and that is to turn to God. God is his only hope to regain his place among the living. In his firm belief that God will break open the doors of his prison, he knows there will be great reason for joyful thanksgiving. Upon witnessing God's saving deed on behalf of the Psalmist, the just will assemble around him to join in the glad expressions of praise and thanks. In the Church's Liturgy of the Hours, this psalm is prayed at First Vespers of Sunday (that is, on Saturday evening). And as each Sunday is a "little Easter," the Church thus employs Psalm 142 in the weekly celebration of God's wondrous rescue of his Son from the prison of death. The opening words of the psalm seem to anticipate Jesus' own situation as he endured the agony of Gethsemane: "Then [Jesus] said to [his disciples], 'I am deeply grieved, even to death; remain here, and stay awake with me.' And going a little farther, he threw himself on the ground and prayed, 'My Father, if it is possible, let this cup pass from me; yet not what I want but what you want'" (Matt 26:38–39). As the Psalms so often make plain, the path of faith and trust always proceeds through suffering to new life, from doubt to faith, from sadness to thanksgiving. The Psalms show us the paschal mystery at work, guiding us on the way to resurrection and glory even in this present life.

PSALM 142 *(141)*

¹ A Maskil *of David when he was in the cave. A Prayer.*

² With all my vóice I crý to the LÓRD;
with all my vóice I entréat the LÓRD.
³ I póur out my tróuble befóre him;
I téll him áll my distréss
⁴ while my spírit fáints withín me.
But yóu, O Lórd, know my páth.

On the wáy where Í shall wálk,
they have hídden a snáre to entráp me.

⁵ Lóok on my right hánd and sée:
there is nó one who páys me héed.
No escápe remains ópen to mé;
nó one cáres for my sóul.

⁶ To yóu I crý, O LÓRD.
I have sáid, "Yóu are my réfuge,
my pórtion in the lánd of the líving."
⁷ Lísten, thén, to my crý,
for Í am brought dówn very lów.

Réscue me from thóse who pursúe me,
for théy are strónger than Í.
⁸ Bríng my sóul out of príson,
and Í shall give thánks to your náme.
Aróund me the júst will assémble,
becáuse of your góodness to mé.

PRAYER

Lord Jesus Christ, Savior and Redeemer, in whose paschal mystery we discern the way to glory and new life, strengthen your followers in times of temptation and trial, that we may witness to the power of your grace at work in our lives. To you be all glory and honor, now and forever. Amen.

Psalm 143

LET ME KNOW YOUR LOVING MERCY

Psalm 143 is the last of the seven Penitential Psalms (see commentary on Pss 6, 51, 130). The Psalmist begins with the familiar request that his prayer be heard, that God "turn his ear" to the appeal brought forward in faith. Immediately following the initial petition is an affirmation that stems from past experience of God's ways: fidelity and justice always mark

God's actions toward those in need. Verse 2b is a profound confession of faith that anticipates St. Paul in its formulation: "In your sight no one living is justified." No one can claim to be righteous or just before God; we all come before the Lord as sinners in utter need of mercy, compassion, forgiveness, and redemption. Quoting this verse, St. Paul articulates his doctrine thus: "'No human being will be justified in his sight' by deeds prescribed by the law, for through the law comes the knowledge of sin" (Rom 3:20); and again, "We have come to believe in Christ Jesus, so that we might be justified by faith in Christ, and not by doing the works of the law, because no one will be justified by the works of the law" (Gal 2:16b). Precisely because we know and acknowledge our sinful state, the only posture we can take before God is one of pleading, with hands outstretched in petition (v. 6a), knowing all that God has done for us in the past and trusting that our prayer will again be heard and our life restored (v. 5). Like so many of its predecessors (cf. Pss 139, 140), this beautiful psalm possesses all the marks of an intimate and personal relationship with God. The Psalmist says, "Like a parched land my soul thirsts for you" (v. 6b). "To thirst" for someone bespeaks a cherished and enduring relationship; the words come from deep within, and are freighted with deep emotion. We might find further clues to the depth of the relationship by considering a term repeated at the beginning and the end of the psalm: "servant." "Do not call your servant to judgment" (v. 2a), and "I am your servant" (v. 12c). To deem oneself God's servant is to adopt an attitude of ready and attentive obedience to the divine voice. For the Christian, this is perfectly modeled by Jesus, and beautifully articulated by St. Paul in the christological hymn of the Letter to the Philippians: "Let the same mind be in you that was in Christ Jesus, who, though he was in the form of God, did not regard equality with God as something to be exploited, but emptied himself, taking the form of a slave, being born in human likeness. And being found in human form, he humbled himself and became obedient to the point of death—even death on a cross" (2:5–8). With each new morning, our hope in the gift of God's loving mercy brings us to assume with the Psalmist and with Christ this faithful posture before the Almighty—attentively waiting and trusting that our prayer will be heard (cf. v. 8).

PSALM 143 (142)

¹ *A Psalm of David.*

O LÓRD, lísten to my práyer;
túrn your éar to my appéal.
You are fáithful, you are júst; give ánswer.
² Do not cáll your sérvant to júdgment,
for in your síght no one líving is jústified.

³ The énemy pursúes my sóul;
he has crúshed my lífe to the gróund.
He has máde me dwéll in dárkness,
like the déad, lóng forgótten.
⁴ Thérefore my spírit fáils;
my héart is désolate withín me.

⁵ I remémber the dáys that are pást;
I pónder áll your wórks.
I múse on what your hánd has wróught,
⁶ and to yóu I strétch out my hánds.
Like a párched land my sóul thirsts for yóu.

⁷ O Lᴏʀᴅ, make háste and ánswer mé,
for my spírit fáils withín me.
Do not híde your fáce from mé,
lest I becóme like thóse
who go dówn into the gráve.

⁸ In the mórning, let me knów your loving mércy,
for in yóu I pláce my trúst.
Make me knów the wáy I should wálk;
to yóu I líft up my sóul.

⁹ Réscue me, O Lᴏ́ʀᴅ, from my fóes;
to yóu have I fléd for réfuge.
¹⁰ Téach me to dó your wíll,
for yóu are my Gód.
Lét your good spírit guíde me
upon gróund that is lével.

¹¹ Lᴏʀᴅ, sáve my lífe for the sáke of your náme;
in your jústice, léad my sóul out of distréss.
¹² In your mércy make an énd of my fóes;
destroy all thóse who oppréss my sóul,
for Í am your sérvant.

PRAYER

Lord our God, faithful and just, who show us mercy and teach us the
way of your will, grant us insight to heed and follow your holy bidding,
that we might experience the joy that comes in serving you in imitation
of Christ Jesus, who is Lord, forever and ever. Amen.

$Psalm$ 144

REACH DOWN FROM HEAVEN

Psalm 144 presents something unique in the Psalter; it appears to be a mélange of different psalms brought together in such a way as to give the texts new meaning and purpose. A glance back at Psalm 18 (especially vv. 3–4, 10, 15, 17, 34–35, 44–48), Psalm 33 (especially v. 12), and Psalm 8 (especially v. 5) provides ideas and images echoed by Psalm 144. In those earlier instances, the texts presented acclamations of praise for God's power and strength, but now they have been given the form of petitions: "Lower your heavens, O LORD, and come down"(v. 5a); "Flash your lightnings, rout the foe" (v. 6a); "Rescue me, save me from the mighty waters" (v. 7b). Such a process brings home an important point for our reflection: our prayer is always to the One who alone can reverse situations of pain and helplessness, who heals the wounds inflicted by others. In the light of this realization, the opening words of praise and blessing (vv. 1–2) are seen as an appropriate prelude to the petitions that follow (vv. 5–8). Note how the Psalmist refers to God himself as "merciful love" (v. 2), using the Hebrew word *hesed*, the covenant love that always remains faithful, loyal, steadfast, and true. While the human response to God's unfaltering and unwavering love is often tepid and faltering, the divine stance is eternally firm and trustworthy. The language of war and battle with which the psalm opens reminds us of St. Paul's admonition in the Letter to the Ephesians: "Finally, be strong in the Lord, and in the strength of His might. Put on the full armor of God, so that you may be able to stand firm against the wiles of the devil. For our struggle is not against enemies of flesh and blood, but against the rulers, against the authorities, against the cosmic powers of this present darkness, against the spiritual forces of evil in the heavenly places. Therefore, take up the full armor of God, so that you may be able to withstand on that evil day, and having done everything, to stand firm" (6:10–13). In the midst of combative struggle, even among his urgent petitions, the Psalmist affirms his intention to "sing a new song to the LORD" (v. 9), for he knows that it is God who brings about the victories in our life, assured that, just as he once "set David free" and brought him to triumph over the evils that beset him (v. 10), so will there be blessings for anyone who trusts in God's saving power. The psalm concludes with the stirring beatitude,

"Blessed the people of whom this is true; blessed the people whose God is the LORD!" (v. 15). Again and again, the Psalms remind us of God's sovereign rule over the universe and all that is in it. When we pray the Psalms we joyfully acknowledge God's protection and care for us, who "routs the foe" and "reaches down from on high" to draw us into the divine reign of peace and blessing.

PSALM 144 (143)

¹ *Of David.*

Blést be the LÓRD, my róck,
who tráins my hánds for báttle,
who prepáres my fíngers for wár.

² He is my mérciful lóve, my fórtress;
hé is my strónghold, my sávior,
my shíeld in whóm I take réfuge.
He brings péoples únder my rúle.

³ LÓRD, what is mán that you regárd him,
the son of mán that you kéep him in mínd,
⁴ mán who is mérely a bréath,
whose dáys are like a pássing shádow?

⁵ Lower your héavens, O LÓRD, and come dówn.
Touch the móuntains; wréathe them in smóke.
⁶ Flash your líghtnings; róut the fóe.
Shoot your árrows, and pút them to flíght.

⁷ Reach dówn with your hánd from on hígh;
rescue me, sáve me from the míghty wáters,
from the hánds of fóreign fóes
⁸ whose móuths speak ónly émptiness,
whose hánds are ráised in pérjury.

⁹ To you, O Gód, will I síng a new sóng;
I will pláy on the tén-stringed hárp
¹⁰ to yóu who give kíngs their víctory,
who set Dávid your sérvant frée
from the évil swórd.

¹¹ Rescue me, frée me from the hánds of foreign fóes,
whose móuths speak ónly émptiness,
whose right hánds are ráised in pérjury.

¹² Let our sóns then flóurish like sáplings,
grown táll and stróng from their yóuth;
our dáughters gráceful as cólumns,
as thóugh they were cárved for a pálace.

¹³ Let our bárns be fílled to overflówing
with cróps of évery kínd;
our shéep incréasing by thóusands,
téns of thóusands in our fields,
¹⁴ our cáttle héavy with yóung.

No rúined wáll, no éxile,
no sóund of wéeping in our stréets.
¹⁵ Blessed the péople of whóm this is trúe;
blessed the péople whose Gód is the LÓRD!

PRAYER

O God, our mighty stronghold and Savior, be our protection against the forces that wage war against us, seeking to destroy your rule over our hearts. May your faithful love and steadfast compassion be our daily strength as we unite ourselves to your Son in his paschal mystery, that we might know too the power of his resurrection, who lives and reigns, forever and ever. Amen.

Psalm 145

YOUR RULE ENDURES FOREVER

In his *Confessions*, St. Augustine writes, "Almighty God, you have made us for yourself, and our hearts are restless until they rest in you." Psalm 145 provides a foundation for the saintly bishop's profound words. From beginning to end, this psalm is an exuberant account of the marvels God works for us, the ways in which the human family experiences the truth of God's love as a continual outpouring of goodness. It is also an acrostic psalm, with consecutive verses beginning with consecutive letters of the Hebrew alphabet; thus Psalm 145 is intended as an expression of fullness and completeness, a verbal symbol of the infinite number of reasons why praise is due to God. It is certainly worth noting that this psalm bears as its superscription the single word *Praise*; it is the only psalm thus designated. The opening lines usher us into a litany of unmeasured and exalted praise of God, whose name is to be blessed forever and ever (vv. 1c, 2b). From a general reference to "awesome deeds" (v. 6) to specifications of compassion, mercy, and goodness (vv. 8–9), the Psalmist proclaims the reasons for exalting God to the heights, reiterating faithfully each day God's justice and holiness. In verses 11–13, the words here rendered "reign" and "kingdom" derive from the same Hebrew root; the implicit repetition may thus underscore the importance of the theme for the Psalmist. With this psalm we are nearing the end of the Psalter, and we are reminded both of God's goodness and of the divine reign that moves and guides all creation. Every person, every creature, every object has its origin in God, and is thus imbued with the divine character. We must not merely stand in immobile awe before our God and his deeds; as God acts, so we must act. We must make a fitting response by returning to God what we ourselves have received: mercy, compassion, forgiveness, patience, justice, understanding, trust. Yes, God has entrusted to us the gifts of the earth to preserve and cultivate. There are inevitably times in our life when pain and suffering come upon us, when we must face hard decisions and suffer loss. It is precisely in those agonizing circumstances that our trust may become the means of our healing, as we turn over to God all that we cannot change or manage. In trust we acknowledge the sovereignty of God over our lives, firm in the belief that even in the most extreme situations, where everything seems fragile and uncertain, God is moving our life in the direction of hope and stability. The Psalmist asserts, "The eyes of all look to you, [O Lord,] and you open your hand to satisfy the desire of every living thing" (vv. 15–16). In his Sermon on the Mount, Jesus reminds us, "Look at the birds of the air; they neither sow nor reap nor gather into barns, and yet your heavenly Father feeds them. Are you not of more value than they?" (Matt 6:26). For every blessing in our life—those we recognize and those we cannot perceive—let us bless the holy name of the Lord, for ages unending (v. 21). Amen.

PSALM 145 *(144)*

¹ *Praise. Of David.*

I will extól you, my Gód and kíng,
and bless your náme foréver and éver.

² I will bléss you dáy after dáy,
and praise your náme foréver and éver.

³ The LORD is gréat and híghly to be práised;
his gréatness cánnot be méasured.

⁴ Age to áge shall procláim your wórks,
shall decláre your míghty déeds.

⁵ They will téll of your great glóry and spléndor,
and recóunt your wónderful wórks.

⁶ They will spéak of your áwesome déeds,
recóunt your gréatness and míght.

⁷ They will recáll your abúndant góodness,
and síng of your just déeds with jóy.

⁸ The LORD is kínd and fúll of compássion,
slow to ánger, abóunding in mércy.

⁹ How góod is the LÓRD to áll,
compássionate to áll his créatures.

¹⁰ All your wórks shall thánk you, O LÓRD,
and áll your fáithful ones bléss you.

¹¹ They shall spéak of the glóry of your réign,
and decláre your míghty déeds,

¹² To make knówn your míght to the chíldren of mén,
and the glórious spléndor of your réign.

¹³ Your kíngdom is an éverlasting kíngdom;
your rule endúres for áll generátions.

The LORD is fáithful in áll his wórds,
and hóly in áll his déeds.

¹⁴ The LÓRD suppórts all who fáll,
and ráises up áll who are bowed dówn.

¹⁵ The éyes of áll look to yóu,
and you gíve them their fóod in due séason.

¹⁶ You ópen your hánd and sátisfy
the desíre of every líving thíng.

¹⁷ The LORD is júst in áll his wáys,
and hóly in áll his déeds.

¹⁸ The LORD is clóse to áll who cáll him,
who cáll on hím in trúth.

¹⁹ He fulfílls the desíres of those who féar him;
he héars their crý and he sáves them.

²⁰ The Lᴏʀᴅ keeps wátch over áll who lóve him;
the wícked he will útterly destróy.

²¹ Let my móuth speak the práise of the Lóʀᴅ;
let all flésh bless his hóly náme
foréver, for áges unénding.

PRAYER

O God, ever close to those who call upon you, receive our praise as a joyful and grateful response to the countless blessings you shower upon us. May your fidelity and compassion, goodness and mercy, be our great hope and encouragement as we make our pilgrimage journey to you, our God, forever and ever. Amen.

Psalm 146

PRAISE FOR THE DIVINE JUSTICE OF GOD

Psalm 146 is first in the series of psalms that conclude the Psalter, each of which begins with the Hebrew word *Alleluia*, which means literally "Praise the Lᴏʀᴅ." Each of these psalms expresses a different reason for lifting up exaltation to God. In Psalm 146, the heart of the matter is divine justice. In its biblical sense, "justice" is understood as right relationship. This is subtly expressed in verses 3–4 by means of a pun. The Hebrew word translated here as "mortal man" is *'ādām* (v. 3b); while the word for "earth" is the Hebrew *ādāmâ* (v. 4a). This play on words is rooted in the connection between human beings and the earth that figures so strongly in Genesis 3:19. As God blew the divine life-breath into Adam, and he became a living being in the divine image, a corresponding relationship of Creator to creature emerged. God must in justice care for the creatures that share his divine image, and likewise, those creatures must in justice acknowledge their bond with God by following the laws and commands he has given them. Psalm 146 lists the many ways in which God shows divine justice to beings created in the divine image.

After beginning with a mandate (v. 1b) and a promise (v. 2) of praise, the Psalmist reminds us that as human beings we cannot ourselves be the foundation of our confidence (vv. 3–4); rather, we can only put our trust in the God whom we praise (vv. 1–2, 5–6). The reason for our trust in God's help is founded on our knowledge and experience of the ways in which the Maker of heaven and earth has always shown faithful love and true compassion for those in need. The oppressed are cared for, the hungry nourished, and the imprisoned set free by the God of Jacob (v. 7). Just as at the time of the great Exodus from Egypt, God continues to hear their cries of subjugation, to free them from oppression, and to provide abundant nourishment, even as he had done in their long desert journey. Further proof of God's saving justice is evident in the opening of blind eyes and the lifting up of the lowly (v. 8). The prophets speak too of the righteousness of God's deeds (cf. Isa 35). And those who are marginalized in this world—the stranger, widow, and orphan—they too have hope in the law that God has ordained for their care by members of the community of the faithful (Deut 24:20–21). God's reign establishes the absolute requirement that compassion, protection, and mercy be extended to all those who are in need; and God accomplishes those acts of kindness, sympathy, and benevolence through us. We share in God's justice when we act in God's stead, follow the promptings of the Spirit within us, working for the well-being of all people. And isn't that what the New Testament tells us the reign of God is all about? "Jesus called the twelve together and gave them power and authority over all demons and to cure diseases, and he sent them out to proclaim the kingdom of God and to heal" (Luke 9:1–2). We are both the recipients and the instruments of God's divine justice. Blessed is our calling!

PSALM 146 *(145)*

¹ *Alleluia!*

My sóul, give práise to the LÓRD;
² I will práise the LÓRD all my lífe,
sing práise to my Gód while I líve.

³ Pút no trúst in prínces,
in mortal mán who cánnot sáve.
⁴ Take their bréath, they retúrn to the éarth,
and their pláns that dáy come to nóthing.

⁵ Blessed is hé who is hélped by Jacob's Gód,
whose hópe is in the LÓRD his Gód,
⁶ who máde the héavens and the éarth,

the séas and áll they contáin,
who presérves fidélity foréver,
⁷ who does jústice to thóse who are oppréssed.

It is hé who gives bréad to the húngry,
the LÓRD who sets prísoners frée,
⁸ the LORD who ópens the éyes of the blínd,
the LORD who ráises up thóse who are bowed dówn.

It is the LÓRD who lóves the júst,
⁹ the LÓRD who protécts the stránger
and uphólds the órphan and the wídow,
but thwárts the páth of the wícked.
¹⁰ The LÓRD will réign foréver,
the God of Síon from áge to áge.

Alleluia!

PRAYER

Lord God, Father of the orphan, Protector of the stranger, and Healer of every ill, hear our prayer: Grant that the experience of your compassion and kindness in our own lives may lead us in paths of generous service of our neighbor and to joyful trust in you, who live and reign forever and ever. Amen.

Psalm 147

THE ALMIGHTY STANDS WITH THE LOWLY

The Hebrew exclamation *kî tôb*, which opens Psalm 147, is similar to the expression *mah tôb* (which opens Ps 133); neither is frequent in the Psalter. They both mean "how good," and their appearance is meant to characterize whatever follows as having a very special quality. Here the Psalmist enlightens our faith with the assertion that lifting up praise to

God ought to be for us a true joy, a genuinely pleasant undertaking (v. 1). Ours is a God who, though infinitely great, is yet always close to those in need of divine assistance. To put into context what God has done in rebuilding Jerusalem and gathering its exiles, the Psalmist tells us that the Almighty One, who created the stars and calls each of them by name (v. 4), is nonetheless near enough to us that he takes on the work of healing broken hearts and binding up every open wound (v. 3). While we may at first think that "lifting up the lowly and casting down the wicked" is merely a display of God's power (v. 6), the Psalmist suggests that the actions of God are in fact guided by his own divine wisdom, himself taking joy in being rich in mercy and plentiful in redemption to those who revere him (v. 11a). Everything in the world manifests its Creator: the heavens covered with clouds, clouds that provide rain, rain that brings forth food (v. 8). Yet such nourishment is not limited to human beings alone; no, God cares for every creature he has made, from human beings to cattle to ravens (vv. 8–9), each of which fulfills its part in God's plan for the peaceful progress of the world. While we might think that God might take particular delight in seeing the vigor of a horse or the strength of a warrior (v. 10), such is not the case. No, God's delight is stirred by those who watch and wait for the divine blessing that flows to us from the covenant. Thus are the faithful and steadfast ways of God revealed. The second half of the psalm (vv. 12–20, which in the Septuagint had been divided from the first half [vv. 1–11] as a separate psalm) continues to demonstrate how God's people, now designated collectively as "Jerusalem," have indeed known abundant blessings. The early Church took from this second half of the psalm two important images that they applied to the Christian mystery. The "finest wheat" (v. 14) came to symbolize the gift of the Eucharist, the nourishment of divine life given to pilgrims on their way to the heavenly kingdom. As with the manna of old, God continues to nourish us richly, with the heavenly bread of the Eucharist. Similarly, drawing from the theology of the Johannine Gospel, "the word sent forth" (v. 18) came to be recognized as referring to the incarnation, by which God takes on our human flesh and shares fully in our human nature. "In the beginning was the Word, and the Word was with God, and the Word was God. And the Word became flesh and lived among us, and we have seen his glory, the glory as of a father's only son, full of grace and truth" (John 1:1, 14). In both these images we discern the divine mystery of Jesus in the Sacrament—for there we are nourished at the table of the Word and the table of the Eucharist. The Psalmist's words anticipate the fuller knowledge of Christ Jesus as our true source of nourishment as we make our way to the heavenly kingdom. How good indeed to praise him!

PSALM 147A *(146:1–11)*

Alleluia!

¹ How góod to sing psálms to our Gód;
how pléasant to chant fítting práise!

² The Lᴏ́ʀᴅ builds úp Jerúsalem
and bríngs back Ísrael's éxiles;
³ he héals the bróken-héarted;
he bínds up áll their wóunds.
⁴ He cóunts out the númber of the stárs;
he cálls each óne by its náme.

⁵ Our Lórd is gréat and almíghty;
his wísdom can néver be méasured.
⁶ The Lᴏ́ʀᴅ lifts úp the lówly;
he casts dówn the wícked to the gróund.
⁷ O síng to the Lᴏ́ʀᴅ, giving thánks;
sing psálms to our Gód with the hárp.

⁸ He cóvers the héavens with clóuds;
he prepáres the ráin for the éarth,
making móuntains spróut with gráss,
and plánts to sérve human néeds.
⁹ He provídes the cáttle with their fóod,
and young rávens that cáll upon hím.

¹⁰ His delíght is nót in hórses,
nor his pléasure in a wárrior's stréngth.
¹¹ The Lᴏʀᴅ delíghts in thóse who revére him,
those who wáit for his mérciful lóve.

PSALM 147B *(147)*

¹² O Jerúsalem, glórify the Lᴏ́ʀᴅ!
O Síon, práise your Gód!
¹³ He has stréngthened the bárs of your gátes;
he has bléssed your chíldren withín you.
¹⁴ He estáblished péace on your bórders;
he gíves you your fíll of finest whéat.

¹⁵ He sénds out his wórd to the éarth,
and swíftly rúns his commánd.

¹⁶ He shówers down snów like wóol;
he scátters hóarfrost like áshes.

¹⁷ He húrls down háilstones like crúmbs;
befóre such cóld, who can stánd?
¹⁸ He sénds forth his wórd and it mélts them;
at the blówing of his bréath the waters flów.

¹⁹ He revéals his wórd to Jácob;
to Ísrael, his decrées and júdgments.
²⁰ He has nót dealt thús with other nátions;
he hás not táught them his júdgments.

Alleluia!

PRAYER

Lord Jesus Christ, who came among us to show us how to live under the gentle yoke of your Father's reign, enliven our faith that we might wait joyfully in expectation of the love and compassion you wish to bestow on us. In knowing your loving mercy may we be the instruments of your love for all whom we meet. To you be glory and honor, now and forever. Amen.

Psalm 148

LET ALL THINGS GIVE PRAISE

Psalm 148 deals with motifs familiar from the opening chapter of the Book of Genesis. The Bible opens with the story of creation, which comes into being, as this psalm reminds us, by the word of the LORD (v. 5). In divine omnipotence, God speaks a word, calling forth creation in all its wonder. The divine word is immediately translated into divine action, accomplishing the end for which it is sent, as the prophet Isaiah observes (55:10–11). In marked contrast to other creation stories of the Ancient Near East, whose gods bring about creation by engaging in fierce cosmic battles, the God of Israel merely speaks, and the world comes forth in harmony and order. All that is in the world is summoned by the Psalmist to praise the Creator for this act of serene magnificence (vv. 1–4). Taking his cue from Genesis 1, the Psalmist first calls on the waters above the heavens (the firmament) and the sun and moon, sources of light (v. 3)—the first things brought into being by God. Such wonders, far beyond the scope of human imagination or influence, reside in the hands of God; in their very being they invite human beings to express delight and wonder at their display of the divine majesty. In verses 7–9, the Psalmist includes those forces and elements of nature that other nations have made into false gods: fire and wind, mountains and trees. How utterly different is Israel's belief: they have not chosen gods from nature, but rather they have themselves been chosen by the One God who brought all nature into being. The nations that surrounded Israel looked to their "gods" in nature because they sought to influence the impact those forces had on their own lives—rains and storms, sun and moon—bringing fertility to their land and warmth to foster growth. But God himself elected Israel, an insignificant group of slaves, revealing the depth of his goodness to them in divine compassion and liberation. This divine favor remains their compelling reason for ready and unending praise, in which those natural forces are called to join. In verses 11–12, the Psalmist finally extends his call to all who belong to the community of believers, whether rulers or judges, young or old. To praise "the name of the LORD" means lifting up acclaim to the One who accomplishes all things, who brings order and peace to creation, and who continues to sustain all life on earth. The psalm closes with an acknowledgment of God's other side: having spoken of the transcendent power of God, who brings creation into being through a single word of power, the Psalmist now affirms that this God, though infinite and omnipotent, yet remains close to Israel—immanent in the lives and experience of all who place their trust in him. In the Acts of the Apostles, St. Paul preaches this same paradoxical message about the omnipotent God to the Athenians: "Indeed [God] is not far from each one of us" (17:27). The mystery of divine immanence and transcendence, the Almighty One who is as near to us as our own breath, is a truth to be pondered each day, if we but have the eyes of faith to see it.

PSALM 148

¹ *Alleluia!*

Práise the LÓRD from the héavens;
práise him in the héights.
² Práise him, áll his ángels;
práise him, áll his hósts.

³ Práise him, sún and móon;
práise him, all shíning stárs.
⁴ Práise him, híghest héavens,
and the wáters abóve the héavens.

⁵ Let them práise the náme of the LÓRD.
He commánded: théy were creáted.
⁶ He estáblished them foréver and éver,
gave a láw which shall nót pass awáy.

⁷ Práise the LÓRD from the éarth,
sea créatures and all ócean dépths,
⁸ fire and háil, snów and míst,
stormy wínds that fulfill his commánd;

⁹ Móuntains ánd all hílls,
frúit trees ánd all cédars,
¹⁰ béasts, both wíld and táme,
réptiles and bírds on the wíng;

¹¹ Kíngs of the éarth and all péoples,
prínces and all júdges of the éarth,
¹² young mén and máidens as wéll,
the óld and the yóung togéther.

¹³ Let them práise the náme of the LÓRD,
for his náme alóne is exálted,
his spléndor above héaven and éarth.

¹⁴ He exálts the stréngth of his péople.
He is the práise of áll his fáithful,
the práise of the chíldren of Ísrael,
of the péople to whóm he is clóse.

Alleluia!

PRAYER

*Eternal God, almighty in power yet rich in love, deepen our insight into
the wonders of your creation, that we might have the wisdom to discern
the guidance of your loving hand in the courses of our lives and all history. Through Christ our Lord. Amen.*

$\mathcal{P}$salm 149

LET THE FAITHFUL REJOICE

With the opening verse of Psalm 149, the Psalmist issues the final instance of his recurring mandate to "sing a new song to the LORD." The decree is here directed to the "assembly of the faithful"—the *hasidîm* in Hebrew—those who have been steadfast and faithful to the covenant God has established with the people of Israel. God gave the Law to Israel as the means by which they would come to know the One who had brought them into being, who had given them first life and then liberation. "Law" is probably best understood as "instruction" here in its Hebrew context. Any time someone tells you what you should do, it provides an insight into what is important for that person; you have a good idea of what means most to him or her. In establishing the covenant, God revealed to Israel a path to life and prosperity through observance of his teaching in the Law, if they would hold fast to it and carry it out with fidelity and conviction. And from those commands Israel came to know their God as One who asks for fidelity and commitment, adherence to those ways of living that promote well-being and peace, marked by high moral standards and clear expectations. To have found life and blessing in God and in the ways of the commandments calls for rejoicing. God has prospered them along the path of life; so, says the Psalmist, let the music be played on timbrel and harp to accompany their joyful singing and dancing (vv. 2–3). The poor are lifted up and crowned with saving grace (v. 4), for God delights in each of his little ones. What a resonant image of divine care and consolation: the poor, the needy, the lowly shall all wear crowns, for in celebration of God's salvation, all bear tokens of the riches that are theirs in God's love. The account in chapter 19 of the Book of Exodus, telling of the arrival of the Hebrew slaves at Mount Sinai, is echoed in the imagery of Psalm 149. God gives to his people a two-edged sword, a symbol of his conquering hand amid the nations that threatened their peace and security. This weapon reminds them of how God's justice in the covenant accompanied them through their whole desert experience on their way to the Promised Land; God fought for them, protected them, and carried them as on an "eagle's wings" (Exod 19:4) in liberating them from Egypt. Well might the people of God "sing a new song" of God's mercy and compassion as they look back, considering how in all their experiences God was with them, guiding them, safeguarding them in the midst of challenge and struggle. The First Letter of Peter reaffirms the truth of these words, reminding the Christian people of their great dignity and blessing: "You are a chosen race, a royal priesthood, a holy nation, God's own people, in order that you may proclaim the mighty acts of him who called you out of darkness into his marvelous light. Once you were not a people, but now you are God's people; once you had not received mercy, but now you have received mercy" (2:9–10).

PSALM 149

¹ *Alleluia!*

Síng a new sóng to the LÓRD,
his práise in the assémbly of the fáithful.
² Let Ísrael rejóice in its Máker;
let Sion's chíldren exúlt in their kíng.
³ Let them práise his náme with dáncing,
and make músic with tímbrel and hárp.

⁴ For the LÓRD takes delíght in his péople;
he crówns the póor with salvátion.
⁵ Let the fáithful exúlt in glóry,
and rejóice as they táke their rést.
⁶ Let the práise of Gód be in their móuths
and a twó-edged swórd in their hánd,

⁷ To déal out véngeance to the nátions
and púnishment upón the péoples;
⁸ to bínd their kíngs in cháins
and their nóbles in fétters of íron;
⁹ to cárry out the júdgment decréed.
This is an hónor for áll his fáithful.

Alleluia!

PRAYER

Lord our God, who delight in the faithful and crown the lowly with saving grace, plant your law of love in our hearts and foster it with your constant care, that we may grow into the full stature of your Son, Jesus Christ, in whom it is perfectly fulfilled. He is Lord with you and the Spirit, forever and ever. Amen.

Psalm 150

DOXOLOGY

Psalm 150 serves as a general doxology to close the Book of Psalms. A doxology is a prayer of pure praise, simply lifting up to God the glory and adoration due the One who has brought all things into being. Psalm 150 gathers up all that has gone before in the Psalms—suffering and lament, praise and thanksgiving, wisdom, hope, and trust: all the human experiences that belong to the story of our salvation in God—and offers a final paean of praise to the God who has inspired these songs, who has shown us such constant and loving fidelity, who has turned our suffering into joy by his healing grace, and revealed himself as One who is majestic in splendor yet utterly close to his people. The opening call to praise in this psalm is cosmic and universal: it focuses our attention on the "holy place," God's temple on earth, while the "mighty firmament" (v. 1) refers to that cosmic structure above the skies that holds the world in its place. It is as if the Psalmist were extending a series of invitations: Call to mind the countless deeds of God to which these psalms refer, and praise the Almighty One who has accomplished these things beyond count (v. 2a). Then behold creation in all its grandeur—skies and seas, mountains and plains, sun and moon—and again, offer the only response that human mind and heart can make: praise (v. 2b)! The Psalmist employs a contrast worth noting in the musical instruments to be used for this great act of praise. The blast of the trumpet (v. 3) would inaugurate the great Year of Jubilee, as indicated in Leviticus 25. As God had once liberated and blessed his people by freeing them from the oppression of the Egyptians, so must the people do to those who had in time become slaves to them: they, too, were to enjoy blessing and liberation at the hands of God's people. Such jubilant praise would then give way to the more delicate strains of the harp, as when David calmed the restless and fearful spirit of King Saul (1 Sam 16:23). The harp brings joy to the praise of God's name (Pss 57:9; 108:3). And "timbrel and dance" must remind us of Miriam as she led the women of Israel in praising God as the Divine Warrior who had fought for the Hebrew slaves against the onslaught of the Egyptian armies (Exod 15:20–21). The Psalmist thus recounts the wondrous ways in which God has cared for and protected the chosen people. The closing line brings together every living creature, all that

bear within themselves the breath of life, in a command performa
praise the LORD of all life and blessing. This final entry in the I
bears a wonderful connection to the final book of the Christian Bi
which these words of gratitude to God for all that he has done for
reechoed: "From the throne came a voice saying, 'Praise our God, .
his servants, and all who fear him, small and great'" (Rev 19:5). T
be all praise and glory, wisdom and strength, honor, blessing
thanksgiving, now and forever. Amen! Alleluia!

PSALM 150

¹ *Alleluia!*

Praise Gód in his hóly pláce;
práise him in his míghty fírmament.
² Práise him for his pówerful déeds;
práise him for his bóundless grándeur.

³ O práise him with sóund of trúmpet;
práise him with lúte and hárp.
⁴ Práise him with tímbrel and dánce;
práise him with stríngs and pípes.

⁵ O práise him with resóunding cýmbals;
práise him with cláshing of cýmbals.
⁶ Let éverything that bréathes praise the LÓRD!

Alleluia!

PRAYER

*O God of might and grandeur, who wondrously sustain creation with
your loving and compassionate hand, create us anew by the goodness
of your saving grace, that in knowing your love in Christ Jesus our
Lord, we may praise you in all that we say and do. To you be all glory
and honor, now and forever. Amen.*

ANNOTATED BIBLIOGRAPHY

Bellinger, W. H. *Psalms: A Guide to Studying the Psalter*. 2nd ed. Grand Rapids: Baker Academic, 2012. [This book by a seasoned author on the Book of Psalms explains the literary genres of the psalms with reference to their original contexts.]

Bergant, Dianne. *Psalms 1-72*. New Collegeville Bible Commentary. Collegeville, MN: Liturgical Press, 2013. [This seasoned author offers literary and historical information on each psalm, illuminating its religious and spiritual meanings with clarity and insight.]

————. *Psalms 73-150*. New Collegeville Bible Commentary. Collegeville, MN: Liturgical Press, 2013. [See above.]

Brueggeman, Walter. *The Message of the Psalms: A Theological Commentary*. Augsburg Old Testament Studies. Minneapolis: Augsburg, 1984. [The book is almost thirty years old, but still valuable; its erudite author provides a treatment combining contemporary experiences of faith with solid scholarship.]

————. *Spirituality of the Psalms*. Minneapolis: Augsburg Fortress, 2002. [This book provides a distillation of the author's method of making the psalms applicable to human experience, focusing on Psalms of Orientation, Disorientation, New Orientation, God's Justice.]

Clifford, Richard J. *Psalms 1-72*. Abingdon Old Testament Commentaries. Nashville: Abingdon Press, 2003. [This two-volume commentary is an excellent guide to reading the psalms in their historical context, with precise exegetical comments along with well-articulated and sensitive theological reflection.]

————. *Psalms 73-150*. Abingdon Old Testament Commentaries. Nashville: Abingdon Press, 2003. [See previous.]

Creach, Jerome F. D. *The Destiny of the Righteous in the Psalms*. St. Louis: Chalice Press, 2008. [The author provides a comprehensive and insightful theology of the psalms, opening with the importance of Psalm 1 for a proper interpretation of the entire Psalter.]

Jacobson, Rolf A., ed. *Sounding in the Theology of Psalms: Perspectives and Methods in Contemporary Scholarship.* Minneapolis: Fortress Press, 2011. [This volume contains a series of well-written articles explaining various theological approaches to the Psalter, with an appreciation for the rhetorical elements of Hebrew poetry.]

Kriegshauser, Laurence, OSB. *Praying the Psalms in Christ.* Notre Dame, IN: University of Notre Dame Press, 2009. [This author surveys the rich tradition of Christian interpretation of the psalms beginning with the early centuries of the Church, providing a prayerful reading founded upon good scholarship.]

Mays, James L. *The Lord Reigns: A Theological Handbook to the Psalms.* Louisville: Westminster-John Knox Press, 1994. [For this author, the expression "The Lord reigns" is the key that unlocks the manifold ways in which the psalms may be read, flowing from a divine rule marked by compassion, benevolence, and true justice.]

McCann, J. Clinton, Jr. "The Book of Psalms: Introduction, Commentary, and Reflections." *The New Interpreter's Bible.* Vol. 5. Nashville: Abingdon Press, 1996. [This commentary brings together solid scholarship, clear analysis of thorny issues, and sound theological reflection in order to meet the needs of today's readers.]

—————. *Great Psalms of the Bible.* Louisville: Westminster-John Knox Press, 2009. [This series of essays by a veteran commentator on the psalms combines a scholarly reading of the text with practical and insightful reflections on what these ancient texts have to say for contemporary people of faith.]

—————. *A Theological Introduction to the Book of Psalms: The Psalms as Torah.* Nashville: Abingdon Press, 1993. [This book employs an approach known as canonical criticism, which draws out connections between psalms and illuminates how these ancient poems of faith may serve as instruction for today's readers.]

Murphy, Roland E., OCarm. *The Gift of the Psalms.* Peabody, MA: Hendrickson, 2000. [This veteran Old Testament scholar provides a concise reading of the Book of Psalms, considering them from several perspectives, addressing first the literary, theological, and devotional riches of the Psalter, then proceeding to a brief commentary on each of the psalms.]

Nowell, Irene, OSB. *Pleading, Cursing, Praising: Conversing with God through the Psalms.* Collegeville, MN: Liturgical Press, 2013. [This enriching and insightful volume captures what is essential to the praying human heart: finding God in every experience of life.]

—————. *Sing a New Song: The Psalms in the Sunday Lectionary.* Collegeville, MN: Liturgical Press, 1993. [The author considers the psalms as a response to the biblical word given in the liturgy, concomitantly opening the broader context of each psalm to the reader.]

Ravasi, Gianfranco. *Il Libro dei Salmi—Commento e Attualizzazione.* Bologna: Edizioni Dehoniane, 1986. [For the Italian reader; this gem of a commentary in three volumes includes an introduction looking at the various literary genres of the Psalter, then provides a remarkably thorough examination of each psalm, covering its place in the Psalter, its place in the liturgy, its literal meaning, poetic elements, symbolic language, personal and communal meanings, and Christian meaning for today.]